Also by Michael Farquhar:

*...ays in History: A Gleefully Grim Chronicle of Misfortune,
Mayhem, and Misery for Every Day of the Year*

*...ives of the Tsars: Three Centuries of Autocracy, Debauchery,
...etrayal, Murder, and Madness From Romanov Russia*

*...hind the Palace Doors: Five Centuries of Sex, Adventure,
Vice, Treachery, and Folly From Royal Britain*

*A Treasury of Foolishly Forgotten Americans: Pirates,
...kinflints, Patriots, and Other Colorful Characters Stuck
in the Footnotes of History*

*A Treasury of Deception: Liars, Misleaders, Hoodwinkers,
...d the Extraordinary True Stories of History's Greatest Hoaxes,
Fakes, and Frauds*

*...Treasury of Great American Scandals: Tantalizing True Tales
of Historic Misbehavior by the Founding Fathers
and Others Who Let Freedom Swing*

*A Treasury of Royal Scandals: The Shocking True Stories
of History's Wickedest, Weirdest, Most Wanton Kings,
Queens, Tsars, Popes, and Emperors*

More
Days
Histo

Bad D

Secret

Be

an

A

More Bad Days *in* History

*The Delightfully Dismal Day-by-Day
Saga of Ignominy, Idiocy, and
Incompetence Continues*

MICHAEL FARQUHAR

ILLUSTRATIONS BY GIULIA GHIGINI

NATIONAL
GEOGRAPHIC

Washington, D.C.

Published by National Geographic Partners, LLC
1145 17th Street, NW, Washington, DC 20036

ISBN: 978-1-4262-2146-0

Since 1888, the National Geographic Society has funded more than 13,000 research, exploration, and preservation projects around the world. National Geographic Partners distributes a portion of the funds it receives from your purchase to National Geographic Society to support programs, including the conservation of animals and their habitats.

Get closer to National Geographic explorers and photographers, and connect with our global community. Join us today at nationalgeographic.com/join

For rights or permissions inquiries, please contact National Geographic Books Subsidiary Rights: bookrights@natgeo.com

Interior design: Melissa Farris and Nicole Miller

Printed in the United States of America

21/VP-PCML/1

To Mary—
January 23, 1968,
was actually a very Good Day.

History . . . is, indeed,
little more than the register of the crimes,
follies, and misfortunes of mankind.
—Edward Gibbon, *The Decline and Fall of the Roman Empire*
(1776–1788)

Or, as Voltaire had already put it:

History is nothing more
than a tableau of crimes and misfortunes.
—*L'Ingénu* (1767)

Contents

Introduction

Let's face it—many book sequels lack the vital essence of the original. Joseph Heller, Louisa May Alcott, and the stand-in for the long-dead Margaret Mitchell all flopped with their follow-ups to the original classics. Even Milton blew it with his all-but-forgotten *Paradise Regained*.

But happily, when it comes to the annals of unfortunate events, we have only to plunge into the past for an endlessly rich source of entertaining material. Thus, far from being condemned to repeat *Bad Days in History*, we get to celebrate *More* of them.

The variety of events in these pages may seem dizzying as we take a daily hop through the centuries—from a deranged emperor's unfortunate boy-bride in ancient Rome (October 13) to a vice president's gag-inducing smooch in modern America (August 17). In between, we drop in to witness the on-set tyranny of an otherwise beloved comedienne (May 14), the romantic cluelessness of a scientific genius (July 29), and the killer hijinks of a genocidal 10th-century saint (July 11).

Genocidal? Yes, some entries teeter a little more toward the dismal than the delightful. Hopefully, though, we can squeeze out a few smirks over some of the racist and otherwise unsavory characters who occasionally make an appearance here. Take the murderous mobsters who get theirs on November 14—right along with the equally loathsome FBI director on the very same day. Or the perpetually forlorn uber-Nazi, into whose aggrieved diary we take a gleeful peek on May 13.

Leaping from the pages of history and into this irreverent collection are horribly behaved heroes, hotheaded sports stars, frosty spouses, floundering Founding Fathers, viciously mean mothers, squabbling generals, disrespected royals, and so many other notable personages who experienced (or caused) some extraordinarily Bad Days. Let them serve as guides—lending perspective to those readers navigating through their own problems, while allowing everyone else a few laughs.

January

Jailhouse Rock Star:
The Assassin's New Year Soiree

"I had a very happy New Year's . . . ," an ebullient Charles Guiteau announced to the courtroom, "and hope every body else did."

It may seem odd to begin a book of Bad Days with someone having a good one. But wait: The merry reveler in question had recently murdered the 20th president of the United States, James A. Garfield. And despite the heinousness of that crime, his jailers allowed Guiteau to host a party in his cell over the holiday weekend. "I had plenty of visitors," the self-satisfied assassin reported, "high-toned, middle-toned and low-toned people . . . They don't, any of them,

want me hung. Everybody was very glad to see me. They all expressed the opinion without one dissenting voice that I would be acquitted."

In what *The New York Herald* branded "a curious and disgusting spectacle," Guiteau had indeed received hundreds of people—"to inflame and gratify the assassin's vanity and indulge their own morbid curiosity." Women as well as men came seeking autographs. "What is stranger still," the *Herald* reported, "there were women unwomanly enough to bring their little children along with them and allow them to shake hands with this vulgar murderer and wish him a 'Happy New Year.'"

While the slain president's widow and five children remained shrouded in grief, Guiteau enjoyed the status of a semi-celebrity in the nation's capital, where he had gunned down Garfield the previous July.* Often described as "a disappointed office seeker," he was in fact a sociopathic loon, convinced that God had ordered him to murder the president and that the fate of the nation rested in his hands. His delusional raving throughout the ensuing trial† spawned quite a following—not unlike those in the 20th century who would become infatuated with killer Charles Manson. Guiteau even used his notoriety to solicit a wife—who should be, he specified, a "nice Christian lady under 30 years of age."

The narcissist's bath in the limelight was a brief one: Contrary to his oft stated conviction that he would be spared the noose, Guiteau died on the gallows a year after achieving infamy. A grandstander to the end, the killer read a poem he had written for the occasion of his execution, "I am Going to the Lordy."

---

* The train station where Guiteau ambushed Garfield, shooting him in the back and the arm, is now the site of the National Gallery of Art in Washington, D.C. Garfield initially survived the attack but ultimately succumbed on September 19, 1881.

† The deranged Guiteau made a rational point when he declared, "The doctors killed Garfield; I just shot him." The president's attending physician—the inaptly named Dr. Willard Bliss—repeatedly plunged his unwashed hands and dirty instruments into the president's abdomen in a bid to locate the bullet lodged there. By the end of Garfield's 79-day ordeal, his body had been almost entirely consumed by infection.

Perhaps his tarnished soul did indeed reach the heavens. But his pickled brain remains earthbound, preserved in Philadelphia's Mütter Museum.

JANUARY 2, 1492

Momsters, Part 1:

A Cold Shoulder to Cry On

January 2, 1492, was unbearably sad for Muhammad XI, sultan of Granada. On that day King Ferdinand of Aragon and Queen Isabella of Castile triumphantly entered his emirate to formally relieve the last Muslim sovereign on the Iberian Peninsula, known as Boabdil, of his realm. After handing the monarchs the ceremonial keys to the city, the vanquished ruler prepared to retreat into exile.

First, however, Boabdil turned around to take one last glance at the magnificent possession he had lost. Overcome with grief, the deposed sultan wept. Fortunately for him, his mother was there to lend him comfort—or something. "You do well, my son, to cry like a woman," she reportedly said, "for what you couldn't defend like a man."

JANUARY 3, 1973

On Second Thought, Part 1:

Well, That Lasted About Half an Inning

"We plan absentee ownership as far as running the Yankees is concerned. We're not going to pretend we're something we aren't. I'll stick to building ships."

*—George Steinbrenner, upon purchasing the New York Yankees
with a group of investors for $10 million, January 3, 1973*

Not since Hitler's assurance that "We want nothing but peace" had a man contradicted himself more blatantly than New York Yankees owner George "The Boss" Steinbrenner did after declaring his intent not to interfere in the day-to-day operations of his newly acquired team. From the minutiae of hair-grooming standards for players to his multiple firings and rehirings of manager Billy Martin, Steinbrenner became baseball's ultimate buttinsky.*

Dallas Green—one of 14 Yankees managers who would come and go (and, in some cases, come and go again) during Steinbrenner's turbulent 37-year stewardship—derisively referred to the Cleveland shipbuilder cum owner as "Manager George." A seemingly endless parade of personnel streamed through the locker room and front office of Yankee Stadium, from pitching coaches and general managers to discarded players and team presidents. The unremitting turnover prompted third baseman Graig Nettles to comment on the passing show: "Every year is like being traded—a new manager and a whole new team."

JANUARY 4, 1987

Oral's Fixation:
Paying Off God the Gangster

God had already threatened to kill the Reverend Granville Oral Roberts once, in 1986. But He apparently let things slide when the diamond-decked, silk-suited televangelist failed to cough up the cash the deity demanded.

---

* As minority owner John McMullen described his own position: "Nothing is as limited as being a limited partner of George's."

This time, however, the Almighty clearly meant business.

On January 4, 1987, Roberts shared with his television audience the Creator's requirements: $8 million for the Oral Roberts University School of Medicine by the end of March . . . or else! Given Roberts's claim that a terrifying 900-foot-tall Jesus had once materialized before him, this newest divine command was not to be taken lightly.

"I desperately need you to come into agreement with me concerning my life being extended beyond March," the charismatic preacher begged his followers in a newsletter after the telecast. Roberts's son Richard—soon to be ousted as president of Oral Roberts University for misappropriation of funds, among other sins—likewise pleaded for his father's life: "Let's not let this [January 24] be my Dad's last birthday!"

With God's deadline drawing nigh and the ministry's coffers still $1.3 million shy of that lofty fundraising goal, the senior Roberts ascended his university's 200-foot-high Prayer Tower on March 22 for a vigil that would end with either the Lord's bill paid off or the pastor smitten by the Eternal Hand. "If I go from [the Tower] to Jesus, I will see you in heaven," Roberts wrote to his followers. "But I believe that won't happen, because I believe our God will do this mighty thing and at the end of March, you and I will know the miracle has happened and the Gospel will go to the nations."

Doubters included *The Tulsa Tribune,* which torched the preacher's tactics in an editorial titled, "Come Off It, Oral." But then, an unlikely savior emerged in the person of Florida dog-track owner Jerry Collins, whose 11th-hour contribution was accompanied by the suggestion that the preacher needed psychiatric care.

None of these propitiations, alas, could keep the Oral Roberts University School of Medicine from closing under its crushing financial burden in 1989. The Creator—a patient avenger apparently—promptly arranged a life extension for Roberts that lasted not just "beyond March" but until December 15, 2009, when the tower-topping televangelist was finally called to account at the age of 91.

Grave Misfortune: The Queen Who Passed to the Odor Side

"No sooner had she drawn her last breath than
nowhere did they pay more notice to her than to a dead goat."
—Contemporary chronicler Pierre de L'Estoile on
the January 5, 1589, death of the French queen, Catherine de' Medici

If Catherine de' Medici had been discarded like a decaying farm animal, in L'Estoile's colorful phrase, it was partly because she smelled like one. (Blame the poor embalming methods practiced at the time.) Indeed, so overwhelming was the stench that the once mighty Queen Mother—far away from Paris at the time—had to be hastily buried, without pomp, in a provincial churchyard. And there she lay, forgotten in an unmarked grave, for more than two decades.

Given the choice, she might have opted to stay there.

In 1610, Catherine de' Medici was finally brought back to Paris and properly buried in the Basilica (now Cathedral) of Saint-Denis. Alas, she would rest not in peace but in pieces: Marauding revolutionaries dug up the queen in 1793 and hurled her putrid corpse into a pit with other unceremoniously exhumed French kings and queens (see October 12).

And, on that occasion, no one could distinguish the stench of a dead ruminant from that of all the other rotting royals.

❧

Get the Drift? Nope, They Didn't

No sooner had German meteorologist Alfred Wegener proposed his revolutionary theory of continental drift on January 6, 1912, than naysaying scientists started to pull *him* apart. "Wegener's hypothesis in general is of the footloose type," harrumphed Dr. Rollin T. Chamberlain, a geologist at the University of Chicago. "It takes considerable liberty with our globe, and is less bound by restrictions or tied down by awkward, ugly facts than most of its rival theories."

Chamberlain's was just one voice in a chorus of scorn directed at the visionary scientist for daring to suggest that the landmasses of Earth had once formed a supercontinent (he called it Pangaea) before gradually drifting apart. Though Wegener would not be vindicated until decades after his death, perhaps he found some posthumous solace—not only in being right, but also in the esteemed company of other innovative scientists rejected and ridiculed in their day:

- Religious reformer Martin Luther branded Nicolaus Copernicus as "that fool," bent on upending "the whole art of astronomy," with his crackpot view that Earth revolves around the sun.
- *Scientific American* magazine dubbed airplane inventors Wilbur and Orville Wright "the Lying Brothers."
- "The world [of microorganisms] into which you wish to take us is really too fantastic," French newspaper *La Presse* directly informed Louis Pasteur in 1860. The French chemist and biologist ignored the scornful skepticism—and developed the pathogen elimination process to which he lent his name.
- American surgeon Samuel D. Gross (the subject of Thomas Eakins's famous painting "The Gross Clinic") arrogantly dismissed Joseph Lister's advocacy of antiseptic surgery in 1876: "Little, if any faith, is placed by an enlightened or experienced surgeon on this side of the Atlantic in the so-called treatment of Professor Lister."
- No fan of Charles Darwin's theory of evolution was his former teacher, geologist Adam Sedgwick. "I have read your book with more pain than pleasure," Sedgwick wrote to Darwin upon the 1859 publication of *On the Origin of Species*. "Parts of it I admired greatly; parts I laughed at till my sides were almost sore; other parts I read with absolute sorrow; because I think them utterly false & grievously mischievous."

- Gregor Mendel died an obscure monk in 1884—and his revolutionary experiments in genetics seemed destined to be buried with him. But near the end of his life, the far-seeing Mendel had the confidence to declare that a more profound legacy awaited him: "My time will come."*

JANUARY 7, 1789

A Load of Number 2: The Veep Who Couldn't Put Up With Shutting Up

"But my Country has in its Wisdom contrived for me,
the most insignificant Office that ever the Invention of Man
contrived or his Imagination conceived."
—*John Adams, on his role as the first vice president of the United States*

John Adams was satisfied with second place. As he saw it, his election as the first vice president of the United States on January 7, 1789, solidified his position in the hierarchy of Revolutionary heroes—not only among his contemporaries, but also in history. He could live with George Washington residing at the very peak of Olympus—albeit grudgingly—because, really, he had no choice. Washington's popular status as a demigod was nearly inviolable, so Adams contented himself with the belief that he was, at the very least, first among mortals. Any other post in the new government was, as his wife Abigail wrote, "beneath himself."

Soon after assuming the position, however, Adams realized his role was almost entirely devoid of significance—an "unprofitable dignity," as James Madison described it (or, put less elegantly by future veep John Nance

---

* See March 23 for a particularly hostile response to Edward Jenner and his smallpox vaccine.

Garner, "not worth a bucket of warm piss"). Aside from assuming the presidency in the event of the incumbent's demise, the only constitutionally mandated role for the vice president was to preside over the Senate—*silently*—and cast the deciding vote there in the event of a tie.

The prospect of staying mute in the Senate rankled Adams as he prepared to take office. "Not wholly without experience in public assemblies," he wrote (an understatement, given the pivotal role he had played in the American quest for independence), "I have been more accustomed to take a share in their debates than to preside over their deliberations."

As matters transpired, the Founding Father couldn't find a way to keep his mouth shut. He seemed to babble most about what to call his boss. Whereas the House of Representatives, in the spirit of republicanism, had settled simply on "President of the United States," Adams—perhaps hoping to share the reflected glory of the position—grumbled this wasn't nearly distinguished enough. Only the most regal of titles would befit the leader of the new nation, he loudly demurred—something like "His Majesty, the President." Any lesser appellation, Adams insisted, would put Washington on par with the president of a mere fire company or cricket club—and he, horror of horrors, a rung beneath that!

So obnoxiously outspoken was Adams on the issue that he earned not just a rebuke from his peers, but also their contempt. Thomas Jefferson, for one, called his colleague's proposed title inflation "the most superlatively ridiculous thing I ever heard of." Others sarcastically suggested a suitable name for the portly vice president: "His Rotundity." And many vilified him—unfairly—as an avowed monarchist, a charge that would plague Adams for the rest of his political career.

Mortified by the fuss, President Washington simply kept his distance from the embarrassing veep for the rest of his time in office. Upon leaving it, he wrote to Adams, recently elected to the position whose title had so consumed him: "I am fairly out, and you are fairly in. See which of us is happiest."

JANUARY 8, 1946

Mrs. Blood and Guts:
Beware the Wrath of Patton's Spouse

"May the Great Worm gnaw your vitals
and may your bones rot joint by little joint."
—*Beatrice Patton, 59-year-old widow of Gen. George
S. Patton, pointing a finger at her late husband's
30-year-old mistress, Jean Gordon, and deliver-
ing an old Hawaiian curse—just days before
Gordon committed suicide on January 8,
1946. Also present during the deadly
imprecation was Beatrice's brother
Fred, who—according to a
third family member—said
"there was so much malevo-
lence in the room that he
jumped up and grabbed his
hat and ran out, and only
slowed down when he
reached the street."*

JANUARY 9, 2003 AND JANUARY 9, 2005

Celebrities on *Surreal Life* Support

Remember when faded celebrities stayed that way? They existed in a sort of post-spotlight limbo, with only the occasional guest turn on *The Love Boat* to sustain them.

All that changed on January 9, 2003, when cable network VH1 exhumed some long-dead careers in a ghastly spectacle called *The Surreal*

Life. It was a celebrity version of *Pet Sematary,* with the once marginally famous grotesquely revived to stagger about in a group house, behaving in the most appalling ways imaginable. (Need an example? How about a drunk and naked Verne "Mini-Me" Troyer, staring stupidly at the camera while urinating on a carpet?)

As viewers feasted on the carcasses featured on *The Surreal Life,* VH1 glimpsed more degrading gold in a second series, which premiered exactly two years later: In *Celebrity Fit Club,* hefty has-beens (or never-really-weres) trundled about in a televised weight-loss competition. To ensure maximum humiliation, "stars" such as Gary Busey and the Snapple Lady were required to wear next to nothing as they exposed their flabby bodies in a 360-degree showcase. They were also subjected to being hoisted onto a giant scale each week.

Being treated like pigs was apparently a less dire fate than dignified obscurity for participants on the seven(!)-season show. Besides, how else could Vincent "Big Pussy" Pastore earn enough to eat once *The Sopranos* fed him to the fishes?

JANUARY 10, 1985

Future Imperfect:
When Marty McFly Got Swatted

Eric Stoltz was a fine actor. A product of the Stella Adler "Method" school, he brought an intense realism to such critically acclaimed films as *Mask*. But regrettably, he simply wasn't funny—an essential requirement for the principal role of time-surfer Marty McFly in the sci-fi romp *Back to the Future*.

Stoltz had been cast because Michael J. Fox, the first choice for the part, was committed to the television series *Family Ties* and thus unavailable. Five weeks into shooting, however, director Robert Zemeckis concluded that Stoltz was all wrong for the part—way too dark and broody for Marty's fun, lighthearted character. (And annoying to work with as well: True to his Method roots, the actorly Stoltz gratingly insisted that others address him as "Marty" on set.)

"It was very agonizing," Zemeckis told author Caseen Gaines. "You don't want to have to admit this horrible truth. There was no moment where it was 'Oh, I know what the problem is.' It was always a gnawing suspicion that just got worse and worse in my mind, and then I finally had to admit to myself that it wasn't working in the way that it needed to."

So the filmmakers cut a deal with the producer of *Family Ties,* and Fox was hired as the new Marty. That meant every Stoltz scene would have to be reshot—including the last one, filmed at the fictional Twin Pines Mall parking lot on January 10, 1985. Hours later, Stoltz received the unwelcome news that his *Future* was now history.*

JANUARY 11, 1913

A Myopic Diagnosis: Look Who's Stupid Now!

One might expect the *Journal of the American Medical Association* to utilize lofty language—jargon well beyond the layman's ken—to share updates with its esteemed members. But a January 11, 1913, report detailing Dr. William Martin Richards's study of public-school children in New York showed just how stupid that assumption would be.

"The forty pupils . . . Dr. Richards examined were the worst that could be found in these schools," the *JAMA* entry read, "eighteen of them being

---

* Eric Stoltz wasn't the only victim of the radical role reshuffle. Melora Hardin, cast as Marty's girlfriend, Jennifer Parker, was deemed too tall to play opposite the five-foot-four Fox, so she too was replaced. Her particular Bad Day was fleeting, however: Hardin wound up playing Jan on *The Office.*

so stupid* that they were in ungraded classes." Unrelentingly blunt, the report went on to note that "eleven were so stupid that it required three terms to do the work of one term [while] eleven were delinquent."

The good news: The study revealed that the little nitwits only needed eyeglasses.

———

JANUARY 12, 1999

O-bitch-uary, Part i:
An Overdose of Venom

"Periwigged lordly decadence, the shadow of aristocracy in the Jungian sense, darkened the life of a man who wore his crest on his chest but was not protected by it. His was the profligacy that exiled Rochester, the privileged hedonism that, in the history of England's landed families, has always caused shame, bankruptcy and death."
—*Obituary of John Hervey, Seventh Marquess of Bristol, published in* The Independent *on January 12, 1999*

Britain's Lord Bristol may indeed have destroyed his reputation with his many excesses. But once the 44-year-old aristocrat was dead, *The Independent*—an online English newspaper claiming to practice "free-thinking journalism"—gleefully continued his ruination.

Yes, the deceased's "thanatoid flamboyance" was notable—a fortune squandered on myriad indulgences, legal and otherwise. But the paper's vicious take on his life was equally extravagant. Penned by Jessica

---

* And speaking of *stupid* . . . It was on this date in 2000 that U.S. president George W. Bush famously pondered, "Rarely is the question asked: Is our children learning?"

Berens, who indicated she'd met Lord Bristol only once,* it savaged an existence the writer deemed thoroughly feckless. Estimated at various times in his life to be worth anywhere from £1 million to £30 million, wrote Berens, "in the end [Hervey] was just a junkie—scabrous, pathetic, helpless, desperate—in and out of court, almost penniless, usually friendless."

A kinder, gentler assessment came from Bill Walrond, the coroner who led the inquest into Lord Bristol's death. After concluding that long-term drug abuse had indeed killed the marquess, Walrond pronounced the case "particularly tragic . . . but I suspect that Lord Bristol is as deserving of sympathy as he is of censure . . . it is easy for people who are not in a situation to condemn one that is."

Especially for someone as bitchy as Jessica Berens.†

JANUARY 13, 1928

First Amendment 1, Decency 0

The masses were welcomed to watch the spectacle of death. But this wasn't the Roman Colosseum, where Christians were torn apart by

---

* Of her sole encounter with Lord Bristol, Berens wrote: "The man had become an exhibition. He sat in his stately dining room beneath his family portraits and he could not eat. He could hardly speak. An all-consuming misery underpinned his drug habit and he accepted both as inevitable rather than rectifiable."

† Berens's intimacy with Britain's underclass may have fired her caustic take on its upper crust: For three years she served as writer-in-residence at HMP (Her Majesty's Prison) Dartmoor in Devon, teaching composition skills to former gang members. Berens herself died on April 12, 2019, eulogized by *The Telegraph* newspaper as "an eccentric and inspiring presence . . . known for her wit, her incisive writing, her elaborate dress sense, her knitting and her impatience."

wild beasts. Nor was it a public beheading in Revolutionary France. Instead, it was the front page of the New York *Daily News*.

A furtively enterprising photographer at New York's Sing Sing prison—a single-shot camera strapped to his ankle and a trip wire running up his pants leg—managed to capture the electric-chair execution of convicted murderer Ruth Snyder on January 12, 1928.

The next day—under the screaming banner headline "DEAD!"—*Daily News* readers were treated to the ghastly image captured by the sneaky shutterbug: It showed the 32-year-old Queens housewife, found guilty of murdering her husband, "as the lethal current surged through [her] body at 11 p.m. last night." The human appetite for deadly entertainment having abated little since Nero's days, sales of the Extra edition predictably soared.

JANUARY 14, 1989

Matchless Prose: The Book That Wouldn't Burn

The Muslim community of Bradford, England, attracted international attention of all the wrong kinds on January 14, 1989, when its members gathered in public to protest—and burn—Salman Rushdie's recently published novel, the allegedly blasphemous *Satanic Verses*.

"How fragile civilization is," the author wrote in the event's aftermath; "how easily, how merrily a book burns."

Metaphorically, Rushdie was right. Mechanically, however, the infernal inferno proved mundane, bordering on farcical. Strung up on a pole, the novel simply refused to ignite. As bemused protest organizer Ishtiaq Ahmed told the BBC in 2009, "It was a very thick book . . . and it was very difficult to actually set fire to it. We had to find a can of petrol to pour on the book."

Far less funny was the fatwa calling for the slaughter of Rushdie and his publishers, issued one month later by Iran's Ayatollah Ruhollah

Khomeini. To this day, Rushdie receives an annual "Valentine" from Iran, reminding him of the country's homicidal vow.

Satanic, indeed!

We Got Yer "New York Values" Right Here, Mac!

The New York *Daily News* delivered an unmistakable message—"DROP DEAD, TED"—to Texas Senator Rafael Edward Cruz on the front page of its January 15, 2016, edition. The funereal invitation (issued by the same newspaper that had featured the high-voltage demise of Ruth Snyder—see January 13) was published in response to presidential candidate Cruz's disparaging remark about the "New York values" he said his Republican rival Donald Trump embodied.

To make certain no one misinterpreted the tabloid's take on the Canadian-born Cruz, the page also depicted a clearly agitated Statue of Liberty, her middle finger defiantly extended.

Fugu the Bell Tolls: The Kabuki Star's Last Supper

Bandō Mitsugorō VIII may have been a brilliant performer—a master of the highly specialized art of Kabuki theater—but when it came to his culinary choices, he had the brains of a blowfish.

On January 16, 1975—two years after being enshrined as a "national treasure"—the acclaimed Japanese actor ordered an extraordinarily dangerous dinner. Pufferfish, or fugu, is a delicacy in Japan, but it must be meticulously prepared to ensure that its highly toxic innards do not contaminate its flesh. Perhaps feeling invincible, Bandō ordered the fish's most lethal

and assiduously avoided organ, the liver—*four* of them, in fact.

Any chef trained adequately in fugu safety would have balked at such a suicidal request, but the diner's honored status may have compelled the preparer to comply in this case. Having ingested an evening meal that amounted to a heaping pile of poison, Bandō Mitsugorō then experienced the agony of slow respiratory failure.

And for this, his final performance—call it "To Liver Die"—the artist secured his unique place on the roster of History's Dumbest Demises.

JANUARY 17, 1833, 1840, 1841, AND 1889

Well, I Do Despair!

For anyone seeking good company and cheer, January 17 might be a day to pull the covers over your head and stay in bed. The 19th-century luminaries below, for example, certainly would have profited from that luxury—as would those unlucky enough to be around them on that frequently miserable January day:

- Less than a month had passed since the severed-ear episode, and Vincent van Gogh had no way to pay the hospital bills stemming from the incident. Among the staggering fees, his biographers note, were charges for the sheets and towels he had bloodied. "What is to be done?" the artist wrote despondently to his younger brother Theo on January 17, 1889. "My pictures are valueless."

- Henry Clay was similarly sullen on January 17, 1833, lamenting the state of the Union as South Carolina threatened secession over tariffs and other issues. Oh, and he had just lost the presidential election to Andrew Jackson. "As to politics, we have no past, no future," Clay wrote to a friend lucky not to find himself face-to-face with the sulky U.S. senator from Kentucky. "After forty-four years of existence under the present Constitution, what single principle is fixed? . . . We are as much at sea, as the day when the Constitution went into operation."

- Composer Robert Schumann was so worn down by the family drama surrounding his betrothal to pianist Clara Wieck—he had sued her father for the right to marry her—that he wrote with an offer to spring her from the engagement. That struck a discordant note with the 20-year-old Clara, who confided her displeasure to her diary on January 17, 1840: "My state of mind is indescribable—I cannot forget the words in Robert's last letter—they torture me. I have endured everything, I have lost my father, I have stood up to him in a court of law, what battles have I fought with myself, but Robert's love made up for all this. I believed his faith was immovable, and now he hurts me so much. I can barely calm myself."*

- Exactly one year after Clara chronicled her romantic woes, Abraham Lincoln was experiencing his own love-induced meltdown. "I have, within the last few days, been making a most discreditable exhibition of myself," the future 16th president wrote on the dreaded 17th. That moment of self-reflection didn't quite capture it. But this one did: "I am now the most miserable man living. If what I feel were equally distributed to the whole human

---

* The Schumanns did finally tie the knot in September of the same year, becoming one of the most famous musical couples in history—until Robert's suicide 16 years later.

family, there would not be one cheerful face on earth. Whether I shall ever be better I can not tell; I awfully forebode I shall not. To remain as I am is impossible; I must die or be better, it appears to me."

Lincoln, then serving in the Illinois House of Representatives, had broken off his engagement to Mary Todd (perhaps wisely; see March 26) and fallen hard for a young woman named Matilda Edwards. Guilt and desire were driving him mad—as in *certifiable*—according to his friends and associates:

"Crazy as a *Loon*," said his law partner, William Herndon.

"We have been very much distressed, on Mr. Lincoln's account," wrote Martinette Hardin McKee, "hearing that he had two Cat fits and a Duck fit."

"The doctors say he came within an inch of being a perfect lunatic for life," reported Jane D. Bell. "He was perfectly crazy for some time, not able to attend to his business at all. They say he does not look like the same person."

According to one friend, Orville H. Browning, Lincoln "was so much affected as to talk incoherently, and to be delirious to the extent that he did not know what he was doing." Another, Joshua Speed, wrote that "they had to remove razors from his room—take away all Knives and other such dangerous things . . . it was terrible."

Luckily, Lincoln kept it together—as he would the Union.

———◆———

JANUARY 18, 1862

John Tyler:
In Death, a Lost-Cause Célèbre

"He has filled a large space in the history of his country . . .
He has secured, we believe, a blissful immortality."

—Preamble to a resolution adopted by the Virginia House of Delegates
upon the death of former president John Tyler on January 18, 1862

The obsequies and honors heaped upon John Tyler befitted a fallen U.S. president. A grieving public filed past his flag-draped coffin, while the president, vice president, and members of Congress accompanied the 150-carriage funeral cortege to Tyler's final resting place.

Alas, the esteemed mourners—from President Jefferson Davis to the authors of so many soaring tributes—were all Confederates, and the standard that shrouded his casket was a Rebel flag. Even the graveyard was in Richmond, the very capital of the Confederacy. Indeed, former president Tyler had died just before taking his seat in the Confederate Congress.

Meanwhile up north—nothing. Not a peep from President Abraham Lincoln on his predecessor's passing. Not one flag lowered to half-staff or a single moment of silence observed. To most, the president catapulted to national prominence as part of the "Tippecanoe and Tyler Too" ticket was a traitor—a vigorous advocate of secession who then abandoned his shattered country to serve an enemy state.

"He ended his life suddenly . . . in Richmond," *The New York Times* editorialized, "going down to death amid the ruins of his native State. He himself was one of the architects of its ruin; and beneath that melancholy wreck his name will be buried."

Oddly, the *Times* placed the ruin of Virginia several years too early. And though the name of John Tyler was indeed buried, it was not "beneath that melancholy wreck." Rather, it was in obscurity.

JANUARY 19, 1970

The Best Meh for the Job

The U.S. Senate had already shot down Richard Nixon's choice of Clement Haynsworth to replace Abe Fortas on the Supreme Court. Then, on January 19, 1970, the president proposed George Harrold Carswell for the same position. But with his less-than-stellar judicial record, the nominee needed all the boosting he could get. So in stepped Nebraska Republican Senator Roman Hruska to offer support that might best be described as flaccid:

"Even if [Carswell] were mediocre, there are a lot of mediocre judges and people and lawyers. They are entitled to a little representation, aren't they? We can't have all Brandeises and Frankfurters and Cardozos."

Nope. Or, as it turned out, a Carswell either: Nixon's *third* nominee, Harry Blackmun, ultimately got the seat.

For the King of England, Death on Deadline

The year 1935 marked the 25th anniversary of George V's ascension to the British throne. The occasion came with an outpouring of love and support for the king who had been so steadfast and self-sacrificing during the darkest days of World War I. "I cannot understand it," the shy, dutiful monarch said of the mass demonstration. "After all, I am only a very ordinary sort of fellow."

And a mortal one, for sadly George V had but a few days to live: As the Silver Jubilee year came to a close, the sovereign's heart and lungs were failing. His gradually ebbing life would come to a shockingly abrupt end.

On January 20, 1936, just before midnight, King George V died. That is to say, he was put to sleep. It was perhaps the most extraordinary royal demise in centuries, for not since the decapitation of Charles I in 1649 had the death of a British monarch been planned and carried out.

Earlier that evening, the king's physician, Lord Dawson, had scrawled a medical bulletin on the back of a menu card from Sandringham House, the royal retreat in Norfolk: "The king's life is moving peacefully toward its close." Less than two hours later, Dawson closed it.

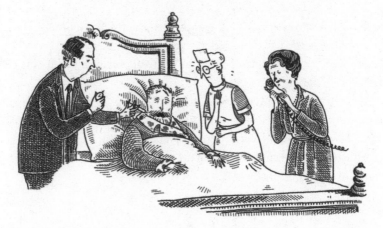

The royal physician made the following note: "At about 11 o'clock, it was evident that the last stage [of death] might endure for many hours, unknown to the Patient, but little comporting with that dignity and serenity which he so richly merited and which demanded a brief final scene." Dawson's version of that "brief final scene" took the form of a lethal dose of morphine and cocaine, which he injected into the dying king's jugular vein.

"Breathing quieter," Dawson noted 15 minutes later. "Appearance more placid—physical struggle gone." Soon after the king's family was summoned to his bedside, George V expired. "Hours of waiting just for the mechanical end," Dawson later wrote, "only exhausts the onlooker and keeps them so strained they cannot avail themselves of the solace of thought, communion or prayer."

Yet Dawson's hastening of the king's death wasn't motivated purely by mercy. He believed the announcement should appear in the morning edition of *The Times* of London, rather than in what he viewed as "the less appropriate field of the evening journals." To that end, Dawson had his wife call the newspaper's editor and urge him to delay publication for as long as possible. "So," wrote royal biographer Robert Lacey, "with the help of his considerate doctor, who did not entertain a moment's doubt that he was doing the right and dignified thing by his royal patient, George V performed the ultimate duty of a media monarch. He died in time for the morning editions."

JANUARY 21, 1993

O Say Can You Screech?
The Star-Mangled "Banner"

For some reason, certain celebrities invited to sing the national anthem feel compelled to put their own personal stamp on a song that requires no additional postage. They seem to think the "star" in "Star-Spangled Banner" refers to them, trampling the hymn with faux soulfulness and spastic octave switches.

Most such "interpretations" fail miserably, but the all-time worst may have been that of Carl Lewis, the Olympic gold medalist with a tin ear. He gallantly butchered the anthem before a Chicago Bulls–New Jersey Nets NBA game on January 21, 1993.

"All right, are we all ready?" Lewis coaxed the crowd. "Here we go."

Then, in what the *Chicago Sun-Times* later called "an unintentionally comical rendition," Lewis started off shakily and went downhill from there. After screeching his way through "the rockets' red glare," Lewis heard his voice crack—and the crowd howl. "Uh-oh," he interrupted himself before gamely soldiering on toward the song's climax, at which point Lewis declared, "I'll make up for it now."

He did not.

ESPN's Charley Steiner delivered the best review of the performance when he invoked Lewis's apparent inspiration: "Francis Scott Off-Key."

JANUARY 22, 1861

Robert Uneasy Lee:
Not Quite a Rebel Yell

Robert E. Lee has come to epitomize the Confederate cause, for which he is frequently excoriated. But there was a time when he was both a steadfast son of Virginia *and* a loyal American. In a letter he wrote on January 22, 1861, Lee was clearly torn, lamenting both the disintegration of the United States and the specter of civil war:

> God alone can save us from our folly, selfishness & short sightedness . . . I am unable to realize that our people will destroy a government inaugurated by the blood & wisdom of our patriot fathers, that has given us peace & prosperity at home, power & security abroad, & under which we have acquired a colossal strength unequalled in the history of mankind. I wish to live under no other government, & there is no sacrifice I am not ready to make for the preservation of the Union save that of honour. If a disruption takes place, I shall go back in sorrow to my people & share the misery of my native state, & save in her defence there will be one soldier less in the world than now. I wish for no other flag than the 'Star spangled banner,' & no other air than 'Hail Columbia.' I still hope that the wisdom & patriotism of the nation will yet save it . . . I see no cause of disunion, strife & civil war & I pray it may be averted.

When his native Virginia seceded from the Union three months later, Lee resigned his commission in the U.S. Army to accept command of the Confederate forces.

JANUARY 23, 1848

The Agony of the Ecstasy

Horace Wells, a notable pioneer in the use of surgical anesthesia, was arrested on his 33rd birthday for hurling sulfuric acid at several streetwalkers.

It turned out the normally mild-mannered dentist was high on chloroform—an anesthetic he originally began using for scientific self-experimentation before embracing the compound for what he described as "the exhilarating effect produced by it." In the disturbing case of Dr. Wells, though, euphoria manifested itself as derangement—and prompted the attacks for which he claimed no memory.

Imprisoned in a cell at New York City's infamous Tombs prison, he made a final testament to the editors of the *Journal of Commerce* on January 23, 1848—the day he sliced open his femoral artery: "Great God! Has it come to this? Is it not all a dream? Before 12 o'clock this night I am to pay the debt of nature. Yet, if I was to go free tomorrow, I could not live and be called a villain."

Instead, he bled to death and was called a groundbreaker.

JANUARY 24, 1996

O. J.'s Interview-mercial: At Least He Wasn't Selling Gloves

In the cable-channel lineup of 1996, Black Entertainment Television (BET) was a bit of a backwater, with programming that most critics dismissed as rinky-dink: reruns, infomercials, raunchy music videos. So it was considered quite a coup when the network landed the first interview with O. J. Simpson more than three months after his acquittal for the murders of his ex-wife, Nicole Brown Simpson, and her friend Ronald Goldman.

Precisely what enticed the controversial football legend to sit down with BET news anchor Ed Gordon on January 24, 1996? (Far more prominent personalities—NBC's Katie Couric, for one—had clamored for the opportunity.) Was it to show solidarity with the black-owned and operated network? Or was it BET's promise to run ads for Simpson's self-produced video on the murders?

Gordon conducted an admirable interview, but Simpson was not exactly in a forthcoming mood. For viewers wondering where O. J. might have been on the night of the killings, for example, the Juice suggested the answer was out there. And there was a simple way for those inquisitive sofa sleuths to find it:

Just buy the video.

JANUARY 25, 1971

The Scariest Clown on Earth: Idi Amin Seizes Power

Idi Amin of Uganda may have been the most ferocious monster to emerge from the collapse of colonial Africa. A sadistic mass murderer, he kept the heads of his enemies in a freezer while the corpses of countless other victims ended up in the gullets of Nile crocodiles. So intense was the slaughter—which began as soon as Amin seized power on January 25, 1971—that no one knows exactly how many people died in the ensuing eight years of terror. (Estimates range from 80,000 to 500,000.) "Even Amin does not know how many people he has ordered to be executed," noted Henry Kyemba, a Ugandan health minister who defected to Britain in 1977. "The country is littered with bodies."

Yet "the Butcher of Uganda" managed to disguise his savagery (at least from Western observers) behind a mask of amiable buffoonery.

It was easy to laugh at this illiterate behemoth of a man, his uniform festooned with medals for imaginary feats and stretched almost beyond endurance by his nearly 300-pound frame. He was the self-proclaimed "Lord of All the Beasts of the Earth and Fishes of the Sea," as his official title read in part, "and Conqueror of the British Empire in Africa in General and Uganda in Particular." There was also Amin's grandiose claim to the throne of Scotland, part of his weird fetish for all things Great Britain. (Including its queen, apparently: To celebrate the silver anniversary of her coronation, Amin asked Elizabeth II to send him a pair of her "25-year-old knickers." The tyrant also generously offered the monarch his services as a stud: "Dear Liz," he cabled, "if you want to know a real man, come to Kampala.")

Reporters relished the colorful quotes supplied by the gregarious despot known as "Big Daddy." In one poolside chat with them early in 1976, for example, Amin—who reputedly sired some 30 children with six wives—revealed the simple secret of his virility: "I am very good at it." And then there was his delectable take on cannibalism: "I tried human flesh, and it's too salty for my taste."

The autocrat's cartoonish side seduced some casual observers. Others, however, glimpsed the cunning depravity beneath the surface. "He is killer and clown, big-hearted buffoon and strutting martinet," *Time* magazine noted in 1977. "He can be as playful as a kitten or as lethal as a lion."

In addition to the genocidal policies that prompted President Richard Nixon to call him "a prehistoric monster," Amin made the international community shudder with his well-publicized praise for Hitler, his support for Palestinian terrorists (including his direct involvement in the 1976 hijacking of an Air France flight originating in Israel), and his expulsion of some 60,000 Asian Ugandans who had been the backbone of the nation's economy.

Thomas Patrick Melady, U.S. ambassador to Uganda, captured the essence of Amin in a 1973 cable to the State Department: "Racist, erratic and unpredictable, brutal, inept, bellicose, irrational, ridiculous, and militaristic." Also, Melady might have added, *invincible.*

Sure, the vicious killer with the playful grin was ousted from power in 1979. Rather than pay for his atrocities, though, Amin spent the rest of his life in luxurious, unrepentant exile, lolling about in Saudi Arabia until his death there from kidney failure in 2003.

In 1996, a *Boston Globe* reporter in search of Amin interviewed the manager of a grocery store in Jeddah where the ex-dictator liked to shop.

"Today, people greet him and say, 'Hello, Mr. President,'" the manager said.

But why? Wasn't he a savage dictator?

"Oh yes. He used to eat people," the manager replied, laughing. "But this is our nature: We forget."

JANUARY 26, 2006

Oprah's Book Clubbing

Upon entering the lions' den known as *The Oprah Winfrey Show* on January 26, 2006, author James Frey was promptly torn into, well, *A Million Little Pieces.*

That was the title of Frey's searing 2003 memoir of his descent into drug addiction and his ultimate redemption. Oprah, the empress of daytime talk, had picked the title for her book club in September 2005, guaranteeing its best-sellerdom. But now here she was, clawing back that honor in a spectacle of lacerating indignation.

Several weeks earlier, in an exposé that began with the words "Oprah Winfrey's been had," The Smoking Gun website had revealed that numerous portions of Frey's story had been fabricated. (He'd actually spent just a few hours in jail, for example, and not 87 days.) But it wasn't so much Frey's fraudulence that prompted Oprah to verbally maul the young author in front of her millions of viewers. Rather, it was the drubbing that Oprah had taken a couple of weeks earlier, when she had defended Frey and his book in the aftermath of the revelations.

"The underlying message of redemption in James Frey's memoir still resonates with me, and I know it resonates with millions of other people who have read this book," Winfrey declared in a phone call broadcast January 11 on CNN's *Larry King Live,* when Frey was a guest on the program. "To me, it seems to be much ado about nothing."

Her "blithe re-endorsement of the book," as Frank Rich described it in *The New York Times,* opened the once sacrosanct Oprah to virulent criticism. "She should have said: 'Had I known that many parts were fake, I wouldn't have recommended the book to millions of loyal viewers. I wouldn't have made this liar a lot of money,'" opined *Times* columnist Maureen Dowd. A third chattering-class sentence was handed down by *The Washington Post's* Richard Cohen, in a column titled "Oprah's Grand Delusion": "[F]ame and wealth has lulled her into believing that she possesses something akin to papal infallibility. She finds herself incapable of seeing that she has been twice fooled—once by Frey, a second time by herself."

All of this was evidently too much for Oprah, who morphed from warm and fuzzy into utterly ferocious on her January 26 program. First came a moment of self-flagellation: Oprah looked into the camera and declared, "I left the impression that truth does not matter . . . To everyone who has challenged me on this issue of truth, you are absolutely right." And then—*ping, zing, ping!*—the claws came out: Amid jeers from the audience, Oprah unleashed an inquisitorial lambasting that left Frey mortified and sputtering on her iconic couch.

It was hard not to pity the hapless liar. Indeed, Frey's publisher Nan Talese, who appeared with him on the program (and received her own share of withering wrath), slammed Oprah for her "fiercely bad manners," adding that "you don't stone someone in public, which is just what she did."

And with that verbal missile, Talese schooled Winfrey in another essential truth about truth: It hurts!

JANUARY 27, 1859

A Hiss-toric Performance

"No reaction at all to the first and second movements. At the end, three pairs of hands tried slowly to clap, whereupon a clear hissing from all sides quickly put an end to any such demonstration."

—Johannes Brahms, on the January 27, 1859, performance in Leipzig of his recently premiered Piano Concerto in D Minor

Having obsessed over the work for six years, the 25-year-old composer tried to take the hostile audience response in stride: "I think it's the best thing that could happen to one; it forces you to collect your thoughts and it raises your courage. But the hissing was really too much, wasn't it?"

JANUARY 28, 2011

On Second Thought, Part 2: Love Hurts!

"All my people love me. They would die to protect me."
—Libyan dictator Muammar Qaddafi, January 28, 2011. Less than nine months later, the self-proclaimed "Godfather of Libya, King of Kings of Africa, and Leader Who Lived in All Libyans' Hearts" would be dragged from the filthy drainpipe in which he had hidden himself, beaten, held down on a car hood, violated with a bayonet, and fatally shot.

JANUARY 29, 1942

I Would Not Trust Them on the Coast, I Would Not Serve Them Buttered Toast

The Japanese attack on Pearl Harbor did more than plunge the United States into World War II. It also unleashed a xenophobic frenzy throughout the land, from the highest echelons of government down to ordinary citizens.

And that included newspaper writers.

"I am for the immediate removal of every Japanese on the West Coast to a point deep in the interior," syndicated columnist Henry McLemore wrote of his fellow American citizens in the *Los Angeles Times* (and other outlets) on January 29, 1942. "I don't mean a nice part of the interior either. Herd 'em up, pack 'em off and give 'em the inside room in the badlands. Let 'em be pinched, hurt, hungry, and dead up against it . . . Let us have no patience with the enemy or with anyone whose veins carry his blood . . . Personally, I hate the Japanese. And that goes for all of them."

Even Theodor Geisel, who would become better known as the beloved children's book author Dr. Seuss, was consumed by the hysterical fear that Japanese Americans living on the West Coast were prepared to form a "fifth column" that would abet an enemy invasion. This was widely deemed an unacceptable risk—and it ultimately led to the mass internment of ethnic Japanese in concentration camps.

Two weeks after McLemore's column appeared in his local paper, Geisel published a crass cartoon showing Japanese residents of California lining up to receive packets of TNT from a shack labeled "Honorable 5th Column."

The cartoon's title: "Waiting for the Signal From Home."

JANUARY 30, 1798

Setting Low Expectorations: The First Congressional Spat

On January 30, 1798—just over a year after George Washington warned his countrymen about "the baneful effects of the Spirit of Party" in his farewell address—a violent partisan clash erupted in Congress.

Representative Matthew Lyon of Vermont—a fiery, Irish-born populist in the emergent Democratic-Republican mold—took to taunting his ideological opponent Roger Griswold, a Federalist (or "aristocrat," as Lyon called members of that party) from Connecticut. Loud enough to be overheard, Lyon called Griswold and his fellow congressmen from the Nutmeg State elitists who blithely ignored the will of their constituents. If Lyon traveled to Griswold's home state, he declared, he could instigate a popular revolt that would "turn out the present representatives."

Duly baited, Griswold retorted: "Will you wear your wooden sword when you come into Connecticut?" It was a withering reference to the widely circulated report that Lyon had been court-martialed for cowardice during the Revolutionary War—and sentenced to carry a wooden sword as a badge of shame.*

At first, Lyon ignored the insult. Griswold repeated it. So Lyon strode up and spewed a mouthful of tobacco juice in Griswold's face.

"Spitting Lyon," as he came to be called, faced a fierce rebuke from the Federalists, who moved to expel him from Congress. His actions, declared Christopher Champlin of Rhode Island, "tended to degrade the members of that House from the rank of men, and to reduce them to the level with the meanest reptile that crawled upon the earth." Samuel Otis of Massachusetts branded Lyon "a kennel of filth" and declared that his conduct "would not be suffered in a brothel or a den of robbers." Lyon, he insisted, should be ousted from the House the way "citizens removed impurities and filth from their docks and wharves."

Despite the maelstrom of Federalist indignation, the motion to expel Lyon failed to pass with the necessary two-thirds majority. And that's when Griswold unleashed his own barbaric reprimand—a full fortnight after being left with Lyon's brown spittle dripping down his face.

---

* A member of Ethan Allen's Green Mountain Boys, Lyon took part in capturing Fort Ticonderoga from the British in 1775. The following year, however, Gen. Horatio Gates cashiered Lyon for having failed to halt a mutinous retreat of soldiers under his command. Belying the controversial charge, Lyon was subsequently appointed paymaster of a new regiment, with the rank of captain. And historians suspect that infamous wooden sword of dishonor was an after-the-fact embroidery.

"As soon as I saw [Lyon] in his seat, I took my cane and walked across the floor in front of the speaker's chair," Griswold recounted. "He saw me before I struck him, and was endeavoring to draw a sword cane when I gave him the first blow. I called him a scoundrel and struck him with my cane, and pursued him with more than twenty blows on his head and back until he got possession of a pair of [fireplace] tongs, when I threw him down after giving him several more blows with my fist, I was taken off by his friends."

Lyon, a smug Griswold concluded, was "very much bruised" and had "blood running down his face."

Thus did Lyon and Griswold get the Spirit of Party started—and it's been a rave ever since.

JANUARY 31, 1969

A Shrine Shame

Imagine a sacred space in today's Germany honoring the souls of Hermann Göring and his fellow reptiles from the Third Reich: a temple where war criminals are not just remembered, but revered. Impossible as that may seem—especially in a nation where it is illegal to mimic the Hitler salute—such a place exists for the top Nazis' Axis counterparts in Japan.

On January 31, 1969, representatives of the Imperial Shrine of Yasukuni in central Tokyo decided that the perpetrators of such atrocities as the Bataan Death March and the Rape of Nanking—men responsible for the agony of millions—were "able to be honored" as *kami,* or sacred spirits, among Japan's war dead at the Shinto temple. The religious rationale for including these mass murderers remains mired in an elusive philosophy, but it apparently boils down to this: Naked aggression and gross inhumanity committed for an emperor's sake aren't so bad after all.

February

Billy Graham Preaches Nixon Values

". . . a lot of the Jews are great friends of mine. They swarm around
me and are friendly to me because they know that I'm friendly
with Israel. But they don't know how I really feel about what
they are doing to this country. And I have no power, no way to
handle them, but I would stand up if under proper circumstances."
—*"America's Pastor" Billy Graham, in conversation with*
President Richard Nixon at the White House on February 1, 1972

Reverend Graham's ugly tirade would not come to light for 22 years:
In 1994, Nixon's former chief of staff, H. R. Haldeman, revealed
in his published diaries that the beloved preacher had engaged the president in a "considerable discus-
sion of the terrible problem
arising from the total Jewish
domination of the media."
Not only that, Haldeman
divulged, but president and
prelate had also agreed that
something needed to be done
about the dominance.

"Those are not my words," an indignant Graham fired back at the time. And there the matter seemed to end—until 2002, that is, when the National Archives released an incriminating tape of the Nixon-Graham exchange. The Jewish "stranglehold has got to be broken or the country's going down the drain," Graham can be clearly heard fulminating.

Only when confronted with this proof of his anti-Semitic aspersions did the spiritual counselor to presidents see fit to apologize.

FEBRUARY 2, 1988

Slurring Words of Support

"This country needs a spear chucker,
and I think we've got him right up here on this podium."
—*Mayor Gene Dorff of Kenosha, Wisconsin, introducing African-
American presidential candidate Jesse Jackson at a rally on February 2, 1988*

Mayor Dorff may have been a supporter of Jesse Jackson, but he had a strange way of showing it—"spear chucker" being a notorious racial epithet. But Dorff had in fact meant to *compliment* Jackson, he insisted—as, you know, a guy who could pierce right through any issue. "I wanted him to chuck a spear to the heart," the mayor later backpedaled, "in the context that it go to the heart of the problem."

Mm-hmm.

FEBRUARY 3, 1857

James Buchanan's Dred-ful Act

James Buchanan was not just one of the nation's worst presidents; he was a terrible president-elect, too.

On February 3, 1857—a month before his Inauguration—Buchanan launched a secret and highly unscrupulous campaign to sway the Supreme Court to render what is widely considered its worst decision. In the *Dred Scott* v. *Sandford* case, the soon-to-be 15th American president prodded, cajoled, and essentially bribed with favors various justices of the Court in an egregious breach of the line supposedly separating the executive and judicial branches of government. Buchanan got his way, pushing a fractured nation ever closer to civil war.

According to historians, the Court had been inclined to consider *Scott* in the most narrow and immediate context of the case—that is, whether or not Dred Scott, having been enslaved in Missouri, was now a free man because of the time he had spent in free territory. A lower court had determined that he was, based on the state's long-held judicial standard of "Once free, always free." The Missouri Supreme Court reversed that decision, however: "Times are not as they were when the former decisions on this subject were made," the high court declared. Scott next filed in federal court, lost, and ultimately appealed to the U.S. Supreme Court.

A year after oral arguments were first heard in *Dred Scott* v. *Sandford,* Buchanan metaphorically slithered into the Court's chambers with emphatic correspondence to present his own case.

The president-elect was after something more than a simple decision on Scott's status as a free or enslaved man. He expected a permanent solution to the nation's most bitterly divisive issue: Did the federal government have the constitutional power to regulate if and where human bondage might exist in U.S. territories, as it had done with the Missouri Compromise of 1820?

"The great object of my administration will be if possible to destroy the dangerous slavery agitation and thus restore peace to our distracted country," Buchanan wrote to Justice Robert Grier.

The president-in-waiting might simply have stated that he didn't need that headache when he took office. And that he wanted the decision to favor the slaveholding southern states, which in his mind would benefit tremendously from unfettered expansion into the territories. In the end, the supposedly independent Court gave James Buchanan a gift-wrapped ruling: Dred Scott was declared barely human, and certainly no citizen of the United States; therefore, he lacked standing to file for his freedom in the first place. Far more ominous, the Court declared the Missouri Compromise unconstitutional. Slavery, in essence, would be allowed to metastasize, unrestrained by federal law.

Though the incendiary decision was handed down on March 6, 1857—two days after Buchanan's Inauguration—the president had known exactly what was coming when he swore the oath of office. Indeed, on that day it was easy for him to announce with all the umble sincerity of Dickens's Uriah Heep: "To their decision, in common with all good citizens, I shall cheerfully submit, whatever this may be."

❦

FEBRUARY 4, 1940

Stalin's Henchman:
Cropping a Killer's Career

Five-foot-tall secret police commissar Nikolai Yezhov was Joseph Stalin's "Mini-Me." A compact mirror of the Soviet tyrant, Yezhov reflected every bit of Stalin's murderous zeal to cleanse his iron regime of perceived political threats.

"Our Soviet people will exterminate to a man all these despicable servants of the capitalist lords, vile enemies of all workers," Yezhov declared in the midst of the Great Purge he orchestrated on behalf of his boss in the mid-1930s. From high-ranking Red Army generals and Communist Party apparatchiks to low-status peasants, more than a million citizens were seized. Hundreds of thousands were summarily shot in a bid to quench Stalin's thirst for blood.

"There will be some innocent victims in this fight against Fascist agents," Yezhov said. "We are launching a major attack on the Enemy;

let there be no resentment if we bump someone with an elbow. Better that ten innocent people should suffer than one spy get away. When you chop wood, chips fly."

Stalin was well pleased with his pet monster, who kept as souvenirs the bullets used to execute his most prominent enemies. In July 1937—with mass arrests and murders in full fury—Yezhov was awarded the Order of Lenin, the Soviet Union's highest civilian decoration. Schools and factories were named in his honor. Paeans were written to "Great Stalin's faithful friend."

But don't expect fealty from a scorpion. As so often happened with those who surrounded the dictator, "Great Stalin" eventually stung Yezhov. Turns out the loyal killer was a bit *too* much like the tyrant, who now wished to distance himself from the fiendish purge he had launched.

On February 4, 1940, Yezhov found himself in the very execution chamber he had designed for maximum efficiency, crying for mercy. According to one official witness, Yezhov "became hysterical" when he learned his appeal had been denied. "He started to hiccup [and] weep, and when he was conveyed to 'the place,' they had to drag him by the hands along the floor. He struggled and screamed terribly."

Yezhov's corpse was incinerated after his execution; his memory was obliterated as well. In a primitive form of Photoshop (call it photo-*chop*), the regime that had encouraged Yezhov's reign of terror proceeded to manually erase the junior reptile from images of him posed next to the master fiend Stalin.

FEBRUARY 5, 2011

Unnecessary Dumbness:
Dallas Venerates Michael Vick

Perhaps inspired by the Detroit officials who had given the key to their city to Saddam Hussein in 1980, a misguided functionary of Dallas,

Texas, bestowed that same honor on Michael Vick on February 5, 2011. Not only was Vick a barbarous animal abuser—owner and operator of the savage dogfighting club Bad Newz Kennels—but he also quarterbacked the Philadelphia Eagles, archrivals of the Dallas Cowboys. Exalting Vick on home turf was therefore roughly the equivalent of a fifth-century Roman emperor celebrating Attila the Hun Day.

"I would like to personally present to Michael Vick the key to the city of Dallas, Texas," announced controversial Mayor Pro Tem Dwaine Caraway, who had apparently made the decision to honor Vick without consulting the actual mayor. "Michael," effused Caraway, "you deserve it. You earned it. We appreciate you, and we love you."*

FEBRUARY 6, 1935

If Your Boyfriend Were Adolf Hitler, Wouldn't *You* Want a Puppy?

Poor Eva Braun: Her boyfriend was a genocidal monster with bad breath, commitment issues, and a fierce addiction to multiple drugs. Worse, he wouldn't give her a puppy for her birthday.

"If I had a dog I would not feel so lonely," Hitler's mistress lamented in her diary on February 6, 1935. Sure, the führer had sent her flowers, but you can't cuddle vegetation. "I suppose I am ungrateful," Braun continued in her birthday entry, "but I did want to be given a dachshund. And I just don't have one. Perhaps I'll get one next year, or much later, when it will be more appropriate for a budding old maid."

---

* No such love and appreciation flowed from the city's denizens toward the flashy politician (who once dressed as a pimp for Halloween): In April 2019, Caraway was sentenced to four years in prison for accepting nearly half a million dollars in kickbacks and bribes from 2011 to 2017.

Less than three months after her doggone birthday, the forlorn mistress tried to kill herself. Hitler got the message, and soon Braun was doting on two Scottish terriers she named Negus (or "King") and Stasi (prophetically, the title of the postwar East German secret police).

But there would be no happy endings for this canine crew. Not only did Eva's dogs despise Hitler's German shepherd, Blondi, but all three animals were killed when their master and mistress committed suicide as the Third Reich collapsed around them in 1945.

FEBRUARY 7, 1940

Jiminy Cricket! This Film Isn't Worth a Wooden Nickel!

"I'd rather have an artistic flop than a box-office smash hit any day," Walt Disney confidently declared during a meeting at the end of January 1940. But that was a week before the February 7 premiere of his company's second full-length animated feature, *Pinocchio*, which bombed: It lost some $18 million (in 2020 dollars) in just the first year of its release.

Like the film's animated leviathan, Monstro the Whale, Disney had to swallow the production's oversize budget. And now—far from the ebullient mastermind behind 1937's enormously successful *Snow White and the Seven Dwarfs*—Uncle Walt was as forlorn as Eeyore. "He was very, very depressed about it," Disney's associate Joe King later told animation historian Michael Barrier. Undeterred, the company founder had hope that another animated extravaganza in the pipeline would recover *Pinocchio*'s losses: *Fantasia* was set for release later in the year.

Alas, it too flopped.*

———

FEBRUARY 8, 1831

He *Really* Dug His Wife

"Time is a physician that heals every grief," the ancient Greek playwright Diphilus wrote. But for Ralph Waldo Emerson, time only exacerbated the emotion—to a disturbing degree. "O willingly, my wife, I would lie down in your tomb," the philosopher and essayist wrote in despair after the death of his young spouse, Ellen, on February 8, 1831.

A year later, Emerson took a literal step in that direction. "I visited Ellen's tomb & opened the coffin," he confided to his diary. The sight of his wife's decaying remains apparently left the leader of America's transcendentalist movement unfazed: Fifteen years after the death of his five-year-old son, Waldo, in 1842, Emerson reportedly cracked open *his* coffin as well.

In a coda crawling with macabre irony, vandals desecrated Emerson's grave at Sleepy Hollow Cemetery in 1889, seven years after his death. Interrupted after digging up the casket, the scoundrels never got their Emersonian peek at the deceased, however—nor the plunder they were apparently seeking.

———

* Both films got off to a slow start because World War II had depressed revenues from the formerly lucrative European and Asian markets. Walt Disney eventually recouped his losses, however, and *Pinocchio* and *Fantasia* went on to become fantastically profitable cinema classics.

FEBRUARY 9, 2014

Zoo-illogical

February 9, 2014, was a perfect day to take the kids to the Copenhagen Zoo—if one happened to be raising a future serial killer.

A special event was staged that day: After being served his favorite meal of rye bread, a perfectly healthy 18-month-old giraffe named Marius—all gangly gracefulness and impossibly long lashes—was shot dead. (His genes had been deemed redundant for the zoo's breeding program.) Then, for the edification of the assembled children, the young giraffe's carcass was dissected in an outdoor space. That gruesome spectacle completed, Marius was chopped into bloody chunks and fed to the zoo's carnivores.

"I'm actually proud," a spokesperson for the Copenhagen Zoo told the Associated Press. "We have given children a huge understanding of the anatomy of a giraffe that they wouldn't have had from watching a giraffe in a photo."

No mention of whether that pride extended to giving the kids some very long-necked nightmares.

FEBRUARY 10, 1940

FDR's Generation Slap

The weather was foul in Washington on February 10, 1940—but far worse that day was President Franklin Roosevelt's mood. Thousands of young people from the communist-leaning American Youth Council had gathered on the front lawn of the White House, invited there by First Lady Eleanor Roosevelt, to set the president straight on social issues. But FDR wasn't about to sit and endure their simplistic nostrums. Adopting the tone of a crusty grandfather who's seen how the world works, the president delivered a lacerating speech from the South Portico—"a verbal spanking," as biographer Joseph P. Lash described it, more stinging than the freezing rain pelting the self-righteous mass.

"The young people had begun to irritate him," Lash wrote. "His wife's leaning over backward to put the best face on their arguments irritated him even more." The resulting speech, therefore, was a rebuke of both the radicalized kids and the first lady's naive embrace of them*—an address devoid of the warmth and charm that were FDR's customary signatures on such occasions.

"Do not as a group pass resolutions on subjects which you have not thought through and on which you cannot possibly have complete knowledge," the president sternly advised—just before dismissing one such Youth Council proclamation as "absolute twaddle."†

Stung by Franklin's verbal frostbite, the red-faced Reds headed for the relative winter warmth to be found *off* the White House lawn.

FEBRUARY 11, 1964

Hey RUDE!

With the shrieking teens now home and in bed, the Beatles probably expected a staid reception at the British Embassy after their first U.S. concert, which had taken place at the Washington Coliseum on February 11, 1964. Not that they relished the prospect. "We always tried

---

* As one astute observer in the crowd noted, "He doesn't like the smell of the albatross that his wife has hung around his neck."

† The Youth Council objected to American aid being sent to Finland—fighting off an attempted Soviet invasion at the time—because the council viewed it as "an attempt to force America into an imperialistic war," as FDR contemptuously quoted its resolution. Such an idea, the president sniffed, "is about the silliest thought that I ever heard advanced in the fifty-eight years of my life."

to get out of those crap things," George Harrison told Beatles biographer Hunter Davies. "But that time we got caught."

A bizarre mix of adulation and condescension ensued. "Just a little quiet party, they tell you," Ringo Starr recalled. "But when you get there, they've got their friends all lined up and you feel like something in a zoo."

Stiff upper lips melted upon the band's arrival: The esteemed guests "shrieked, squealed, pushed and kicked each other to get a look at what one stately diplomatic wife termed 'those darling little baby boys,'" *The Washington Post* reported. One "bloody animal," said John Lennon, attacked Ringo's hair with a pair of scissors, intent on taking home a tonsorial souvenir. "I walked out of that," Lennon later told *Rolling Stone* magazine. "Swearing at all of them, and . . . left in the middle of it."

Those not falling over themselves to embrace or assault a Beatle treated the Fab Four with contempt. "There was more than a hint of the master-servant relationship in one [bureaucrat's] voice when he said: 'Come along, you there, you've got to come and do your stuff,'" observed journalist Bruce Phillips. When guests demanded autographs, officials insisted that the lads oblige. "Sign this," one said to Lennon, who declined, prompting the command: "You'll sign this and like it."

"The Beatles were treated like yobs!" recalled photographer Harry Benson, who traveled with the band. "They were very sad. They looked as if they wanted to cry. John in particular. They weren't pugnacious, they were humiliated!"

Perhaps Lennon had that night at the embassy in mind when he wrote the alienated lyrics to "I'll Cry Instead," released six months later.

FEBRUARY 12, 1976

When the Fist Is Mightier Than the Pen: A Nobel Prizefight

Colombian novelist Gabriel García Márquez seemed genuinely delighted to spot his friend, the Peruvian writer Mario Vargas Llosa, at a Mexico

City film premiere on February 12, 1976. "Mario!" the author of *One Hundred Years of Solitude* boomed across the room.

Vargas Llosa returned the greeting with a balled fist, punching his old friend square in the face. "How dare you come and greet me after what you did to Patricia in Barcelona!" the *Conversation in the Cathedral* writer roared at García Márquez. It was the spark that ignited an epic literary feud between two future winners of the Nobel Prize in Literature.

What triggered Vargas Llosa's eruption? That's a mystery—"a real Gordian knot for their biographers to unravel," as García Márquez expert Dasso Saldivar told the Associated Press in 2007.

Some speculate it was a political rift or professional jealousy. But in that case, what to make of "Patricia"? Photographer Rodrigo Moya shed some light on the truth in an essay recounting his photo session with a black-eyed García Márquez two days after the blowup. According to Moya, the novelist told him the details: Vargas Llosa had left his wife, Patricia, for a Swedish flight attendant, whereupon Patricia came crying to García Márquez. The latter comforted her—and urged her to file for divorce.

What degree of comfort did García Márquez provide Patricia? That may have to remain a surprise ending.

FEBRUARY 13, 1818

The Royal Obstetrician's Labor Pains

Nearly two centuries before the tragic death of Diana, Princess of Wales, a similar pall of grief fell over Britain when another beloved princess—Charlotte of Wales—died while giving birth in the fall of 1817. No mourner felt the loss more keenly than Sir Richard Croft, Princess Charlotte's obstetrician. After all, it was his responsibility to see that she gave birth safely, and in that he had failed.

Public calumny was then heaped atop Sir Richard's private anguish. "These arrows, shot by premeditated malice, pierced into a spirit peculiarly sensitive of honor," read one contemporary account, "and ultimately led to that catastrophe which feeling and candid mind must regret." For it was on February 13, 1818, that the despondent Sir Richard Croft took two guns and shot himself.*

The Eyesore Tower

"We shall see stretching out like a black blot, the odious shadow of the odious column built up of riveted iron plates."
— *"Protest against the Tower of Monsieur Eiffel,"*
published in Le Temps, *February 14, 1887*

Barely had the foundation for the Eiffel Tower been poured in Paris when an elite group of French writers and artists launched an all-out attack on the soon-to-be-iconic structure. The "useless and monstrous" monolith would dominate the French capital, they warned in a letter published in the newspaper *Le Temps* on February 14, 1887, "like a gigantic, black factory chimney, crushing with its barbaric mass" the city's most cherished edifices. Notre-Dame, the Arc de Triomphe—all of them were sure to be "humiliated" and "shrunken . . . disappearing affrighted in this bewildering dream."

---

* Sir Richard's fatal regret had a peculiar precedent in British royal history. One day in the summer of 1640, Abraham van der Doort, the first Surveyor of the King's Pictures, was mortified to discover that a miniature painting by English artist Richard Gibson had gone missing from the collection of Charles I. Rather than face the shame of losing one of Charles's favorite artworks, van der Doort hanged himself. The miniature would later be recovered—but not before German poet Georg Rudolf Weckherlin had penned this poisonous epitaph: "Anxious to do his duty well / Van Dort [sic] there, conscientious elf / from hanging up his pictures, fell / One day to hanging up himself."

Being French, the critics couldn't resist dragging those notoriously boorish Americans into the fray: "The Eiffel Tower, which even the United States would not countenance, is surely going to dishonor Paris."

The siege of the tower didn't end with that broadside of collective indignation. Indeed, engineer Gustave Eiffel's revolutionary design raised a number of French writers to new heights of individual invective: To pamphleteer Léon Bloy, the tower was a "truly tragic street lamp." To poet Paul Verlaine, it was nothing more than the "skeleton of a belfry." Playwright François Coppée found the "iron gymnasium apparatus" to be "incomplete, confused and deformed," while novelist J. K. Huysmans couldn't resist blasting away with metaphors both necrotic and scatological: The Eiffel Tower was "a carcass waiting to be fleshed out with free-stone or brick," Huysmans inveighed, to say nothing of its resemblance to "a hole-riddled suppository."

The acclaimed short-story writer Guy de Maupassant, who had attached his name to the *Le Temps* letter, remained relentless in his criticism of the Eiffel Tower—"This high and skinny pyramid of iron ladders," as he described it, "this giant ungainly skeleton upon a base that looks built to carry a colossal monument of Cyclops, but which just peters out into a ridiculous thin shape like a factory chimney."

Much as he hated the tower, however, Maupassant often ate lunch in its restaurant. "It's the only place in Paris," he explained, "where I don't have to see it."

FEBRUARY 15, 1924

We Interrupt This Decade...

R eaders of the February 15, 1924, edition of *Maclean's* magazine—reveling in the relative peace and prosperity of the Roaring Twenties—were rudely doused with the pessimistic predictions of the author and journalist Sir Philip Gibbs, acclaimed for his frontline reporting during World War I. Although that horrific conflict had concluded six years earlier, Gibbs nevertheless insisted there was little expectation for a lasting peace:

"I had hoped—and by that hope I believed—that after the dreadful lessons of war and its overwhelming costs to victors and vanquished, there would be a growing allegiance to some new code of international law, such as that possessed in the League of Nations, which would substitute arbitration for the old argument of force, and justice for the brutal claim that might is right," he observed gloomily. "That hope must now, I think, be postponed."

Sir Philip then became frighteningly specific:

"The groundwork of the new order laid down by the treaty of Versailles is beginning to crack and crumble above a boiling lava of human passion," he declared, a full decade before Hitler assumed dictatorial powers in Germany. "Europe is once more slipping downhill and gathering speed on the slope."

(As it happens, the writer had been made cynical by experience. On the commencement of the Battle of the Somme, which took a million lives, he informed his readers, "It is, on balance, a good day for England and France. It is a day of promise in this war.")

Incidentally, on the same day Gibbs's dismal prognostication was published in *Maclean's*, Senator Frank L. Greene of Vermont was facing a more immediate crisis—one arising from the contemporaneous Prohibition era.

Strolling with his wife near the U.S. Capitol, Greene found himself in the midst of a gun battle between government agents and a band of bootleggers. A stray bullet entered his skull, leaving the senator partially paralyzed for the rest of his life.

He died six years later—just as clouds of the cataclysmic storm predicted by Sir Philip Gibbs gathered ominously over Europe.

FEBRUARY 16, 1948

Time's Cold-Blooded Response

"So fierce is the world's ridicule we cannot speak
or show our tenderness . . ."
—*Truman Capote,* Other Voices, Other Rooms

Time magazine printed an especially nasty review of Truman Capote's otherwise acclaimed first novel, 1948's *Other Voices, Other Rooms,* declaring that the book was "calculated to make the flesh crawl . . . The distasteful trappings of its homosexual theme overhang it like Spanish moss."

At least one reader of the weekly newsmagazine was left choking on the vitriol dripping from the page. In a letter to the editor published on February 16, 1948, one R. E. Berg of San Francisco objected to the tone of the review and questioned why the magazine—so progressive on other social issues—remained stubbornly puritanical about same-sex attraction: "I do not believe you have ever made a reference to homosexuality . . . without going specifically out of your way to make a vicious insinuation, caustic remark, or 'dirty dig' . . . I have seen a great deal of Spanish moss in a lot of places . . . and I must confess that some of it is quite beautiful."

The editors' response, printed below Berg's letter:

"It gives TIME the creeps."

FEBRUARY 17, 1921

When Henry Ford
Mass-Produced Hate

"The only statement I care to make about *The Protocols* is that
they fit in with what is going on. They are sixteen years old and
they have fitted the world situation up to this time. They fit it now."
—*Auto pioneer Henry Ford, in a* New York World *interview
published on February 17, 1921, praising an anti-Semitic screed
known as* The Protocols of the Elders of Zion

The Protocols, detailing a supposed Jewish plot for world domination,
were a proven forgery—the 1905 handiwork of the Russian tsar's
secret police, consisting largely of passages plagiarized from other works.
But that didn't stop Henry Ford from running a series of anti-Jewish
diatribes based on *The Protocols* in the weekly newspaper he owned, *The
Dearborn Independent.* The inflammatory columns would later be compiled into a best-selling and highly influential book, *The International Jew.*

Most modern scholars agree that Ford's aggressive promotion of *The
Protocols* helped spread the virus of anti-Semitism worldwide. In Germany, for example, Adolf Hitler awarded Ford the Nazi Iron Cross and
declared, "You can tell Herr Ford that I am a great admirer of his. I shall
do my best to put his theories into practice."

Tragically, *The Protocols* remain the bible of bigots everywhere.

———◆———

FEBRUARY 18, 1885

A Tad Too Much Tumescence

"If Mr. Clemens cannot think of something better to tell our
pure-minded lads and lasses he had best stop writing for them."

—Little Women *author Louisa May Alcott on*
Mark Twain's Adventures of Huckleberry Finn

February 18, 1885, was definitely *not* the date Samuel Clemens (aka Mark Twain) chose for the publication of the American edition of *Adventures of Huckleberry Finn*. He had hoped the picaresque novel would be out in time for the previous Christmas season—"the best time in the year to tumble a big pile into the trade," as he put it. That goal became impossible, however, thanks to a cheeky saboteur who caused a two-month production delay by etching an obscene bit of erect anatomy onto one of the illustration plates.

"Had the mistake not been discovered," noted Twain's publishing director (and nephew by marriage), Charles L. Webster, "Mr. Clemens's credit for decency and morality would have been destroyed." Although the public was ultimately spared the sight of an aroused Uncle Silas Phelps—the subject of the enhanced illustration—Twain's decency was nevertheless called into question when *Huckleberry Finn* was finally released.

The now classic novel was greeted in some quarters by "genteel recoiling," wrote Robert B. Brown in *American Heritage.* Indeed, within one short month of its publication, *Huck Finn* had been banned from the shelves of the Concord Free Public Library in Massachusetts. "I regard it as the veriest trash," said an unnamed member of the library committee. In the eyes of another, "The whole book is of a class that is more profitable for the slums than it is for respectable people."

More libraries (and eventually schools) followed Concord's lead. And over the decades that followed, objections to the novel gradually moved from priggish condemnations of its subject matter to outraged denunciations of the perceived racism at its core. In 1982, for example, an education official in Virginia branded *Huckleberry Finn* a "grotesque example of racist trash." He then tried to have it removed from the curriculum—missing the irony, perhaps, that he was an administrator at Mark Twain Intermediate School.

It's intriguing to speculate how all the moral histrionics might have fueled Twain's satirical genius. As Henry Allen wrote in *The Washington*

Post a century after *Huck* was first expelled from Concord, "That novel remains one of the finest litmus tests yet devised for fools, school administrators, purveyors of racial prudery and others inflated by the gas of purest sanctimony."

How to Make Lame Duck in Mere Minutes

On February 19, 1913, Pedro José Domingo de la Calzada Manuel María Lascuráin Paredes served as president of Mexico for less than 60 minutes—not much more time than it took to utter his full name.

Lascuráin exerted his glancing grip on power during "the tragic 10 days" of the Mexican Revolution, when a U.S.-backed coup by Victoriano Huerta toppled sitting President Francisco Madero.

To claim his prize—the presidency—Huerta had to maintain a pretense of legality. Enter Lascuráin: According to the Mexican Constitution, the nation's vice president and attorney general would have been next in line for the top job once Madero was removed. But Huerta had ousted them as well, so it fell to Lascuráin—as foreign secretary, he was third in the line of succession—to become the president of Mexico.

This perfectly suited Huerta's agenda. He forced Lascuráin to name him interior secretary, thus positioning himself fourth in the constitutionally mandated order. Then, immediately after the appointment, Lascuráin obligingly resigned.

Mexico's minutes-long president was fortunate to survive the coup; both Madero and his toppled vice president, José María Pino Suárez, were murdered in its aftermath. In fact, Lascuráin lived another four decades, dying in 1952 at the age of 96. His political agility thus distinguished him as having the shortest presidency in world history—but his durability made him Mexico's second longest-lived former president.

You *Can* Go Home Again—
But Should You?

General Hussein Kamel al-Majid was wise enough to get the hell out of Iraq after running afoul of his cousin and brother-in-law Uday, the savagely homicidal son of Iraqi dictator Saddam Hussein. But six months after defecting to Jordan in August 1995, Kamel was dumb enough to return—lured to his doom by a promise of amnesty. "You ass," his brother and fellow defector reportedly shouted at him, "you want us to go back to our deaths!"

Having served high up in Saddam's murderous regime, Kamel should have known that any hands welcoming him back to Iraq would soon be encircling his throat. Consider the facts: If Iraqi athletes could be fed into Uday's torture chambers merely for losing a game—and they were— what fate but extermination could possibly await a high-status defector such as Kamel? Hadn't the country's onetime oil minister and head of weapons-development programs spoken a bit too impulsively when he publicly advocated the overthrow of his father-in-law's "treacherous and oppressive regime"?

Sure enough, Uday came to greet Hussein and his brother, along with their spouses, Raghad and Rana—both sisters of Uday—when the foursome crossed back over the Iraqi border from Jordan on February 20, 1996. Uday whisked his sisters away in his Mercedes, leaving the brothers to make their own way home. Raghad and Rana were immediately granted divorces because, as the official line had it, the women "could not live with those who have been traitors and have been unfaithful to their country and the noble values of their family."

Three days later came the predictable denouement. On February 23, machine-gun bullets, mortar shells, and grenades began to rain down on the al-Majid homestead in Baghdad. Both brothers, their father, another brother, their sister, and two of her children were killed in the ensuing 13-hour firefight. Kamel's corpse was reportedly desecrated afterward.

Two attackers slain in the fray were declared martyrs—and given an official state funeral. Leading the solemn mourning procession? Uday, of course.

FEBRUARY 21, 1437

The *James* Jinx:
Scotland's Royal Shit Show

It's good to be the king—unless your name happens to be "James" and Scotland is your realm. Then you're dealing with something akin to a curse.

It all began on February 21, 1437, when James I tried to flee his assassins by climbing down into a sewage tunnel beneath the royal chambers. The king might have escaped his ghastly demise—he was stabbed to death in a stinking stream of waste—but for two key mistakes: Weeks earlier, frustrated by the loss of some tennis balls in that same tunnel, James had ordered the passage blocked off, thus depriving himself of an emergency exit. Then, having successfully concealed himself in this crappy conduit, James mistakenly judged that his killers had left his bedroom; his cries for help fatally alerted the assassins to his presence below.

James I's execrable end was emblematic of his family's future.

The king's son, James II, fared almost as badly as his hapless father.

A proponent of modernizing Scottish artillery, he imported a number of cannons from Flanders and, in 1460, laid siege to Roxburgh Castle, held by the English. Unfortunately, one of the new cannons, known as "The Lion," exploded as the 29-year-old monarch—"more curious than became him, or the majesty of a king," as Robert Lindsay of Pitscottie reported—stood next to it. His "thigh-bone was dung in two with a piece of misframed gun that brake in shooting," Lindsay elaborated, "by which he was stricken to the ground and died hastily."

James II was succeeded by his preteen son, who was still too young and inexperienced to rule on his own. Alas, once he came of age, James III was an ineffective ruler: He endured rebellion and even imprisonment before a final clash with his nobles (led by his own son) claimed his life at the Battle of Sauchieburn in 1488.

Accounts vary as to precisely how James III died. One story has it that he found refuge with a local peasant after the battle, only to be slaughtered there by a rebel disguised as a priest. Others indicate he died in battle. Whatever happened, James III had joined his father and grandfather in a ghastly heritage—one that his own son would unluckily carry forward.

The fourth James made the fatal mistake of invading England while his brother-in-law, Henry VIII,* was off fighting in France. Little did James IV know that Henry's queen, Katharine of Aragon—more familiar in history as the pious victim of her husband's lust for Anne Boleyn—was a bit of a savage when it came to warfare. After English troops killed James at the Battle of Flodden in 1513, Katharine, serving as regent during Henry's absence, yearned to send her husband his enemy's pierced corpse as a trophy. But, she wrote regretfully, "our Englishmen's hearts would not suffer it." Katharine therefore had to settle for sending Henry the Scottish king's bloodied coat—which, she suggested in an accompanying letter, would make a fine banner. Thus, while James IV avoided the posthumous shame of having his carcass indecorously displayed in France, it was nonetheless left to rot unburied.

---

* James IV was married to Henry VIII's sister, Margaret Tudor.

The saga of the jinxed Jameses seemed to conclude in 1542, when James V died in his own bed—though of a broken heart, it was said, after Scotland lost yet another battle to the English at Solway Moss. Had the Caledonian curse finally been dispelled? Perhaps not. James V's six-day-old daughter, Mary, inherited not only her father's throne but his woebegone legacy: This Queen of Scots died more ignominiously than any of her forebears—on a chopping block, in a notoriously botched beheading.

There would be one last James—No. VII—on the Scottish throne, and he brought the feculent legacy of the first James full circle: This king, who also ruled England as James II, was deposed by his own daughter and son-in-law, who went on to rule as William and Mary. James tried to win his crown back in 1690, but he was defeated by William's forces at the Battle of the Boyne in Ireland. The ex-king deserted his Irish supporters so hurriedly afterward that they concocted an enduring epithet for him: Séamus an Chaca, or James the Shit.

FEBRUARY 22, 1900

The Poppycock Cure: Take Two Doses and Call Me *If* There's a Morning

Before being outlawed in the United States in 1924, heroin was enthusiastically embraced by some unlikely merchants of death: family physicians.

Doctors routinely touted the opium derivative as a nonaddictive alternative to morphine. They prescribed it for any number of ailments—especially the common cough. "No other drug can compare with heroin in this particular," one general practitioner declared in the February 22, 1900, edition of the *Boston Medical and Surgical Journal.* "It does not cause unpleasant disturbance of the stomach or intestine," the article continued. "It can be prescribed in cases in which heart complications occur without risk of any deleterious effect upon that organ."

Other than, you know, stopping it.*

❦

Inaugural Digress:
Lincoln Makes Quiet an Entrance

"We cannot believe that a man of his bold and open bearing,
who has hewn his way by strength of arm, and will,
and force of character to his present high position,
would blench at the first show of danger."
—New York World *editorial, February 1861, condemning President-elect
Abraham Lincoln's backdoor arrival in Washington to take office*

Early in 1861, with a simmering nation on the cusp of civil war, Abraham Lincoln's friends were concerned that the president-elect would be assassinated before he could be sworn into office that March. They were right to be alarmed. Allan Pinkerton—the renowned detective charged with the security of the railroads on which Lincoln was traveling from his home in Springfield, Illinois, to Washington, D.C.—had sniffed out evidence of a murder plot brewing in Baltimore, Maryland, just 40 miles north of the capital.

"The opposition to Mr. Lincoln's inauguration was most violent and bitter," Pinkerton wrote, "and a few days' sojourn in this city convinced me that great danger was to be apprehended."

---

* Bayer, the German company in whose labs heroin was first synthesized, marketed the drug more aggressively than its other new product, aspirin. Countless patients became addicted as a result.

Baltimore at the time was a violence-prone town surging with seces-sionist sentiment,* but Lincoln's first reaction was to ignore the rum-blings of menace. He likewise rebuffed Gen. Winfield Scott's suggestion that he alter his scheduled stop in Baltimore, the last before Washington, by boarding a diversionary train that would take him through the city under cover of darkness. That would make the opposite of a reassuring impression of leadership in these fraught times, Lincoln argued: "What would the nation think of its President stealing into its capital like a thief in the night?"

Not much, it turned out.

Lincoln's worried advisers eventually persuaded him that more was at stake than his personal safety: It was the Union itself, the nation he had been charged to preserve. Thus the soon-to-be 16th president—thinly disguised in an old overcoat, with a soft cap replacing his trademark stovepipe hat—reluctantly allowed himself to be hidden in a sleeping car and whisked away in the early morning hours of February 23, 1861. He quietly arrived in Washington at 6 a.m.—safe, sound, and soon very sorry.

"This surreptitious nocturnal dodging or sneaking of the president-elect into his capital city, under cloud of night, will be used to damage his moral position and throw ridicule on his administration," lawyer George Templeton Strong correctly predicted in his diary.

Press reaction across the country, both in print and in caricature, was merciless—the president-elect's cowardice a recurring editorial theme. "Had we any respect for Mr. Lincoln," *The Baltimore Sun* harrumphed, "the final escapade by which he reached the capital would have utterly demolished [it], and overwhelmed us with mortification."

The *Sun*'s stance was hardly surprising, given the insult delivered to the bypassed city, but Lincoln took fire from his home state as well: "The dignity of his station, and regard for the character of his country, should have forbidden that he sneak to the nation's capital incog., like a refugee from justice," the *Illinois State Register* opined.

---

* Although Maryland refrained from the secession march of other states after Lincoln's election, it remained strongly pro-slavery.

One of the few voices raised in Lincoln's defense belonged to abolitionist Frederick Douglass. "He reached the Capital as the poor, hunted fugitive slave reaches the North, in disguise, seeking concealment, evading pursuers, by the underground railroad, between two days, not during the sunlight, but crawling and dodging under the sable wing of night," Douglass wrote in a benevolent comparison. "He changed his programme, took another route, started at another hour, traveled in other company, and arrived at another time in Washington . . . We have no censure for the President at this point. He only did what braver men have done."

But that endorsement provided little solace to Abraham Lincoln. "You . . . know that the way we skulked into this city . . . has been a source of shame and regret to me," the president told his friend Ward Hill Lamon years later, "for it did look so cowardly!"

FEBRUARY 24, 1902

Guess Who's *Not* Coming to Dinner?

"The President regrets that he is compelled to withdraw the invitation to you to dine to-night at the White House."
—*Message from Theodore Roosevelt's secretary to Senator Benjamin Tillman of South Carolina, delivered on February 24, 1902—two days after Tillman had socked a fellow congressman on the Senate floor*

The president's snub—based on the congressional brawl he considered to be an egregious breach of decorum—mortified Tillman. South Carolina's senior senator had been treated "in a cowardly and ungentlemanly way" by "this ill-bred creature who is accidentally President," Tillman indignantly claimed in a letter to Charleston mayor James A. Smyth.

But buried in the dinner cancellation was an even more detestable slight for the homicidally racist senator: Four months earlier, Booker T. Washington—a black man!—had been welcomed to dine where Tillman had just been refused.

Appalled at Washington's invitation to the White House, Tillman railed at the time: "We shall have to kill a thousand niggers to get them back in their places."

Instead, Teddy firmly put Tillman back in *his* place.

FEBRUARY 25, 628

A Quickie Reign of Ruin

Shah Kavad II, ruler of a vast empire encompassing most of the Middle East, had a very brief reign.

It began on February 25, 628, after Kavad's father was deposed (and subsequently executed by his son); it ended about six months later when the shah was felled by a plague. But his time on the throne wasn't nearly short enough for his many brothers and half brothers, most of whom were slaughtered by their tyrannical sibling. Or for his stepmother—who, legend has it, committed suicide, rather than be forced into marrying him. Or for the Sasanian Empire itself, whose precipitate decline is often attributed to Kavad II's abbreviated but reckless rule.

FEBRUARY 26, 1972

Crying Foul: The Fake News That Felled Ed Muskie

"Boy! That's not the man I want to have
with his finger on the nuclear button."
—*William Loeb, publisher of the Manchester* Union Leader

A mong the oft told tales of presidential campaign implosions, Edmund Muskie's tearful breakdown at an outdoor news conference on February 26, 1972, is one of the most notorious.

The well-regarded senator from Maine, leading a large field of Democrats, was thought to have a decent chance of unseating President Richard Nixon in the fall election—until that fateful snowy day when he allegedly broke down and wept, coming off as weak and unsteady. *The Washington Post*'s David Broder, considered the dean of political reporting and punditry, filed a report of the event. And it was his front-page account—written, as Broder later acknowledged, "in an unrestrained fashion"—that became definitive.

Regrettably, it was also wrong—or at least seriously misleading.

"With tears streaming down his face and his voice choked with emotion, Sen. Edmund S. Muskie (D-Maine) stood in the snow outside the Manchester *Union Leader* this morning and accused its publisher of making vicious attacks on him and his wife, Jane," Broder's story began. "In defending his wife, Muskie broke down three times in as many minutes—uttering a few words and then standing silent in the near blizzard, rubbing at his face, his shoulders heaving, while he attempted to regain his composure sufficiently to speak."

Muskie was undeniably angry that day. The *Union Leader*'s far right publisher, William Loeb, had indeed been smearing the candidate and his wife in a series of front-page editorials. Muskie, Loeb had written, was a hypocrite who, according to an account sent to Loeb from an unnamed letter writer in Florida, had used the derogatory term "Canucks" to describe French Canadians—a significant voting bloc in New Hampshire. And Muskie's wife, Loeb added, was a crude slob.

Outraged by the attacks, Muskie rented a flatbed truck upon which he stood right in front of the *Union Leader*'s Manchester headquarters and railed against Loeb, calling him a "gutless coward" (among other epithets). The harsh words were sometimes choked, but witnesses standing directly before the candidate reported that Muskie never cried. Instead, he merely wiped falling snow from his face as he spoke.

Other press accounts from the day made only passing reference to Muskie's supposedly overflowing emotions as he defended his wife.

Broder's was virtually the only chronicle that had him sputtering and sobbing—a version of events that the journalist repeated in an op-ed column several days later. (That piece would be included in a collection that won Broder the Pulitzer Prize that year.)

"If David Broder had not been there, no one would have ever remembered this," Tony Podesta, one of Muskie's chief campaign aides, asserted in a 2002 interview with another Muskie confidant, Donald Nicoll. "It was only because of David Broder . . . that Ed Muskie crying became a kind of . . . history-changing political event."

Muskie's campaign came to an end two months later.

Broder continued to defend his reporting, but the story would forever haunt him. What the *Post* correspondent couldn't know at the time: The letter Loeb received from Florida detailing Muskie's supposed Canuck slurs was a forgery. It had been concocted by one of the evil elves in Nixon's dirty-tricks factory, intended to discredit the president's surging opponent.

"Had those facts been known," Broder reflected in his 1987 book *Behind the Front Page,* "I might have described Muskie in different terms: not as a victim of his own overambitious campaign strategy and his own too-human temperament but as the victim of a fraud, managed by operatives of a frightened and unscrupulous President. That story surely would have had a different impact.

"Unwittingly, I did my part in the work of the Nixon operatives in helping destroy the credibility of the Muskie candidacy."

———•——

FEBRUARY 27, 1962

Frankly Furious:
When JFK Snubbed Sinatra

O l' Blue Eyes was seeing red in late February 1962.
Frank Sinatra had just learned that his invited guest, President John F. Kennedy, had reversed his decision to stay at the singer's Palm Springs

compound. So, farewell, weeks of frenzied preparation. Worse, Sinatra had to surrender the dream that his estate would become the western White House, granting the mob-connected "Chairman of the Board" the entrée to gilded respectability he felt his friendship with the president merited.

"The cancellation made a big splash in the newspapers," wrote Sinatra's daughter Tina in her 2012 memoir. "Had the Kennedys sought deliberately to humiliate my father, they couldn't have done a better job."

Sinatra had no way of knowing that FBI Director J. Edgar Hoover had essentially pulled the plug on what was expected to be a swinging bachelors' weekend (the first lady being out of the country at the time). On February 27, as Sinatra was merrily bustling about preparing his pad, the president's brother Robert (also the attorney general of the United States) received a disturbing memo from Hoover: It confirmed that Jack's mistress, Judith Campbell, was simultaneously the girlfriend of Chicago mafioso (and RFK target) Sam Giancana.* Having introduced the president to Campbell in the first place, Sinatra therefore emerged as an undeniable link between Kennedy and the mob. "Johnny, you can't associate with this guy," the attorney general informed his brother.

But who would break the news of his banishment to The Voice? That distasteful task fell to Kennedy in-law (and Sinatra's fellow Rat Packer) Peter Lawford, who must have winced as Sinatra smashed the telephone to pieces in reply. Reaching Robert Kennedy on a second phone and finding him coolly unapologetic, Sinatra destroyed that instrument as well.

---

* Hoover had even more compromising information about another of the president's mistresses, Ellen Rometsch, which prompted a terrible decision by Robert Kennedy the following year (see October 10).

"I felt sorry for Mr. S," wrote the singer's longtime valet, George Jacobs. "He was like the girl who got stood up for the prom, all dressed up with no place to go. He had spent a fortune on the house, just for JFK, and now the house was off-limits."

Sinatra's tantrum only intensified upon learning that Kennedy was indeed still coming to Palm Springs but would be staying at the nearby home of Bing Crosby—a Republican, no less. "They might as well have stuck a poker in dad's eye," wrote Tina Sinatra.

Her father reacted like a gored bull indeed, going "on the most violent rampage I had seen," Jacobs revealed. He ripped pictures of the president and others in his circle off the walls and shattered them on the floor. Kicking open the door to the Presidential Suite, Sinatra tried to pry off the plaque he had proudly mounted inside: JOHN F. KENNEDY SLEPT HERE. But it wouldn't budge, wrote Jacobs, remaining "a bitter reminder of how he had been used and dumped."*

"I followed Mr. S around the house on his search-and-destroy mission, just to make sure he didn't die of a cerebral hemorrhage," Jacobs concluded. "I didn't dare try to stop him, or even say, 'Cool it, boss. This ain't worth it.' He probably would have killed me."

FEBRUARY 28, 1983

*M*A*S*H*E*D*

The two-hour series finale of *M*A*S*H* that aired on February 28, 1983, was a ratings spectacular—watched by more Americans than any other television program previously produced. Such a triumphal exit

---

* There were even reports (denied by Tina Sinatra in her book) that the raging singer—who, just a year before, had arranged one of the most glittering Inaugural Balls ever witnessed in Washington—took a sledgehammer to the presidential helipad he had installed in the yard.

might have given the stars of the show bright hopes for their future prospects in Hollywood. But the last *M*A*S*H* episode—ironically titled "Goodbye, Farewell and Amen"—slapped a Code Blue on the careers of many cast members and became their final bow before oblivion.

Co-stars Harry Morgan, William Christopher, and Jamie Farr signed on for the notoriously atrocious spin-off *AfterMASH,* in which they reprised their decidedly nonessential roles as, respectively, Colonel Potter, Father Mulcahy, and that one-note cross-dresser (except now minus the side-splitting dress) Corporal Klinger.

"Take the three weakest characters of *M*A*S*H,* put them in the hilarious confines of a Veteran's Hospital, and you have a recipe for classic comedy," snarked Ken Levine, one of the show's executive producers.

Although *AfterMASH* undoubtedly deserves its enshrinement among *TV Guide'*s worst shows ever, it still fared better than yet another post-*M*A*S*H* miscarriage: *W*A*L*T*E*R* featured Gary Burghoff returning to his role as the lovable Walter "Radar" O'Reilly.* The fate of that single-episode fiasco might have spared audiences the horror that could have been *H*O*T*L*I*P*S.*

⊰——⊱

FEBRUARY 29, 1968

A Leap-Year Waterloo: McNamara's Other Quagmire

There's only a 1-in-4 chance you'll find a Bad Day in History on February 29. But those odds couldn't spare U.S. Secretary of Defense

---

* Burghoff left *M*A*S*H* several years before the series concluded. So did McLean "Colonel Henry Blake" Stevenson, whose name became almost synonymous with failed sitcoms; witness the junkyard of stalled Stevenson vehicles *Hello, Larry; The McLean Stevenson Show; In the Beginning;* and *Condo.*

Robert McNamara some leap year misfortune in 1968. Having resigned from Lyndon Johnson's Cabinet over disagreements with the president on the conduct of the Vietnam War, McNamara departed from the Pentagon that day in a style that ingloriously symbolized the conflict he had helped steer to a dismal stalemate.

"For some reason the Furies turned the mask comic," Paul Hendrickson wrote in his book *The Living and the Dead: Robert McNamara and Five Lives of a Lost War.* It started when the Pentagon's parking-garage elevator—number 13, fittingly—seized up in mid-haul. Among the 13 people trapped inside were McNamara and the president, with whom he had fallen out of favor, there to see him off. Johnson joked that he would now have to scrub his planned farewell speech of its references to McNamara's vaunted efficiency. Not funny, really—but something to break the rising tension in the tightly enclosed space. After about 15 minutes, the elevator doors were pried apart enough for the president, the secretary, and their rattled retinue to climb out.

But the hits just kept on coming.

As the party emerged onto the Pentagon's River Terrace parade ground, the morning's gloomy skies opened up. "There was some kid holding an umbrella over my head which had a hole in it," President Johnson remembered. "The water was running down the shoulder of my coat. He was also holding it so that all the water . . . fell on McNamara's glasses, who was standing at attention going blind."

The president had nice things to say about the outgoing secretary, but none of those gathered could hear them: The downpour had short-circuited the PA system. Likewise rained out was the planned flyover by a formation of the fighter jets that McNamara had championed during his troubled tenure: the *all-weather* F-111.

March

On Second Thought, Part 3:
Lobbing a Lie

"No lobbying, no lobbying."
—*Retiring U.S. Senator Christopher Dodd in August 2010,*
when asked what he would do next after his three-decade legislative career.
Six months later, on March 1, 2011, The Hill *reported that Dodd would*
become "Hollywood's leading man in Washington, taking the most
prestigious job on K Street." In other words—as chairman and CEO
of the Motion Picture Association of America—a lobbyist.

Unholy Matrimony, Part 1:
After the Wedding, No Reception

Unlike so many arranged marriages (see June 12, for example), the union between Vincenzo Gonzaga, future Duke of Mantua, and

Margherita Farnese, granddaughter of the Duke of Parma, swelled with promise. Despite being herded to the altar for political and dynastic reasons, the couple enjoyed a rare benefit in the coldly calculated business of royal matchmaking: They actually liked each other. Vincenzo was thrilled to find his teenage bride-to-be sweet—and even prettier than her portrait. As for Margherita, having climbed into bed on her wedding night to await her prince, "she thanked God infinitely for having been given such a suitable husband," a lady-in-waiting reported, "and so much to her liking."

Yet the marriage essentially ended later that evening on March 2, 1581.

The nuts and bolts of the matter was that their nuts and bolts didn't fit: Something about the bride and groom's plumbing kept the union from being consummated, imperiling political stability to such an extent that the pope got involved. Both the Gonzagas and the Farneses were determined to maintain honor and fortune—and each ducal family blamed the other's offspring for the nuptial no-go. This necessitated a much closer examination—an anatomical farce that would have made Masters and Johnson blush.

Vincenzo was summoned to strut his stuff. But, given the clinical circumstances, he wasn't quite up to it. No matter—the future ruler (and reported model for the licentious Duke of Mantua in Giuseppe Verdi's opera *Rigoletto*) had already proven himself to be a successful seducer of other women. Besides, a cast of his princely package revealed no obvious physical deformities. Though Margherita's family remained unconvinced of Vincenzo's capabilities, most of the doctors who had been called in concluded that she, not he, was the impediment.

Perhaps that was because Margherita was a mere 13 years old at the time. Despite this more-than-mitigating factor, Margherita was subjected to a mortifying series of examinations—"'probed and investigated' by the fingers of so many doctors and surgeons that hardly a province in Italy was left unrepresented," historian Valeria Finucci noted in her book *The Prince's Body: Vincenzo Gonzaga and Renaissance Medicine*. Some found what they believed to be a physical barrier "such that no virile member, even one of iron, could penetrate it," as Mantuan physician Cesare Pendasio graphically put it.

With the risk of infection ruling out corrective surgery, Pope Gregory XIII simply annulled the marriage instead. Young Margherita Farnese was then clapped into a convent—urged to renewed chastity by the future saint Charles Borromeo—and there she remained confined for the rest of her life.

The newly single Vincenzo Gonzaga, meanwhile, set out to prove his priapic prowess. "With Vincenzo unleashed, possessing a hymen in the duchy of Mantua suddenly became a liability," Finucci wrote. "Defloration having become part of the prince's agenda," including at least one reported case of hospitalization for his victim.

Yet there would be one more sex test for this loathsome lothario. Before he would permit Vincenzo to conduct another advantageous marriage—this one to his daughter, Eleanor de' Medici—the Grand Duke of Tuscany confided that "My purpose is to remain assured that the [potential groom] can consummate the marriage with a virgin, and therefore let's do the test, and let's choose carefully a healthy maiden who we know for sure is a virgin."

Vincenzo passed his audition and went on to father six children with Eleanor. The test maiden was never heard from again.

MARCH 3, 2018

Barry in Bronze:
A Statue of Staggering Limitations

When we last visited with Washington, D.C.'s crack-smoking "Mayor for Life" Marion Barry was bragging to the *Los Angeles Times* about his invincibility. "I'm gonna be like that lion the Romans had," the soon-to-be-convicted felon crowed. "They can just keep throwin' stuff at me, you know? . . . In the end, I be sittin' there, lickin' my paws."

Well, as it turned out, "the Night Owl," as he called himself—a reference to his penchant for after-dark prowling—was correct. On March 3, 2018,

an eight-foot statue of Barry was unveiled on Pennsylvania Avenue, where his likeness stands proudly among those of actual luminaries.

As might be expected, there is no pipe raised to the mouth of the looming bronze figure, no sign of the African kente cloth the four-term mayor would don for the benefit of his loyal constituents every time he got in trouble, and no inscription of what were perhaps his most memorable words, "I'll be goddam . . . Bitch set me up"—muttered repeatedly about the woman who cooperated in the FBI sting operation that captured hizzoner smoking the very drug that was creating such mayhem in the city he was ostensibly leading. Indeed, the Barry statue is entirely sanitized: Just the smiling mayor in a conservative suit, arm raised in a wave, emblematically lickin' his paws.

MARCH 4, 1829

White House or Animal House?

A new age was dawning in Washington when, on March 4, 1829, Andrew Jackson was inaugurated the nation's seventh president. The Virginia coterie of chief executives, along with their Massachusetts brethren, had, at last, been eclipsed by a down-home son of Tennessee. Gentility was giving way to just plain folks.

Jacksonites ecstatic over the 61-year-old general's ascendancy jammed the city streets. "Old Hickory" was their man, and they his adoring myrmidons. Horsemen galloped up and down Pennsylvania Avenue displaying hickory bridles and hickory stirrups, while women adorned themselves with hickory-nut necklaces and barbers advertised "haircutting in the Jackson style." Democratic victory was in the air.

Then it was on to the President's House, its elite soirees suddenly outmoded. Jackson was thronged as he slowly made his way on horseback from the Capitol to the Executive Mansion. And contrary to the legend of what came next, the new president's household staff had indeed prepared for the onslaught: Three long tables of food had been set up in the East Room, large quantities of lemonade and orange punch had been mixed (and liberally laced with whiskey, alas), and gallons of ice cream stood awaiting the scoop.

It was a noble try.

The mansion was stormed like an American Bastille, with the rowdy crowd roaming every room of the house. The refreshments were gobbled up and chugged down in an instant, while the crush in the East Room became suffocating. China was dropped and broken. Fistfights erupted. Muddy-booted partygoers climbed on delicate tables and chairs for breathing room and a view.

"What a scene did we witness!" wrote Margaret Bayard Smith, a ranking member of Washington society. "The majesty of the People had disappeared, and a rabble, a mob of boys, negros [sic], women, children, scrambling, fighting, romping. What a pity, what a pity!"

Pressed against a wall and "sinking into a listless state of exhaustion," according to one report, the evening's host was overcome. Several men fought their way through the mob to reach Jackson, then locked their arms around the new president and helped him escape through a window. Hardly a reveler realized he had left. The crowds were finally dispersed only by the promise of replenished refreshments on the lawn.

The refined Bayard Smith, though appalled by the ruinous rabble, acknowledged that a shift had occurred: "It was the People's day, and the People's President and the People would rule."

Samurai Biography:
Woodward Dissects Belushi

Death came for John Belushi in the form of a drug overdose on March 5, 1982. Then, entwining itself with that sad day—smothering it, in fact—came *Wired: The Short Life & Fast Times of John Belushi* by Bob Woodward. Many felt the famed Watergate journalist had produced little more than a biographical autopsy of the comedian—a corpse-on-a-slab account, cold and clinical, that focused less on the man than on the excesses that had destroyed him.

"Yeah, Woodward did a really nice job of making John look like a Bluto junkie," Belushi's brother Jim bitterly observed in an interview with authors Tom Shales and James Andrew Miller. "I don't think Woodward's capable of understanding what love is, or compassion, or relationships. He is one cold fish."

Indeed, Woodward's pathologist approach to *Wired,* published in 1984, evoked the reporting he and Carl Bernstein had employed so successfully in *All the President's Men*—using, as his publisher trumpeted, "diaries, accountants' records, phone bills, travel records, medical records and interviews with firsthand witnesses."

But the hard facts marshaled to bring down a president, said critics, were far less effective at capturing the dazzling and dark facets of John Belushi. "Mr. Woodward reconstitutes an endless series of endless nights with his subject," *The New York Times* noted, "but so much of this is done with a deadpan objectivity that it becomes repetitious and monotonous. We tire of reading about the cocaine shots, the Quaaludes, the arguments with producers and directors."

It wasn't a life that emerged from the pages of *Wired.* Rather it was a remorseless chronicle of degradation, designed to spotlight the single smoking gun that seemed of any real interest to Bob Woodward: a star's drug-induced death in a dirty hotel room.

MARCH 6, 2000

With a Name Like "Banana," You Really Should Avoid Sex Scandals

In 1982, a law was enacted in Zimbabwe making it a crime to poke fun at the name of the newly independent nation's first president: Canaan Banana. That ordinance would prove impossible to enforce outside the African nation, however, when ex-president Banana figured in a sensational sex scandal a decade after leaving office.

Though Banana had once blasted homosexual behavior as "deviant, abominable and wrong," in 1998, he was convicted on 11 charges of "sodomy and indecent assault" involving numerous male staffers, including his bodyguard. No law on earth could spare Banana the headlines that followed, even as he steadfastly denied both his guilt and the implication that he was gay. "Man Raped by Banana," the *Herald* reported, while the *Guardian* trumpeted, "Banana Forced Officer to Have Sex."

The relatively staid BBC News, on the other hand, *may* have been playing it straight with its literally correct website banner on March 6, 2000: "Banana Appeals Against Sodomy Conviction." But a follow-up story headline in May makes that rather doubtful: "Banana Sex Appeal Rejected."

———

MARCH 7, 2016

On Second Thought, Part 4: Going to the Mat for the Wrong Guy

Pity Leo Kocher's unfortunate sense of timing.

The head wrestling coach at the University of Chicago sent an impassioned defense of his old pal, disgraced Speaker of the House Dennis Hastert, to a sentencing judge on March 7, 2016. Though Hastert had pleaded guilty to structuring bank withdrawals to avoid reporting requirements, Kocher extolled him as "an outstanding human being who has made enormous contributions to Society—particularly the youth of society—over his lifetime."

His testimonial to Hastert's sterling personal qualities, written on university letterhead, continued in this same effusive vein: "[He] is a good man—and is universally regarded as such by those who have gotten to know him. Please note that you can count on that as fact."

A mere seven weeks later, Hastert—a former wrestling coach himself—confessed in court to having also been what the judge termed "a serial child molester."

For his failure to recognize the depths of Hastert's depravity, Kocher's well-meaning but poorly timed letter might best be pedo-philed under "Whoops!"*

MARCH 8, 1966

Lord Half Nelson

Admiral Horatio Nelson lost an eye in Corsica, his forearm in the Canary Islands, and a good number of his teeth to scurvy. Then, when a sniper's bullet tore through his spine at the Battle of Trafalgar in 1805, he lost his life.

But fate hadn't finished with the British naval hero.

---

* Kocher's bona fides as a true, albeit woefully ill-informed friend were also demonstrated a decade earlier when he wrote to the nationwide wrestling community, urging them to stand up for Hastert, who was then under fire for his failure to properly investigate lewd and lascivious messages that Representative Mark Foley had been sending to teenage Capitol Hill pages.

On March 8, 1966, Nelson lost his perch high atop a monumental column in Dublin, known as Nelson's Pillar. Explosives detonated by a group of Irish republican activists—resentful that this stone relic of British sovereignty still stood in a free Ireland—brought his statue crashing down.

In the aftermath of the sabotage—aptly named "Operation Humpty Dumpty"—the street was littered with fragments of Lord Nelson. These included the statue's head, which was subjected to a rather indecorous post-explosive ordeal: After being stolen by a group of university students, the stone noggin was variously posed on a beach for a commercial fashion shoot, featured onstage during a concert by The Dubliners, and smeared with lipstick while displayed in the window of a London antiques store.

In 2005 Lord Nelson's head was returned to Ireland, where it now resides in the Dublin City Library—battered and broken, much like Lord Nelson himself.

MARCH 9, 1917

Nicholas II: Happily Never After

"My brain feels rested here—no ministers &
no fidgety questions to think over."
—*Tsar Nicholas II, writing to his wife, Alexandra, from
Russia's military headquarters in Mogilev on March 9, 1917*

Mar ch 9 was the worst possible day for the autocrat to feel at ease. Although revolution was erupting on the streets of St. Petersburg, all that seemed to concern Nicholas was the case of measles recently contracted by his children. Perhaps, he suggested to Alexandra that day—less than a week before he was swept off his throne—they could recover in the warmth of the Crimea?

As usual, his wife abetted the tsar's colossal cluelessness. Even without the diabolical machinations of her corrupt confidant and soothsayer, Grigori Rasputin—assassinated two months earlier by a group of conservative nobles—Empress Alexandra maintained a dangerously ill-informed sway over her weak and vacillating husband. The troubles in the capital were merely "a hooligan movement," she purred in a letter to Nicholas the next day, "young boys & girls running about & screaming that they have no bread, only to excite . . . if it were very cold they wld. probably stay in doors. But this will all pass & quieten down."

A day later—having prayed at Rasputin's graveside—Alexandra shared more of her profound insights: "It seems to me it will be all right—the sun shines so brightly—I felt such peace & calm on His dear grave—He died to save us." Plus, she wrote, "all adore you & only want bread."

Alexandra's empty reassurances may have placated Nicholas, but 400 miles away in Moscow a political realist was forming a much more accurate read of the situation. Mikhail Rodzianko, chairman of the Duma (Russia's legislative assembly from 1906 to 1917), sent the tsar an urgent telegram:

> Situation serious. Anarchy reigns in the capital. Government is paralyzed. Transport, food, and fuel supplies are utterly disorganized. General discontent is growing. Disorderly firing is going on in the streets. Various companies of soldiers are shooting at each other. It is absolutely necessary to invest someone who enjoys the confidence of the people to form a new government. No time must be lost. Any delay may be fatal. I pray God that at this hour responsibility may not fall on the wearer of the crown.

Alas, the wearer of the crown elected to ignore the minister's dire warning. "That fat Rodzianko has sent me some nonsense," the soon to be ex (and ultimately executed) tsar burbled to his wife, "which I shall not even bother to answer."

Suffragette Mars "Venus"

Diego Velázquez's languorously reclined "Venus" had a backside to behold—which is one reason why Mary Richardson went to London's National Gallery on March 10, 1914, and repeatedly hacked the famous nude with a meat cleaver.

Richardson's ostensible intent: to strike a blow for fellow suffragette Emmeline Pankhurst, who had been violently removed from a speaker's platform in Scotland the day before and arrested. "I have tried to destroy the picture of the most beautiful woman in mythological history as a protest against the Government for destroying Mrs. Pankhurst, who is the most beautiful character in modern history," Richardson declared in a statement after her arrest. "Justice is an element of beauty as much as colour and outline on canvas."

Yet "Slasher Mary," as she was dubbed, later admitted that the goddess of love's alluring derrière had likewise motivated her frenzied attack on the masterpiece: "I didn't like the way men visitors gaped at it all day long."

Hope Springs Infernal

Is it really a Bad Day in History when delusion and unfounded hope appear to comfort the man who harbors them? Probably not—so perhaps file this one under Pathetic Days in History.

On March 11, 1861, just a week after leaving office, President James Buchanan—now widely regarded as one of the nation's worst chief executives (see February 3)—shared his laughably sanguine thoughts in a private letter to James Gordon Bennett, editor and publisher of *The New York Herald*.

"Under Heaven's blessing [my] administration has been eminently successful in its foreign and domestic policy," Buchanan wrote, adding, "unless we may except the sad events which have recently occurred." Buchanan's recent "sad events" referred to the small matter of seven states having seceded from the Union under his watch—a harbinger of the coming Civil War. (A bit like saying, "Other than that iceberg, the *Titanic* voyage was terrific!")

"Whether I have done all I could consistently with my duty to give them a wise and peaceful direction towards the preservation or reconstruction of the Union, will be for the public and posterity to judge," Buchanan blithely continued. "I feel conscious that I have done my duty in this respect and that I shall at last receive justice."

If justice is the opprobrium of generations to come, Mission Accomplished!

MARCH 12, 1956

The Southern Manifesto:

101 Damnations

On March 12, 1956, a repugnant document commonly known as the Southern Manifesto was presented on Capitol Hill. It was the declaration of a band of exasperated congressional racists, decrying the U.S. Supreme Court's 1954 *Brown* v. *Board of Education* decision. (The Court had ruled unanimously that any state law establishing racially segregated public schools was a violation of the equal-protection clause of the 14th Amendment.)

Here's just one enlightened excerpt:

> We regard the decision of the Supreme Court in the school cases as a clear abuse of judicial power . . . This unwarranted exercise of power by the Court . . . is creating chaos and confusion in the States principally affected. It is destroying the amicable relations between the white and Negro races that have been created through 90 years of patient effort by the good people of both races. It has planted hatred and suspicion where there has been heretofore friendship and understanding . . . We decry the Supreme Court's encroachments on rights reserved to the States and to the people, contrary to established law and to the Constitution.

The manifesto was signed by 101 members of Congress—the majority of them Southern Democrats deluded enough to believe that a century's worth of terror and segregation constituted "amicable relations."

MARCH 13, 1852

Not-So-Great Expectations

"I am happy to say that Mrs. Dickens and the seventh son—
whom I cannot afford to receive with perfect cordiality, as on the
whole I could have dispensed with him—are as well as possible . . .
I had been in an unsettled and anxious condition for a week or so,
but may now shut myself up in Bleak House again."
—*Charles Dickens, unenthusiastically announcing the birth of his
10th and final child, Edward Bulwer Lytton Dickens,
known to his family as Plorn, on March 13, 1852*

MARCH 14, 1950

Burned Up Over Bergman:
Here's Looking Down at You, Kid

Fresh from being burned alive in the film *Joan of Arc,* Ingrid Bergman was put on the hot seat again on March 14, 1950—this time, on the floor of the United States Senate. The actress was condemned by Senator Edwin C. Johnson of Colorado as "a powerful influence for evil"—not for any alleged communist associations (the red-hot charge of the day) but for being an adulteress. Or, as Johnson called the *Casablanca* star: an "apostle of degradation . . . [a] free-love cultist . . . a horrible example of womanhood . . . [a] moral outlaw."

Bergman had attracted the senator's wrath by abandoning her husband and young daughter to run off with a "love pirate"—Italian film director Roberto Rossellini, who was also married at the time. Johnson regarded the affair not only as "an assault upon the institution of marriage" and "a direct challenge to the family unit as the basis for our civilization" but also as a personal betrayal by someone he *thought* he knew: *The Bells of St. Mary's* Bergman, not the "common mistress" the Swedish actress had become.

"She was by very long odds my own favorite actress of all time, and I have been enjoying motion pictures for more than 40 years," cineast Johnson declared. "Millions of American movie fans adored and idolized her. Not only was her interpretation magnificent beyond description, but her home life was ideal, where she lived quietly and happily with her devoted little family. She was a sweet and understanding person with an attractive personality which captivated everyone on and off the screen."

It was clear, Johnson concluded, that the actress had not only sold her soul—"the soul of Hollywood's greatest star"—but that she had also lost her mind. How else to explain the cruel abandonment of her daughter? "Even mothers among the dumb beasts defend their brood with their lives," the senator insisted. "Her unnatural attitude toward her own little girl surely indicates a mental abnormality."

To ensure that the likes of Bergman would never pollute another movie screen with her corrupted morals, Johnson introduced legislation that day requiring the licensing of actors, actresses, producers, and films by a division of the Department of Commerce. In essence, bad people would be banned from making or appearing in movies.

It was too late for his fallen heroine to redeem herself, Johnson said. But "out of her ashes may come a better Hollywood."*

MARCH 15, 1992

Cultural Vandalism, Part 1: The Cleanup Mission That Should've Been Scrubbed

On March 15, 1992, members of a youth group—armed with brushes and other cleaning equipment—descended on the Upper Cave of Mayrières in southern France to help rid the culturally rich heritage site of graffiti. Amid all the scrawl were two bison images, which happened to have been applied some 15,000 years earlier. Thorough in their job, the volunteer cleaning corps gave the prehistoric drawings—priceless archaeological treasures—a good scrubbing as well.

By the time they realized their mistake, only bits of bison remained—prompting this scouring response from René Gachet, the local director of cultural affairs: "Absolutely stupid!"

---

* Twenty-two years after Johnson introduced his failed legislation with a fiery assault on Bergman, Senator Charles Percy of Illinois read an apology to the exiled actress on the Senate floor. Bergman responded with her trademark grace: "Dear Senator Percy, my war with America was over long ago. The wounds, however, remained. Now, because of your gallant gesture with your generous and understanding address to the Senate, they are healed forever."

MARCH 16, 2003

On Second Thought, Part 5: Dick Cheney, Weapon of Mass Distraction?

"We believe he has, in fact, reconstituted nuclear weapons."
—Vice President Dick Cheney, discussing Iraqi dictator Saddam Hussein on NBC's Meet the Press, *March 16, 2003. Six months later, on the same program, Cheney came clean: "I did misspeak . . . We never had any evidence that he had acquired a nuclear weapon."*

This clarification didn't cover another misspoken statement from the vice president, made that same bad day in March, when he had this to say about the U.S. invasion of Iraq: "My belief is we will, in fact, be greeted as liberators."

———

MARCH 17, 2010

Not Quite on Top o' the Mournin'

"His mom lived in Long Island for ten years or so. God rest her soul. And, ah, um, she's, wait, your mom's still . . . your mom's still alive. It's your dad who passed. God *bless* her soul."
—Vice President Joseph Biden, introducing Prime Minister Brian Cowen of Ireland at a White House celebration of St. Patrick's Day, March 17, 2010

Biden's premature burial of Mrs. Cowen was embarrassing, sure, but it was hardly an aberration. Here's another characteristically cringe-worthy Bidenism, selected (somewhat) at random: "I'm told Chuck Graham is here," Biden shouted at a campaign rally on September 9, 2008, addressing the wheelchair-bound Missouri state senator. "Stand up, Chuck, let 'em see you!" Instantly recognizing his mistake, the gaffe-prone politician recovered from the mortifying moment—sort of: "Oh, God love you. What am I talking about? I'll tell you what, you're making everybody else stand up, though, pal . . . I tell you what [to the crowd]: Stand up for Chuck!"

MARCH 18, 1314

Knights Take Kings:
Revenge of the Templars

"God knows who is in the wrong and who has sinned," Jacques de Molay shouted from the stake on March 18, 1314, as flames engulfed him. "Soon misfortune will come to those who have wrongly condemned us: God will avenge our death."

De Molay was the last Grand Master of the monastic military order known as the Knights Templar, and his curse proved prescient for the two men most responsible for brutally suppressing the group: King Philip IV of France and his lapdog, Pope Clement V. Both would be dead within the year. And for Philip, the end would come with a heaping dose of humiliation.

Philip IV, known as "the Fair" (for his looks, not his decency), was a notoriously remote, calculating, and cruel monarch with one singular passion: gold. And the Knights Templar were sitting atop mounds of the stuff. (The group, initially founded two centuries earlier as crusaders, had eventually come to control vast wealth.) Using his two favorite instruments—slander and persecution—Philip set out to relieve the Templars of their riches.

First, the diabolical king spread rumors of the group's supposed sexual deviance, along with their heretical, even satanic behavior. He then had his agents round up various Templars and extract confessions under torture. Finally, Fair Philip—good Christian monarch that he was—extirpated these monstrous defilers of all that was holy by burning them alive. Pope Clement was forced to put his imprimatur on the terror campaign, ultimately dissolving the order.

By the time de Molay was immolated, the Templars were all but finished—but so was Clement. The Gascon pope, who had moved the Holy See from Rome to Avignon in what became known as "the Babylonian captivity," died a month after the execution. (His body was then unintentionally cremated when the church in which it was resting caught fire.) Perhaps Clement's reluctant role in the French king's schemes had spared him further degradation?

No such luck for Philip, who lived long enough to see his family implode in a scandal known as the Tour de Nesle affair.

Shortly after de Molay's agony at the stake, word reached the king that three of his daughters-in-law had been conducting adulterous affairs in Nesle's Tower, a guardhouse along the River Seine. (The blabbermouth is believed to have been Philip's daughter Isabela, who was married to King Edward II of England but happened to be home in France for a visit.)* Philip's reprisals were characteristically heartless: Two of the wayward princesses, Blanche and Margaret, were shorn of their hair and thrown into squalid dungeons. (A third, Blanche's sister Joan, was found innocent but kept under close watch for having failed to reveal the liaisons.) Blanche and Margaret's lovers, two sibling knights, fared far worse. They were skinned alive and their bones were broken to bits.

Only at the close of this tawdry cascade was Philip himself allowed to die, felled by a cerebral aneurysm in November 1314. De Molay's curse lived on, however: Each of the king's three sons died without a male heir, and the ancient Capetian dynasty of French monarchs—sharing the fate of the Templars—soon withered away.

---

* Isabela, the infamous "She-Wolf of France," later conspired with her lover, Roger Mortimer, to have her husband murdered.

MARCH 19, 1798

Take *That*, Your Royal Hindness!
Cutting Britain's Big Cheese
Down to Size

The king of England was once held sacred as God's representative on earth . . . until he wasn't. In a cartoon by Richard Newton, drawn on March 19, 1798, John Bull—a figure representing the English people—bares his behind to explosively break wind in the face of King George III.

And all this after those unruly Americans had already cut loose on their king!

MARCH 20, 1781

Momsters, Part 2:
Hail Mary, Full of Greed

"Mary, the Mother of Washington."
Thus reads the spare tombstone of George Washington's mother. But a more fitting epitaph would have been "Mary, the Bother of Washington." The Grandmother of Our Country proved to be wolfish in trying to keep her son—and his fat purse—at her disposal.

Ample historical evidence indicates that Washington was generous to his mother. But while she lived quite comfortably, the rapacious matriarch never ceased digging deeper into his pockets, loudly protesting his financial neglect all the while. Indeed, Mary Washington seemed to delight in humiliating George as publicly as possible.

"I learn from very good authority that she is upon all occasions, & in all Companies complaining of the hardness of the times—of her wants & distresses," Washington wrote to his brother John Augustine. "That she can have no *real* wants that may not be supplied I am sure of—*imaginary* wants are indefinite, & oftentimes insatiable, because they are boundless & always changing."

Indeed, on March 20, 1781, Washington was mortified to receive a letter from Benjamin Harrison, the speaker of the Virginia House of Delegates, advising him of a movement in the house, in response to Mary Washington's cries of penury, for the state to come to her fiscal rescue.

The Revolutionary commander was forced to make an excruciating defense of his treatment of his mom: "Before I left Virginia, I answered all her calls for money; and since that period, have directed my Steward to do the same," he wrote back. "Whence her distress can arise, therefore, I know not, never having received any complaint . . . Confident I am that she has not a child that would not divide the last sixpence to relieve her from *real* distress. This she has been repeatedly assured of by me: and all of us, I am certain, would feel much hurt at having our mother a pensioner, while we had the means of supporting her; but in fact she has an ample income of her own."

Washington did write his mother to suggest that if she was feeling that impecunious, she was welcome to live at any of her children's homes—except his own.

MARCH 21, 1986

On Second Thought, Part 6:
The Best Friend He Never Had

During his ill-fated campaign for the presidency in 2012, former House Speaker Newt Gingrich did his darnedest to paint himself as an acolyte of Ronald Reagan. They were two Cold Warriors, as he would have it, united in their effort to defeat the evil Soviet empire. Indeed, Gingrich couldn't drop the Gipper's name often enough during the Republican primary debates. (Call it Reagan Reflux Syndrome—a condition so severe that political observers actually began tracking Gingrich's regurgitative embrace of the 40th president.)

Yet the onetime history professor flunked Newt 101 when it came to recalling his own past. Some three decades earlier—on March 21, 1986—Gingrich had taken to the floor of the U.S. House of Representatives and bashed the very president with whom he would later claim common cause: "Measured against the scale and momentum of the Soviet empire's challenge," Gingrich groused, "the Reagan administration has failed, is failing, and without a dramatic change in strategy will continue to fail . . . President Reagan is clearly failing."

As for the 40th president's thoughts on his self-proclaimed ally? His biographer Lou Cannon told *Bloomberg* in 2012: "I'm not sure Reagan even knew who Gingrich was."

MARCH 22, 1966

They Auto Have Known Better: When GM Reached Its Nader

Was consumer crusader Ralph Nader a sexual deviant? An anti-Semite? Did he drink to excess? Do drugs?

Private detective Vincent Gillen pursued the answers to these questions on behalf of General Motors, the megacorporation that had hired him to dig up dirt on the pesky auto-safety advocate.

Nader had made the company's Chevrolet Corvair a subject of ridicule in his 1965 book *Unsafe at Any Speed*—"the leading candidate for the un-safest-car title," as he described the crash-prone vehicle during subsequent congressional testimony.* With Corvair sales deflating, GM tried to run Nader off the road. "They want to get something somewhere on this guy," Gillen claimed he was told by a lawyer retained by the company, "to get him out of their hair and to shut him up."

The investigation was as thorough as it was unsavory. Scores of Nader's family members and associates were interviewed about every aspect of his private life, having been assured it was part of a routine background check. Some suspected Gillen of surreptitiously recording their answers. "Surely," said Nader, "the questioning by private detectives of people who know and who have worked with me as to my personal life in an attempt to obtain lurid details and grist for the invidious use and metastasis of slurs and slanders goes well beyond affront and becomes generalizable as an encroachment upon a more public interest."

Even slimier, though, was the harassment Nader endured—threatening late-night calls, crude attempts to bait sex traps, and men shadowing him, even into the halls of Congress. "What are we coming to when a great and powerful corporation will engage in such unethical and scandalous activity in an effort to discredit a citizen who is a witness before a Congressional committee?" railed Democratic Senator Gaylord Nelson of Wisconsin. "It is an assault upon freedom in America."

On March 22, 1966, a congressional hearing was held on the General Motors campaign to discredit Nader. GM chairman and CEO James Roche, maintaining that the investigations were simply an effort to discern whether Nader had any connection to the lawsuits filed against GM for the Corvair's safety failures, apologized—sort of—at the hearing: He would concede only that the scope of the company probe had perhaps been a bit too broad.

Roche's classic non-apology apology backfired: It attracted the attention of a lawyer named Stuart Speiser, who immediately contacted Nader.

---

* GM could have stabilized the Corvair's problematic rear suspension, argues classic-car historian Mark Trotta, by simply including an inexpensive part known as a sway bar. The episode is eerily reminiscent of Ford's later decision to omit a rubber bladder costing all of $5.08 from its firetrap Pinto.

"I told Ralph I was sure GM expected to be sued," Speiser recounted in his 1980 book *Lawsuit,* "and that they were probably prepared to pay a large sum . . . to bury their mistakes."

Speiser's instinct was accurate, yielding an unprecedented $425,000 invasion-of-privacy settlement. Nader announced he would use the money to keep checking under GM's hood: "They are going to be financing their own ombudsman."

<hr />

MARCH 23, 1885

The First Anti-Vaxxers:
Taking Pox-Shots at Jenner

"I am not surprised that men are not thankful to me; but I
wonder that they are not grateful to God for the good which he
has made me the instrument of conveying to my fellow-creatures."
—*British scientist Edward Jenner*

When it comes to serving humanity, Edward Jenner ranks among history's greatest benefactors. His pioneering vaccination experiments at the dawn of the 19th century ultimately resulted in the nearly global eradication of the devastating scourge of smallpox.

To his detractors, however, the acclaimed scientist may as well have been Satan. People feared and despised Jenner's smallpox vaccination for both religious and health-related reasons, as well as for the law that mandated it—all despite the proven efficacy of inoculation.

Among the masses of misguided anti-vaccinators, those in Leicester, England, were perhaps the most virulent: On March 23, 1885, an estimated 20,000 people crowded the city to unleash their wrath. In what was described at the time as "a perfect carnival of public merriment," the lifesaving scientist was dragged through town, hanged on a gibbet, then chopped up and burned.

Fortunately for Jenner, he had died 62 years earlier. That left the madding crowd only his straw effigy to brutalize—and a deadly pox to circulate among them.

MARCH 24, 1841

Put to the Testes, Part ɪ:
Hands Christian Andersen

"My penis is giving me trouble, and, heaven knows, it isn't my fault."
—*A diary entry by Hans Christian Andersen, March 24, 1841*

Beloved children's author (and houseguest from hell; see July 5) Hans Christian Andersen was a bona fide hypochondriac, plagued by all manner of imaginary ailments. His priapic problems, on the other hand, were very real. And they had a simple cause: Andersen was an energetic onanist.

Page after page of his diary contains coded references to sessions of what actually did amount to self-abuse, along with predictably related complaints such as "penis tender," "penis hurts," "penis sick," "penis very bad," and "sore penis and worried about it." Contrary to Andersen's diary declaration, therefore, it must be concluded that the chronically aching appendage was in fact entirely his own fault.

MARCH 25, 1995

Supreme Court Swoon:
A Texas Toady's Gush to Judgment

"Thank you for taking the time to visit the office and on the plane back. Cool! Keep up all the great work. The state is in great hands."

—Harriet Miers, personal attorney to then governor
George W. Bush, in a note dated March 25, 1995

President George W. Bush was taken aback when his 2005 nominee for the Supreme Court, White House counsel (and slavering pen pal) Harriet Miers, met unexpected resistance from the right.

"I think it's a disaster on every level," Judge Robert Bork declared on CNN (his own nomination to the High Court having been rejected by the Senate in 1987). "This is a woman [who] so far as anyone can tell . . . has no experience with constitutional law whatever."

Indeed, the record on Miers was relatively blank, reducing the president to proffering bland assurances of her qualifications. "She is plenty bright," he insisted. "People are going to be amazed at her strength of character and intellect."

Miers had left no paper trail documenting her judicial philosophy. There was, however, a smattering of mash notes she had written to then governor Bush, and they displayed all the nuance of a 12-year-old girl with a crush:

"You and Laura are the greatest!"

"Texas has a very popular Governor and First Lady!"

"Hopefully Jenna and Barbara recognize that their parents are 'cool'— as do the rest of us."

"You are the best Governor ever—deserving of great respect!"

Bush withdrew the nomination.

MARCH 26, 1865

Mary, Mary, Downright Scary

Abraham Lincoln, looking haggard and drawn, the weight of war carved into his face, walked among the dead and dying in the aftermath of battle. "He remarked that he had seen enough of the horrors of war," reported an officer accompanying the president, "that he hoped this was the beginning of the end, and that there would be no more bloodshed or ruin of homes."

It was late March 1865, and the Civil War was, in fact, rapidly concluding; the wreckage and gore the president witnessed near Petersburg, Virginia, was the result of a desperate and doomed attempt by Robert E. Lee's depleted forces to break the Union choke hold on the Confederate capital of Richmond. But in the waning weeks of the horrific conflict, Lincoln faced a new and especially ferocious battle on the home front.

The president and his wife, Mary, accompanied by their youngest son, Tad, had traveled to central Virginia aboard the steamboat *River Queen* at the invitation of Gen. Ulysses S. Grant. "He was really most anxious to see the army," Grant explained, "and be with it in its final struggle."

By all accounts, the trip was a much-needed tonic for the careworn president, recently inaugurated for a second term. Grant, whose respect for Lincoln only deepened during the interlude, described the refreshed president sitting among the men around a campfire. He "talked, and talked, and talked," the general recalled. "The old man seemed to enjoy it, and said: 'How grateful I feel to be with the boys and see what is being done at Richmond . . .' He would sit for hours, tilted back in his chair, with his hand shading his eyes, watching the movements of the men with the greatest interest."

But then along came Mary to ruin it all.

The first lady might be charitably described as a bit high-strung.* "This woman was to me a terror," remarked Lincoln's former law partner, William Herndon: "imperious, proud, aristocratic, insolent, witty and bitter." Though capable of great kindness, Mary Lincoln was subject to violent mood swings (possibly due to intense migraines or a bipolar disorder) and could detonate at the slightest trigger. "The Hellcat is

---

* But not insane—and most certainly not deserving of the committal to an asylum that her son Robert would arrange a decade later.

getting more Hellcattical, day by day," one of President Lincoln's secretaries, John Hay, wrote to the other, John George Nicolay, in 1862. Alas, "Her Satanic Majesty"—another fond moniker for the mercurial first lady—unleashed her most savage fury right in the middle of her husband's much needed Virginia sojourn.

It all began during a review of Gen. Edward Ord's troops along the James River on March 26, 1865. Mrs. Ord was to ride on horseback with the other men beside the president, while Mary Lincoln and General Grant's wife, Julia, would be relegated to trailing behind in an ambulance carriage. Learning of the arrangement, the first lady was livid. "What does that woman mean by riding by the side of the President?" she stormed. "And ahead of me? Does she suppose that he wants her by the side of him?" As Mrs. Lincoln's fury mounted, Mrs. Grant tried to calm her and defend Mrs. Ord at the same time. Her two-pronged effort was doused with neck-snapping venom: "I suppose you think you'll get to the White House yourself, don't you?" the first lady hissed. When Mrs. Grant politely demurred, out spewed more invective from Mrs. Lincoln: "Oh! You had better take it if you can get it. 'Tis very nice."

When the ambulance carriage reached the parade ground at Malvern Hill, Mrs. Ord rode up to greet the president's wife—utterly unprepared for the fusillade that awaited her. "Mrs. Lincoln positively insulted her, called her vile names in the presence of a crowd of officers, and asked what she meant by following up the President," reported Adam Badeau, a member of General Grant's staff. "The poor woman burst into tears and inquired what she had done, but Mrs. Lincoln refused to be appeased, and stormed till she was tired. Mrs. Grant still tried to stand by her friend, and everybody was shocked and horrified."

Though depleted after her vicious tirade, the first lady was apparently rejuvenated enough to resume it that evening. During a reception aboard the *River Queen,* she attacked General Ord as incompetent and insisted he be removed from command. Then she turned her rage on the president, accusing him of shamelessly flirting with Mrs. Ord.

Lincoln bore the outburst "as Christ might have done," Badeau wrote, "with an expression of pain and sadness that cut one to the heart, but with supreme calmness and dignity." Then, Badeau continued, "he walked away, hiding that noble, ugly face that we might [not] catch the full expression of his misery."

Less than three weeks later, Lincoln was assassinated.

MARCH 27, 1964

Never Let the Facts Get in the Way
of a Good Story, Exhibit 38

"For more than half an hour 38 respectable, law-abiding citizens in Queens watched a killer stalk and stab a woman in three separate attacks in Kew Gardens," read the introduction to a front-page story published in *The New York Times* on March 27, 1964. "Twice, the sound of their voices and the sudden glow of their bedroom lights interrupted him and frightened him off. Each time he returned, sought her out and stabbed her again. Not one person telephoned the police during the assault; one witness called after the woman was dead."

The world came to know the name Catherine "Kitty" Genovese thanks to that *Times* report, and it shuddered at the callousness of the neighbors who reportedly stood idly by, watching the 28-year-old woman die screaming in terror. That horrific indifference—epitomized by one man the paper quoted as "sheepishly" telling police "I didn't want to get involved"—deeply resonated. Societal soul-searching, academic analysis, even emergency-response reform followed as the *Times* story and its frightening implications seeped into the national consciousness and remained there for decades.

Problem was, very little of the *Times* report was true.

"While there was no question that the attack occurred, and that some neighbors ignored cries for help, the portrayal of 38 witnesses as fully aware and unresponsive was erroneous," *Times* reporter Robert McFadden wrote in a 2016 obituary of Kitty Genovese's killer. "The article grossly exaggerated the number of witnesses and what they had perceived. None saw the attack in its entirety. Only a few had glimpsed parts of it or recognized the cries for help. Many thought they had heard lovers or drunks quarreling. There were two attacks, not three. And afterward, two people did call the police. A 70-year-old woman ventured out and cradled the dying victim in her arms until they arrived. Ms. Genovese died on the way to a hospital."

Kitty Genovese had been dead for 10 days, her murder having merited only a few paragraphs in the *Times,* when the paper's metropolitan editor and future executive editor, Abe Rosenthal, received a sensational scoop while lunching with Police Commissioner Michael J. Murphy. "Brother," Rosenthal recounted Murphy telling him, "that Queens story is one for the books. Thirty-eight witnesses . . . I've been in this business a long time, but this beats everything." Before even leaving the restaurant, Rosenthal had gotten one of the most significant elements of the case wrong.

"Thirty-eight," author Kevin Cook wrote in his examination of the case. "A number so definitive that it would help define the story for fifty years, and so arbitrary that Murphy may as well have picked it out of a hat."

The police commissioner, it turned out, had been misinformed about the number of witnesses. But Rosenthal, who used that bogus figure as the title of his 1964 book, and Martin Gansberg, the *Times* reporter assigned to follow up on Murphy's tip, both swallowed it unquestioningly. The two journalists then proceeded to craft the misleading indictment of apathy and inhumanity that followed.

One skeptic of the *Times* account—the late Daniel Meenan, a reporter for WMCA radio at the time—did some digging of his own. According to his notes, read on camera by his colleague Gabe Pressman in the documentary *The Witness,* Meenan had irately confronted Gansberg about the distortions in his piece: "Why didn't you include in your story the fact that many witnesses did not believe a murder was taking place?" Meenan demanded.

Replied Gansberg: "It would have ruined the story."

MARCH 28, 2019

Pugh! Something Stank
Around This Baltimore Mayor

O nce upon a time there was a children's author named Catherine
Pugh, who wrote a series of books about a little girl named Healthy
Holly. They were silly stories with lots of mistakes—like a laid-back
approach to spelling—"vegetale" in a book about vegetables, for example, or a title character whose name toggled from "Herbie" to "Herby"
at random. Also, our hale little heroine tended to be a bit . . . dense:
Informed by her mother that skipping rope is exercising and that exercising is fun, Holly responds, "I will be healthy. I like having fun."

For all their flaws, the books sold hundreds of thousands of copies—
which is where the story of Healthy Holly gets interesting.

You see, kids, author Catherine Pugh—let's call her Conflict of Interest
Cathy—had another career: She was the mayor of Baltimore. She also
happened to be a trustee of the University of Maryland Medical System,
which found the Healthy Holly books so captivating that it paid Pugh
half a million dollars for 100,000 copies of her self-published series. And
Kaiser Permanente, coincidentally seeking a lucrative contract to provide
health insurance to city workers, shelled out more than $100,000 to buy
about 20,000 more.

Whereas Healthy Holly would never sit around doing nothing—after
all, she just *adored* exercise—the books apparently did: Some 9,000 of
them were left to rot in a warehouse. Meanwhile, the location of any
others that may have been printed became a celebrated local mystery. A
search by *Baltimore Sun* reporters in schools, libraries, and other likely
places turned up nothing. An Amber Alert for Holly?

Around the ides of March, Mayor Pugh found herself deep in the
stink when the *Sun* began publishing stories about the hinky Healthy
Holly deals. At first, Pugh dismissed the allegations of impropriety as a
"witch hunt." Then, on March 28, she held a hastily arranged press
conference that betrayed how fuzzy she was on the notion of contrition:

"I sincerely want to say that I apologize that I have done something to upset the people of Baltimore. I never intended to do anything that could not stand up to scrutiny."

The clueless (or was it shameless?) Pugh then turned her public mea culpa into a sales opportunity, saying she intended to expand the "Healthy Holly" brand to include fun baby apparel. Items planned for production included onesies and bibs, printed with the encouraging words "walk, run, crawl, skip, dance."

Comedian John Oliver gleefully skewered Pugh on his HBO program *Last Week Tonight:* "[It] might be better for her to read the writing on the onesie and walk, run, crawl, skip, or dance her way out of office."

Pugh opted to slink. In the wake of FBI raids on her office and two homes, she quietly resigned on May 2, and on November 21, pleaded guilty to four charges of conspiracy and tax evasion. Finally, the following February, Pugh was sentenced to three years in prison and a big fat fine. But at least there was literary fodder for another potential best seller: *Healthy Holly Heads Up the River.*

MARCH 29, 1989

Carr Crash at the Oscars

Allan Carr was a caftan-clad, coke-snorting colossus in Hollywood. The girthful impresario threw legendary parties and produced *Grease,* one of the most successful movie musicals in history. Subsequent kowtowing to Carr by the entertainment industry made him believe he was a glittering star in their firmament: "I'm dreaming all this," he told *People* magazine in 1979, "and I'll kill the son of a bitch who tries to wake me up."

Carr's fantasy world crashed spectacularly with a single ill-advised production, beamed around the globe on March 29, 1989, and watched by perhaps a billion eyewitnesses. His 61st Academy Awards ceremony "began by creating the impression that there would never be a 62nd,"

New York Times critic Janet Maslin wrote of the debacle. The show opened with Snow White, "played as a simpering ninny" (Maslin again), entering the theater behind dancing stars and greeting mortified celebrities in the audience while chirping a variation of the tune "I Only Have Eyes for You" ("We Only Have Stars for You").

From there, things only got worse. The curtain opened to reveal a re-creation of the famed Coconut Grove nightclub, with Merv Griffin crooning his 40-year-old novelty hit, "I've Got a Lovely Bunch of Coconuts" (cue dancing coconuts!). Griffin then informed Snow White that he had found her a blind date: heartthrob Rob Lowe, whose infamous sex tape would soon surface in real life. Lowe and Snow proceeded to butcher John Fogerty's "Proud Mary," its lyrics bowdlerized to honor the occasion: "Rollin', Rollin' . . . keep those cameras rollin'"! And roll they did, capturing shock, horror, and disgust on famous faces throughout the audience.

In the weeks that followed, the dreamy Carr was forced to confront the full extent of the fiasco he had created. For starters, Disney sued for the misappropriation of their character Snow White. But especially galling for Carr, who subsisted on celebrity oxygen, was the scathing letter that arrived days later at the headquarters of the Academy of Motion Picture Arts and Sciences: Signed by 17 Hollywood luminaries (among them Paul Newman, Julie Andrews, and Gregory Peck), it blasted the awards show as "an embarrassment to . . . the entire motion picture industry . . . It is neither fitting nor acceptable that the best work in motion pictures be acknowledged in such a demeaning fashion. We urge the president and governors of the Academy to ensure that future award presentations reflect the same standard of excellence as that set by the films and filmmakers they honor."

Carr was left to console himself with this clunky bit of psycho-sartorial advice from one of his calamity's own numbers: "Whenever you're down in the dumps, / Try putting on Judy's red pumps."

Then again, look what happened to poor Judy.

<hr>

MARCH 30, 1826

The Shrieking Sound and Clay's Fury

"His assaults were so gross, repeated, and unprovoked I could no longer bear them . . . Submission, on my part, to the unmerited injury . . . would have made existence intolerable."
—*Secretary of State Henry Clay, in a letter recounting his duel with Senator John Randolph*

Historians have dubbed the decade from roughly 1815 to 1825 the "Era of Good Feelings" for the sense of shared national purpose that seemed to animate Americans in the aftermath of the War of 1812. But those noble urges evaporated in the vitriol of a vicious tirade directed at President John Quincy Adams and Secretary of State Henry Clay on the floor of the United States Senate on March 30, 1826.

Bitterness still lingered from early the year before, when the House of Representatives had conferred the presidency on Adams, despite the fact that Andrew Jackson had won more popular *and* electoral votes.* Adding to the ire was that the Jacksonians believed Adams and Clay had concocted a conspiracy: In the so-called "corrupt bargain," Clay—then the influential speaker of the House—had supposedly agreed to

<hr>

* Jackson had indeed won the popular vote and gained the most electoral votes. But he had not obtained the required majority, thus throwing the outcome of the election to the House of Representatives. The Tennessee statesman did prevail in the next election, however; see March 4.

rally votes for Adams in exchange for his own appointment as secretary of state.

The verbal attack came from Senator John Randolph of Virginia, already well known for his over-the-top oratory. His "high-toned and thin voice," as the *Boston Journal* described it, "would ring through the Senate Chamber like the shrill scream of an angry vixen."* It led many listeners to conclude that Randolph was entirely out of his mind.

But the caustic, opium-consuming senator outdid himself with his piercing fulmination of March 30—notorious not only for its malice but for the potentially mortal encounter it led to with Clay.

As he was accustomed to doing, Randolph inserted seemingly irrelevant historical references into his meandering speech—invoking, in this case, both the Carthaginian general Hannibal and England's royal House of Stuart. The allusions left many senators scratching their heads. Few could mistake Randolph's meaning, though, when he summoned two unsavory characters from Henry Fielding's widely read novel *Tom Jones:* Blifil and Black George—a "combination unheard of till then," Randolph declared, "of the puritan with the black leg."

Blifil, outwardly pious but inwardly consumed by greed, was clearly a cutting reference to Adams—"the puritan." And the dishonest Black George ("the black leg" being contemporary slang for a card cheat) was an unmistakable slur on Clay. Alluding to the two literary scoundrels was therefore inflammatory by the standards of the day.

"Malignant passions abound in him," George D. Prentice, editor of the *Louisville Journal,* wrote of Randolph's harangue. "His tongue is little scrupulous in giving vent to them. They overflowed in epithets of even more than his usual venom and scurrility on Mr. Clay."

---

* Randolph was often described as a startlingly androgynous figure—"a pale, meagre, ghostly man," as Senator William Plumer of New Hampshire wrote, "who has the appearance of a beardless boy more than a full grown man." As for that high-pitched voice, Representative Samuel Taggart of Massachusetts had a theory: "One would suppose him to be either by nature, or manual operation fixed for an Italian singer" (that is to say, a castrato; see September 27).

And for that, the nation's top diplomat sought a blood solution.

A week after the incendiary speech, Randolph accepted Clay's challenge to a duel. They met on the Virginia side of the Potomac River to engage in what became a rather absurd affair of honor. Both men took their positions, fired—and missed. But rather than calling it a day, as Senator Thomas Hart Benton suggested to the aggrieved parties, Clay insisted on another round. "This is child's play," he harrumphed—before firing a second errant shot. Randolph, for his part, simply gave up, signaling his concession by discharging his pistol into the air and approaching Clay to shake hands.

"And so ended this ludicrous duel," biographer Robert Remini wrote. "Two days later Clay and Randolph exchanged cards, and social relations were formally and courteously restored."

Turned out poor aim was the better part of valor.

MARCH 31, 2016

Those Who Cannot Remember the Past ... Wing It

"Well, I think Lincoln succeeded for numerous reasons. He was a man who was of great intelligence, which most presidents would be. But he was a man of great intelligence, but he was also a man that did something that was a very vital thing to do at that time. Ten years before or twenty years before, what he was doing would never have even been thought possible. So he did something that was a very important thing to do, and especially at that time."

—*Presidential candidate Donald Trump, in an interview with* Washington Post *reporters Bob Woodward and Robert Costa on March 31, 2016, when asked to explain Abraham Lincoln's success as a Republican president*

April

Fool's Day, All Right

Puritan fanatic Cotton Mather—fresh off his triumphal purge of witches from Salem, Massachusetts—had a sense that the devil's minions weren't quite finished with him. His four-day-old son had just died of a bowel obstruction, and on April 1, 1693, Mather confided to his diary what he believed to be the cause of the infant's demise:

> I had great Reason to suspect a *Witchcraft,* in this praeternatural Accident; because my Wife, a few weeks before her Deliverance, was affrighted with a horrible *Spectre,* in our Porch, which Fright caused her Bowels to turn within her; and the *Spectres* which both before and after, tormented a young Woman in our Neighborhood, brag'd of their giving my Wife that Fright, in hopes, they said, of doing Mischief unto her *Infant* at least, if not unto the *Mother:* and besides all this, the

Child was no sooner born, but a suspected Woman sent unto my Father, a Letter full of railing against myself, wherein shee told him, *Hee little knew, what might quickly befall some of his Posterity.*

And no, Cotton wasn't kidding.

— ◆ —

APRIL 2, 1915

Birth Defect: The Mistruths of a Malicious "Masterpiece"

D. W. Griffith's 1915 silent feature *The Birth of a Nation* was Hollywood's first mega-production—a technically brilliant, three-hour celluloid extravaganza. It was also breathtakingly racist—"a great film that argues for evil," as critic Roger Ebert described it in 2003.*

The sweeping epic's version of history boiled down to this: Destroyed in the Civil War and overrun by rapaciously inferior, sex-crazed blacks, the once halcyon American South had been gloriously rescued by the white knights of the Ku Klux Klan.

And that was precisely how the Reverend Thomas B. Gregory preferred to view the past. In a piece published in the *New York American* on April 2, 1915, the Universalist minister (and regular contributor to the Hearst press) swooned over the film's alleged historic significance: "As an educator, its value is well-nigh inconceivable and its chief value in this direction lies in its truthfulness. That the story as told by the picture is

---

* In either a long-overdue response to a virulently racist film or a retrospective capitulation to modern sensibilities, the name of actress Lillian Gish—who starred in *The Birth of a Nation*—was removed from the campus theater at Ohio's Bowling Green State University in 2019.

true I am ready to swear on the Bible, the Koran, the Zend, and all other 'Holy Scriptures' put together."

And we swear Reverend Gregory had gone right around the Zend when he wrote this one.

APRIL 3, 1847

Bigotry on the High Seas:
Frederick Douglass's Stolen Berth Right

"I have travelled in this country 19 months, and have always
enjoyed equal rights and privileges with other passengers,
and it was not until I turned my face towards America that
I met anything like proscription on account of my colour."
—*Frederick Douglass, writing from Liverpool to the editor
of* The Times *of London on April 3, 1847*

Earlier that day, the former slave turned famed abolitionist had discovered—"to my surprise and mortification"—that his prepaid accommodations for passage back to the United States aboard the Cunard steamship *Cambria* had been given to another passenger. Douglass was informed that the agent who sold him his ticket had done so without authority, and "that I should not go on board the ship unless I agreed to take my meals alone, not to mix with the saloon company, and to give up the berth for which I had paid."

It's impossible to say which was worse for Douglass—the discrimination and isolation he endured returning to America, or the pro-slavery mob he faced on his equally fraught journey to Britain aboard the same ship in 1845. "Yes," he recounted, "they actually got up a MOB—a real, American, republican, democratic, Christian mob—and that, too, on the deck of a British steamer, and in sight of the beautiful high lands of Dungarvan!"

APRIL 4, 1846

Thumbs-Down on
Benjamin Haydon's Art

"They rush by thousands to see Thumb. They push, they fight,
they scream, they faint, they cry help and murder! and oh! and ah!
They see my bills, my boards, my caravans, and don't read them,
but their sense is shut. It is an insanity, a *rabies,* a madness, a *furor,*
a dream. I would not have believed it of the English people."
—*Benjamin Haydon, April 1846*

Benjamin Haydon fancied himself a master: an artist gifted enough
to establish, and represent, a preeminent school of British historical
painting. "I trust my merciful Creator will not let me leave this world
without an opportunity to put forth . . . the talents with which He has
blessed me," Haydon once confided to his journal.

Alas, his "merciful Creator" never got the call.

After a decidedly non-illustrious career filled with disappointments,
unseemly squabbles with the art establishment, and occasional stints in
debtors' prison, Haydon was subjected to what biographer Paul O'Keeffe
described as "a failure tuned to so exquisite a pitch of cruelty and humiliation as to make it, perversely, a thing of genius."

Ironically, the dreadful occasion in April 1846 was supposed to be a
redemption. A decade earlier, Haydon's sketched ideas for artworks to
adorn the newly rebuilt Houses of Parliament had been rejected. Undeterred, the artist simply transferred his rebuffed proposals to canvas.
Then—as a means of bestowing his overlooked genius upon the world—
Haydon crafted a plan to exhibit the paintings, choosing what he
believed would be an auspicious venue: the Egyptian Hall at Piccadilly
Circus. After all, it had been the site of his greatest artistic (and financial)
achievement way back in 1820, when enthusiastic crowds and generous
critics had embraced his epic painting, "Christ's Triumphant Entry into
Jerusalem."

April 4, 1846—the day on which Haydon hosted a private preview of his exhibit—dawned damp and dreary: a perfect prelude to the coming disaster. Of the 400 guests invited, four showed up. "Twenty-six years ago, the rain would not have prevented them," the artist lamented. "But now it is not so." His daughter's words, recorded in Haydon's journal entry for that day, expressed an inescapable truth: "People are more disposed to seek after Curiosities than attend to Science and Art."

The "curiosity" in this case was circus impresario P. T. Barnum's three-foot-three performer, General Tom Thumb—who, to the lofty artist's regret, was likewise booked at the Egyptian Hall. Despite Haydon's published appeal to "let every Briton who has pluck in his bosom and a shilling in his pocket crowd to his works during Easter week," visitors whizzed by to marvel at Tom instead. Meanwhile in Haydon's exhibition space, crickets chirped. "Tom Thumb had 12,000 people last week," the incredulous artist wrote on April 21. "B. R. Haydon 133½ (the ½ a little girl). Exquisite taste of the English people!"

And yet their taste was apparently better than Haydon's. Charles Dickens, for one, described the artist as "unquestionably . . . a very bad painter." Of those drawn to view his works, Dickens expressed his amazement "not that they were so few, but that they were so many."

Six weeks later, Haydon closed his exhibit at a significant loss. "Next to victory is a skillful retreat," he wrote that day, "and I marched out before General Tom Thumb, a beaten but not conquered exhibitor."

Haydon would die by his own hand just over a month later.

APRIL 5, 1531

Bring to a Rapid Boil . . . Add Chef

Richard Roose, a cook in the household of Bishop John Fisher, found himself in hot water—a boiling vat of it, to be precise—on April 5, 1531, as he was slowly scalded to death by special order of England's Henry VIII.

The punishment was novel, even for those barbaric times. The king had pushed it through Parliament in response to what he viewed as a particularly appalling crime: Roose was accused of trying to poison the Bishop of Rochester by mixing purgatives into his meal. The prelate survived, albeit with dangerously depleted bowels. But two other household members succumbed to the effects of the stool-loosening soup.

Roose swore his deed was just meant to be a joke. Others detected something more sinister, however. Fisher was a staunch opponent of King Henry's plan to discard his first wife, Katharine of Aragon, in order to marry Anne Boleyn. The would-be queen's grasping family, therefore, had every reason to seek the obdurate bishop's destruction. Though historians largely discount the Boleyns' involvement in such a messy form of assassination, suspicion still lingers in popular retellings of the story.

Regardless of what motivated Roose—a warped sense of humor, or pressure from a powerful clique—the poor cook paid the terrible price of being poached. "He roared mighty loud," a contemporary reported as the chained unfortunate was repeatedly dunked into the bubbling cauldron "until he was dead." And though crowds normally enjoyed the spectacle of death at Smithfield—the infamous execution site in London, where burning and disemboweling regularly took place—there was something about this new method of dispatch that made some of them sick.

Fortunately for the queasy, the bishop, who had escaped the worst effects of Roose's concoction (but not Henry VIII's wrath for his refusal to recognize the king as Supreme Head of the Church in England), would later endure a more conventional death, by axe—a crow-pecked head, spiked and perched on a bridge, presumably being more palatable than human fondue.

<hr />

APRIL 6, 1856

The Charge of the Tight Brigade

Nicholas I, Russia's iron-fisted tsar, was in despair as he lay dying in the spring of 1855. His vast empire was facing certain defeat in the

Crimean War, and there was nothing this once fearsome grandson of Catherine the Great could do about it.

The fate of his troops weighed especially heavy on the failing tsar. "Tell them that in the other world I shall continue to pray for them," he gasped. "I have always tried to work for their good. If I failed in that, this was not because of a lack of good will, but because of a lack of knowledge and ability. I beg them to pardon me."

A year later—just one week after Nicholas's son and successor, Alexander II, signed the humiliating Treaty of Paris, ending not only the war but any illusion of Russian preeminence—the dead emperor's promised blessings undoubtedly turned to spits and curses. For it was from his heavenly perch that the "condescending Jupiter," as the late tsar was once described, watched a mortifying scene unfold on April 6, 1856: The defeated soldiers for whom he had voiced so much concern got spectacularly drunk and proceeded to degrade themselves before their erstwhile enemies.

"The great objects of attraction to-day were the Russians, who crowded over the Tchernaya [River], and wandered into every part of our camp, where they soon made out the canteens," a British soldier recorded. "Their drunken salute to passing officers is very ludicrous; and one could laugh, only he is disgusted at the abject cringe with which they remove their caps, and bow, bareheaded, with horrid gravity in their bleary leaden eyes and wooden faces, at the sight of a piece of gold lace."

But what must really have repulsed the ghost of Tsar Nicholas was the plastered soldiers' trip back across the river that evening—"on balks of timber," the British witness noted, "which looked double to their vision but in reality were narrow enough for a sober man to find some difficulty in crossing."

The result of the effort was both predictable and pathetic: "Ever and anon the Ruski tumbled off amid shouts of laughter and was pulled out half drowned. A grim guard, with fixed bayonets, envious probably of the happy condition of their comrades, was waiting for them at the other side; and the bank was controlled by Cossacks, with ropes, all ready to tie up any 'incapable' and take him homewards.

"Down they came, staggering and roaring through the bones of their countrymen (which in common decency I hope they will bury as soon as possible) . . . [British] General Codrington was down at the ford, and did not seem to know whether to be amused or scandalized at the scene."

Nicholas I, assuredly, would have struggled with no such perplexity.

APRIL 7, 2003

Not by Feith Alone

Secretary of Defense Donald Rumsfeld had a little task for Undersecretary Doug Feith, which he sent in the form of a Monday-morning memo on April 7, 2003. Rummy's directive seemed to demand that his subordinate solve half the world's problems. Here's the verbatim text of what *The Atlantic* described as "perhaps the least enviable weekday to-do list imaginable":

> TO: Doug Feith
> FROM: Donald Rumsfeld
> SUBJECT: Issues w/Various Countries
> We need more coercive diplomacy with respect to Syria and Libya, and we need it fast. If they mess up Iraq, it will delay bringing our troops home.
> We also need to solve the Pakistan problem.
> And Korea doesn't seem to be going well.
> Are you coming up with proposals for me to send around?
> Thanks.

APRIL 8, 2013

Cruel Britannia:
Turning Munchkins Into Meanies

"When we were filming the movie no one intended it to be

used in this way. I am ashamed, I really am . . . I thought British
people were better than that. I don't understand them."
—*Actress Ruth Duccini, a Munchkin portrayer*
in the 1939 film The Wizard of Oz

The exultant anti-dirge "Ding-Dong! The Witch Is Dead!" was racing up the British pop charts—not in 1939, when *The Wizard of Oz* was released, but in 2013, when former British prime minister Margaret Thatcher passed away.

Thatcher had not been universally beloved by her people. Yet amid the many unseemly celebrations of her death on April 8, 2013—the crude graffiti, the spontaneous street parties, the burning effigies of the deceased—one stood out as singularly appalling: the successful campaign to have the melted-witch tune climb the pop-music charts.

"It is shocking that the song is being used to celebrate the death of someone," former Munchkin portrayer Jerry Maren told the *Sun*. "It's a shame that the song is being used in this way."

Wicked, in fact.

APRIL 9, 1922

Put to the Testes, Part 2:

The Nuttiest Cure You've Ever Heard

"New Life in New Glands"
—*Headline in the April 9, 1922, issue of the* Los Angeles
Sunday Times, *heralding the "remarkable results" from goat testicles*
being implanted in the scrotums of men suffering various
ailments from low libido to high blood pressure

Journalistic ethics, along with an untold number of *L.A. Times* readers, took a punch below the belt when the newspaper's publisher,

Harry Chandler, sponsored and promoted the highly questionable medical procedures of a quack named John R. Brinkley. Chandler even arranged for Brinkley to be granted a temporary medical license in California, allowing the charlatan to perform his bizarre surgery on the paper's managing editor, Harry E. Andrews. Soon afterward, Brinkley reported, Andrews was "able to ride horse-back, and recently took a hundred-mile auto ride without fatigue. Mr. Chandler will vouch for the truth of this statement, as will Mr. Andrews himself, if called upon, or any other member of the *Times* staff."

Yet as Mr. Chandler was probably aware, the procedure was no more efficacious than grafting testes onto a tree. And whereas he was happy to recommend the testicular treatment for others, there is no evidence that the legendary *Times* man ever underwent the transplant himself.

On the other hand, U.S. Circuit Judge Erskine M. Ross did go for the gonadal gusto. "I cannot understand why anyone should be any more ashamed to have goat glands implanted in his body than to put any edible part of the goat into his stomach, which many do," the esteemed jurist said in a newspaper interview (proudly excerpted by—get this—*Goat World* magazine). "And while I can well understand that the medical profession seeks to keep quacks and humbugs out of it . . . it is well . . . to remember that new and most valuable discoveries in all sciences . . . are being constantly made."

And, as the "rejuvenated" judge should have known, so are hucksters.

APRIL 10, 1848

Unholy Matrimony, Part 2:
Spouse of Horror

Poor Euphemia ("Effie") Gray. Her self-esteem took quite a hit on her wedding night—April 10, 1848—when the vivacious 19-year-old presented herself to her new husband, the British social thinker, writer, and critic John Ruskin, who was nearly a decade her senior. There is no record of precisely how Ruskin reacted when he beheld her naked form, only that he didn't sleep with her that night—or ever.

Ruskin advanced various explanations for the nonconsummation, Effie reported, including "hatred to children, religious motives, [and] a desire to preserve my beauty." Finally, after months of waffling, he came clean with his "true reason": According to Effie, "he had imagined women were quite different to what he saw I was, and that the reason he did not make me his Wife is that he was disgusted with my person the first evening."

What could possibly have repulsed the writer so? Some historians have speculated that Ruskin was sexually repressed, with desires that tipped perilously close to pedophilia. Others have theorized that he was put off by Effie's pubic hair, or that she was menstruating on her wedding night.

No one will ever know what really happened on that night of shocking revelation. But the aftermath of the marital collapse and subsequent annulment may be telling. Ruskin became besotted with a nine-year-old girl, Rose La Touche, whose later rejection of him (and subsequent death at age 27 in 1875) was said to have contributed to the insanity of his later years. Effie, on the other hand, married John Everett Millais—a painter Ruskin had long championed, whose romance with Effie he supposedly engineered—and apparently enjoyed the vigorous intimacy of which she had been long deprived:

The couple had eight children.

APRIL 11, 1979

Khomeini's Bad Gratitude

Years before he became Iran's supreme leader, Ayatollah Ruhollah Khomeini was a prisoner—arrested in 1963 for having led an uprising against the regime of Shah Mohammad Reza Pahlavi. Happily for Khomeini, the tedium of internment was relieved by a regular visitor—one who became an unlikely advocate.

General Hassan Pakravan, Iran's deputy prime minister (and chief of SAVAK, the shah's dreaded secret police), popped in once a week to have lunch, over which the two men would chat genially about history, philosophy, and religion.

"Teamsar [General]," the religious leader would say, "I count the days until we reach our lunch day." Pakravan told his wife, Fatemeh, that the conversations were "very good, very cordial. Very friendly," according to the oral history she provided Harvard University. But, he added, Khomeini's ignorance of philosophy and history was appalling, his naked ambition unsettling. "It made my hair stand on my head," he said of the ayatollah's ferocious drive. "It was frightening."

He should have heeded his raised hackles.

Yet subduing his misgivings, Pakravan—a relative moderate despite SAVAK's reputation for torturing and killing opponents of the Pahlavi regime—persuaded the shah to spare Khomeini's life. To execute him, Pakravan successfully argued, would only inflame the ayatollah's legions of loyal followers. Khomeini was sent into exile instead.

And there he lay in wait for the next 16 years, roaring back in the midst of the 1979 revolution that toppled the shah. Upon ascending to the post of supreme leader, the ayatollah was reminded of all that Hassan Pakravan had done to save his life. Khomeini's laconic reply: "He should not have."

"Khomeini is an unforgiving man," Fatemeh Pakraven related. "The more he owes someone, the more he hates him, and he owed everything to my husband."

Thus, on April 11, 1979, Pakravan was among the first officials of the old regime to be executed—shot by a firing squad, with photos of the deed triumphantly published in the Iranian press.

A most unjust dessert after all those edifying lunches.

APRIL 12, 2013

Unbeliebable!

For young diarist Anne Frank, nothing could have been worse than Nazis knocking at her door. But bratty teen sensation Justin Bieber may be in line for second worst.

"Truly inspiring to be able to come here," the singer wrote in a guest book at the Anne Frank House Museum in Amsterdam during his visit of April 12, 2013. "Anne was a great girl."

Very sweet—so far. But the staggeringly self-absorbed heartthrob couldn't resist adding this postscript, a wink to the nickname his fawning female fans gave themselves: "Hopefully she would have been a belieber."

Bieber's message prompted a slew of hilarious celebrity clap-backs: "I

agree with Justin Bieber," tweeted British comic Ricky Gervais. "Anne Frank would've loved his stuff. It's perfect for being played really really quietly so no one can hear it." Actor Rainn Wilson, meanwhile—mock quoting "93% of beliebers"—tweeted, "Who's this Anne Frank & why is he visiting her HOUSE? Are they dating?! OMG!"

APRIL 13, 1986

"Mother of the Nation" Miscarries

"Together, hand in hand, with our boxes of matches
and our necklaces, we shall liberate this country."
—*Winnie Mandela, wife of imprisoned South African anti-apartheid
leader Nelson Mandela, in a speech delivered on April 13, 1986*

Those "matches" and "necklaces" championed by Mrs. Mandela, the so-called "Mother of the Nation," were commonly used to commit an unspeakable barbarity. South Africans condemned to be "neck-laced"—usually blacks accused of collaborating with the nation's apartheid government—suffered an agonizing ordeal: A gasoline-filled rubber tire was forced down around the victim's chest, immobilizing the arms, then set ablaze.

Just five months before publicly endorsing this brand of mob savagery, Winnie Mandela had received the Robert F. Kennedy Human Rights Award.

⋅——⋅

APRIL 14, 1968

What a Putts!

Roberto De Vicenzo was feeling the love on April 14, 1968, serenaded on his 45th birthday by crowds watching him dominate the Masters Tournament. Even more uplifting, the Argentinian golfer could justifiably picture himself being fitted for the victor's coveted green jacket: After 72 holes, De Vicenzo—who had won the British Open the previous year—was tied for the lead with American Bob Goalby. An 18-hole playoff the following day would determine the winner.

Or so De Vicenzo believed.

Caught up in the excitement of the day, De Vicenzo hastily signed the scorecard that had been filled out by his playing partner, Tommy Aaron. What he failed to notice in doing so would cost him the tournament—and haunt him the rest of his life.

De Vicenzo had birdied the 17th hole of the final round, earning a score of 3. But Aaron mistakenly entered a 4 on their shared scorecard. Never mind that the incorrect figure had been written in pencil; once players sign their cards, according to PGA tournament rules, the numbers they display might just as well be etched in stone.

The undetected one-point difference handed Goalby the tournament—and landed De Vicenzo in the annals of agonizing defeat.

De Vincenzo dejectedly called himself "stupid." But Goalby was equally aggrieved, later telling the *Los Angeles Times*, "I have forever been singled out as the guy who won the Masters because of some damn clerical mistake."

APRIL 15, 1865

The Booths: Tragically Upstaged at Ford's Theatre

"A fearful calamity is upon us. The President of the
United States has fallen by the hand of an assassin, and I am
shocked to say, suspicion points to one nearly related
to you as the perpetrator of this horrid deed."
—*Henry Jarrett, manager of the Boston Theater, informing
actor Edwin Booth on April 15, 1865, that his remaining
performances at the venue had been canceled*

Edwin Booth was basking in the triumph of his unprecedented, 100-night run as Hamlet when, on April 15, 1865, he learned that his status as one of America's most acclaimed actors had been eclipsed by the fanatical act of his younger brother. The night before, John Wilkes Booth had shot President Abraham Lincoln in the head.

Ever the dramatic artist, Edwin immediately associated the horror of the deed with the role he had been playing in George Colman's *The Iron Chest* on the night of the assassination. In a letter to his friend Adam Badeau, Booth wrote: "Oh, how little did I dream my boy when on Friday [April 14], I was, as Sir Edward Mortimer, exclaiming, 'Where is my honor now? Mountains of shame are piled upon me!' that I was not acting but uttering the fearful truth."

Though undoubtedly horrified by the murder of Lincoln, whom he had unreservedly supported,* Edwin Booth also recognized that his brother's infamy would derail his career. Accordingly, he took out an advertisement, which was published in numerous papers, expressing the sorrow and regret he and the rest of the Booth family felt:

> It has pleased God to lay at the door of my afflicted family the lifeblood of our great, good, and martyred President. Prostrated to the very earth by this dreadful event, I am yet but too sensible that other mourners fill the land. To them, to you, one and all, go forth our deep, unutterable sympathy; our abhorrence and detestation for this most foul and atrocious of crimes. For my mother and sisters, for my remaining brothers and my own poor self, there is nothing to be said except that we are thus placed without any power of our own. For our present position we are not responsible. For the future—alas, I shall struggle on in my retirement bearing a heavy heart, an oppressed memory; and a wounded name, dreadful burdens, to my too welcome grave.

Edwin Booth did retire from acting—temporarily. He had received death threats and other abusive missives, but then as now, celebrity conferred a certain immunity. In the immediate aftermath of the assassination, the authorities largely left Edwin alone. And less than a year later—after "chewing my heart in solitude," as he put it—Booth was raucously welcomed back to the stage.

The rest of his family, by contrast, endured unrelenting distress.

Edwin's older brother, Junius Brutus Booth, Jr.—namesake of his famous father, but significantly less skilled in the family acting profession—narrowly avoided being lynched in Cincinnati, where he had been performing

---

* "Abraham Lincoln was my president," Edwin wrote, "for in pure admiration of his noble career and Christian principles I owe what I never did before—I *voted* & FOR HIM!"

at Pike's Opera House. A mob gathered at his hotel on the morning of April 15, just after Junius learned what John had done, braying for his blood. "They would have hanged him in a minute if they could have laid their hands on him, so great was their rage," recalled Emil Benlier, a clerk at the hotel who hid Booth and eventually helped smuggle him out. Soon afterward, Junius was arrested at the Philadelphia home of his sister, Asia Booth Clarke, and taken to the Old Capitol prison in Washington, D.C.

Asia's husband, a comedic actor named John Sleeper Clarke, was thrown into the same jail as Junius, joining several others swept up in the post-assassination frenzy. One of them, John Ford, owner of the theater where Lincoln was murdered, recalled that Clarke was "brought in, kept like a malefactor in a small room & on prison fare, forbid to speak to any one or see a paper."

Embittered by the degrading experience, as well as by the stain on his reputation from his link to the Booth family, Clarke sought a divorce—"which would be [his] only salvation now," as Asia reported him saying. (Ironically, John Wilkes Booth had warned his sister at her wedding that Clarke was using her and the Booth name to advance his own career: "Always bear in mind you're a professional stepping-stone," John had reportedly cautioned Asia.)

Abandoned by friends and betrayed by her husband, Asia—who avoided arrest only because of her advanced pregnancy—chronicled the effects of her brother's notorious crime upon her family. "Those who have passed through such an ordeal," she wrote, "never relearn to trust in human nature, they never resume their old place in the world, and they forget only in death."

APRIL 16, 1913

Mauling Matisse

Henri Matisse was having a hell of a time finding an appreciative audience in 1913. His work was on display at the International

Exhibition of Modern Art among fellow avant-garde painters and sculptors such as Pablo Picasso and Auguste Rodin. The Armory Show, as it was known—the first of its kind in the United States—opened in New York, where Matisse was flensed by the *Times:* "We may as well say in the first place that his pictures are ugly, that they are coarse, that they are narrow, that to us they are revolting in their inhumanity."

Then it was on to Chicago—where Matisse was further splattered. On April 16, students at the Art Institute of Chicago burned copies of Matisse's now legendary 1907 "Blue Nude" and other works. They then staged a mock trial in which a manacled student, playing the role of "Henry Hair Mattress," was led to the docket at bayonet point.

The visionary's crime? "You are charged with artistic murder, pictorial arson, artistic rapine, total degeneracy of color, criminal misuse of line, general esthetic aberration, and contumacious abuse of title," the indictment read.

The jury found the defendant guilty—after which, the *Chicago Daily Tribune* reported, "The executioner stepped forward, but the shivering futurist, overcome by his own conscience, fell dead."*

———❦———

APRIL 17, 2010

A Two-Letter Blunder:
Penguin's Peppery Response

"We're mortified that this has become an issue of any kind
and why anyone would be offended, we don't know."

---

* Fortunately, wealthy sisters Etta and Claribel Cone revived him. "My two Baltimore ladies," as Matisse had affectionately dubbed the pair, championed the artist and his works, including that burned-in-effigy "Blue Nude." The impressive collection the sisters Cone amassed is now proudly on display at the Baltimore Museum of Art.

—*Robert Sessions, head of publishing for Penguin Group Australia,*
quoted by The Sydney Morning Herald *on April 17, 2010,*
in response to a highly offensive misprint in The Pasta Bible,
a cookbook published by his company

It was quite an error. The antepenultimate ingredient in the recipe for "Spelt tagliatelle with sardines & prosciutto" was supposed to be salt and freshly ground black pepper. Instead, the cookbook called for "salt and freshly ground black people," prompting Penguin's costly decision to pulp and reprint all 7,000 copies of the book.

They should have tossed Sessions into that pulverizing machine as well.

The unrepentant publisher just couldn't seem to grasp why his company's "silly mistake" might have upset people. "When it comes to the proofreader, of course they should have picked it up," he told the *Herald*. "But proofreading a cookbook is an extremely difficult task. I find that quite forgivable."

Unless that was a typo for "unforgivable," we're adding freshly ground Penguin to our recipe for cream of shame soup.

APRIL 18, 1970

Ono You Don't!

Yoko Orders John to "Get Back"

John Lennon was all about peace and love, love, love. His pacifist sensibilities and songwriting talent had made him not only a global superstar, but also a musical guru the world could embrace.

His private behavior, however, belied his beatific reputation. Lennon's first wife, Cynthia, and their son, Julian, would experience this firsthand as the rock star life began to supplant his role as husband and father. Indeed, when it came to caring for his little family, which he abandoned in 1968, Lennon was one Mean Mr. Mustard. His neglect of five-year-old

Julian was so egregious that Paul McCartney famously wrote "Hey Jude" as a way of comforting the lonely child.

"Dad could talk about peace and love out loud to the world, but he could never show it to the people who supposedly meant the most to him: his wife and son," Julian told the *Daily Telegraph* in 2015. "How can you talk about peace and love and have a family in bits and pieces—no communication, adultery, divorce? You can't do it—not if you're being true and honest with yourself."

His authorship of "Strawberry Fields Forever" notwithstanding, Lennon was never the most blissful Beatle; his cynicism and bitter sarcasm reflected a deeper psychic pain. Hoping to help resolve these issues, Arthur Janov, author of *The Primal Scream*, suggested a therapeutic visit from Lennon to his forsaken family. The now ex-Beatle agreed, and on April 18, 1970, he went to see Cynthia and Julian. But the reunion was abruptly terminated, courtesy of Lennon's new wife, Yoko Ono.

Perhaps sensing a threat, the avant-garde artist telephoned Cynthia's home with a pointed message for John. Although not delivered in Yoko's own primal scream of a singing voice (the housekeeper relayed Yoko's demand), the meaning was clear: "Yoko has just called and is threatening to commit suicide unless John returns home immediately."

Dutifully, John rushed back into the arms of Yoko. And away from Julian—yet again.

APRIL 19, 797

Momsters, Part 3: Irene the Mean

Ferocious as they are, mother crocodiles do carefully carry their young in their jaws. But Byzantine empress Irene didn't possess even this most rudimentary reptilian instinct. Indeed, she chomped right down on her son, Constantine VI.

The empress, whose name ironically means "peace" in Greek, had become intoxicated by the power she wielded while serving as regent for

Constantine, who inherited the throne of the Eastern Roman Empire at the age of nine. As the boy grew up and started to assert himself, Irene correctly saw threats to the authority she had amassed. So she began to sabotage Constantine by urging him to make decisions that would sap his popularity—dumping his wife and marrying his mistress, say, or ripping out the tongues of his uncles.

When this Byzantine maneuvering failed to do the trick, Mean Irene took even more savage measures—call them "the ties that blind": On April 19, 797, she had her son's eyes gouged out. And with that maternal touch, Irene became the first woman to rule the empire in her own right.

APRIL 20, 1991

A Host of Problems: *SNL* Under Siege

Steven Seagal arrived at New York's 30 Rockefeller Plaza with a greasy ponytail, a bad attitude, and a debilitating lack of humor. For some reason the self-adoring action-film star had been invited to host the April 20, 1991, episode of NBC's *Saturday Night Live.* Thanks to his inability to play well with others, however, the broadcast proved to be one of the show's most problematic.

In interviews for the 2002 book *Live From New York* by Tom Shales and James Andrew Miller, cast members recalled the fiasco: "The biggest problem with Steven Seagal was that he would complain about jokes that he didn't get, so it was like—you can't explain something to somebody in German if they don't speak German," said cast member Tim Meadows. "He just wasn't funny, and he was very critical of the cast and the writing staff. He didn't realize that you can't tell someone they're stupid on Wednesday and expect them to continue writing for you on Saturday."

"He didn't want to go along with what the plan was that week," observed David Spade. "As a result I think that was the first week that I heard talk about replacing the host and just doing a cast show."

"Some of his sketch ideas were so heinous, but so hilariously awful, it was like we were on *Candid Camera*," noted Julia Sweeney.

SNL producer Lorne Michaels got his revenge about a year after Seagal's famously unfunny performance. In the show's 18th season opener, host Nicolas Cage was in the middle of a comically offensive monologue when, as part of the sketch, he was summoned to a backstage reprimand by Michaels. Said Cage, pretending to be horrified at his effect on the audience: "They probably think I'm the biggest jerk who's ever been on the show."

"No, no," Michaels replied. "That would be Steven Seagal."

APRIL 21, 1912

The Wages of Sin—
If You've Got the Wages

One week after the sinking of the *Titanic,* the congregation of New York's Madison Square Presbyterian Church may have been looking for solace in their Sunday sermon.

Pastor C. H. Parkhurst had other ideas.

The tragedy that had claimed 1,517 innocent lives, Parkhurst informed his flock, was a "terrific and ghastly illustration" of the dangers of decadence, "when men throw God out of the door and take a golden calf in at the window."

The good pastor continued to conjure a vivid image of the finery swallowed by the icy Atlantic: "The picture which presents itself before my eyes is that of the glassy, glaring eyes of the victims, staring meaninglessly at the gilded furnishings of this sunken palace of the sea; dead helplessness wrapped in priceless luxury; jewels valued in seven figures becoming the strange playthings of the queer creatures that sport in the dark depths . . . Grand men, charming women, beautiful babies, all becoming horrible in the midst of the glittering splendor of a $10,000,000 casket!"

But an inconvenient truth torpedoed the reverend's wrathful-deity message: Many of those who perished were traveling in austere third-class quarters that became austere third-class graves. Without even a porthole in steerage, there was never an opportunity to take in that golden calf at the window.

———

APRIL 22, 2003

Remember the Mane!

By 2003, the many incarnations of the Breck Girl, whose shiny, full-bodied tresses adorned shampoo advertisements from the 1930s on, had fallen flat as a cultural icon. But on April 22 of that year, *The New York Times* revived her—now with testosterone and presidential ambitions—in the person of Senator John Edwards of North Carolina.

In a front-page story about the campaign strategies being deployed for the reelection of President George W. Bush, *Times* reporters Adam Nagourney and Richard W. Stevenson quoted an anonymous Bush insider who described Edwards, a potential Democratic rival, as "the Breck Girl of politics." The lustrous metaphor stuck to the well-coiffed candidate like greasy buildup.

The Edwards campaign tried to soften the sting of that label by taking ownership of it: Staffers handed out bottles of Breck shampoo at the official launch of Edwards's White House bid that September.

But by the time he made a second run for the presidency four years later, the impeccably styled politician had apparently learned nothing about the perils of being perceived as a looks-obsessed lightweight. With the Breck Girl epithet still clinging to him (thanks in part to conservative commentator Rush Limbaugh, who co-opted the phrase and repeated it in countless broadcasts), Edwards was swept up in another hair to-do when it was disclosed that he had used campaign funds for salon visits costing $400. Meanwhile, a leaked video of the candidate meticulously tending his locks—set to the tune of "I Feel Pretty"—was going viral.

"Appearances matter in politics," Adam Nagourney wrote in a retrospective of his original piece in the *Times,* "and four years after the Breck Girl line first appeared in print, Mr. Edwards continues to have trouble leaving it behind."

Hmm, perhaps a scandalous distraction? When the *National Enquirer* revealed that Edwards had a mistress—who bore him a love child while his wife, Elizabeth, was dying of breast cancer—the Breck Girl of politics became the Alfred E. Neuman of ethics.

APRIL 23, 2017

Boared to Death

The Islamic State in Iraq and Syria, aka ISIS, has been notoriously inventive in finding new ways to kill people. So it was only fitting that on April 23, 2017, a band of these militant sadists were treated to a unique demise of their own.

Concealing themselves among marsh reeds while preparing a surprise attack on some Iraqi tribesmen, at least eight ISIS members were reportedly set upon by a pack of wild boars. The ferocious animals mauled three of the terrorists to death and injured five others.

Alas, these porcine special forces have yet to be recruited for further duty.

APRIL 24, 1967

Senselessly Lost in Space:
The Soviets' Doomed Cosmonaut

The 50th anniversary of the Bolshevik Revolution was fast approaching in the spring of 1967, spurring Soviet leaders to cast about for something spectacular to mark the occasion. A fresh triumph in the heavens would serve well, they decided, especially now that the once dominant Soviet space program had begun to lag behind that of the United States.

Alas, a revival of the glory days, when Yuri Gagarin became the first human to sail through outer space, wasn't simply a dream; it was a demand—and one that brooked no dissent. As a result of the Kremlin's extreme pressure, cosmonaut Vladimir Komarov—the 40-year-old father of two—would become the first person to die on a spaceflight.

The plan was a complicated twin-docking mission: Soyuz 1, the spaceship Komarov piloted, would link up with a second, three-man ship; the two vessels would then swap crews.

There were only several hundred hitches with this scheme, the most notable being that three crewless test launches had ended in catastrophe. But with the anniversary celebrations looming, there was no time to conduct a fourth trial run. Komarov would be hurtled into space aboard a craft that historian Asif Siddiqi has condemned as "incontrovertibly not ready for crewed flight."

Serious technical problems arose almost immediately after the launch of Soyuz 1 on April 23, 1967. First a solar panel failed to unfurl, starving the craft of power. Then the capsule's auto-stabilizing system crapped out. Ground control opted to scrub the mission, but one final glitch proved fatal: The descent module's main parachute failed to deploy on reentry, and Soyuz 1 smashed back to Earth the day after its rushed launch—at 90 miles an hour.

The high-speed impact and resulting explosion reduced Komarov to a charred lump. In the years following, wildly unsubstantiated tales of the cosmonaut's final moments began to appear: Komarov cursing the callous leaders who had sent him to his death; Komarov tearfully bidding his wife farewell via radio; Komarov insisting that his obliterated remains be displayed in an open coffin so the world might witness what had been done to him.*

Yet the horrific fate of a good man—"conscientious, highly intelligent, modest and reserved . . . one of the most erudite of the cosmonauts," as Siddiqi described him—needed no such embroidering. Vladimir Komarov died valiantly, serving a state that had failed him.

APRIL 25, 1973

On Second Thought, Part 7: Rewind Me Next Time

"I always wondered about that taping equipment
but I'm damn glad we have it, aren't you?"
—*President Richard M. Nixon to his chief of staff (and
Watergate co-conspirator) H. R. Haldeman, on the Oval Office
recording devices that would soon doom them both, April 25, 1973*

For most of their White House tenure, both Nixon and Haldeman seem simply to have overlooked the fact that their words were being recorded for posterity—and prosecution. As Haldeman himself revealed in a paper published by the National Archives' *Prologue* magazine in the summer of 1988, "It is amazing to me when I think back to the first days,

---

* A picture circulating on the internet shows Komarov's charred corpse in an open casket, but the leaked image is of an early viewing by colleagues. Komarov was, in fact, cremated before his state funeral; his ashes were then deposited in the Kremlin Wall beside those of fellow Soviet heroes.

weeks, and months of the taping system's existence how quickly I forgot about it.. . . . I think Nixon lost his awareness of the system even more quickly than I did . . . I sometimes ask myself if I would have said some things differently if I had consciously considered the fact that my words were being taped . . . But my confidence that the tapes were never going to be heard by anyone except Nixon and myself was so great that I really do suspect I would have . . . spoken just as I did."

And to think: Everyone else believes *they* sound terrible on tape!

APRIL 26, 1836

Why So Proudly He Railed: Francis Scott Key's Perilous Fight Against Free Speech

Delve into history a little bit and you soon start to uncover certain inconvenient truths—such as the fact that the author of "The Star-Spangled Banner" favored institutionalized slavery over the First Amendment.

Francis Scott Key, whose stirring 1814 poem "Defence of Fort M'Henry" furnished the lyrics for the national anthem, was serving as U.S. Attorney for the District of Columbia in 1836, when he was called upon to prosecute one Reuben Crandall, a botanist charged with carrying subversive and libelous antislavery papers.

Key's closing appeal to the jurors in the case, delivered in court on April 26, was a demand that the land of the free and the home of the brave remain gallantly white: "Are you willing, gentlemen, to abandon your country, to permit it to be taken from you, and occupied by the abolitionist, according to whose taste it is to associate and amalgamate with the negro? Or, gentlemen, on the other hand, are there laws in this community to defend you from the immediate abolitionist, who would open upon you the floodgates of such extensive wickedness and mischief?"

Providentially, Key's gift for poetry eclipsed his hortatory skill: The defendant—whom Key had described in his indictment as a "malicious, seditious and evil disposed person disaffected to the law and government of the United States"—was found not guilty the same day.

Crandall's redemption, alas, was short-lived. He died less than two years later, largely from the effects of his arbitrary imprisonment of nearly nine months.

APRIL 27, 1908

Black and White and Shredded All Over

"It was a sober gathering," Mary White Ovington wrote of the dinner held by the Cosmopolitan Club, a progressive interracial group, in New York City on April 27, 1908. "The beauty of human brotherhood, the thought that all men can work together for good, was the dominant word."

That lofty message was lost, however, in the lurid press reports that followed. Both white and—*gasp!*—"Negro" people had attended the event, a racial mix as toxic as arsenic and soda to many at the time. "We have bitter contempt for the whites who participated in it and illustrated that degeneracy will seek its level," scolded the Richmond *Leader*. The St. Louis *Dispatch*, meanwhile, spewed outright venom: "This miscegenation dinner was loathsome enough to consign the whole fraternity who participated in it to undying infamy."

As for Miss Ovington—"the high priestess" of the event, who had taken "white girls into that den," as the Savannah *News* fumed—no vile obscenity was spared her when the press rashly printed her home address. "My mail was very heavy," she recounted. "I was smothered in mud."

Civil rights pioneer W. E. B. DuBois was horrified by the vilification of Ovington, his ardent supporter. (The two would be among the co-founders of the National Association for the Advancement of Colored People the following year.) "You have my sincere sympathy," he wrote to her that May. "I trust the good work isn't altogether dead."

By contrast, Booker T. Washington—a DuBois rival in the movement*—was delighted with the attacks. After all, Washington himself had secretly orchestrated the slurs and slander by alerting the press that the mixed-race dinner would take place.

So successful was Washington's ploy that he repeated it when Ovington and fellow club members tried to host another dinner at New York's Cafe Boulevard in 1911.

"One needs only to glance over this invitation . . . and note the names of the speakers and the long-winded topics they are to discuss, to be convinced that they are a bunch of freaks," Washington's close associate Charles Anderson wrote to him on January 19, 1911. "I shall do my best to see the movement gets a full newspaper report." In response, Washington delivered this command: "Would see that all copies of printed announcement reach all city editors in advance. Think *New York Times* will work in harmony with you."

Though the *Times* ignored the story, other outlets pounced. "THREE RACES MIX AT BANQUET FOR MAN'S BROTHERHOOD," screamed the headline in the *New York Press*. "Fashionable White Women Sit at Board with Negroes, Japs and Chinamen to Promote 'Cause' of Miscegenation . . . Intermarriage of Kinky-Haired Peoples with Caucasians Keynote of Blow-Out at Cafe Boulevard—Africans Have Time of Their Life, But the Waiters Are Sorely Puzzled."

"Thus you see," wrote a satisfied Charles Anderson, "the function was well handled by the papers."

---

* DuBois and Washington had radically differing approaches to achieving civil rights: Whereas DuBois advocated making gains from within the Jim Crow system, Washington worked to upend it entirely.

Voyage of the Yammed:
No Bounty for Bligh

It all came down to coconuts. Whereas British Lt. (not Capt.) William Bligh had been a strict disciplinarian from the start of H.M.S. *Bounty*'s botanical mission to the West Indies, he reportedly evolved into something of an ogre as the crew grew lax in their duties during a hedonistic five-month anchorage in Tahiti. Fletcher Christian, Bligh's erstwhile friend and unofficial second-in-command, became a special target of the commander's shaking-fist-in-the-face rages. "Sir," Christian declared at one point, "your abuse is so bad that I cannot do my duty with any pleasure. I have been in hell for weeks with you."

Which brings us to the coconuts.

On the return voyage, the day before the infamous mutiny on the *Bounty*, Bligh accused Christian and a few others of filching some of the palm fruits from his personal supply. "I suppose you'll steal my yams next," he screamed at Christian before ordering a ship-wide punishment: "Stop these villains' grog, and give them but half a pound of yams tomorrow, and if they steal then, I'll reduce them to a quarter."

That did it. In the early morning hours of April 28, 1789, Bligh was rousted from his bed and hauled onto the ship's deck. There he stood helplessly, half naked in his nightshirt, arms bound behind his back, pleading for mercy.

He would be accorded none.

"Damn his eyes!" shouted one of the mutineers. "Put him into the boat, and let the Bugger see if he can live on three-fourths of a pound of yams a day!"

And with that Bligh was forced aboard a launch, accompanied by the 18 members of his crew who had remained loyal. The party was then cast adrift.

Being marooned on the open ocean was normally a death sentence, but Christian had seen to it that his nemesis was at least provisioned with survival rations. (The records do not indicate whether this bounty included coconuts.) Miraculously, Bligh safely made landfall more than 4,000 miles away.

His historical reputation, by contrast, was sunk.

APRIL 29, 1945

Mussolini: Condemned to Repeat History—Upside Down

"No previous event in Italian history comes close to the horror at Piazzale Loreto. Even tribes of cannibals do not visit such atrocities on the dead."
—Benito Mussolini, founder and editor of the fascist daily
Il Popolo d'Italia, *writing in 1920 on the brutal killing of a Carabinieri officer in Milan's Piazzale Loreto—a quarter century before his own corpse was dumped at the very same place on April 29, 1945. There, the body of the deposed and executed Italian dictator was utterly defiled—spat and urinated upon, kicked, hammered, and pumped with bullets—all before Il Duce was strung up like a side of beef, upside down, beside his mistress and other executed fascists.*

APRIL 30, 1892

Mrs. Grant's Untold Tales of Ulysses

"My book, my book, on which I have worked so hard for the last three long years, my book, in which I took so much pride and so much pleasure, my book, on which I have built so many castles, is by the critics pronounced *too* near, *too* close to the private life of the Genl [Ulysses S. Grant] for the public, and I thought this was just what was wanted. You can imagine my great disappointment and sorrow."

—*Former first lady Julia Grant, writing to a friend on April 30, 1892, lamenting the failure to have her memoirs published. Not until the manuscript was finally released in 1975 would the public be privy to* The Personal Memoirs of Julia Dent Grant (Mrs. Ulysses S. Grant). *(But by then, did anyone really care?)*

May

Mayday! Mayday!
The Poison Rain on Kiev's Parade

"To hell with it. Let's start the parade."
—*Volodymyr Shcherbytsky, first secretary of the Communist Party
of the Ukrainian Soviet Socialist Republic, giving the order
to march through a malignant miasma*

It was the perfect day for a parade—except for those invisible clouds of radioactive death enveloping Kiev on May 1, 1986.

Four days earlier and just 80 miles north, an explosion and fire at the Chernobyl Nuclear Power Plant had begun spewing radiological contamination into the air. Caution and basic concern for the citizens of Ukraine's capital city might therefore have dictated a cancellation of the traditional May Day festivities. But Soviet leaders, intent on concealing the true extent of the disaster, wouldn't countenance that: Secrecy must be maintained at all costs—including human lives.

So shortly after 10 a.m., the parade kicked off. Thousands of happy, cheering people turned out in the warm sunshine, unaware of the nuclear fallout precipitating on their heads as they sang and danced. It's possible that a few of the revelers paused long enough to notice the party leaders perched in the reviewing stand above them. "Some on the rostrum that morning had armed themselves with dosimeters [radiation-exposure monitors] and consulted them discreetly, but constantly," wrote Adam Higginbotham in his account of the Chernobyl catastrophe. "Others simply stole occasional glances at the sky."

The forecast for the rest of the merry month? Thyroid cancer.

MAY 2, 1927

Breeding Contempt

"Three generations of imbeciles are enough."
—*Supreme Court Justice Oliver Wendell Holmes, Jr., in his majority opinion on* Buck v. Bell, *delivered on May 2, 1927, affirming the state of Virginia's right to sterilize a young woman named Carrie Buck against her will*

Holmes and his judicial brethren (minus dissenting Justice Pierce Butler) never questioned the state of Virginia's conclusion that Carrie Buck, her mother (with whom she was institutionalized), and her infant daughter were all "feebleminded."

In his remarkably callous opinion—cited a few years later by Nazi defendants at Nuremberg—Holmes argued: "It is better for all the world if, instead of waiting to execute degenerate offspring for crime or to let them starve for their imbecility, society can prevent those who are manifestly unfit from continuing their kind. The principle that sustains compulsory vaccination is broad enough to cover cutting the Fallopian tubes."

And apparently broad enough to cover axing ethics, too.

MAY 3, 1927

Silent Majority: Charles King's Spectral Interest Group

Liberian president Charles D. B. King was popular with the masses—but even more so with the phantom masses. After all, some 234,000 citizens had voted to reelect him for a third term on May 3, 1927—an extraordinary mandate, given that the West African nation then had just 15,000 registered voters.

No wonder *Guinness World Records* took note—though only to throw cold water on President King's stunning achievement. In an obvious effort to disenfranchise the disembodied, the editors sourly declared the election the most fraudulent in history.

MAY 4, 2010

Postcard From Europe: And Here I Am With My … Um … Ward

"I had surgery and I can't lift luggage. That's why I hired him."
—*Self-proclaimed "gay conversion" guru George Rekers, struggling to explain why he was traveling around Europe with a young male prostitute he had hired on the adults-only website Rentboy.com*

After the *Miami New Times* reported his European adventures on May 4, 2010, Rekers—a Southern Baptist minister and co-founder of the homophobic lobbying group Family Research Council—strenuously denied that he was gay. Oh, and nothing untoward had happened on the trip.

Indeed, Reverend Rekers claimed that his youthful companion—whose online ad boasted he was "willing to do anything" (except, apparently, carry luggage, which Rekers was photographed hauling himself)—was a lost sheep, and that something special had emerged from their journey together.

He revealed what that was to *Christianity Today* magazine: "One thing for which I am grateful is that my travel assistant openly shared his spiritual doubts with me during the trip and he did let me share the gospel of Jesus Christ with him with many Scriptures in three extended conversations."

In other media outlets, meanwhile, the "travel assistant" offered an entirely different view of what the two men had shared. And it sure wasn't Scripture.

MAY 5, 1900

Sugar and Spite:
Nothing Nice From Dr. Howard

"The female possessed of masculine ideas of independence . . .
who would sit in the public highways and lift up her pseudo-virile
voice, proclaiming her sole right to decide questions of war
or religion, or the value of celibacy and the curse of woman's
impurity, and that disgusting antisocial being, the sexual pervert,
are simply different degrees of the same class—degenerates."
—*William Lee Howard, M.D., "Effeminate Men and Masculine
Women," published in the* New York Medical Journal *on May 5, 1900*

The sex-obsessed Dr. Howard viewed this type of "antisocial creature"— the woman who defied the socially prescribed behavior of her gender, which was supposed to be sweet, demure, and above all *quiet*—as "more amusing than dangerous." The only real peril came when she reproduced: "She is then a menace to civilization, a producer of nonentities, the mother of mental and physical monstrosities who exist as a class of true degenerates until disgusted Nature, no longer tolerant of the woman who would be a man, or the man who would be a woman, allows them to shrink unto death."

And lest nonconventional boys get lost in this ludicrous screed, here's a sample of the snips and snails Dr. Howard sent their way: "He grows up physically unsexed, detested by the vigorous male, utilized as a willing servitor by the society of women, and sternly admonished by a true father if he finds him dancing attendance with all his mincing manners upon a daughter."

The root cause of the "indifferent boy who grows up to be an effeminate man"? Why, the mother, of course!

MAY 6, 2018

The (Pre)Tension Is Unbearable

On May 6, 2018, the pages of *The Washington Post* were graced with a paid wedding announcement from one of society's most esteemed personages (at least in her eyes): Savile Collins de Montenay FitzAlan de Dinan Lord. With the *Post* charging by the word, the bride's name alone must have cost a fortune. Ah, but such is the price of pretension—and oh so worth it! How else might the public have been informed of Ms. Lord's distinguished pedigree?

"She is a member of the DAR," the announcement read, "the Daughters of the Colonial Wars, the Society of the Friends of St. George's and Descendants of the Knights of the Garter, and the Metropolitan Club in Washington, D.C. She is descended from the French Count Guarin de

Metz and the English Baron Fulque FitzWarin, who was at Magna Carta. They were the subjects of the famous 13th-century manuscript, *The Romance of Fulque Fitzwarenne.* She was presented to society at the Infirmary Ball and International Debutante Ball in New York City, Bachelor's Cotillion in Baltimore, Queen Charlotte's Ball in London, and was chosen to represent the United States at the Opera Ball in Vienna Austria."*

Juggling all those balls must have been a chore for Collins de Montenay FitzAlan de Dinan Lord—like finding a towel large enough for her monogram, or a check signature line long enough for her sesquipedalian autograph. And with a lineage as exalted as hers—just imagine, an ancestor actually "at" Magna Carta!—it was always going to be a challenge to maintain the dignity of her noble clan. Yet the multisyllabic bride managed to do just that, as the *Post* announcement made clear: "Ms. Lord is the Director of the SPAM® Museum in Austin, Minnesota."

⊶⊷

MAY 7, 1912

Frostier Than the Iceberg

James Moody, 24, was a junior officer who went down with the *Titanic,* having refused numerous appeals to board one of its lifeboats. His corpse was never recovered—a small detail that the owners of the White Star Line neglected to mention on May 7, 1912, in response to an inquiry from the dead man's brother, Christopher, about bringing the body back to England.

Instead, Ismay, Imrie, & Co. presented a discouragingly expensive invoice for the return service, along with its cold "regret that it is not

---

* One name shy of his bride, the groom—Kenneth Lowell Harvey Oscar Johnson— must have had the good sense to avoid mockery by keeping his printed pedigree short: After all, the announcement identifies him as "a member of Mensa International."

possible for us to do any more" about the proposed shipment. But the company did offer an alternative (if mythical) means of accommodating the deceased, lost forever in the frigid Atlantic: "While sympathising with your inclination [to bury Moody in his homeland] we trust, however, that you will eventually decide to allow the remains to be interred with the others which we can assure you will be carried out on your behalf by our people with all due reverence, and if you would care for a photograph of the grave or if there are some words you would like included on the tombstone we shall be happy to have your wish complied with on hearing from you."*

With the wreck of the *Titanic* lying on the ocean floor nearly 2.5 miles beneath the surface, of course, the promised "photograph of the grave" would have required submersible technology that would not be developed for another half century.

MAY 8, 1771

Momsters, Part 4: Well, Marie Antoinette, at Least You Have a Good Head on Your Shoulders (For Now)

Years before the guillotine literally knocked Marie Antoinette down a few notches, her mother, the Austrian empress Maria Theresa, did so figuratively with pen and paper.

---

* Andrew Hume, father of one of the musicians who died aboard the *Titanic*, received an equally chilly notice from the music agency that had employed his son, John: "Dear Sir, We shall be obliged if you will remit us the sum of 5 shillings 4 pence, which is owing to us as per enclosed statement. We shall also be obliged if you will settle the enclosed uniform account."

On May 8, 1771, this harpy of a parent was in a particularly cutting mood: "I write now before the miniature [portrait] which represents my very dear daughter but do not find it has that look of youth she had eleven months ago." Although the future queen of France was only 15 years old at the time, her mother confessed herself mortified that Marie was still not expecting an heir after a year of marriage: "Unfortunately," the empress sniped, "a change in condition"—pregnancy—was "not the cause" of the girl's fading looks.

Having shredded her daughter's appearance and fecundity, the empress turned to Marie Antoinette's personality. Reports had reached her in Vienna that the queen-to-be was not engaging the proper people in the French court, thus squandering the only real gift she possessed: an appealing vivacity. "Do not lose it by neglecting that which gave it to you," the empress warned: "You owe it neither to your beauty (which in fact is not so great), nor to your talents or culture (you know very well you have neither)." Rather, Maria Theresa wrote, "it is your kind heart, your frankness, your amiability, all exerted with your good judgment."

That last part was a rare lapse into maternal tenderness. The empress recovered her scathing tone in her very next epistle.

MAY 9, 1864

Famous Last Wo—

"They couldn't hit an elephant at this distance."

That was Union Gen. John Sedgwick's confident assertion just moments before a Confederate sharpshooter's bullet struck him down at the Battle of Spotsylvania Court House on May 9, 1864.

So delectable was Sedgwick's premature declaration that we couldn't resist adding another inductee into the Hubris Hall of Fame: During a taping of *The Dick Cavett Show* on June 8, 1971, Jerome Irving Rodale—an early advocate of organic diets and the publisher of such health-focused magazines as *Prevention* and *Organic Gardening*—blithely underestimated his own mortality: "I never felt better in my life!" he crowed. "I've decided to live to be a hundred." Then, with the cameras rolling, Rodale dropped dead of a heart attack.

The episode of karmic comeuppance never aired.

What a Drag:
The Capture of Jefferson Davis

"Intelligence was received this morning of the capture of
Jefferson Davis in southern Georgia. I met Stanton this Sunday P.M.
at Seward's, who says Davis was taken disguised in women's clothes.
A tame and ignoble letting-down of the traitor."
—*Diary entry by Secretary of the Navy Gideon Welles (referencing
Secretary of War Edwin Stanton and Secretary of State
William H. Seward) on the capture of the Confederate president*

"Clothes make the man," the adage has it. But after a regrettable sartorial choice on May 10, 1865, they threatened to unman Jefferson Davis.

Five weeks after fleeing Richmond as the Confederacy collapsed, the president and his family were surrounded by Union cavalry at their wooded campsite in Irwinville, Georgia. An instant escape in the early morning darkness was Davis's only option to avoid capture. Clad in his customary gray coat, trousers, boots, and spurs, however—having fallen asleep in them earlier in the night—Davis was easily identifiable. What happened next, as he prepared to slip out of his tent toward his horse, would plague the proud southern leader forever.

"Knowing he would be recognized," wrote Davis's wife, Varina, "I pleaded with him to let me throw over him a large waterproof which had often served him in sickness during the summer as a dressing gown, and which I hoped might so cover his person that in the grey of the morning he would not be recognized." Then Varina added a fatal finishing touch: "As he strode off I threw over his head a little black shawl which was round my own shoulders." It was, alas, a fringed number, with a figured band colored red-orange, light blue, green, and gold.

The fugitive president, dressed in Varina's hastily assembled getup, was captured almost immediately. Soon enough, exaggerated stories began to filter north. "The captors report that he hastily put on one of Mrs. Davis' dresses and started for the woods," Maj. Gen. James H. Wilson telegraphed Secretary Stanton. The next day, Wilson went even further (though he didn't elaborate): "The device adopted by Davis was even more ignoble than I reported at first."

A gleeful northern press made its own assumptions: Jefferson Davis suddenly became Scarlett O'Hara. In what the fallen president bitterly called "the staple of so many malignant diatribes and pictorials," he was caricatured as having been caught wearing a hoopskirt and bonnet.*

As Davis would later write in *The Rise and Fall of the Confederate Government,* he remained sickened by "the story and its variations, all the

---

* Showman P. T. Barnum could not resist setting up a display in his American Museum—a wax figure of Jefferson Davis in a dress he called "the Belle of Richmond." Soon after, a fire broke out in the museum and the Davis mannequin was tossed from an upstairs window. "As Jeff made his perilous descent," *The New York Times* reported, "his petticoats again played him false, and as the wind blew them about, the imposture of the figure was exposed." Landing to "cheers and uncontrollable laughter," the statue was then promptly hanged by the gathered crowd.

spawn of a malignity that shames the civilization of the age." Indeed, Davis biographer Robert McElroy observed that "probably no single incident of his career caused him such poignant anguish."

Yet beyond the dishonor and humiliation, historians Mark E. Neely, Jr., Harold Holzer, and Gabor S. Boritt noted something else about the unflattering tale that disturbed Jefferson Davis: "at some level of consciousness" both he and his wife "knew that there was a kernel of truth to it."

MAY 11, 1950

Ted Williams Fans the Flames by Flaming the Fans

"I'm the guy they love to hate. For these 'sports-men,'
I can only extend my heartiest contempt."
—*Ted Williams, writing in* The Saturday Evening Post, *1954*

Like a shark detecting a drop of blood in the ocean, Red Sox legend Ted Williams had an uncanny sense for even a whisper of criticism from Boston fans. "I believe I have the best pair of 'rabbit ears' ever developed in the majors," he wrote in his *Evening Post* article. "There might be 30,000 people in the stands, some of them cheering and some of them talking to their neighbors. But if there are a half-dozen giving the old razoo, I can spot them in a matter of seconds . . . A lot of the regulars at Fenway Park make a practice of giving me the business every time they come out to see a game."

Playing his own part in what became a spiraling cycle of abuse, "the Splendid Splinter" never hesitated to give it right back to the surly naysayers—"those damned New England buzzards," as he called them, "those wolves in the left-field stands."

It all began during Williams's rookie season in 1940. When the young star made a rare fielding error and then struck out, the crowd assailed him with boos. On the spot, the thin-skinned slugger resolved never again to doff his cap to Red Sox fans.

The cold war between the famous outfielder and the Fenway faithful grew only more frigid from there, with nearly every jeer prompting an on-field tantrum. Helping matters not at all, an unforgiving press stoked the standoff—"poking, prowling, and trolling for trouble," as biographer Ben Bradlee, Jr., put it—eager to puncture the player who respected sportswriters about as much as he did the boo-birds in the stands.

The tripartite tension reached an absurd climax on May 11, 1950, during a doubleheader against the Detroit Tigers at Boston's Fenway Park. In the first game, Williams dropped a routine fly ball. It was no big deal—the game was ultimately a Tigers blowout—but the fans razzed him anyway. Williams returned their appreciation with his usual scorn.

Then, in the second game, things really turned ugly.

With two outs and the Sox up 2–0 in the eighth, Detroit loaded the bases for Vic Wertz, who smashed a grounder toward Williams in left field. As "Teddy Ballgame" charged the ball, however, it took a bad bounce and rolled past him to the wall. The three Detroit runners scored, yielding an eventual Tigers sweep, while "The Kid" endured a stadium-size wave of abuse.

Boston Globe reporter Larry Whiteside described his inelegant response: "With thunderous boos descending upon him, Williams bowed three times to various sections, then made an obscene gesture."

Yet it was more than just an extended middle finger. There were two of them, in fact—one from each fist—raised defiantly to all quadrants of the stadium. And that was followed with another unmistakable message to the fans—in the form of a hot loogie hocked their way.

"It was by far the biggest and most extreme tantrum of his career," Bradlee wrote, "and the papers savaged him for it." *Boston Evening American* columnist Austen Lake wrote that Williams had "removed himself from the ranks of decent sportsmen. Yesterday he was a little man, and in his ungovernable rage, a dirty little man."

Said the unrepentant Williams after the game, "I didn't mind the errors, but those damn fans; they can go fuck themselves, and you can quote me in all the papers."

The rest of Williams's career was equally fraught with tension, but a cooler head eventually prevailed: His noggin was cryogenically frozen upon his death in 2002.

━━◆━━

Who's Minding the Snore?
Keeping President Taft Awake

A t well over 300 pounds, William Howard Taft was large enough to get stuck in a bathtub, according to White House chief usher Irwin "Ike" Hoover. The portly president was also given to explosive flatulence, expelled at the most inopportune times. Yet the 27th chief executive had an even more embarrassing proclivity: No matter how significant the occasion, he tended to fall asleep in the middle of it. ("Sleeping Beauty," his wife, Nellie, would call him.)

The task of keeping the drowsy president out of dreamland in public usually fell to his loyal aide, Archibald "Archie" Butt,* who remained constantly by his boss's side—ready with an elbow or a loud cough should Taft drift off and start snoring. "It is my duty, as I construe my duty, to protect him from such situations as to guard his person from anarchists," Butt wrote.

Alas, on May 12, 1909, a narcoleptic episode eluded the grasp of the ever vigilant aide. It was the funeral of a congressman's wife, and Butt's customary seat beside the president was filled on this occasion by Supreme Court Justice Edward D. White. "In the midst of the services I saw the President fall asleep," Butt recalled in a letter written the same day, "and

---

* Archie Butt found himself in far more dire circumstances aboard the *Titanic* three years later. Like that of James Moody (see May 7), his body was never recovered.

I stood horrified when I heard an incipient snore. I could not wake him up, I was not near enough to him."

The situation was mitigated somewhat when Justice White fell asleep as well. Both men snoozed silently, but Butt was prepared to use their tandem slumber to Taft's advantage: Had *either* of them snored loudly, Butt wrote, "I made up my mind to lay it to the justice."

MAY 13, 1941

Another Grim Day for Goebbels

When we peeked into the diary of Joseph Goebbels in the first volume of *Bad Days,* it was 1928 and the epically unlucky super-Nazi was complaining about his sore feet, his lack of friends or a wife, and persistent rumors about his sexuality.

Happily, things weren't much better on May 13, 1941, when the perpetually aggrieved propaganda minister confided to his journal how distraught he was over the arrest in Scotland three days earlier of Deputy Führer Rudolf Hess, who had flown there on an unsanctioned peace mission. "A hard, almost unbearable blow," Goebbels wrote. "The Führer is quite shattered. What a sight for the world's eyes: the Führer's deputy a mentally disturbed man. Dreadful and unthinkable. Now we shall have to grit our teeth."

And we shall have to grin.

MAY 14, 1970

I Loathe Lucy

On-screen, Lucille Ball was a delight—a wacky television icon adored by millions. Off-screen, however, she could be something of a shrew—at least while producing her popular 1968–74 sitcom, *Here's Lucy.*

The comedienne was the star of the show, but she was also the executive in charge of its production. To this second, behind-the-scenes role, she brought all the tact and grace of a Komodo dragon. "I've never *seen* anybody so bossy," recalled actress Jayne Meadows, whose experiences on the *Here's Lucy* set frayed what had once been a warm personal friendship with Ball. Directors were preempted by Lucy's own barking command to  "*Cut!*" Writers were routinely shredded. Even the long parade of famous stars making guest appearances on the program, such as Meadows, faced the wrath of the tyrannical redhead. "My God, they tell me *I'm* a bitch," said Joan Crawford, who was reportedly reduced to tears after a thorough Lucy-lashing. "[She] can outbitch me any day of the week!"

Ball's on-set savagery proved too much for Richard Burton, who—along with his wife at the time, Elizabeth Taylor—was featured in a memorable episode where Lucy gets Taylor's massive diamond ring stuck on her finger. The laughs generated by the ensuing shenanigans were paid for in blood-boiling irritation by Burton, an acclaimed Shakespearean actor who found himself being lectured by Lucy—"Milady Balls," he called her—on how to deliver his lines.

After one particularly trying day on the set, Burton vented his frustrations in his diary: "Those who had told us that Lucille Ball was 'very wearing' were not exaggerating," the actor wrote on May 14, 1970, noting that Lucy was lucky he hadn't killed her. "She is a monster of staggering charmlessness and monumental lack of humour . . . A machine of enormous energy, which driven by a stupid driver who has forgotten that a machine runs on oil as well as gasoline and who has neglected the former, is creaking badly towards a final convulsive seize-up. I loathed her the first day. I loathed her the second day and the third. I loathe her today but now I also pity her. After tonight I shall make a point of never seeing her again."

And with that, Burton was done 'splainin'.

MAY 15, 1862

The Uncivil War, Part 1:
Don't Call That New Orleans Woman
a Lady—Call Her "the Big Easy"

"As the officers and soldiers of the United States have been
subject to repeated insults from the women (calling themselves
ladies) of New Orleans, in return for the most scrupulous
non-interference and courtesy on our part, it is ordered that
hereafter when any female shall, by word, gesture or movement,
insult or show contempt for any officer or soldier of the
United States, she shall be regarded and held liable to be treated
as a woman of the town plying her avocation."
—Maj. Gen. Benjamin Butler, General Order No. 28
(commonly known as the "Woman Order"), issued May 15, 1862

General Butler was thoroughly unimpressed with the southern belles
of New Orleans—particularly the one responsible for hurling the
contents of a chamber pot from an upper-story window. The vile excreta
landed right on the head of Rear Adm. David Farragut, the U.S. naval
hero who had recently captured the pivotal port city.

After jeers, snubs, and even hocked spittle had greeted the Union
occupiers of New Orleans, the assault on Farragut was about the last
insult that General Butler, the military governor, was willing to countenance from the city's defiant female population. On May 15, 1862,
he therefore issued General Order No. 28, which decreed that any
woman engaging in such offensive behavior would essentially be considered a common prostitute.

For a society that held a woman's honor and virtue as sacred as its
"right" to enslave its fellow human beings, Butler's order was deemed
tyrannical—especially because it was understood to mean that the
women of New Orleans would now be subject to degradation by maraud-

ing Union soldiers. Confederate president Jefferson Davis denounced Butler in a proclamation, ordering "that he be no longer considered . . . simply as a public enemy of the Confederate States of America but as an outlaw and common enemy of mankind, and that in the event of his capture . . . [he] be immediately executed by hanging."

A little extreme—but then, so was General Order No. 28.

Butler denied that his order contained any implicit sexual threat, claiming in his autobiography that it "executed itself." He insisted that "the ladies in New Orleans forebore to insult our troops because they didn't want to be deemed common women, and all the common women forebore to insult our troops because they wanted to be deemed ladies, and of those two classes were all the women secessionists of the city." According to the general, "there was no case of aggression after that order was issued, no case of insult by word or look against our officer or soldier while in New Orleans."

But that wasn't quite true. Eugenia Levy Phillips was among the prominent ladies of New Orleans to run afoul of "the Beast," as Butler's enemies called him after the order was issued. Charged with laughing as the funeral cortege of a Union officer passed in front of her house, she was hauled into his office. Her defense: "I was simply in good spirits the day of the funeral." The Beast wasn't buying it. "I do not call you a common woman of the town, but an uncommonly vulgar one," he roared. And with that Butler sentenced Mrs. Phillips to spend the duration of the war on a desolate barrier island off the coast of Mississippi.

By her account, it was hell. "Not a tree or blade of grass shades the eye or person from the fearful heat," she wrote. The bugs were unbearable, the food sparse and barely edible, her cell filthy, her captors abusive.

Butler quickly recognized his mistake in making Mrs. Phillips a rebel martyr. He ordered her release after just a few months, but by then it was too late to preserve his job—or his legacy. The general, recalled to Washington that December, would remain forever tarnished by his infamously misogynistic order.

MAY 16, 1571

Planet Parenthood

Most people would rather not learn the details of their conception, but German astronomer (and part-time astrologist) Johannes Kepler was an exception. He meticulously charted the magical moment back to May 16, 1571, at 4:31 in the morning.

How could he be so precise? Kepler never explained.

But while timing the act was one thing, the thought of the two people committing it surely must have given Kepler a shudder: By his own account, neither parent was pleasant or attractive. His mother, later charged with witchcraft,* was "small, thin, swarthy, gossiping and quarrelsome, of a bad disposition," while his father, a wife-beating brute who eventually abandoned the family, was "vicious, inflexible, quarrelsome, and doomed to a bad end."

Credited with developing the first laws of planetary motion, Kepler clearly knew a little *too* much about unheavenly bodies as well.

———

MAY 17, 1814

Here's a Thought: MOVE OUT!

German philosopher Arthur Schopenhauer may have influenced the likes of Nietzsche, Freud, Einstein, and Tolstoy. But in 1814, he was just a surly 26-year-old living at home with his mother, Johanna,

---

* Katharina Kepler, accused of poisoning another woman and biting a young girl, was imprisoned for witchcraft and threatened with the instruments of torture used to elicit confessions. Given her surly disposition, this was hardly unexpected in witch-crazed Europe. Katharina was saved only by the rhetorical brilliance of her son, who suspended his scientific endeavors to defend her in court.

whose life he made unbearable. Indeed, the evolving genius was a Grade A jerk to his maternal landlady. No matter that Johanna—a best-selling author who counted Goethe among her friends and admirers—had encouraged her son to pursue his intellectual passions, rather than the family's mercantile business as his late father had wished.

Schopenhauer still held his mother in contempt. He dismissed Johanna's writing, as well as what he viewed as her pedestrian German patriotism; railed against her spending; and loudly blamed her for his father's probable suicide by drowning in 1805. Plus, he loathed her friend, Georg Friedrich Konrad Ludwig Müller von Gerstenbergk, who he feared would take his father's place in the marital bed. All of this made for an excruciatingly tense household, culminating in a decisive, door-slamming explosion on May 16, 1814. The details of this final clash are lost, but the result was made explicit in a letter Johanna left for Arthur the following day—her final farewell:

"The door which yesterday . . . you slammed so noisily is closed forever between you and me . . . I owe this to my health, for another scene like yesterday's would bring on a stroke that might prove fatal . . . My duty towards you is at an end, go your way . . . Live and be as happy as you can be."

Mother and son never saw one another again.

———◆———

MAY 18, 2001

Putting His Lies on the Line

Despite his extraordinary literary success, Pulitzer Prize–winning historian Joseph Ellis must have felt insignificant compared with the *Founding Brothers* whose lives he profiled. Why else would he have manufactured stories—both in the classroom and in the press—about his military service in Vietnam when, as that war raged, he had actually been a graduate student at Yale and then a teacher at West Point?

Perhaps, as some have suggested, Professor Ellis felt guilty that his cadet students were marching off to the very battles he had managed to sidestep. Or maybe some deeper psychological disturbance prompted his lies. Whatever the cause of his decades-long deception, it was finally exposed by *The Boston Globe* on May 18, 2001.

And with the ensuing assault upon his reputation, Ellis finally got his first taste of combat.*

MAY 19, 1622

Put to the Testes, Part 3:
The Sultan Gets Sacked

L ike most adolescents, Osman II was infatuated with himself. And with titles such as "Shadow of God on Earth" and "Caliph of the Face of the Earth," how could he not be?

Problem was, the young sultan didn't feel quite exalted enough—a child's pique that became a young adult's nightmare at the end of his reign on May 19, 1622. Barely a teen when he came to the Ottoman throne in February 1618, Osman knew little of his empire's realpolitik. But he had learned plenty about its legendary past—tales of conquest and glory, of great sultans such as Suleiman the Magnificent and his own

---

* Ellis wasn't the only prominent man to fabricate wartime service overseas. Ronald Reagan may have wanted to fight during World War II, but his poor eyesight made that impossible. Instead, he spent most of the war at the First Motion Picture Unit of the Army Air Corps in Culver City. Still, the future president fancied himself a combatant, writing in his 1965 autobiography, *Where's the Rest of Me?*: "By the time I got out of the Army Air Corps, all I wanted to do—in common with several million other veterans—was to rest up awhile, make love to my wife, and come up refreshed to a better job in an ideal world."

namesake, Osman I, the myth-shrouded founder of the ruling dynasty. For a boy so immersed in Ottoman history and lore—something like a modern teen's perception of a galaxy far, far away—the present seemed little more than a dim reflection.

Osman was justified in feeling jaded. After all, he had to wait three months after the death of his father, Ahmed I, to ascend the throne, having been supplanted by his unstable uncle, Mustafa "the Mad." The usurpation was unprecedented: In the good old days, Osman knew, Uncle Mustafa would never have made it so far. Sultans' brothers were routinely strangled to avoid precisely such rivalries.

With Ottoman affairs in such a sorry state, the new sultan was convinced that the empire must return to its golden era. In the words of historian Baki Tezcan, he wanted to be "a new Osman for a new age."

Alas, this new Osman was a mere child: an idealistic lad about to tread upon some very entrenched interests, especially those in the military. And, in the end, he would be crushed.

Dreaming of a martial greatness that would eclipse his forebears, the 16-year-old Osman led Ottoman forces to war with the Polish-Lithuanian Commonwealth in 1621—right after doing away with his brother Mehmed, old-style. Osman tried to pin the failure of the pointless excursion on the military, specifically the elite, centuries-old infantry units known as the Janissaries.

He had a point. The Janissaries had grown soft over the years—no longer the rigidly disciplined, Spartan force they had once been. It was rumored that the sultan wanted to replace them with a more dedicated, more professional army, which may have been true. But he never got the chance.

On May 19, 1622, Osman II was deposed, publicly degraded, and imprisoned at the Yedikule Fortress, where he was strangled to death the next day.

In a twist to the story of the first regicide in Ottoman history, Mustafa I—the usurping uncle whose continued existence had defied tradition—was placed back upon his nephew's throne as a puppet. And there was one final twist—to Osman's testicles, which were seized and compressed in the iron grip of one of his assassins, just before the cord around his neck ended the ex-sultan's agony at age 17.

MAY 20, 2001

Another Reason "Jerry Lewis" Will Never Be Synonymous With "Dignity"

"You don't want to be pitied because you're a
cripple in a wheelchair, stay in your house."
—*Comedian Jerry Lewis, longtime host of the Muscular Dystrophy
Association's annual Labor Day telethon, responding to criticism of
his fundraising style on* CBS Sunday Morning, *May 20, 2001*

Despite raising billions for the cause over four decades, Jerry Lewis never seemed to grasp that some of those he sought to help might object to being reduced to "half a person," as he referred to people with muscular dystrophy. Or that they would take issue with the notion that a disease could somehow compromise their humanity. "God goofed," Lewis declared during the 1973 telethon, holding an adorably doomed tot in front of the camera, "and it's up to us to correct His mistake."

In the end, it was up to the Muscular Dystrophy Association to correct *its* mistake: After some of Jerry's "Kids" campaigned against his cloying paternalism, Lewis was removed as the telethon host in 2010.

———

MAY 21, 1963

Willy Wonka's Chocolate-Covered Racism

Virginie Fowler, the Knopf editor of internationally renowned children's-book author Roald Dahl, crafted a rather schoolmarmish memo for the writer on May 21, 1963. Among other issues Fowler had with Dahl's manuscript for *Charlie and the Chocolate Factory,* she objected to the description of Veruca Salt's (well-deserved) disposal down a garbage chute. "This whole image of smelling, stinking garbage makes for a crude image," Fowler scolded. "Fish heads and cabbage have no place in a chocolate factory."

On the other hand, the fastidious editor apparently had no problem with Dahl's portrait of the chocolate factory workers, the Oompa-Loompas, as black pygmies whom Willy Wonka had "brought over from Africa" himself—"the whole tribe of them, three thousand in all" . . . from "the very deepest and darkest part of the African jungle where no white man had been before." Wonka "shipped them over here," Dahl went on, "every man, woman, and child in the Oompa-Loompa tribe. It was easy. I smuggled them over in large packing cases with holes in them, and they all got here safely."

For eight years—beginning with the book's publication in 1964—the Oompa-Loompas remained the African pseudo-slaves as originally written. However, mounting criticism of the author's offensive portrayal prompted a revision in 1972. That's when the pygmies became "dwarfish hippies," as Dahl biographer Jeremy Treglown described them, "with long 'golden-brown' hair and 'rosy-white' skin."

Crowd-favorite villain Veruca Salt, by contrast, remained an unreconstructed spoiled brat.

MAY 22, 1863

The Uncivil War, Part 2:
Piling on After Chancellorsville

Other than a torturously sore rear end, Maj. Gen. George Stoneman, Jr., was feeling triumphant during the Civil War's Battle of Chancellorsville, which took place in the spring of 1863. He and the Union cavalrymen under his command had completed their mission: to ride behind enemy lines and destroy Robert E. Lee's vital supply and communication channels to Richmond.

Upon rejoining the main body of the Army of the Potomac, however, Stoneman learned the horrible truth: Not only had the Confederates crushed the U.S. forces under Gen. Joseph "Fighting Joe" Hooker in the battle's main arena, but Hooker was now loudly blaming Stoneman for the devastating loss. "I sent him out to destroy the bridges behind Lee," Hooker seethed. "He rode 150 miles without seeing the bridges he should have destroyed . . . His purposeless ride had all the result of a defeat."

In need of a scapegoat for his subpar performance against Lee's much smaller force, Hooker went after Stoneman with unrelenting fury. "No officer never [sic] made a greater mistake in construing his orders," he later testified before the congressional Joint Committee on the Conduct of the War, "and no one ever accomplished less in so doing."

The defeated General Hooker conjured up all manner of reasons for the failure of the "wooden man," as he called Stoneman, among them the "cantankerous influence" of notoriously cautious Gen. George B. McClellan. There was also Stoneman's southern-sympathizing wife, to say nothing of that most excruciating torment for a cavalryman—hemorrhoids, or "the piles," as the ailment was called. "[B]etween the two he had become completely emasculated," Hooker charged. "I might as well have had a wet shirt in command of my cavalry."

Stoneman did indeed suffer from a stinging case of the piles, and it's true he had not achieved as much as he liked to believe he had (one critic faulted him for leading his cavalry "to raid on smoke-houses and capture henroosts"). Yet the bulk of Hooker's accusations were unfounded. Nevertheless, recognizing the inevitable, Stoneman slunk back to Washington, D.C., on May 20, 1863, to receive treatment for his hemorrhoids. Two days later, he was replaced by the self-promoting Alfred Pleasonton.

If Hooker imagined that Stoneman's fall* would vindicate his own shoddy performance at Chancellorsville, he was quickly disabused of that notion: The following month he, too, was replaced.

———◆———

MAY 23, 2019

Naomi Wolf:

Howling Up the Wrong Tree

As a woman who imputes mystical qualities to her own vagina—"a gateway to, and medium of, female self-knowledge and consciousness"—author Naomi Wolf has frequently shown signs of malfunctioning shame receptors, both in her brain and in the nether regions she has declared nearly sentient.† But Wolf's apparent immunity to embarrassment was put to a severe test on May 23, 2019, when she appeared live

---

* Stoneman was immortalized in The Band's 1969 song "The Night They Drove Old Dixie Down": "Virgil Kane is the name / and I served on the Danville train / Till Stoneman's cavalry came / and tore up the tracks again." Hooker's name has been equally (if less honorably) durable; reflecting his favorite wartime activity, it lives on as a crude term for prostitute.

† Wolf's paean to her privates—"part of the female soul"—appeared in her book *Vagina: A New Biography,* hailed by its publisher as "an astonishing work of cutting-edge science and cultural history that radically reframes how we understand the vagina." Critic Katha Pollitt, for one, came away unastonished: "It's lucky vaginas can't read," Pollitt wrote in a review for *The Nation,* "or mine would be cringing in embarrassment."

on BBC radio to shill her most recent book, *Outrages: Sex, Censorship, and the Criminalization of Love.*

While researching the book, Wolf told interviewer Matthew Sweet, she had uncovered evidence that "several dozen executions" occurred during the frenzied persecution of homosexuality in Britain during the mid-19th century.

"Several dozen executions?" Sweet challenged.

"Correct," Wolf responded, forging ahead with her assertion that British executions for sodomy had not ended by 1830, as commonly believed, but had continued for several more decades—as revealed by her foray into the criminal archives.

"I don't . . . I don't think you're right about this," Sweet interjected again. He informed Wolf that she had fundamentally misunderstood the legal term "death recorded," which appeared beside the names of the men convicted of the same-sex crimes that Wolf referenced in *Outrages.* "It was a category that was created in 1823 that allowed judges to *abstain* from pronouncing a sentence of death," Sweet explained. "I don't think any of the executions you've identified here actually happened."

"Well that's a really important thing to investigate," Wolf calmly replied. "What is your understanding of what 'death recorded' means?"

Sweet reiterated the definition, then further shattered Wolf's scholarship by pointing out her incorrect assumption that sodomy was synonymous with homosexual expressions of love: "I can't find any evidence that any of the relationships you describe were consensual."

Media reports of the encounter—a book-tour implosion that would have mortified a more shame-bound author—remarked upon Wolf's poise as the pillar of her central treatise crumbled. But this was genitalia-touting Naomi Wolf, remember. So, of course, there wasn't a blush of abashment to be detected—even when her publisher eventually withdrew the book. As she proclaimed in the immediate aftermath of the debacle:

"I don't feel humiliated."

Davy Crockett Rassles
the Political Bears

D avid, David Crockett (the "King of the Wild Frontier" reportedly hated the diminutive Davy) faced an adversary far more savage than those bears he famously hunted when he boldly defied fellow Tennessean Andrew Jackson in Congress on May 24, 1830.

The president's pet bill—the Indian Removal Act, which authorized the banishment of Native Americans ("Savages," in Jackson's parlance) from their ancestral lands in the southeastern states—was up for a vote in the House of Representatives. Crockett voted against it, making him the only member of the Tennessee delegation to do so. It was an act of conscience against what he later described as "a wicked, unjust measure"—and, perhaps, a deliberate poke at Jackson, from whom Crockett had become increasingly estranged.

Whatever Crockett's motive, it proved costly. Once the bill passed, he found himself in a political wilderness more hostile than anything he'd encountered on the western frontier—and the animus came from on high: "I trust, for the honor of the state, your Congressional District will not disgrace themselves longer by sending that profligate man Crockett back to Congress," the president warned Samuel Jackson Hayes.

Jackson and his allies moved against the recalcitrant congressman with murderous precision. "I found the storm had raised against me sure enough," Crockett wrote of his 1831 homecoming after the close of Congress that session, "and it was echoed from side to side, and from end to end in my district, that I had turned against Jackson. This was considered the unpardonable sin. I was hunted down like a wild varment [sic], and in this hunt every little newspaper in the district, and every little pin-hook lawyer was engaged. Indeed, they were ready to print any and every thing that the ingenuity of man could invent against me."

In his campaign for reelection, Crockett faced William Fitzgerald—"a little country lawyer with very little standing," as the incumbent described him, "a perfect lick spittle." But Fitzgerald had strong backing from the Jackson machine, whose ferocity began to deplete Crockett of his customary good nature.

Representative Crockett became so prickly as to threaten his opponent with a thrashing if he dared spread any more scurrilous stories. But Fitzgerald remained unrelenting in his attacks. So after yet another negative blast delivered during a shared campaign stop, Crockett stood up to make good on his warning. That's when Fitzgerald pulled a gun on him. Unarmed and utterly stunned, Crockett could only slink back to his seat—and, ultimately, out of the U.S. Capitol. Many historians believe that mortifying moment onstage doomed Crockett's hopes of returning to Washington in 1831.

"I would rather be beaten and be a man than to be elected and be a little puppy dog," Crockett wrote with a defiance that belied his post-election bitterness. "I have always supported measures and principles and not men. I have acted fearless and independent and I never will regret my course. I would rather be politically buried than to be hypocritically immortalized."

As it happened, Crockett got the last laugh—briefly. He beat his gun-toting nemesis in the next election and served another term in Congress, only to die at the Alamo in 1836.

MAY 25, 675

Momsters, Part 5:
The Woes of Wu's Tang Clan

A gal had to be plenty fierce to get anywhere in seventh-century China, but Wu Zetian (known as Empress Wu) fit that qualification precisely. Nothing was going to block her path to becoming China's sole female ruler, not even her own children. *Especially* not her own children.

The first of Wu's offspring to suffer, legend has it, was an infant daughter, Princess Si of Anding. When the princess was born in 654, Wu was a mere consort, or lesser wife, of Emperor Gaozong of the Tang Dynasty. But not for long: Wu cunningly strangled her baby and blamed the murder on the emperor's main wife, the childless and presumably envious Empress Wang. Soon enough, Wu replaced Wang as No. 1 Spouse and came to wield extraordinary power behind her sickly husband's throne. And she didn't like to share it—a fact that her eldest son, Li Hong, elevated to crown prince, foolishly failed to grasp.

Li Hong had already dangerously irked his mother when he took pity on the two imprisoned daughters of an imperial concubine whom Empress Wu had swept out of her way, and asked his father to free them. But she truly became incensed when the crown prince dared question his mother's vast authority in government matters—so much so that on May 25, 675, she had Li Hong poisoned.

A single instance of filicide would qualify for a Bad Day in this collection, yet the evil-tempered empress was far from finished with finishing off her brood.

A second son, Li Xian, became crown prince after his brother's lethal last meal. But he, too, quickly ran afoul of his maleficent mother. The emperor had delegated a measure of responsibility to his new male heir—which, of course, Empress Wu found threatening. Li Xian might have known that his mom was mad when she had the court scholars prepare a set of books on filial obedience for his instruction. Alas, he missed the hint. Next, Empress Wu accused him of murdering the imperial soothsayer, who had prophesied his unworthiness as a future emperor.

What ultimately doomed Li Xian, though, was a treason charge. Several hundred suits of armor were found in his palace—clear evidence, the empress concluded, that her son was planning a rebellion. In retaliation, Li Xian was stripped of his title, reduced to the status of a commoner, and shipped off to the provinces. Sometime later, he was forced to commit suicide.

After the death of Emperor Gaozong in December 683, a third son inherited the throne as Emperor Zhongzong. Adept by now at neutralizing her rivals, Mommy Wu disposed of him in a few scant months, replacing him with her more malleable fourth son, Emperor Ruizong. She allowed him to play pretend ruler until 690—the year the master puppeteer stepped out from behind the throne and seized it for herself. As leader of the new Zhou dynasty, Empress Wu ruled effectively if ruthlessly until 705, when she was defanged, declawed, and finally forced into retirement.

MAY 26, 1219

Ja Better Watch Out!

The missionary monks of the new religious order founded by St. Francis of Assisi spoke of peace. They spoke of Christ's love. Regrettably, they spoke none of it in German.

According to a contemporary account by Jordan of Giano, Francis sent 60 or so of his followers—Italians all—to establish a chapter in Germany on May 26, 1219. Upon arriving, the friars were asked if they were heretics come to breed religious dissent. Lacking the first clue as to what the question meant, they responded with one of the few German words in their vocabulary: *"Ja."* ("Yes.")

Outraged by the innocently uttered response, the Germans stripped the monks naked and beat them to the point where they were lucky to escape with their lives. Saint that he was, Francis was sufficiently moved by the fiasco to suspend the obedience requirement of his order; the next mission to Germany, Francis declared, would be entirely voluntary.

MAY 27, 2004

Repentance? Nun for Cardinal Law

With a trail of shattered souls as his shameful legacy, Bernard Cardinal Law—the disgraced Archbishop of Boston who systematically enabled pedophile priests to thrive and prey in his diocese—might have spent the rest of his life in quiet penance.

But he didn't.

Instead of the monk's cell where he belonged, Law glided into a luxuriously ceremonial post in Rome as archpriest of St. Mary Major Basilica on May 27, 2004. There he immediately started bossing nuns around—and not just the ones assigned to him as household servants inside his cushy Eternal City pad. (The fancy digs were just one of the many perks he received upon his controversial appointment.) Law also tried to put 57,000 American nuns under his thumb. The good sisters were simply too liberal for the complicit cardinal's liking—misguidedly addressing social ills, rather than adhering strictly to the conservative hierarchy's agenda.

Law's threatened crackdown had largely dissipated by the time of his death in December 2017. Still, he probably would have relished the sight of two sisters bowing over his coffin in obeisance at his funeral.

Or were they just puking?

MAY 28, 1962

Jimi Hendrix's Army Stint: Let's Just Call It Hazy

The U.S. Army was fed up with Pvt. James M. Hendrix, known to his friends as Jimi. "Hendrix is poorly motivated for the military, has no regard for regulations, requires excessive supervision while performing his duties, [and] pays no heed to counseling from his supervisors as to his shortcomings," read a scathing fitness-for-duty appraisal from May 28, 1962, nearly a year after the future rock god's enlistment. "He is a habitual offender when it comes to making bed check, having missed bed check in March, April and May."

Indeed, the report suggested, something was seriously amiss with Hendrix. "At times [he] isn't able to carry on an intelligent conversation, paying little attention to having been spoken to. At one point it was thought perhaps Hendrix was taking dope and was sent to a medical examiner to be examined[,] with negative results."

Despite the bleak assessment, there was one harbinger of Hendrix's future glory: "Pvt Hendrix plays a musical instrument during his off duty hours, or so he says. This is one of his faults, because his mind apparently cannot function while performing duties and thinking about his guitar."

The last lick came when Hendrix was discovered practicing on a different solo instrument in the latrine. "I recommend with out [sic] hesitancy that Hendrix be eliminated from the service," the May 28 report concluded, "as expeditious as possible."

Three days later, both the left-handed virtuoso and his guitar were gone.

MAY 29, 1921

When the Pulitzer Board
Paved Over *Main Street*

The Pulitzer verdict was in: The jury's unanimous choice for the year's best novel was *Main Street,* Sinclair Lewis's best-selling evisceration of small-town America. But when the prize was announced on May 29, 1921, *Main Street* had been supplanted as the winner by Edith Wharton's *The Age of Innocence.*

Overriding the jury's selection was the Pulitzer Board, led by the arch-conservative president of Columbia University, Nicholas Murray Butler. For starters, Butler was, as his biographer noted, "out of his intellectual depth in rendering aesthetic and critical judgments." Worse, *Main Street* was simply not to his liking—and he tweaked the wording of the prize's original mandate to give himself the ammunition to shoot it down.

Upon creating the prize for American novels in 1904, Joseph Pulitzer had stipulated that the winning book "shall best present the whole atmosphere of American life." But Butler craftily changed "whole" to "whole-some," setting a standard of positivity that the aggressively satirical *Main Street* could never meet.

Lewis called the decision "the Main Street burglary"— but he wasn't the only one peeved. The three-man jury had its own issues, among them the wording of the announcement: "The jury recommends . . . *The Age of Innocence*." (Which it most certainly had not!)

Journalist John L. Heaton sent a letter to the board insisting that the misrepresentation be corrected, while juror Robert Morss Lovett set the record straight in *The New Republic:* "The public . . . has the right to know that the award was made in the face of a recommendation . . . in favor of *[Main Street],*" he wrote. "The decision of the [jury] . . . was confirmed by the fact that the book through its social criticism had led its readers to formulate for themselves a higher standard of life and purge the small town atmosphere of certain unwholesome tendencies."

Wharton herself was upset that her novel had edged *Main Street:* "When I discovered that I was being rewarded—by one of our leading Universities [Columbia]—for uplifting American morals, I confess I did despair," she wrote to Lewis in response to his gracious congratulatory note. "Subsequently, when I found the prize shd really have been yours but was withdrawn because your book (I quote from memory) had 'offended a number of prominent persons in the Middle West,' disgust was added to despair."

In gratitude, Lewis dedicated his next work, *Babbitt* (1923), to Wharton. It too was nominated for the Pulitzer, but again the board overruled the jury's endorsement—this time in favor of Willa Cather's *One of Ours*. "I'm quite sure I never shall get the Pulitzer," Lewis wrote to his father. Finally, three years later, Sinclair Lewis's *Arrowsmith* won the 1926 prize.

Out of pique or principle, Lewis declined to accept it. "All prizes, like all titles, are dangerous," he wrote to the Pulitzer committee. "The seekers for prizes tend to labor not for inherent excellence but for alien rewards: they tend to write this, or timorously to avoid writing that, in order to tickle the prejudices of a haphazard committee."

Lewis had transcended his ticklishness by 1930, however, when he accepted the Nobel Prize in Literature.

MAY 30, 1896

A Tsar-Crossed Day

After the slaughter of Russia's Tsar Nicholas II and his family in 1918, it was all too easy to look back and pinpoint the seeds of his destruction. Hindsight decreed that a deadly human stampede on May 30, 1896—just four days after the coronation of Nicholas and his wife, Alexandra—had been the dark but certain portent of the catastrophe to come.

Nearly half a million people had gathered on a meadow outside Moscow that fateful May day to celebrate the new reign and to receive the tsar's bounty of beer, sausages, and commemorative enameled cups. Then horror struck: Word spread through the crowd that supplies were running out, sparking a terrible, unstoppable surge toward the gift booths. The field, normally used as a military training ground and therefore crisscrossed by trenches, became a sea of suffocating congestion as thousands fell and were trampled.

All around, people were "fighting for breath, vomiting, succumbing to the irresistible pushing and jostling," a reporter from the *Russian Gazette* recounted.

Later that day, with mangled corpses stacked high and awaiting burial, Nicholas II made a dreadful decision—the first in a reign that would be plagued by them: He agreed to attend a glittering ball hosted by the French ambassador that night. The acceptance went against the distraught tsar's better instincts, but he was a weak and pliable man—traits that would ultimately lead him to ruin—and so he caved in to his overbearing uncles, who held that protocol demanded he attend the festivities. Nicholas and Alexandra opened the evening by dancing a quadrille.

"The dreadful accident [on the field] . . . was appalling beyond all description," wrote the tsar's mother, the Dowager Empress Marie, "and has . . . draped a black veil over all the splendor and glory!"

But the pall cast by the disaster was far more encompassing than the dowager empress could imagine. "It is true that the most modern historical method takes small account of portents and evil signs," the *Saturday Review* noted at the time, "but the human mind has by no means outgrown their spell. In Russia the supernatural point of view is practically universal . . . Such a people, who shape their daily lives by the events of comets and eclipses, would see in this event at Moscow a baleful portent."

The article's prescient conclusion: "The new reign will be thought of as one foredoomed to calamity."

MAY 31, 1880

Helping Hands Off

Sunanda Kumariratana, queen consort of Siam (now Thailand), had it all: palaces, personal servants, precious jewels. All, that is, except a life preserver.

On May 31, 1880, the royal barge ferrying the 19-year-old pregnant queen and her infant daughter to the Summer Palace capsized in the turbulent waters of the Chao Phraya River. With guards and officials swarming the scene, Sunanda and the baby princess easily could have been rescued. But a strict law forbade anyone from touching a royal

personage—as in *ever, for any reason.* (How strict? The penalty was death.)

So as the queen floundered in the water, no one dared reach out a hand. Instead, legally paralyzed, everyone present watched in horror as she slipped beneath the surface and drowned.

June

---·◆·---

Raisa and Nancy's Cold War: Reaching
the Icy Summits of Pettiness

"Who does that dame think she is?"
—*Nancy Reagan on Raisa Gorbachev*

Not since Princess Pauline Metternich and Countess Anastasia Kiel-mannsegg famously resorted to dueling rapiers in 1892 have two highly placed women fought quite as ferociously as Nancy Reagan and Raisa Gorbachev did during the 1980s. Though neither first lady drew blood or battled topless (as did the princess and the countess), their rivalry was no less intense—a frosty sideshow at the very summits where their husbands struggled to conclude quite a different Cold War.

The clash began in November 1985, during the first U.S.–Soviet conference in Geneva. Nancy and Raisa had tea while the two world leaders convened privately. They failed to bond. "From the moment we met, she talked and talked and *talked*," Mrs. Reagan wrote in her autobiography, *My Turn*—"so much that I could barely get a word in, edgewise or otherwise." Her loquacious interlocutor focused almost entirely on the glories of the Soviet system. "I wasn't prepared for this," she wrote, "and I didn't like it."

The U.S. first lady rarely concealed her unhappiness with any given situation—a characteristic not lost on Mrs. Gorbachev, likewise famed for her *froideur.* Raisa had "a Soviet way of behavior," Russian journalist Lyudmila Telen told *The New York Times* in 1999—abrupt, sometimes to the point of rudeness, no-nonsense, and gratingly didactic.

While Nancy Reagan vented in *My Turn* about the Soviet first lady's imperious ways, Raisa Gorbachev was far more circumspect in her own autobiography, *I Hope.* Still, more than mere words can convey feelings. "The Russian, as her body language made abundantly clear, considered her American counterpart vapid and foolish," noted Rupert Cornwell in *The Independent.*

Some sort of détente might have been reached at the next meeting, held in October 1986 in Reykjavík, Iceland—after all, only one of the feuding first ladies was there. But even then, Nancy and Raisa sparred from afar. "There must be a cause for her not coming," Mrs. Gorbachev replied when asked if she was upset that Mrs. Reagan was absent. "Maybe she had something else to do. Or maybe she is sick."

Or maybe Raisa decided to attend the conference at the last minute? After all, it had been arranged exclusively for President Reagan and General Secretary Gorbachev. "This put me in an awkward position," Mrs. Reagan wrote of the news that her rival would travel to Iceland: "Should I go simply because she was going? No, I decided. Raisa's last-minute reversal struck me as a bit of one-upmanship. I had a full schedule in Washington, as I'm sure she knew, and I didn't want to change it.

"Besides, I thought it was important, as my son Ron put it, not to be jerked around. I felt that Raisa was testing me, to see if I would cave in and change my mind. But she had to know that schedules are made out long in advance, and I was determined not to give in."

Meanwhile, keep in mind, nuclear disarmament was at stake.

The next summit was in Washington, D.C. "Raisa and I hadn't seen each other in two years," Mrs. Reagan wrote of the December 1987 encounter, "but nothing much had changed." Indeed, the American first lady was as prickly as ever—resentful that Mrs. Gorbachev had failed to acknowledge both Nancy's recent breast-cancer surgery and the death of her mother—while Raisa resumed her incessant lecturing. This was most evident during a White House tour, which the Soviet first lady commandeered with commentary of her own. "A human being would like to live in a regular house," Raisa declared, despite not having visited the family quarters. "[The White House] is like a museum."

The first ladies appeared to have reached an accord at the final summit, held in Moscow six months later. They were even spotted holding hands. But, as betrayed by their confrontation on June 1, 1988, that cordiality was fleeting. The scene that day—a final showdown of sorts—was the Tretyakov Gallery, where Mrs. Reagan was to view a collection of historic Russian icons. Mrs. Gorbachev arrived first. Having unilaterally changed the planned meeting spot at the gallery, she informed the assembled press that her American counterpart was late. Raisa then lectured them on the artistic virtues of the various icons. In the midst of her talk, Mrs. Reagan arrived.

Cue "Flight of the Valkyries."

The Soviet first lady tried to bustle her away to begin the tour, but Mrs. Reagan wouldn't have it. "Now wait a minute," she said. "I want to say something, okay?"

Nancy then made a show of thanking Mrs. Gorbachev—now conspicuously checking her watch—for the chance to see the icons. But when a journalist tried to ask her a question, Mrs. Gorbachev cut him off. "We have decided there would not be any interviews in the Tretyakov Gallery," Raisa said, apparently forgetting her own impromptu chat. "Please allow us to show Mrs. Reagan the Russian ancient arts in the remaining time."

Tipped off that Raisa had already held the floor, Nancy ignored her rival's plea and fielded questions from the press. Her response to one inquiry about the conflicting ideologies of Soviet communism and American capitalism neatly distilled her strained relationship with Mrs. Gorbachev: "I'd call it a Mexican standoff."

JUNE 2, 1780

We Will Not Tolerate Tolerance

Lord George Gordon—the notoriously eccentric member of Parliament distinguished by his long red hair and rambling speeches—was usually a passionate champion of the oppressed. The Scotsman decried the abuse of sailors in the British Navy, for example. He was appalled by the injustice of sugar planters in Jamaica "growing rich at the expense of the whipped, hungry, bleeding bodies of their slaves." And he condemned Britain's "mad, cruel, and accursed" war against the American colonies.

Yet Gordon attacked Roman Catholics—among the most marginalized members of British society at the time—with splenetic fury. And in his prejudicial zeal, the Presbyterian statesman—"the lunatic apostle," diarist Horace Walpole called him—inadvertently triggered one of the most violent riots in Britain's history. All because Parliament had restored to Catholics a smattering of rights, such as owning land.

As president of the Protestant Association, Gordon called forth members to rally "in a firm, manly, and resolute manner" to present a petition demanding a repeal of the Catholic Relief Act of 1778. Some 60,000 people answered his summons, marching en masse to the Houses of Parliament on June 2, 1780. Disorder ensued almost immediately. Periwigs were ripped off the heads of arriving lords, clothes torn, carriages smashed. Yet all that was a mere prelude to the mayhem to come after the House of Commons declined to consider the petition until the following week.

London erupted.

Rampaging mobs set fire to Catholic churches, businesses, and homes—the furious assault largely unhampered by law enforcement and fueled by an intoxicating mix of religious bigotry and raw plunder. "Such a scene my eyes never beheld, and I pray God I never may again," Lady Anne Erskine wrote from her perch at the chapel house at Spa Fields, in the London borough of Islington. "The situation of the place which is high and very open gave us an awful prospect of it. We were surrounded by flames . . . The sky was like blood with the reflection of the fires."

The destructive surge continued for a week, with an estimated 500 people killed, before finally being quelled by various militia. "Our danger is at an end, but our disgrace will be lasting," wrote historian Edward Gibbon, "and the month of June 1780 will ever be marked by a dark and diabolical fanaticism which I had supposed to be extinct."

Gordon was ultimately acquitted of treason: He had undeniably mustered the crowds on June 2, a court ruled, but he had not encouraged the frenzy of violence that followed. In an ironic aftermath of the riots that bear his name, this most rabid of Protestants had himself circumcised and converted to Judaism.

JUNE 3, 1938

Sop-Ed Page: *The Times* Pushes Appeasement

In the run-up to World War II, *The Times* of London was frequently accused of being a media tool of British prime minister Neville Chamberlain's conservative government and its policy of appeasing Nazi Germany. Bolstering that charge was an editorial the paper ran on June 3, 1938, which argued that the best way to preserve peace in Europe was to feed the führer a large chunk of Czechoslovakia, Britain's nominal ally.

This recommendation sat rather uneasily with *Times* manager John

Walter. "I feel that our [lead editorial] yesterday must have come as a shock to many readers of *The Times*," he wrote to editor Geoffrey Dawson, "advocating as it did the cause of the Wolf against the Lamb, on the grounds of Justice. No wonder there is rejoicing in Berlin."

Four months later, the Berlin celebrations reached a euphoric crescendo when Chamberlain did indeed sell out Czechoslovakia with his declaration that he had achieved "peace for our time." Yet as history would soon prove, the Wolf was still ravenous.

JUNE 4, 1974

Batter(ed) Up! The Old Brawl Game

"That's probably the closest we'll ever come
to seeing someone get killed in the game of baseball."
—*Texas Rangers manager Billy Martin on the riot that erupted
during a game between his team and the Cleveland Indians*

Attendance was nearly triple its normal number at Cleveland's Municipal Stadium on the night of June 4, 1974. Had the historically woeful Indians suddenly awoken? No, it was an unforced error by team management: In a bid to fill seats at the fan-forsaken field once likened to an "open-air mausoleum," the front office had promised ticket holders a boundless supply of 10-cent beers.

The evening began wholesomely enough. A woman bounded down to the field, bared her breasts in the on-deck circle, then tried to kiss umpire Nestor Chylak, who managed to evade the overture. That impromptu burlesque inspired others to shed their clothes and streak across the field (a cultural craze in 1974). One man left the stands and slid into second base—a risky prospect with balls in play—while a father-son team opted to moon the opposing outfielders.

The baseball bacchanal continued amid clouds of marijuana and firecracker smoke. But then the carnival atmosphere—more typical of a 1970s outdoor concert—began to give way to raw, booze-fueled aggression. Missiles ranging from rocks to radio batteries were hurled onto the field, while cherry bombs exploded in the Texas dugout. The hometown fans spit on Rangers first baseman (and future Indian player and manager) Mike Hargrove, who narrowly missed being hit in the head by a flying gallon jug of Thunderbird wine.

By the bottom of the ninth inning, lives were at stake. What *Newsweek* magazine described as "one of the ugliest incidents in the 105-year history of the game" began when a drunken idiot ran onto the field and swiped the cap off the head of Rangers outfielder Jeff Burroughs, who retaliated by kicking the kid in the thigh, and falling over in the follow-through. From his obstructed-view seat in the dugout, Rangers manager Billy Martin concluded that Burroughs was being attacked. Grabbing a fungo bat, he rallied his team to the fallen player's rescue: "Let's go get 'em, boys!"

The resulting charge of Martin's fright brigade galvanized the hammered horde in the bleachers. A number of them descended on the field, brandishing chains, knives, and clubs. Menacingly, they surrounded the Texas players. Cleveland manager Ken Aspromonte, recognizing the mortal peril of the situation, ordered his own Indians to defend the ambushed Rangers. Then, amid the discordant organ strains of "Take Me Out to the Ball Game," a riot ensued.

"We got hit with everything you can think of," Martin told reporter Mike Shropshire. "Chairs were flying down out of the upper deck. Cleveland players were fighting their own fans. First they were protecting the Rangers, and then they were fighting to protect themselves. Somebody hit [Indians pitcher] Tom Hilgendorf with a chair and cut his head open."

With all the bases stolen—literally—a battered and bloodied umpire Chylak declared the game a Cleveland forfeit. No doubt he felt nostalgic for a more innocent era of professional baseball: the one that existed just seven innings earlier, when he had survived that Sadie Hawkins encounter.

Fortunately, American League president Lee MacPhail was on hand to sift through the complexities of the fiasco and offer this trenchant postmortem analysis: "There was no question that beer played a part in the riot."

Warhol's OlFactory Reception

"She was wearing the same green Oscar de la Renta she wore the last time I went out with her, and when we got into the elevator I noticed she had underarm b.o., like she hadn't taken a shower before she got dressed. So Mick must like b.o. . . . Down at the World Trade Center the wind was really blowing so that's when I was really noticing the b.o."
—*Pop artist Andy Warhol, to his diary on June 5, 1978. Earlier that evening, Warhol had squired Rolling Stone Mick Jagger's girlfriend, the apparently malodorous supermodel Jerry Hall, to a party at New York City's World Trade Center. "The food was rotten," Warhol reported, "but the sunset was so beautiful. Everybody was trying to make Jerry."*

E-I-E-I-*Ewww*

They were jezebels of the barnyard—a cow, two heifers, three sheep, and a pair of sows. Each of the eight animals, wrote Puritan minister (and witch hunter turned target; see April 1) Cotton Mather, had committed unspeakable sins with "a most unparalleled wretch, one Potter by name . . . executed for 'damnable bestialities.'"

Goodman Potter, Mather charged, was a hypocrite—"devout in worship, gifted in prayer, forward in edifying discourse among the religious, and zealous in reforming the sins of other people," but also a diabolical defiler of his livestock. In fact—again, according to the breathless

Mather—Potter had "lived in most infandous [sic] Buggeries for no less than fifty years." Yet he wasn't the only culpable one—at least not by Puritan standards.

In this case, it took nine to tango. And as far as the courts were concerned, the carnal cow, the harlot heifers, the seductive sheep, and the slutty sows were all equally responsible for the gross indecencies that Potter had taken with them. It was only natural, therefore, that Potter's cloven-hoofed paramours should join him on the gallows on June 6, 1662, where each was executed in turn.*

———✦———

JUNE 7, 1998

Falling Flat on His As...pirations

A certain member of the *Bad Days* team was thrilled as a young man to get a job at *The Washington Post*. After that—and beyond anything he ever dared dream—he got to collaborate with one of the newspaper's top editors: future two-time Pulitzer Prize winner Gene Weingarten, who created a weekly humor contest for *Post* readers known as "The Style Invitational."

Weingarten beamed with pride over his young protege's progress at the paper, gushing in print, "Why, in a few years, if Michael keeps his nose to the grindstone, he might rise to be chief executive *Washington Post* urinal attendant!"

Then, on June 7, 1998, Gene's exuberance exceeded all previous plaudits. "Michael is a fine lad," he wrote after receiving a particularly inspired

---

* Nearly a century later, a court in France would take a more merciful view of bestiality. In 1750 one Jacques Ferron was sentenced to death after being caught mid-coitus with a donkey. But when a local priest and others swore in court that she was a "most honest creature," with no prior whiff of scandal about her, the ass's life was spared.

contest idea, "a man of irreproachable moral character, a highly compe-
tent professional who, with just a few career 'breaks' along the way, might
have made something of himself instead of becoming a simpering lick-
spittle. Also—and we mean no disrespect here—Michael has absolutely
no behind. It is as though God simply forgot, for a moment, at the birth
of Michael Farquhar, that humans must sit, wear pants, and in his case,
display the occasional 'Kick Me' sign."

JUNE 8, 1998

The General's Final Salute:
Sani Abacha's Hard Fall

Sitting on a pile of plundered billions, Nigeria's military dictator
Sani Abacha had plenty of reason to celebrate. In fact, he was doing
just that on June 8, 1998—in the company of three prostitutes, it was
reported, and a heaping dose of "performance-enhancing" Viagra. But
it was all too much fun for the 54-year-old's heart, which suddenly
gave out, leaving Abacha (one imagines) a quite-contented corpse.

His wife, Maryam, on the other hand, got no such happy ending:
She was busted at the airport several weeks later, attempting to flee the
country with 30 suitcases stuffed with cash.

JUNE 9, 1936

June Bugged

The first five months of 1936 were frenzied ones for Democratic
congressman Marion Zioncheck of Washington State. But the sixth
month—especially its ninth day—would be an apogee.

The year began with a drunken bender, when Zioncheck commandeered the telephone switchboard at his apartment building and woke up all his neighbors. Next he rashly eloped with Rubye Nix, a 21-year-old government stenographer he had just met. Reporters relished the couple's increasingly bizarre behavior—which included high-speed police chases, a honeymoon riot in Puerto Rico, and recitals by a dancing pet turtle—as they literally lapped up the "Zioncheck Zingers" (rye whiskey, honey, and a sprig of mint) served up by the congressman at his apartment while sporting a Native American headdress.

Around the beginning of June, the already erratic Zioncheck snapped when Rubye left him after only a month of marriage. He began a frantic search for her, driving wildly all over the streets and sidewalks of Washington, D.C., with a brief detour onto the White House lawn in a bid to deliver a gift of Ping-Pong balls to President Franklin Roosevelt. Although Marion tracked down Rubye and the lovebirds reconciled, the congressman was arrested on a lunacy charge and packed off to a hospital asylum.

There he simmered down, but only until June 9—when, as the Associated Press reported, he "lost his reputation as the institution's model patient."

Zioncheck managed to free himself from confinement by kicking out two window screens and scampering away in his white bathrobe. "He galloped about the grounds," the AP story elaborated, "whooping and puffing at a long black cigar, until caught by guards."

Tragically, the escapade was one of Marion Zioncheck's last bursts of . . . *exuberance.* Upon returning to Seattle later that summer, the congressman (who had long denied mental illness) found that his political support had all but evaporated: Men he had trusted as friends were now vying for his seat in Congress. The discovery drove him to the roof of his downtown office building, from which he jumped—while Rubye, unaware of the depth of her troubled husband's despair, stood waiting for him on the sidewalk below.

JUNE 10, 1845

Andrew Jackson's %*#&-ing Funeral

If pets often take on the characteristics of their human masters, there's little mystery to why Andrew Jackson's parrot, Poll, was such a foul-mouthed little monster. The seventh president was famously salty himself—consistent with his hot temper and homicidal tendencies. And though Old Hickory may have tolerated his imprecatory pet, the mourners at his funeral—held on June 10, 1845—were "horrified and awed at the bird's lack of reverence" when the parrot began screeching obscenities during the service.

Poll was quickly removed from the proceedings—no doubt responding to the banishment with some choice words that would have made his late owner proud.

JUNE 11, 1943

A Bridge Party Too Far

What appeared to be an ordinary ladies' bridge party in Cleveland, Ohio, was, according to the FBI, something far more seditious: a dire threat to the institution charged with protecting the American people and upholding the Constitution of the United States. During this seemingly innocuous gathering on June 11, 1943, a certain woman—whose name has been removed from the files, sparing her eternal infamy—uttered a word that might have sabotaged a nation at war. She called the bureau's heroic director, J. Edgar Hoover, "queer."

Happily for the health of the Republic, a patriot among the bridge players conveyed the treasonous allegation to the FBI. The woman who had leveled it—"an old maid school teacher," according to the bureau report, at least until her marriage five years prior—was then summoned to the FBI's Cleveland office. There, Special Agent in Charge L. V. Boardman succeeded in breaking the domestic agitator. According to a dossier on the matter—sent to Hoover's daily dining partner, Assistant FBI Director Clyde Tolson—Boardman "severely chastised her, pointing out that he personally resented such a malicious and unfounded statement as she had made and that he could not understand what would lead her to make any such libelous statement concerning a man in such a responsible position as the Director."

Having babbled out a lame explanation for her treachery—that she had overheard a group of young men disparaging the director at a Baltimore diner, and had repeated the rumor when one of her bridge partners wondered aloud why Hoover was a bachelor—the woman promised to make amends.

"She stated that those in attendance at the bridge party had been gathering like this for a period of eleven years," the report to Hoover's companion continued, "and she was going to point out to each of those present that her statement was not founded on fact and that she was deeply sorry that she had made it and it should not have been made at all. She is going to advise Boardman when this has been done."

And with that subversive blabbermouth silenced at last, the triumphant director could finally enjoy a nice, quiet bachelors' dinner with Clyde.

JUNE 12, 1733

Unholy Matrimony, Part 3: With This Ring, I Thee Dread

"I pity this poor person, for she will be
one more unhappy princess in the world."
—*Prince Frederick of Prussia on his bride-to-be,*
Elisabeth Christine of Brunswick-Wolfenbüttel-Bevern

Prussia's prince, the future Frederick the Great, didn't want to get married—as in, really, *really* didn't want to get married. It wasn't so much his betrothed's looks or personality (though he didn't think much of either). It was that poor Elisabeth Christine happened to be female.

"If I am forced to marry her, I will reject her away as soon as I am master," the unhappy heir insisted, "and no man can blame me for it, knowing that I was forced to do something that was totally against my inclinations."

But Frederick had virtually no say in the matter. His formidable father, King Frederick William I, wanted a wedding. And—as was made evident when the bully king ordered the beheading of his son's close friend, right in front of Frederick, whom he then imprisoned for four months—this was a monarch who meant business.

Thus, on June 12, 1733, the distasteful wedding took place—with the prince literally pushed into the marital bed that night by his implacable pop. True to his word, Frederick refused to consort with Elisabeth Christine, consigning her to a separate household.

There were no children.

Frederick did, however, deign to dine with his neglected spouse—once every year.

❦

JUNE 13, 1978

Her Majesty's Hideous Houseguests:
When the Ceaușescus Came Calling

The sovereign enjoys certain privileges under the British Constitution. Choice of houseguests, however, is not one of them. That was made painfully evident in the summer of 1978, when Queen Elizabeth II was compelled by her government to host Romanian despot Nicolae Ceaușescu and his equally odious wife, Elena, at Buckingham Palace.

The state visit—the first to Britain by the leader of a communist country—was supposed to be a warming gesture in the midst of the Cold War: a hand extended to a dictator perceived to be independent of Soviet influence, as well as a way to promote British business interests in Romania. Aware that the Ceauşescus had pillaged their own country and left its people starving, however, the monarch was not pleased to welcome them. "They have blood on their hands," she reportedly remarked to her staff, later describing the visit as the worst three days of her life.

Even before the cruel couple's red-carpet arrival on June 13, the queen had been warned by French president Valéry Giscard d'Estaing that the Ceauşescus were a bit light-fingered; the pair had removed expensive vases and other valuables from their rooms during an official visit to Paris. "It was as if burglars had moved in for a whole summer," Giscard told the BBC.

Larceny alerts aside, Queen Elizabeth soon found out for herself just how boorish these two barbarians really were. It's not clear exactly what the couple did to confirm the queen's distaste. (Perhaps it was their staggering body odor.) In any event, she quickly came to loathe them. Such was her revulsion that one day while walking her dogs, she ducked behind some bushes to avoid encountering the detestable duo as they strolled in her palace gardens.

As it turned out, the government that had foisted the Ceauşescus on the queen found them equally problematic. Despite lacking certain qualifications—like, say, a high school education—Elena fancied herself a chemist and insisted that she be honored as such during the state visit. But the prestigious Royal Society bluntly denied her a fellowship. Desperate to avoid a diplomatic incident, the British government scrambled to find some other scientific group willing to oblige. To their eventual mortification, both the Royal Institute of Chemistry and the Polytechnic of Central London willingly heaped honors upon the woman who barely knew the chemical formula for water.

Nicolae, for his part, appeared satisfied with his honorary knighthood in the Order of the Bath (which some privately renamed "Order of the Bloodbath" in his honor). Obligated to attach this badge of "merit" to his chest, the unamused monarch doubtlessly would have preferred to pin it to his eye. Upon Ceauşescu's overthrow 11 years later, Her Majesty's government recovered its senses and revoked the ill-considered honor.

A far worse indignity awaited the tyrant and his spouse: Nicolae and Elena were executed by firing squad on Christmas Day of 1989.

❖

JUNE 14, 2001

When Pigs Buy

Nothing says "class" quite like Stolichnaya vodka pouring from the penis of an ice statue. Or how about a life-size cake in the shape of a woman, replete with exploding breasts? Those were just a few fun features of the $2 million 40th-birthday bacchanal that Tyco CEO Dennis Kozlowski threw for his second wife, Karen, on June 14, 2001. Company funds paid for half of it.

Of course, nothing says "retribution" quite like the six-year prison term that Kozlowski served after being convicted of looting nearly $100 million from Tyco to pay for the party and other absurd extravagances—among them a $6,000 shower curtain. "I was piggy," the disgraced CEO later admitted to *The New York Times.*

That self-aware comment may have been the only time Kozlowski's name was ever linked with the word "understatement."

❖

JUNE 15, 1845

Queen Ranavalona I:
Madagascar's Head Case

When it came to discipline, Ranavalona I, the 19th-century queen of Madagascar, tended to go medieval on her subjects—especially

the Christian ones, whom she burned, beheaded, or even boiled for their faith. Nor were foreigners immune to her old-school wrath, as a group of them discovered on June 15, 1845.

Fed up with the rapacity of European powers on the African island nation, Ranavalona at one point banned any further commerce with the imperialists. In retaliation, a joint English and French force sailed to the island's trading center at Tamatave and attempted to bombard its fort into submission. They underestimated the defenses, however, and upon storming the citadel found themselves dangerously exposed. Retreating to their ships, the assailants were forced to leave a number of their dead onshore.

What happened next was reminiscent of the sort of message European kings and queens had sent their enemies centuries before.

The heads of the fallen were hacked off, stuck on poles, and perched on the beach to serve as a reminder (and a taunt) that Queen Ranavalona meant business. She deemed it "very strange and highly impertinent" that the Europeans would dare protest these gruesome totems; she was mistress of her country, just as Queen Victoria was mistress of her own. One local official did take it upon himself to order the heads taken down and buried—which, as author Ian Hernon wrote, was ill-advised in the extreme: "His reward for this humane act was that the heads were exhumed and put back on the beach—along with his own."

And there they would remain for the next eight years.

JUNE 16, 2001

Praisin' Putin: The Gullibility That Dogged George Bush

"I looked the man in the eye. I found him to be very straightforward and trustworthy . . . I was able to get a sense of his soul."
—*President George W. Bush, on first meeting Russian president Vladimir Putin at a summit in Slovenia, June 16, 2001*

It seemed to be the beginning of a beautiful friendship—like when Caesar met Brutus. But the 43rd president's myopic view of his new-found pal was not universally shared among his associates.

"A lot of us were kind of rolling our eyes about that," Eric Edelman, then Vice President Dick Cheney's deputy national security adviser, later told journalist Peter Baker. As for the veep himself, Putin's former position as head of the Soviet Union's notoriously brutal security services made Cheney shudder every time he laid eyes on the Russian president: "I think *KGB, KGB, KGB.*"

President Bush's dreamy conception of his Russian counterpart finally darkened four months after that first enchanted encounter, when Putin dared to disparage Bush's beloved Scottish terrier, Barney. "Putin kind of dissed him," the former president recalled in an interview with his daughter Jenna in 2014. "'You call that a dog?' A year later, your mom and I go to visit Vladimir at his dacha outside of Moscow and he says, 'Would you like to meet my dog?' Out bounds this huge hound, obviously much bigger than a Scottish terrier. And Putin looks at me and says, 'Bigger, stronger, and faster than Barney.'"

The scene had all the makings of a canine cold war, but Dubya coolly weathered this first strike: "I took it in. I didn't react," Bush recalled. "I said [to myself], 'Wow, anybody who thinks *My dog is bigger than your dog* is an interesting character."

JUNE 17, 1991

Exhuming the Worst: A Conspiracy Theory With Grave Consequences

Amateur historian Clara Rising had a hunch: President Zachary Taylor hadn't died from simple gastroenteritis after consuming a heaping bowl of cherries and iced milk in July 1850, as was commonly believed. Rather, she posited, Old Rough and Ready, hero of the recently won war with Mexico and president for only 16 months, had been poisoned—a victim, she suspected, of pro-slavery factionalists furious over Taylor's opposition to the Fugitive Slave Act and the Compromise of 1850, both of which became law after his untimely death.

"This man may have, if not prevented it, delayed or somehow solved the problems that caused the Civil War," Rising ventured in *The New York Times*. And if he had indeed been murdered, that would make Taylor—not Abraham Lincoln—the nation's first assassinated president.

Armed with little more than a letter from a Taylor descendant—and abetted by a compliant county coroner—Rising was able to test her hypothesis by having the corpse of the 12th president exhumed and examined for arsenic poisoning. On June 17, 1991, under the prying gaze of hundreds, Taylor's tomb in Louisville, Kentucky, was opened, and his rotting coffin—newly draped with a flag in the day's single nod to decorum—was taken to the Jefferson County coroner's office. There, President Taylor (or what was left of him) became the subject of a rather intrusive, if not grotesque, evaluation.

"The former President had been totally skeletonized," reported William Maples, a forensic anthropologist who assisted the coroner. "He presented an austere picture of simple mortality: a skeleton, clad in his funeral attire, his skull pillowed on a bunch of straw stuffed beneath the casket liner." Despite the advanced decay, Taylor was still somewhat recognizable by his prominent eyebrows. And enough remained of his corpse—including, Maples noted, "pubic hair, even"—to be sampled for arsenic poisoning.

For Rising, viewing the subject of her fervent imaginings was "a sacred moment," she told *Newsweek* magazine. "I had at last met Zachary. And if someone had done him in, we were damn sure going to find out."

But the indignity the dead president endured was for naught. Nine days after the exhumation, the lab results came back: The only traces of arsenic, ruled Dr. George Nichols, Kentucky's chief medical examiner, were those "consistent with being a human being on the planet Earth." No other toxic metals were found. (It *was* determined, however, that President Taylor had probably been a teeth grinder.)

Death, in this case, really was just a bowl of cherries.

But the negative results did little to dampen Rising's zeal. "I still feel that this doesn't change the fact that his political enemies were delighted at his removal," she told the Louisville *Courier-Journal.* "Whether they did him in or not, they certainly celebrated" his demise.

Three years before her own death in 2010, Rising's self-published alternative-history book *The Taylor File* garnered at least one rave review on Amazon: "I thought this book was fascinating and informative, but I am a necrophile, so my opinion is slanted. The descriptions of the conditions of the Presidents' [sic] corpse was [sic] . . . arousing [sick]."

❧

JUNE 18, 1815

At Waterloo, They Gave Their Lives . . . and Their Front Teeth

As night descended over the carnage of the Waterloo battlefield on June 18, 1815, the smoke and thunder of cannon fire and the screams of slaughter gave way to an eerie, moonlit stillness. Only the anguished cries of the dying punctuated the calm.

It was the day of Napoleon's last stand, and some 50,000 men had fallen in a space only a few miles square. "The number of the dead was far greater than I had ever seen on any former battlefield," Sgt. D. Robertson of the Gordon Highlanders recorded in his diary. "The bodies were not scattered over the ground but were lying in heaps—men and horses mixed promiscuously together."

And creeping among them in the shadows were human scavengers seeking a treasure most gruesome.

The dead and the dying were frequently subject to after-action pillaging—stripped of any item of value, including their clothes, by local residents and fellow soldiers alike. Waterloo was no different. "It is one of the worst results of a life of violence that it renders such as follow it selfish and mercenary," confessed Pvt. George Farmer of the 11th Light Dragoons. "When the bloody work of the day is over, the survivor's first wish is to secure, in the shape of plunder, some recompense for the risks which he has run and the exertions which he has made. Neither does it enter into [his] mind . . . to consider whether it is the dead body of a friend or of a foe from which he is seeking his booty."

In addition to watches, rings, and boots, the Waterloo dead offered up a new and highly lucrative commodity. Recent advances in the fabrication of realistic-looking dentures had rendered some old items obsolescent: Ivory, lacking enamel, tended to stink as it deteriorated, while brittle porcelain produced a grating sound and an unnaturally white gleam. When it comes to human teeth there really is no substitute quite like . . . *other* human teeth.

Procuring said chompers presented problems, however. Out of desperation, the indigent would occasionally agree to have theirs yanked out for pay. Alternatively, a denture manufacturer might consort with grave robbers—inviting predictable questions of quality control. Ah, but a freshly sown battlefield: Here lay a sure and ready supply from young men lost in their prime. And that's where the ghoulish opportunists amassed, swooping in to pry them out.

"Only let there be a battle and there will be no want of teeth," Bransby Blake Cooper quoted one such marauder in his 1843 book, *The Life of Sir Astley Cooper*. "I'll draw them as fast as the men are knocked down."

JUNE 19, 1984

A Nose Would Have Been a Better Pick

On June 19, 1984, NBA commissioner David Stern announced what is widely considered professional basketball's biggest recruiting blunder: The Portland Trail Blazers picked the University of Kentucky's Sam Bowie in the second round—notwithstanding a stress fracture in his left leg, which had forced the seven-foot-one player to sit out several college seasons.

Bowie's bad leg only worsened once he joined the Blazers, compounded by additional fractures and other osteo ailments that left the once golden prospect warming the bench—and his team managers boiling over with regret. Perhaps they were thinking of the future legend they had declined in selecting Bowie: Michael Jordan.

JUNE 20, 1997

Cowabungle!

Hollywood has produced its share of duds over the decades. But *Batman & Robin* was so bad it got trashed even by the people who made it.

When this fourth installment of the revived Batman franchise was released on June 20, 1997, mainstream critics blasted everything from the film's cartoonish quality and groan-inducing dialogue to its homoerotic undertones (the dynamic duo's costumes featured prominent man-nipples and bulging codpieces). But that was merely a preview of the barbs unleashed by the cast itself. "I felt like I was making a kid's toy commercial," recalled Chris O'Donnell, who played Robin (and became notorious for shouting "Cowabunga!" without a hint of irony in one space-surfing scene).

George Clooney was similarly unsparing of his own performance as Batman—which, he admitted, had nearly killed the franchise: "With hindsight, it's easy to look back at this and go, 'Whoa, that was really shit, and I was really bad in it.' . . . Batman is still the biggest break I ever had and it completely changed my career, even if it was weak and I was weak in it. It was a difficult film to be good in."

Even director Joel Schumacher tried to make amends for the pain he had caused: "If there's anybody watching this [on DVD] that . . . loved *Batman Forever* [the preceding film] and went into *Batman & Robin* with great anticipation . . . then I really want to apologize. Because it wasn't my intention. My intention was just to entertain them."

Oh, well—at least the fallout was funny.

JUNE 21, 2011

A Seriously Subprime Conscience

"I have no regrets about . . .
how Countrywide was run. It was a world-class company."
—*Angelo Mozilo, former chairman and CEO, Countrywide Financial
Corporation, after running his company into the ground*

Mozilo, the overly tanned face of the subprime-mortgage crisis, had been granted plenty of time to reflect between the 2008 demise of his "baby" (as he called Countrywide) and a deposition he delivered on June 21, 2011.

Apparently, he did not use the time wisely.

Issuing wildly irresponsible loans that Mozilo himself had privately labeled as "toxic," Countrywide had contributed disproportionately to the worldwide financial implosion. Yet in addition to using his deposition to trumpet his lack of regrets, the fallen CEO had the chutzpah to blame Countrywide's customers—not the actual "baby" teething with fangs: "[Borrowers] left their homes because the values went below the mortgage. That's what caused the problem."

TenniZZZ, Anyone?

Wimbledon line judge Dorothy Cavis Brown had just enjoyed a nip or two at the tournament's annual cocktail party for umpires and line judges when she teetered over to Court 3 for a first-round match between South Africa's Abe Segal and Clark Graebner of the United States. Then, right in the middle of play, she dozed off—head tilted sideways, arms and legs crossed, like a weary railroad traveler.

Cavis Brown's sudden snooze might have gone unremarked had it not been match point. Graebner had hit the ball out and Segal ran to the net to shake his hand. A smiling Graebner, aware that his ball had landed beyond the line, nevertheless pointed out the game wasn't *officially* over until the line judge made the call. After a ball boy failed to rouse the slumbering official—the crowd tittering in delight—Segal himself approached Cavis Brown and, as he remembered the moment, shouted "Out!" beside her ear. Only then did the startled woman awake to make the call—and discover she had netted Wimbledon infamy.

Babe Ruth: The Sox Slugger

"I just went crazy."
—*George Herman "Babe" Ruth, Jr.*

Back when he was still pitching for the Boston Red Sox, Babe Ruth took violent exception to a call made on June 23, 1917. After umpire Clarence "Brick" Owens shouted "Ball four!" on a Ruth pitch to Washington Senators leadoff hitter Ray Morgan, the future Sultan of Swat unleashed an obscenity-laced protest against the ump, including threats of bodily harm.

No mere threats, these; the Babe then rushed the plate and dropped Owens to the dirt with a punch.

Policemen escorted Ruth off the field. He was suspended 10 games and fined $100. But the ump got to make the final call, for in Owens's estimation, Babe Ruth had not exactly earned the nickname "Slugger" that day: "Ruth's blow did not hurt me and the swing did not come particularly hard," the umpire said afterward. "His conduct was in no way justified, and I cannot understand how a man who has been in the game so long as he has could have so completely lost his head."

JUNE 24, 1961

Truth Defects: The Tragically Duplicitous Ad for Thalidomide

"Put your mind at rest. Depend on the safety of 'Distaval.'"
—*Advertisement for Distaval, a brand name for thalidomide, published in the June 24, 1961, edition of the* British Medical Journal. *The man-*

ufacturer was touting the fact that overdoses of the drug, even in children, had no harmful effects. Not mentioned, however, were the thousands of devastating birth defects that had already ensued when pregnant women took the sedative.

Momsters, Part 6:
Catherine de' Medici,
Queen of Clubbing

The only thing more putrescent than Catherine de' Medici in death (see January 5) was her parenting style in life. For France's Queen Mother, maintaining power was far more important than making her children happy. So when Catherine learned that her teenage daughter Marguerite was carrying on a secret romance with the royal family's rival, the Duke of Guise, she made her disapproval known far more savagely than might your average boyfriend-averse mom.

Early on the morning of June 25, 1570, Marguerite was summoned to her mother's bedroom. There she encountered the fist-flying, hair-pulling fury of Catherine, who—joined by Marguerite's own brother, King Charles IX—brutally pummeled the terrified princess, shredding her spirits along with her nightgown. When the violent frenzy abated, the poor girl was left sobbing and abandoned on the floor.

Catherine returned to the scene to make amends, but they were merely cosmetic: She covered the girl's bruises with makeup, rearranged her hair to hide the bald spots on her scalp, and provided her a fresh new gown. After all, a battered princess did not match the image of royal dignity the Queen Mother was always careful to convey.

Recognizing the royal wrath, the Duke of Guise had the good sense to immediately betroth himself to Catherine de Clèves,* while Marguerite went on to wed King Henri of Navarre in 1572. Though their union marked a joining of Catholic and Protestant royal houses, it sparked mayhem on a far grander scale than that bedside beatdown of Marguerite:

---

* The dallying duke was later assassinated by order of another of Catherine de' Medici's sons, Henri, who became king after the death of Charles IX in 1574.

The nuptials were followed almost immediately by the infamous St. Bartholomew's Day massacre, which ultimately claimed the lives of as many as 30,000 Huguenots, or French Protestants.

JUNE 26, 1953

The Dumping of "the Kremlin Monster"

"He dropped a load in his pants."
—*Nikita Khrushchev, first secretary of the Communist Party of the Soviet Union (and later premier), on the June 26, 1953, arrest of his rival Lavrentiy Beria*

To the howling laughter of a group of party leaders, Khrushchev gleefully shared other humiliating details of Beria's downfall—including the Soviet premier's final encounter with "the scoundrel" on the eve of his arrest: "I shook him warmly by the hand, thinking to myself, *Well, you swine, this is your last handshake. Tomorrow at 2 o'clock we'll really shake you!*"

Beria, who had succeeded the snuffed and primitively photo-chopped Nikolai Yezhov as Joseph Stalin's killer-in-chief (see February 4), was arguably an even more vicious henchman than his predecessor. But when the executioner came calling, "the Kremlin monster" behaved every bit as pathetically as Yezhov had: Beria crawled across the floor of his prison cell on his knees, begging for mercy in such a piercing screech that a rag was shoved in his mouth before the bullet entered his brain.

"In all that you have done, so loathsome, mean, and nasty," executioner Pavel Batitsky reportedly demanded of Beria, "can you not find enough courage in yourself to accept your punishment in silence?"

The rag and the bullet stifled any response from the abominable Beria.

JUNE 27, 1882

Not Too Wild About Wilde

History is filled with unlikely celebrity encounters—like when a drug-addled Elvis Presley dropped in on President Richard Nixon in 1970 to offer up his services as a federal drug enforcement agent. But nothing was quite as incongruous as a meeting a century earlier, on June 27, 1882, when Oscar Wilde—the witty, flitty Irish playwright—paid a visit to the Mississippi home of Jefferson Davis, the grizzled, ultramasculine ex-president of the Confederacy. "It's like a butterfly making a formal visit to an eagle," a local newspaper opined.

Despite their obvious differences in temperament and manner, the meeting should have gone well, given Wilde's open expressions of sympathy for the South. It did not. As the 27-year-old literary celebrity prattled on enthusiastically, charming the women at the table, Davis, 74, remained aloof and frosty. Then he retired early to bed. The next morning, Davis tersely explained himself: "I did not like the man."

JUNE 28, 1997

Sudden Fame: More Than He Could Chew

They are history's bystanders—ordinary men and women thrust suddenly into renown as unwitting participants in events they never anticipated, much less welcomed. Their stories are often unhappy ones.

On June 28, 1997, Mitchell Libonati played an unsought role in one of sports history's grisliest spectacles when boxer Mike Tyson tore off a chunk of opponent Evander Holyfield's ear with his teeth.

Libonati, who had dreams of one day becoming a pro boxing manager, was working as a house cornerman at the MGM Grand Garden Arena in Las Vegas on the night of the WBA Heavyweight Championship fight. Standing at the ring apron, he saw the feral bite up close, then watched

Tyson spit something from his bloodied mouth. When it was all over—after Tyson's disqualification in Round 3, and after the arena had been cleared—Libonati searched the canvas for the mystery projectile. "Whatever it was, I knew it was down there somewhere," he told author George Willis.

Just as he was about to abandon his search, Libonati spotted a shriveled bit of flesh about half an inch long. It was a severed portion of Holyfield's ear. He raced it to the mauled boxer's locker room, frantically knocking on the door and announcing, "I have something he probably wants."

With that, Libonati became part of the story—and part of history. He even appeared on the *Late Show with David Letterman.* The sudden fame wasn't to Libonati's liking, however. "My phone was ringing like crazy and for what? Finding an ear," he told Willis. "I became insecure and didn't show up for work anymore. I haven't had my face around the game since bite night."

JUNE 29, 1937

On Second Thought, Part 8: The Prime Minister's Super-Duped Day

"My sizing up of the man as I sat and talked with him was that
he is really one who truly loves his fellow-men, and his country,
and would make any sacrifice for their good. That he feels himself
to be a deliverer of his people from tyranny . . . As I talked with him,
I could not but think of Joan of Arc. He is distinctly a mystic."
—*Canada's prime minister, William Mackenzie King,*
after meeting Adolf Hitler

William Mackenzie King awoke in Berlin on the morning of June 29, 1937, filled with a biblical zeal. The Scriptures he had read the night before—some aloud to his dead mother, with whom he often communicated in seances (along with his dead dogs)—portended success for the day's interviews. First he was to meet with top Nazi Hermann Göring, and then with Adolf Hitler himself. "Certainly it would seem to be the day for which I was born," King concluded after considering the providential signs.

And what a day it turned out to be—one in which the fiendish führer swept the gullible Canadian prime minister off his feet.

The morning meeting with Göring went splendidly. Hitler's right-hand man probed King about Canada's possible reaction to a theoretical annexation of Austria, then reassured him that no such plan was being considered. (It was executed the following March.) "He also spoke of the cramped position of Germany," the prime minister dispassionately noted in his diary, "and the necessity of her having opportunity for expansion in Europe."

Göring had just laid out a preview of coming events, after which King unwittingly provided one of his own: British prime minister Neville Chamberlain was a man of peace and would do nothing to interfere with Germany's ambitions (which, as it turned out, included chewing apart Czechoslovakia; see June 3).

Next it was off to see the führer, with whom King was instantly smitten. Hitler's features, he rhapsodized, were those of a "calm, passive man, deeply and thoughtfully in earnest. His skin was smooth; his face did not present lines of fatigue or weariness." Hitler's "very nice, sweet" smile left little doubt why the German people loved him so much. But the monster's dreamy eyes captivated King most of all: "There was a liquid quality about them which indicates keen perception and profound sympathy."

King gushed over Hitler throughout their meeting—which took place two weeks before the grand opening of Buchenwald, Germany's newest concentration camp. "I spoke . . . of what I had seen of the constructive work of his regime, and said that I hoped that that work might continue," the prime minister reported. "That nothing would be prepared to destroy that work. That it was bound to be followed in other countries to the great advantage of mankind."

Clearly enchanted with his fellow bachelor (and, as he saw it, his mystical soul mate), King was prepared to swallow just about any steaming rot the führer cared to spew about peace: "Hitler said to me, 'my support comes from the people—the people don't want war.' This impressed me very much & a real note of humility."

After an hour and a quarter—thrilled by "the privilege of so long an interview"—King departed, clutching a personally inscribed silver-framed picture of the führer. "I let him see that I was most appreciative of it, shook him by the hand, and thanked him warmly for it, saying that I greatly appreciated all that it expressed of his friendship, and would always deeply value this gift."

Then, "I wished him well in his efforts to help mankind."

<hr />

JUNE 30, 1882

OK! But Aside From *That,* How Did You Like the Opera?

J ohn Ruskin, the renowned English critic (and famously repulsed newlywed; see April 10), attended a performance of Richard Wagner's epically lengthy opera *Die Meistersinger von Nürnberg* on the evening of June 29, 1882. He enjoyed it no more than his bride's bed.

The next day, Ruskin indulged in some epically loquacious bashing: "Of all the *bête,* clumsy, blundering, boggling, baboon-blooded stuff I ever saw on a human stage, that thing last night beat—as far as the acting and story went—and of all the affected, sapless, soulless, beginningless, endless, topless, bottomless, topsiturviest, tuneless and scrannelpipiest— tongs and boniest—doggerel of sounds I ever endured the deadliness of, that eternity of nothing was the deadliest, so far as the sound went. I never was so relieved, so far as I can remember in my life, by the stopping of any sound—not excepting railway whistles—as I was by the cessation of the cobbler's bellowing."

Half a century later, baboon-blooded Hitler had a far more positive impression of *Die Meistersinger,* which he adored. It became the scrannelpipiest walk-on music at many a Nazi rally.

July

Enron's Code Blue of Ethics

"We are responsible for conducting the business affairs
of the companies in accordance with all applicable laws
and in a moral and honest manner."
—*Kenneth L. Lay, chairman and CEO, Enron Corporation, July 1, 2000*

April Fools' Day had come and gone, but the publication of the Enron "Code of Ethics" on July 1, 2000, was nevertheless a colossal joke—like Hitler's "Tips on Tolerance," or Henry VIII's "Manual of Monogamy." Chairman and CEO Kenneth L. Lay ("Kenny Boy" to pal and financial beneficiary George W. Bush) had taken a break from his daily routine—committing fraud designed to hide the energy giant's staggering debts and financial losses—to compose the code's foreword himself.

"We want to be proud of Enron and to know that it enjoys a reputation for fairness and honesty, and that it is respected," Lay wrote. "Gaining such respect is one aim of our advertising and public relations activities. But no matter how effective they may be, Enron's reputation finally depends on its people, on you and me. Let's keep that reputation high."

You could almost hear him snickering between the lines.

Lauded by the likes of *Businessweek, Forbes,* and *Fortune,* Enron had seen its reputation soar in 2000—along with the price of its stock. The only thing missing was actual performance. In fact, the company adored by Wall Street had losses of $591 million that year and a debt burden of $628 million—all cleverly disguised by Kenny Boy and his cohorts.

Not until 2001 did the facade begin to crumble. "Something is rotten with the state of Enron," *The New York Times* declared on September 9. Three months later, Enron filed what was then the largest corporate bankruptcy in American history.

For those employees who lost millions in worthless stock options and obliterated pensions, Kenny Boy's "Code of Ethics" offered only cruel irony: "The great fun here will be for all of us to discover just how good we can really be."

❖

JULY 2, 2017

The Fat of the Sand:
Chris Christie's Beach Breach

Was that a beached beluga on an empty stretch of sand at the Jersey Shore? Nope, it was Chris Christie, the roly-poly governor of New Jersey, sunning himself on July 2, 2017—smug along the shoreline that had just been closed to the public because of a budgetary impasse.

The images of Christie lolling in front of his state-provided retreat—caught by photographer Andrew Mills from the open doorway of a low-flying plane—outraged residents of the Garden State. But perhaps even more appalling than his gross abuse of power was Christie's media appearance the following day. How was it fair, his critics wanted to know, that taxpayers had been denied access to the very

CLOSED BEACH
No Trespassing
No Boats

same seashore on which he was spotted basking with a coterie of family and friends?

Christie's response: "I'm sorry they're not the governor."

Soon enough, however, the pudgy pol would have reason to rue that *he* was the governor: The aerial shots of Christie hogging the beach when no one else could quickly became an internet sensation, with the governor cleverly photoshopped into hundreds of memes: Christie on a box of Wheaties®, Christie floating on the water directly above the shark from *Jaws,* even Christie calmly witnessing the moon landing.

One meme resonated in particular: Christie perched mid-span on the George Washington Bridge, which had been partially closed to cars in the summer of 2013 as an act of political revenge by the governor's administration.* This spiteful move resulted in massive snarls on the world's busiest span and ultimately left Christie's career stuck on a sandbar.

<hr>

JULY 3, 1912

He Forgot to Mention Their Terrible Teeth

"Curse the blasted, jelly-boned swines, the slimy, the belly-wriggling invertebrates, the miserable sodding rotters, the flaming sods, the sniveling, dribbling, dithering palsied pulse-less lot that make up England today. They've got white of egg in their veins, and their spunk is that watery it's a marvel they can breed . . . They *can* nothing but frog-spawn—the gibberers! God, how I hate them! God curse them, funkers. God blast them, wish-wash. Exterminate them, slime.

I could curse for hours and hours—God help me."

---

*"Time for some traffic problems in Fort Lee [N.J.]," Christie's ironically named deputy chief of staff, Bridget Anne Kelly, wrote in an email.

—British novelist D. H. Lawrence, in a ferociously cranky letter written to his friend and literary advocate, Edward Garnett, on July 3, 1912*

JULY 4, 1762

The Rice and Fall of
Korea's Murderous Crown Prince

Prince Sado, heir to the throne of Korea, stood trembling on a steamy July 4, 1762, begging his father, King Yeongjo, to spare his life. Before him was a wooden rice chest, measuring approximately 4 by 4 by 4 feet, that would serve as his death chamber. "Father, Father. I have done wrong," the doomed prince cried, according to the memoirs of his wife, Lady Hyegyong. "Herewith, I will do everything you say. I will study, I will obey you in everything, I promise. Please do not do this to me."

The king was unresponsive—except for the incessant rapping of his sword. Beyond salvation, Prince Sado then did what was expected of him: He climbed into the chest to await his end. It would take him eight days to die.

Lady Hyegyong's account of her husband's horrific demise, and the events leading up to it, is an invaluable historic resource. However, her assessment of the events is a bit baffling, just as her self-centered, woe-is-me narration is distracting—as if *she* were the one who'd ended up starved to death in a rice chest. From the crown princess's perspective, punctuated throughout the text by her wails of despair, all of her husband's prob-

---

* In the same missive, Lawrence went on to bemoan not only his fraught relationship with his married mistress, Frieda Weekley (whom he would soon marry), but also the recent rejection of his novel *Paul Morel* by British publisher William Heinemann, whose harsh critique of the work Lawrence included in his screed. After being edited by Garnett, *Paul Morel* was published as *Sons and Lovers* and became one of Lawrence's most acclaimed works.

lems—serial rape and murder, specifically—began in childhood, when the little boy felt intimidated and unloved by his remote, undemonstrative father.

"Prince Sado was endowed with a strong and fine bearing, a filial and affectionate nature, and extraordinary intelligence," Lady Hyegyong wrote. But, according to her, the king's constant criticism and disapproval of his heir gradually unbalanced the young man. "As his illness tightened its grip," she wrote, "his behavior often fell short of propriety"—a nice way of saying he became a homicidal maniac. Apparently Sado's daddy issues prompted the deranged prince to hack off the head of a eunuch, beat his mistress to death, rape ladies-in-waiting, and slaughter scores of servants who displeased him.

"It reached the point where every day many dead bodies and victims of injury had to be carried out from the palace," Lady Hyegyong related. "Both in and out of the palace, people were terrified and angry, not knowing when they might meet their death or where they might find safe haven." As she frequently reminds her readers, the crown princess shuddered to recall it all. "Ah! Grief and sorrow."

Oddly enough, the killings did not seem to bother the king—not as much, say, as his son's choice of mistress. On one occasion, he asked the prince what made him so murderous:

"Because I am deeply hurt," was the reply.

"Why are you so hurt?" the king wondered.

"I am sad that Your Majesty does not love me and terrified when you criticize me," Prince Sado answered. "All this turns to anger."

King Yeongjo assuaged his heir's hurt feeling, but his tolerance did not extend to threats to his *own* life. When informed that the prince was plotting his murder (a charge made by Prince Sado's own mother yet denied by his wife in her memoirs), Yeongjo called for the rice chest—or "that thing," as Lady Hyegyong referred to it. "As the days passed, it was just too horrid to imagine the Prince's state," she wrote—concluding the account, of course, with a few final words about her *own* ordeal: "Calling upon Heaven and weeping in pain, I lament my fate."

Poor soul—must have been rough eating from a rice chest, rather than starving in one.

Less a Fairy Tale Than a Bleak House:
Dickens Hosts Andersen

"Fish and guests in three days are stale."
—*John Lyly*, Euphues, *1579*

On July 5, 1856, Charles Dickens extended an invitation he would sorely regret. "You ought to come to me . . . and stay in my house," the novelist wrote to fellow writer (and avid onanist; see March 24) Hans Christian Andersen, whom he hadn't seen since they first met nine years earlier. "We would all do our best to make you happy."

Such invites are often tossed out halfheartedly, but in this case Dickens seemed sincere—if a tad excessive: "I assure you that I love and esteem you more than I could tell you on as much paper as would pave the whole road" from London to Andersen's home in Copenhagen. Little wonder, then, that the *Ugly Duckling* author felt welcomed enough to accept. "That you and your wife are always in my thoughts, you will perceive from my intention, God willing, of visiting you in England this summer to spend a short time with you," Andersen replied the following March, "about a week." If his proposed summer visit was inconvenient, he added, he would go to Switzerland instead.

Had Dickens taken advantage of Andersen's opening to wriggle out of his overture, a burgeoning friendship between two literary geniuses might have been preserved. Instead, Dickens opened the door even wider, enticing the Dane with the beauty and ease of his home in the Kentish countryside. "You shall have a pleasant room there with a charming view," Dickens wrote on April 3, "and shall live as quietly and wholesomely as in Copenhagen itself." The novelist offered Andersen free run of his London home as well, with a servant at his disposal. "Mind," he concluded the missive, "you must not think any more of going to Switzerland. You must come to us."

Andersen did come that June—but not for "about a week." He stayed

. . . and stayed . . . and stayed. What had at first appealed to Dickens about the lanky, childlike storyteller quickly began to grate as the weeks wore on. Behind the superficial charm was, in essence, the cloying self-centeredness of a man-child who threw a fit in Dickens's front yard over a bad review and requested that his host's sons shave him in the morning. He was, Dickens's daughter declared, "a bony bore." (And an incomprehensible one to boot: "He spoke French like Peter the Wild Boy,"* Dickens later wrote Britain's former prime minister, Lord John Russell, "and English like the Deaf and Dumb School.")

Despite the (literal) chill in the house, about which he constantly complained (while apparently oblivious to the metaphorical one that existed between Dickens and his wife, whose marriage was on the verge of collapse), Andersen was happily ensconced. What prompted his departure after five weeks is uncertain. But whatever it was, Dickens—who abruptly ended their friendship in the aftermath—was ecstatic when it finally happened. "Hans Andersen slept in this room for five weeks," he reportedly scrawled on the guest-room mirror, "which seemed to the family AGES!"

JULY 6, 1796

Washington's Bad Press: More of a Pain Than His False Teeth

"If ever a nation was debauched by a man,
the American nation has been debauched by WASHINGTON."
—Aurora General Advertiser, *1796*

---

* Peter the Wild Boy, a popular curiosity at the court of Britain's George I, had been discovered living a feral existence in a German forest and could never be taught to speak.

George Washington was in a snit as his second presidential term neared its end. The cloak of esteem that once made him nearly invincible to criticism had long since been torn away. Now, as he prepared to retire to Mount Vernon after decades of devoted service to his country, he was being trampled in the partisan muck ("buffeted in the public prints by a set of infamous scribblers," he wrote) and betrayed by men such as Thomas Jefferson and James Madison, whom he had once considered close friends.

"Saint Washington," as the *Aurora General Advertiser** sarcastically referred to the nation's first president, was accused of having monarchical pretensions, particularly in the aftermath of the Jay Treaty, which some viewed as overly favorable to "aristocratic" Britain and detrimental to revolutionary France. "He holds levees like a King," Philip Freneau wrote in the *Jersey Chronicle;* "receives congratulations on his birthday like a King; receives ambassadors like a King; makes treaties like a King; answers petitions like a King; employs old enemies like a King . . . swallows adulation like a King, and vomits offensive truths in your face." (No wonder Washington called Freneau "that rascal.")

Critics were relentless in their attacks—"always working, like bees, to distill their poison," the president wrote. Published cartoons showed him being marched off to the guillotine, while some toasted "a speedy death to General Washington." But as future president Woodrow Wilson would write in *Harper's* magazine in 1896, "The men who sneered and stormed, talked of usurpation and impeachment, called him base, incompetent, traitorous even, were permitted to see not so much as the quiver of an eyelid as they watched him go steadily from step to step in the course he had chosen."

Indeed, Washington did remain mostly silent in the face of this venomous censure—at least publicly. Privately, however, he maintained a less-

---

* At a time when virulent partisanship was becoming commonplace in the press, the *Aurora*—published by Benjamin Franklin's grandson—was a particularly anti-Federalist paper. "If you read the *Aurora* . . . or those Gazettes which are under the same influence," Washington wrote, "you cannot but have perceived with what malignant industry, and persevering falsehoods I am assailed, in order to weaken, if not to destroy, the confidence of the Public."

than-stoic stance. Tired, ailing, and deeply wounded, Washington lashed out in a letter to Thomas Jefferson,* whom he blamed for secretly inciting much of the invective: "Until the last year or two ago, I had no conception that Parties would, or even could go, to the length I have been witness to," Washington wrote on July 6, 1796. The president then expressed disbelief and consternation that after all his efforts to keep the United States strictly neutral in the endless clash between Britain and France, "I should be accused of being the enemy of one nation and subject to the influence of another." The president was further appalled by the incendiary misrepresentations used to "prove" foreign entanglements on the part of his administration—delivered, he wrote, "in such exaggerated and indecent terms as could scarcely be applied to a Nero, a notorious defaulter, or even to a common pickpocket."

"But enough of this," Washington concluded his missive; "I have already gone farther in the expression of my feelings, than I intended."

The wearied and disgusted president restrained his feelings even further in his farewell address, published three months later. The original draft pulsed with Washington's anger at his mistreatment, especially in sharply partisan press of the era.

"Some of the Gazettes of the United States have teemed with all the invective that disappointment, ignorance of facts, and malicious falsehoods could invent," he vented in one peevish version of the address, "to misrepresent my politics and affections; to wound my reputation and feelings; and to weaken, if not entirely destroy the confidence you had been pleased to repose in me."

In the final draft, though, Washington was nothing but magnanimous as he prepared to step down and cede power—*willingly,* unlike those monarchs with whom he had been so unfairly compared.

He would leave the endless squabbling to future generations.

---

* Martha Washington, who blamed her husband's declining health on the relentless attacks he endured, had a particular hatred for Jefferson. The two worst days of her life, she reportedly said, were when the president died—and when Jefferson came to Mount Vernon to offer his condolences.

JULY 7, 1938

The Not-So-Great Dadsby: Fitzgerald Disses His Daughter

"To sum up: what you have done to please me or make me proud
is practically negligible since the time you made yourself
a good diver at camp . . . When I do not feel you are 'going
somewhere,' your company tends to depress me
for the silly waste and triviality involved."
—*Acclaimed novelist F. Scott Fitzgerald, in a July 7, 1938, letter
to his 16-year-old daughter, Frances. (No role model he,
the disapproving pop was also a notorious drunk.)*

JULY 8, 1971

Chicken Pox Colonel Sanders Delivers a Middle Finger Lickin'

"People see me up there doing those commercials
and they wonder how I could ever let such products
bear my name. It's downright embarrassing."
—*Harland Sanders, the founder (and face) of Kentucky Fried Chicken,
in a 1976* New York Times *interview, years after he sold the company*

When Heublein Inc., a Connecticut-based liquor distributor, purchased Kentucky Fried Chicken on July 8, 1971, it also acquired a very cranky Colonel Sanders—the white-maned, white-suited octogenarian whose instantly recognizable features and top-secret spice recipe were the very fabric of the chain he had established nearly two decades before. He no longer controlled the company, but the Colonel (an honorary title awarded in Kentucky) remained its paid ambassador—and, it turned out, Heublein's biggest headache.

The living icon took every opportunity to criticize the liquor conglomerate. At one point Colonel Sanders even sued the company for putting his name on what he saw as substandard menu items: "The damn SOBs don't know anything but peddling booze," Sanders said of Heublein's executives. "And they sure as hell don't know a damn thing about good food."

To be sure, the quality of the once prized product had declined under Heublein's stewardship—and Sanders resented it. "It's my face that's shown on that box of chicken and in the advertising," he fumed. "It's me that people recognize, and they stop me everywhere I go to complain." The fraught relationship between the fastidious founder and the cocktail company seemingly indifferent to what had made his food so special emerged in a *New York Times* piece published in September 1976, when Colonel Sanders and a reporter visited a Kentucky Fried Chicken outlet in New York City.

The Colonel, celebrating his 86th birthday, popped into the restaurant's kitchen for a spur-of-the-moment inspection. "That's much too black," he informed the manager after observing a vat of frying chicken. "It should be golden brown. You're frying for 12 minutes—that's six minutes too long. What's more, your frying fat should have been changed a week ago. That's the worst fried chicken I've ever seen."

When the uncompromising Colonel demanded to see how the franchise was preparing its mashed potatoes with gravy, the spuds fared little better. As the manager started to explain Step 1—mix boiling water into instant powdered potatoes—the Colonel cut him off: "And then you have wallpaper paste," he said. "Next suppose you add some of this brown gravy stuff and then you have sludge.

"There's no way anyone can get me to swallow those potatoes," he said after tasting some. "And this cole slaw. This cole slaw! They just won't listen to me. It should he chopped, not shredded, and it should be made with Miracle Whip. Anything else turns gray. And there should be nothing in it but cabbage. No carrots!"

Having trashed the manager's entire operation, the Colonel tried to reassure the stunned man. "Well, it's not your fault," he said. "You're just working for a company that doesn't know what it's doing."

For a corporation presumably accustomed to the Colonel's persistent pecking, Heublein was caught with its public-relations pants down. Informed by the *Times* of the exchange in the New York restaurant, a PR director seemed to validate everything that Sanders had complained about: "We're very grateful to have the Colonel around to keep us on our toes, but he is a purist and his standards were all right when he was operating just a few stores . . . The Colonel has very high standards of personal conduct and for his products, but we need wider parameters to adapt to the real-life world."

In other words, when it comes to tasty chicken, we couldn't give a flying cluck.

JULY 9, 2002

Put to the Testes, Part 4:
Taking the Ball by the Horns

The myth of the bullring is endlessly alluring: man and beast engaged in the primal struggle between life and death. Yet everyone knows there's nothing noble about this rigged contest. The bull almost invariably comes away the loser—taunted and then stabbed to death in a grotesque spectacle that amounts to little more than ritualized animal sacrifice.

Except, that is, on certain occasions—for example, when the matador happened to be Antonio Barrera, who holds the dubious distinction of Most Gored Man in the history of modern bullfighting.

During a less-than-stellar career that ended with his retirement in 2012, Barrera found himself on the wrong end of the horns, or *cuernos,* no fewer than 23 times.

"*Carne de toros,*" some called him—"bulls' meat."

As medical specialists in the field have attested, these bacteria-laden protuberances are uniquely destructive: They can easily snap human bones, tear through muscle and ligaments, and—in what was doubtless Barrera's worst experience of all—rip open a man's scrotum. At a bullfight in Pamplona, Spain, on July 9, 2002, Barrera was rammed in the thigh and hurled through the air, crashing to the sand of the arena floor with a thud. Although the impact disoriented the oft impaled toreador, it sapped his bravado not one bit; he insisted on returning to the ring to finish the kill.

And that's when he got the *cuernos* right in the *cojones.*

Years later, with no apparent irony, Barrera shared this strange sentiment with the makers of the documentary film *Gored:* "I've never had a relationship, even with a woman, as intimate as the one I have with a bull."

JULY 10, 1969

The *Village* Idiot Finds His *Voice*

"The Great Faggot Rebellion"
—*Walter Troy Spencer's description of the Stonewall riots—*
a milestone of the gay rights movement—in a July 10, 1969,
column for the supposedly progressive Village Voice

JULY 11, 969

Sadistic Saint:
The Murderous Olga of Kiev

Olga of Kiev could be called a "super saint"—not simply holy but, according to the Orthodox Church, "equal to the Apostles." That's a pretty lofty label for the vengeance-filled mass murderer who obliterated an entire Slavic tribe in the 10th century.

Yet when Olga was canonized as Russia's first official saint in 1547, that potentially disqualifying episode of genocide was conveniently overlooked; her conversion to Christianity was deemed a more decisive factor. Indeed, the homicidal princess's baptism is considered the first step in the Christianization of what became Russia—a process completed by Olga's grandson (and fellow saint), Vladimir the Great.

"Harbinger of Christianity," wrote Nestor, the renowned 11th-century chronicler, "she was like the morning-star which goes before the sun [Vladimir], like the dawn which proceeds the day. She shone like the moon on a dark night, like a diamond in the mire."

Got it. Now, about that mass slaughter . . .

For Saint Olga, it was all about revenge. A tribe known as the Drevlians had killed her husband, Igor, ruler of Kievan Rus (the realm out of which emerged Russia and Ukraine, among other territories). The contemporary Byzantine annalist Leo the Deacon described how the Drevlians did away with Igor: "They had bent down two birch trees to the prince's feet and tied them to his legs; then they let the trees straighten again, thus tearing the prince's body apart." Ghastly as that demise must have been, it was nothing compared with what Olga had in store for the rebellious tribe that inflicted it. Christlike forgiveness was definitely not part of her plan.

Having murdered Igor, the Drevlians sought to marry Olga to their leader, Prince Mal. When a delegation of 20 tribal leaders arrived to pursue the match, Olga—serving as regent for her young son—welcomed the men. She then had them buried alive. Next she sent word to Prince

Mal that she was prepared to accept his hand and requested that he send his best people to accompany her to his realm. When they arrived, Olga made the men comfortable and offered them hot baths to wash away the grime of their long journey. Exhausted and grateful, the men piled into Olga's bathhouse. She locked its doors and set the place on fire.

As it turned out, Olga's Bathhouse Barbecue was a mere warm-up for the savagery to come. She invited the *still* unwitting Drevlians to a funeral feast at her late husband's tomb. The gracious hostess saw to it that the wine flowed freely. Then, with her guests thoroughly soused, Olga had some five thousand of them butchered and laid siege to their city.

Now comes the point in the story where history and legend elide, as they often do in the lives of the saints. It is said that Olga disposed of the remaining Drevlians with a diabolically clever plan: She announced that all she wanted as tribute from the cowering citizens were pigeons and sparrows from each household. Jubilant at her seeming clemency, the people readily complied. Alas, the birds they produced were immediately weaponized—each fitted with a taper that was lit just as the animals were released. Transformed into flying fireballs, the birds returned to their roosts, setting the town ablaze. And with that, Olga's thirst for vengeance was slaked.

Olga of Kiev died on July 11, 969. The Orthodox faith still celebrates her feast day on that anniversary and recognizes her as the patron saint of widows and religious converts. (But not, oddly enough, of serial killers.)

JULY 12, 1174

Well, Sorreeeee!

Thomas Becket, the temporarily exiled Archbishop of Canterbury, was no doubt amused by a report he received from England in 1166, detailing his sovereign Henry II's latest hissy fit. After all, it could have described the tantrum of a two-year-old: "And the king, flying into his usual temper, flung his cap from his head, pulled off his belt, threw off his cloak and clothes, grabbed the silken coverlet off the couch, and sitting as it might be on a dung heap started chewing pieces of straw."

In another episode several years later, however, the English monarch's notorious fury had far more serious consequences—and not just for Becket, who wound up with his brains splattered on the floor of Canterbury Cathedral after Henry's famously rash remark, "Will no one rid me of this turbulent priest!" (Henry and Becket had been contesting whether monarch or archbishop held ultimate power over the Church in England.) This time the king, too, paid for his lethal fit of pique—with a mortifying penance.

Becket's shocking murder by four hit-man knights, carried out within the sacred confines of his own cathedral, reverberated throughout Christendom. A cult of martyrdom quickly developed around the slain archbishop, who, just two years after his death in 1170, was canonized by Pope Alexander III. Thus King Henry was faced with the dreadful responsibility of having caused the slaughter of a saint, even if inadvertently. Historians disagree on whether Henry's atonement was a public-relations gesture designed to quell near-universal condemnation or an act of genuine remorse.

On July 12, 1174, having traveled within two miles of Canterbury while subsisting on bread and water, Henry dismounted at Harbledown and walked to the chapel of St. Dunstan, just outside the city walls. There the king removed his shoes, donned the rough cloak of the penitent, and, "barefoot and weeping," walked through the 60-foot-high Westgate of Canterbury town. Clad in nothing but his underwear and prostrate before Becket's tomb, Henry allowed himself to be scourged with hundreds of lashes from the bishop, abbot, and monks of Canterbury. For the rest of that day and all through the night, the king remained prone, never responding to the call of nature, and in full view of the pilgrims that he insisted be permitted inside the cathedral. Only after all that—and a vow to restore the Church's ecclesiastical privileges—did the utterly humbled Henry II return to London.

Three and a half centuries later, another hotheaded Henry (the Eighth) avenged his ancestor's penitential disgrace. Having arrogated the power of the Church as his own, the king swooped into Canterbury Cathedral, destroyed Becket's shrine, snatched its precious jewels, and burned the bones of the saint who had caused his mighty forebear to forget himself in such unseemly fashion.

And so concluded this sordid Canterbury tale.

——◆——

JULY 13, 2018

Richie Incognito's Bogus Bully Pulpit

Fresh from an involuntary psychiatric evaluation after hurling a dumbbell at another patron inside a Florida gym, former Miami Dolphins/Buffalo Bills offensive lineman Richie Incognito was named the "first national ambassador" of Boo2Bullying, a Los Angeles–based anti-bullying organization. The announcement, made on July 13, 2018, came nearly five years after Incognito infamously drove his teammate Jonathan Martin to quit the Dolphins and seek mental-health treatment after a vicious two-year harassment campaign detailed in a report commissioned by the NFL.

"Martin was taunted on a persistent basis," the report read, "with sexually explicit remarks about his sister and mother and at times ridiculed with racial insults and other offensive comments."*

Just over a month after his Boo2Bullying appointment, Ambassador Incognito was arrested after an altercation at a funeral home in Scottsdale, Arizona. Seems the newly clement-minded crusader wanted the head of his deceased father cut off for research purposes. He became "upset with staff and began to damage property inside the business and shout at employees," according to a police statement. "At several points during his contact with staff, Incognito threatened to retrieve guns from his vehicle and return to shoot the employees."

---

* The "sexually explicit remarks" and "offensive comments" were specified throughout the report. However, most of them are too vile to cite as examples.

Apparently you can't take the offensive out of this lineman. Or the offensive lineman out of the game: In 2019 Incognito signed with the Oakland Raiders.

———◆———

Put to the Testes, Part 5: Liberté, Egalité—Ow-ee!

The fall of the Bastille prison-fortress in Paris on July 14, 1789, kicked off the French Revolution. It was also the day when the Bastille's governor, Bernard-René Jourdan de Launay, administered a more intimate assault—a testicular strike that resulted in his savage slaughter and the kind of grotesque display for which France would become infamous.

De Launay had been beaten and bloodied since surrendering the Bastille earlier in the day. Weary of the ordeal, he cried out to his tormentors, "Let me die!" Yet De Launay still had enough sangfroid in him to land his boot squarely between the legs of a cook named Desnot, who collapsed to the ground, howling in agony. That was all the prompting his frenzied captors required: They fell upon De Launay with knives, swords, and bayonets, stabbing him again and again before finally shooting him.

Then came the coup de grâce.

The murderous mob presented the crotch-compromised Desnot with a sword to decapitate his dead assailant. Instead, Desnot broke out his own pocketknife and began furiously hacking his way through De Launay's neck. When at last the head was separated, the rabble raised it high atop a pike.

"It was a chilling and a horrid sight!" an English witness reported of the ensuing perched head parade. "An idea of savageness and ferocity was impressed on the spectators, and instantly checked those emotions of joy which had before prevailed [with the storming of the Bastille]. Many others, as well as ourselves, shocked and disgusted at this scene, retired immediately from the streets."

Soon enough, the entire city would go nuts.

—◆—

Deranged Liaisons?

Sir Charles Mordaunt returned home to England from a fishing trip in Norway on July 15, 1868—earlier than expected by his wife, Harriet, who was just then hosting the notoriously rakish Prince of Wales. Nothing untoward was immediately evident—Lady Mordaunt was merely showing the future king Edward VII (known as "Bertie" to his family) her pair of fine white carriage ponies. But Sir Charles, a member of Parliament, was rightly suspicious and utterly infuriated, for the prince was a professional playboy. Harriet, too, had provoked whispers regarding her virtue.

With the specter of cuckoldry looming over him, Sir Charles lost it. Grabbing his wife by the wrist after Bertie's hasty departure, he dragged her along to her prized ponies and shot the animals dead before her eyes.

Seven months after Bertie's pop-in, the real troubles began when Lady Mordaunt gave birth to a baby girl. No scandal attended the delivery, but Harriet created one as soon as she noticed a discharge from the child's eyes. She became convinced that the infant had contracted venereal disease from the father—who, she declared in a distraught confession, was most certainly *not* Sir Charles. She suspected it was Lowry Cole, the Earl of Enniskillen, just one of the men (among them the Prince of Wales) she admitted to having entertained behind her husband's back, "often and in open day."

A sensational divorce trial followed, during which Bertie was compelled to appear as a witness. It was a humiliating ordeal for the heir to the throne—just as Sir Charles intended it to be. Mordaunt "has shown such a spirit of vindictiveness agst me—& such a bad spirit," the prince wrote to Queen Victoria, later adding: "He took care to mention my name so often,—& in order to compromise me in every way—that I fear I have no other alternative but to come forward and clear myself of the imputations wh[ich] he has cast upon me."

Whether the Prince of Wales ever bedded Harriet Mordaunt remains uncertain. His private letters to her, for example, betray nothing suspicious. Historians largely agree, however, that Bertie almost certainly conspired to have her declared insane, rendering her confession of adultery with him the mere ravings of a lunatic. It was enough to legally prohibit her testimony in court and thus vindicate the heir's vigorous denial. Yet it also resulted in the poor woman's confinement for the rest of her life.

Perhaps she indeed had a mental illness—would a sane person smear her feces on the wall?—but Harriet left no doubt as to whom she blamed for her troubles. Hurling a cup of tea at a portrait of the prince, she screamed: "That has been the ruin of me! You have been the curse of my life, damn you."

JULY 16, 1830

O-bitch-uary, Part 2: *Times* to Dis-member the Legacy of a Monarch

"The truth is—and it speaks volumes about the man—that there was never an individual less regretted by his fellow-creatures than this deceased King. What eye has wept for him? What heart has heaved one throb of unmercenary sorrow? . . . If George the Fourth ever had a friend—a devoted friend—in any rank of life, we protest that the name of him or her has not yet reached us."

—The Times *of London's obituary of Britain's George IV, published on July 16, 1830, one day after he died*

The phrase "late and unlamented"* might have been coined to describe England's self-centered and dissolute King George IV, who blocked his own wife from attending his 1820 coronation. Citizens genuinely grieving were scarce on the ground at his funeral a decade later: According to one eyewitness, "the whole demeanour of the people betokened rather an inclination to be joyous and merry than mournful and sad . . . We did not hear any one word of praise of his late Majesty, nor one syllable of regret."

JULY 17, 1845

Broken Bondage:
Dolley Madison's Antebellum Bummer

Dolley Madison was fed up. The summer heat was bothering the former first lady, who was then residing in Washington, D.C., almost 30 years after her husband's presidency and nine years after his death. Worse, according to Mrs. Madison, her slave Paul Jennings was acting downright impertinent.

Dolley's summer snit was expressed in a letter she wrote on July 17, 1845, to John Payne Todd—her alcoholic, ne'er-do-well son from her first marriage. In it she boasted that she had been so gracious as to grant Jennings "the privilege of 2 or 3 weeks to visit his family—when he was to have returned & entered upon his duties again." Yet for some mysterious reason, she went on, Jennings had neglected to return promptly to human bondage: "It was of importance to me that he shd. have been punctual, but he has not appeared or written an apology—of course he will lose the best place and his mistress' convenient resources."

---

* Contrast this to the national outpouring of grief upon the death of the king's daughter and heir, Charlotte of Wales; see February 13.

The "convenient resources" to which the chronically impecunious Dolley referred was presumably the money she received from renting Jennings out to James K. Polk, whose residence—the White House—was just down the street. The same executive abode, incidentally, whose treasures the impudent Paul Jennings had helped Mrs. Madison rescue when the British came calling with torches in 1814.*

JULY 18, 1926

Valentino's "Pink Powder Puff" Huff

"A powder vending machine! In a men's washroom!
Homo Americanus! Why didn't someone quietly drown
Rudolph Guglielmo, alias Valentino, years ago? . . . Do women like
the type of 'man' who pats pink powder on his face in a public
washroom and arranges his coiffure in a public elevator? . . .
Hollywood is the national school of masculinity. Rudy, the beautiful
gardener's boy, is the prototype of the American male."
—Chicago Tribune *editorial, headlined*
"Pink Powder Puffs," published July 18, 1926

I talian-born screen idol Rudolph Valentino was undeniably handsome—a bit *too* handsome, some said. Maybe even . . . pretty?

While women swooned over the young actor's dark, brooding looks, some men were creeped out by the makeup and eyeliner he wore in films such as *The Sheik*. Among them, presumably, was the anonymous *Chicago Tribune* editorial writer, who questioned Valentino's masculinity while railing against the installation of a face-powder dispenser in a North Side

---

* Once famed orator Daniel Webster secured his freedom, Jennings did go back to Mrs. Madison—not in servitude, but to lend his ever broke former owner a financial helping hand.

men's room. The silent-screen star was left seething over the editorial until the end of his life—which, as it turned out, was just 36 days away.

"He was generally burned up about it," Oscar Doob, publicist for Valentino's scheduled film *The Son of the Sheik,* recalled in a 1938 interview. Sensing opportunity in the star's near-obsessive resentment of the editorial smear, Doob suggested he issue a public challenge to the nameless writer. Accordingly, Valentino posted his dare in the Chicago *Herald-Examiner,* the *Tribune*'s competitor: "To the man (?) who wrote the editorial headed 'Pink Powder Puffs' in Sunday's *Tribune,* I call you in return, a contemptible coward and to prove which of us is a better man, challenge you to a personal test." A boxing ring would be their proving ground.

Valentino was serious enough about the Powder Puff Challenge that he engaged his pal Jack Dempsey to help him train. The boxing great was impressed by the thespian's pugilism. "Valentino's no sissy, believe me," Dempsey told sportswriter and boxing authority Frank "Buck" O'Neil. "In case you're interested, let me tell you he packs a pretty mean punch."

Though skeptical that the long-lashed Sheik was in fighting trim, O'Neil had good-naturedly agreed to meet him in the ring for a few rounds. Valentino greeted reporters on the morning of the bout wearing orchid trunks and a lavender lounging robe—not your standard tough-guy getup. But O'Neil came away convinced. "That boy has a punch like a mule's kick," he told the actor's business manager and close friend, S. George Ullman. "I'd sure hate to have him sore at me."

Despite having showcased his jabs and hooks—except against his editorial antagonist, who never revealed himself—the powder-puff insult clung to Valentino, mostly because he wouldn't shut up about it. Journalist H. L. Mencken, whom the movie star consulted about the matter, sagely suggested that the best course of action might be to simply drop it. Alas, Valentino wouldn't listen. Instead, amid increasing snickers, he continued to publicly wrest with the issue of his masculinity until he succumbed to a burst gastric ulcer on August 23.

"Here was a young man who was living daily the dream of millions of other young men," Mencken wrote shortly after Valentino's death. "Here was one who was catnip to women. Here was one who had wealth and fame. And here was one who was very unhappy."

Unholy Matrimony, Part 4: Sorry, Napoleon—She's Just Not That Into You

Napoleon was smitten—not so much with himself, for once, but with his new bride, Josephine. It was an unruly, intense passion, if the future emperor's avalanche of letters in the wake of the wedding is any indication: obsessive, violent, lustful . . . and, alas, unreciprocated.

Josephine, a widow six years Napoleon's senior, had led a vigorous social life before meeting her second husband, and she did not see their marriage as an impediment to continuing it. Indeed, while her new spouse was amassing glory abroad, Josephine was making a few conquests of her own at home. And everyone but Napoleon seemed to know it.

"My happiness is being near you," he wrote to Josephine after a blissful (for him) reunion in Milan during the summer of 1796, four months into their marriage. "What nights together, *ma bonne amie!* . . . Oh, but surely you must have some faults in your character. Tell me!"

Josephine did not respond to the French general's entreaty to reveal herself. That would be left to others.

Whispers of infidelity had reached Napoleon for some time, but he either dismissed them or buried them. Then, on July 19, 1798, as Napoleon was campaigning in Egypt, the inconvenient truth emerged: His aide-de-camp, Andoche Junot, presented definitive evidence that Josephine was engaged in a flagrant affair with an army officer named Hippolyte Charles.

Upon receiving the news, "the general's pale face had turned paler than ever," reported his private secretary, Louis Antoine Fauvelet de Bourrienne. "His features were suddenly convulsed, a wild look came into his eyes, and several times he struck his head with his fists." "Divorce!" Napoleon cried in an anguished rage. It was the only option to restore his honor. "I can't bear to be the laughingstock of Paris."

That would have been a tolerable humiliation compared with what history actually had in store for the man who would soon become First Consul of the French Republic. In the aftermath of the revelation about Josephine, Napoleon had written a tormented letter to his brother Joseph: "The veil has been completely lifted . . . I am weary of human nature. I need solitude and isolation. Greatness no longer interests me. All feeling in me is dried up. My thirst for glory has faded at the age of twenty-nine. I am completely worn out . . . There is nothing left for me but to think only of myself."

Regrettably for Napoleon and his *amour propre,* that sorrow-laden missive never reached Joseph. Instead, it was intercepted by a British cruiser in the Mediterranean, then later published in London to the mirth of a nation.

—◆—

JULY 20, 1939

Steinbeck Harvests the Grapes of Wrath

John Steinbeck was not savoring the recent success of *The Grapes of Wrath* in the summer of 1939. Instead, he lamented the bitter response he had received from a segment of society represented less than favorably in the novel—his classic account of the fictional Joad family's struggle to survive the twin disasters of the Great Depression and the Dust Bowl—published three months before.

"The vilification out there from the large landowners and bankers is pretty bad," Steinbeck wrote in a letter to his literary agent, Elizabeth Otis, on July 20. "The latest is a rumor started by them that the Okies hate me and have threatened to kill me for lying about them . . . I'm frightened of the rolling might of this damned thing. It is completely out of hand—I mean . . . a kind of hysteria about the book is growing that is not healthy."

Indeed, there had been some sharp resistance from entrenched interests, which took various forms. The book was banned in libraries and actually burned in Kern County, California (ironically, the end point of the Joad family's journey).

Steinbeck probably should have expected the backlash—a critical harvest of seeds he himself had sown. In 1938, while reporting on the miserable conditions migrants endured in California, the author had written to Otis: "I want to put a tag of shame on the greedy bastards who are responsible for this."*

JULY 21, 356 B.C.

Hey, Look at Meeeeeee!

In this fame-obsessed Instagram era, let's not forget that human beings have always been willing to do just about anything for notoriety—from serial killing to simply being a Kardashian. Indeed, there's a fancy name for such desperate attention-seeking, no matter the means: *herostratus,*

---

* Steinbeck's advocacy of the common laborer naturally attracted the attention of the subversive-sniffing FBI director J. Edgar Hoover, who created a fat file on the author and prevented him from getting an Army commission after Pearl Harbor. "Do you suppose you could ask Edgar's boys to stop stepping on my heels?" Steinbeck wrote to Attorney General Livingston Biddle. "They think I'm an enemy alien. It's getting tiresome."

lent by the ancient Greek arsonist who, on July 21, 356 B.C., deliberately set fire to the Temple of Artemis, one of the Seven Wonders of the Ancient World. Herostratus paid with his life for this incendiary moment in the spotlight. But no doubt having his name repeated here—nearly 24 centuries later—made it all worthwhile.

JULY 22, 1969

Act of Con-trition: Not the Place to Gripe About Your Sore Neck

Senator Edward M. Kennedy was received like a rock star when he and his entourage arrived at St. Vincent's Roman Catholic Church in Plymouth, Pennsylvania, on July 22, 1969. Crowds pushed to get a glimpse of the celebrity in their midst. Girls squealed with excitement. Cameras flashed. One woman even carried a sign that read, "Kennedy for President, 1972."

Alas, the demonstration was wildly inappropriate for the occasion. It was the funeral for Mary Jo Kopechne, the young woman the senator had left to drown (or suffocate*) in his submerged vehicle after he drove it off a bridge on Chappaquiddick Island four days earlier.

Lest anyone forget that he, too, had suffered in the accident (from which he escaped but failed to report for the next nine hours), Kennedy sported a neck brace as a pity prop—similar to the way he used his

---

* "It looked as if she were holding herself up to get a last breath of air," recovery diver John Farrar testified in a 1970 inquest into Kopechne's death. "It was a consciously assumed position. . . . She didn't drown. She died of suffocation in her own air void. It took her at least three or four hours to die. I could have had her out of that car twenty-five minutes after I got the call. But he [Kennedy] didn't call."

long-suffering wife, Joan, as an ornament in his portrayal of the bereft family man. Not only did Teddy drag along Joan, who suffered a miscarriage in the aftermath, but he also brought his high-wattage sister-in-law, Ethel, and other members of his inner circle. Seemingly lost amid the hoopla were Mary Jo's grieving parents, about to bury their only child.

Although the neck brace was never seen again after the funeral, Kennedy's sympathy ploys continued. In a televised address three days later, the senator shared with viewers his thoughts as he swam away from the wreck while his doomed passenger struggled in vain to free herself, wondering "whether some awful curse did actually hang over all the Kennedys."

Or was it the Kopechnes?

<hr>

JULY 23, 1863

The Uncivil War, Part 3:
Pickett's Unwelcome Charge

"Would that we had never crossed the Potomac, or that the splendid army which we had on our arrival in Pennsylvania had not been fought in detail. If the charge made by my gallant Virginians on the fatal third of July had been supported, or even if my other two brigades . . . had been with me, we would now, I believe, have been in Washington, and the war practically over."
—*Confederate Maj. Gen. George Pickett, writing on July 23, 1863, in the aftermath of the bloody and futile Confederate charge at the Battle of Gettysburg that popularly bears his name*

Pickett was apparently so bitter and despairing over the staggering defeat and loss of life at Gettysburg that Gen. Robert E. Lee asked him to censor a scathing report he had written on the failed offensive.

"You and your men have crowned yourselves with glory," Lee wrote, "but we have the enemy to fight, and must carefully, at this critical moment, guard against dissensions which the reflections in your report will create. I will therefore suggest that you destroy both copy and original, substituting one confined to casualties merely."

A new report was never prepared, and the original is lost. Nevertheless, Pickett loudly blamed Lee for the disaster. And though Lee had already embraced his failures—"This was all my fault, General Pickett," he said at the time. "Your men did all men could do."—Pickett remained hostile. Col. John S. Mosby, the "Gray Ghost" famed for his lightning raids on Union positions, recalled an "embarrassing" meeting between Pickett and Lee in 1870, well after the war was over. "That old man had my division massacred at Gettysburg," he quoted Pickett saying after Lee left.

Mosby's response: "Well, it made you immortal."

JULY 24, 1915

On Second Thought, Part 9:
In Tippy-Top Shape

"Won't Sink. Won't Burn."
—*An advertisement for the S.S.* Eastland *that was intended to
dispel passenger concerns about the top-heavy steamer's tendency
to list. Alas, on July 24, 1915, the* Eastland *did just that:
While docked on the Chicago River, it rolled onto its port side
and sank, killing 844 passengers and crew.**

---

* In a macabre twist, postcards depicting the horrors of the day sold briskly in the catastrophe's aftermath; some can still be found for sale on various internet sites. What could the sender of such a necrogram possibly have written, though? "Bodies being recovered . . . having a ball."?

"I looked across the river," recalled writer Jack Wood-ford in his autobiography. "As I watched in disoriented stupefaction a steamer large as an ocean liner slowly turned over on its side as though it were a whale going to take a nap. I didn't believe a huge steamer had done this before my eyes, lashed to a dock, in perfectly calm water, in excellent weather, with no explosion, no fire, nothing. I thought I had gone crazy."

JULY 25, 1999

Never Trust Any Festival
Over 30 Years Old

"It was dangerous to be around. The whole scene was scary.
There were just waves of hatred bouncing around the place . . .
To get in, you get frisked to make sure you're not bringing in
any water or food that would prevent you from buying from
their outrageously priced booths. You wallow around in garbage
and human waste. There was a palpable mood of anger."
—*Kurt Loder of MTV, quoted by* USA Today, *on Woodstock '99*

Far from the bucolic fields of Max Yasgur's farm, at a toxic, treeless Superfund site one hundred miles away in Rome, New York, organizers tried to re-create the groovy Woodstock vibe of 1969. With the exception of the mud and the sewage, they utterly failed to get themselves—or anyone else, for that matter—back to the garden.

Where the original festival celebrated peace and love, Woodstock 2.0 was stained by gang rapes and looting. Instead of refuge tents to shelter lost children and those who had missed the stage announcement about the brown acid, corporate sponsors set up huts to shill their goods. In 1969, Jimi Hendrix had woken the crowd with his early morning strains of "The Star-Spangled Banner." The 1999 analogue of that slyly patriotic gesture came when Rage Against the Machine saw fit to burn an American flag onstage.

Stewing in 100-degree heat, the crowd picked up on and amplified the aggression incited by Rage and other bands. "Musically and politically," Rob Sheffield reported in *Rolling Stone,* Woodstock '99 was "the triumph of the bullies, with the fighters winning out over the lovers."

The culmination of the three-day debacle came on July 25, when the Red Hot Chili Peppers took the stage as the final act. Candles distributed by a peace group—and intended to be lit during the band's performance of "Under the Bridge"—were instead used to torch nearly everything flammable. "Holy shit, it looks like *Apocalypse Now* out there," singer Anthony Kiedis shouted as Woodstock burned.

Ironically, the conflagration occurred near the end of the Peppers' set, as they honored Hendrix with their cover of his classic "Fire."

❧

JULY 26, 1861

The Uncivil War, Part 4:
Stanton's Bull Run-In With Lincoln

"The dreadful disaster of Sunday can scarcely be mentioned. The imbecility of this administration has culminated in that catastrophe, and irretrievable misfortune and national disgrace are to be added to the ruin of all peaceful pursuits and national bankruptcy as the result of Lincoln's 'running the machine' for five months."

—*Edwin Stanton, former president James Buchanan's attorney general, writing to his ex-boss about Abraham Lincoln, on July 26, 1861, five days after the stunning Union defeat at the Battle of Bull Run*

Less than six months after composing this disparaging letter, Stanton joined the Lincoln administration as secretary of war and grew to admire the president. "There lies the most perfect ruler of men the world has ever seen," Stanton proclaimed at Lincoln's deathbed. "Now he belongs to the ages." It was quite the attitudinal about-face for an administrator who had been in the habit of calling the 16th president "the original gorilla."

O-bitch-uary, Part 3: Mencken Makin' a Mockery of the Dead

"Bryan was a vulgar and common man, a cad undiluted. He was ignorant, bigoted, self-seeking, blatant and dishonest . . . He seemed only a poor clod like those around him, deluded by a childish theology, full of an almost pathological hatred of all learning, all human dignity, all beauty, all fine and noble things. He was a peasant come home to the dung-pile. Imagine a gentleman, and you have imagined everything that he was not."
—*H. L. Mencken, writing about William Jennings Bryan in the* Baltimore Evening Sun *of July 27, 1925. Bryan, a former secretary of state and three-time Democratic nominee for president (see November 3), had died just a day earlier.*

The Road Too Often Traveled: Another Crack in the Melting Pot

"The committee can not be unmindful of the tone of public opinion, voiced by the press of our country, as to the turning loose in the midst of our honest laborers and intelligent and religious people the hordes of vicious, depraved, criminal, and pauper elements of humanity now permitted to invade our land. We can not shut our eyes to the growth of crime, pauperism, and insanity that is traceable from foreign countries to our prisons, almshouses, hospitals, and insane asylums."

—*Report by the Select Committee on Immigration and Naturalization, submitted to Congress on July 28, 1892—just another in the long history of assaults upon [pick a scorned "alien" from any era] yearning to be free*

———◆———

JULY 29, 1914

Unholy Matrimony, Part 5:
A Brilliant Way to Ruin the Mood

Albert Einstein was not just upset; he was bawling. It was July 29, 1914, the day the revered scientist's wife, Mileva Marić, boarded a Zurich-bound train with their two sons and left his life forever. "It was the most wrenching personal moment for a man who took perverse pride in avoiding personal moments," wrote Einstein biographer Walter Isaacson. "For all his reputation of being inured to deep human attachments, he had been madly in love with Mileva Marić and bonded to his children."

No genius was required, however, to see why the marriage failed: Einstein, the master of relativity, was a moron when it came to relationships.

Physics was Einstein's mistress—as was his first cousin, Elsa—

and that left little room for his spouse. "I am starved for love," Mileva wrote, "and I almost believe wicked science is guilty." But rather than attempting to relieve (or at least understand) her emotional deprivation, Einstein dismissed his wife as "an unfriendly, humorless creature who . . . undermines others' joy of living through her mere presence," adding that she "gets nothing out of life" and is "the most sour of sourpusses."

By July 1914, the marriage was in shambles. It was then that Einstein conceived a brilliant plan to salvage it, detailed in the following letter sent to Mileva on July 18:

Conditions.

A. You will make sure

1. my clothes and laundry are to be kept in good order;
2. that I will receive my three meals regularly *in my room.*
3. that my bedroom and study are kept neat, and especially my desk is left for *my use only.*

B. You will renounce all personal relations with me insofar as they are not completely necessary for social reasons. Specifically, you will forego

1. my sitting at home with you;
2. my going out or traveling with you.

C. You will obey the following points in relations with me:

1. you will not expect any intimacy with me, nor will you reproach me in any way;
2. you will stop talking to me if I request it;
3. you will leave my bedroom or study immediately without protest if I request it.

D. You will undertake not to belittle me in front of our children, either through words or behavior.

Less than two weeks later, Mileva Marić departed for good.

JULY 30, 1996

Tarnished Jewell: *The Atlanta Journal*'s Scorning Edition

On July 30, 1996, *The Atlanta Journal* took a bona fide hero and twisted him into some sort of psychotic Barney Fife: a glory-seeking goofball, willing to maim and kill to reap acclaim as the savior from what he himself had wrought.

"Richard Jewell, 33, a former law enforcement officer, fits the profile of the lone bomber," the newspaper authoritatively wrote of the security guard who, just three days earlier, had spotted an explosive-laden knapsack during the Atlanta Olympic Games and immediately reported it to the Georgia Bureau of Investigation. He then helped evacuate the area before the device detonated, saving hundreds of lives. (The blast killed one person—a second later died of a heart attack—and injured 111 others.)

Acting on an FBI tip that Jewell was a suspect in the explosion, the *Journal* caricaturized him as the very picture of the self-important and overzealous rent-a-cop—"a frustrated white man who is a former police officer, member of the military or police 'wannabe' who seeks to become a hero."

As it emerged, that "profile" was unsubstantiated, and the paper's charge that Jewell had sought out the media attention he received in the bombing's aftermath was a lie. As Jewell later told CBS's Mike Wallace, the *Journal* report—printed in an "Extra" edition beneath the screaming headline "FBI SUSPECTS 'HERO' GUARD MAY HAVE PLANTED BOMB"—"pretty much started the whirlwind" that followed.

During a relentless media maelstrom, the hapless security guard, lauded at first, suddenly became a much derided suspect, tried and found guilty in the court of public—or at least newspaper—opinion. Jewell was portrayed as a loser who lived with his mother, had no friends, and took his pseudo-law-enforcement duties way too seriously—"the Una-doofus," as Jay Leno called him on *The Tonight Show,* referencing murderous "Unabomber" Ted Kaczynski.

Journal columnist Dave Kindred even went so far as to compare Jewell to Atlanta's infamous child serial killer, Wayne Williams: "Once upon a terrible time, federal agents came to this town to deal with another suspect who lived with his mother. Like this one, that suspect was drawn to the blue lights and sirens of police work. Like this one, he became famous in the aftermath of murder. His name was Wayne Williams. This one is Richard Jewell."

"The news media just jumped on it like piranha on a bleeding cow," Jewell told *The New York Times*. And for three months his bones were picked clean, until finally the FBI exonerated him—inexcusably late, given how obvious it was from the beginning that the heroic guard could not have committed the atrocious crime. (Domestic terrorist Eric Robert Rudolph was later found to have planted the bomb.)

The torment he endured while trapped in the media frenzy may have dissipated, but not the cloud over his reputation. "There will not only always be a shadow, but I think there's going to be a deep hole and river to cross everywhere I go," Jewell (who died in 2007) told the *Times*.

"There will be a nonhealing scar that is always affixed to my name. I don't know if that will ever be cleared up."

JULY 31, 1942

When General MacArthur
Proved Himself a Petty Officer

"MacArthur could never see another sun, or even a moon
for that matter, in the heavens, as long as *he* was the sun."
—*Dwight D. Eisenhower*

Gen. Douglas MacArthur was safe and snug at his new headquarters in Australia—enjoying Brisbane's refreshing breezes and basking in the acclaim heaped upon him by an adoring American public—when, on July 31, 1942, he ruthlessly backstabbed his loyal subordinate, Gen. Jonathan Wainwright. The latter had been left in command of the Philippines after MacArthur's evacuation less than five months earlier. Now, in the aftermath of the islands' surrender, Wainwright was a captive of the Japanese.

By all accounts, Wainwright's efforts to stave off the enemy attack had been heroic. Thanks to MacArthur's poor planning, however, Wainwright's troops were starving, diseased, and ill equipped. (MacArthur's strategic vision, historian John C. McManus noted, "was, at best, based on overweening optimism and, at worst, in conflict with reality.")

Wainwright faced two options: Surrender, or subject his men to mass slaughter. In choosing to capitulate, the general became the highest-ranking American prisoner of war—sharing with his men all the cruelty, deprivation, and humiliation the Japanese inflicted on their captives. (He was spared the Bataan Death March, however.)

Military leaders in Washington recognized Wainwright's valor. "In this critical hour I have nothing but praise and admiration for the conduct of yourself and your troops in handling a desperate situation," Secretary of War Henry Stimson had written at the peak of the crisis, echoing numerous reports of the besieged general's extraordinary fortitude. But when Army Chief of Staff Gen. George Marshall proposed awarding Wainwright the Medal of Honor, the response he got from MacArthur in Australia was a flak burst of stunning betrayal.

"The citation proposed does not . . . represent the truth," MacArthur wired Marshall. "As a relative matter award of the Medal of Honor to General Wainwright would be a grave injustice to a number of other general officers of practically equally responsible positions who not only distinguished themselves by fully as great personal gallantry . . . but exhibited powers of leadership and inspiration to a degree greatly superior to that of General Wainwright, thereby contributing much more to the stability of the command and to the successful conduct of the campaign." MacArthur concluded by insinuating, but not specifying, a defect in Wainwright's character: "It would be a grave mistake which later on might well lead to embarrassing repercussions to make this award."

Marshall was shocked by the reply. (MacArthur's "animosity toward Wainwright was tremendous," he later wrote.) His deputy, Maj. Gen. Joseph McNarney, added this note on the medal memorandum: "Personally, I question Gen. MacArthur's motives . . . I also question Gen. MacArthur's judgment where matters of personal prestige are concerned." Yet despite the two men's skepticism and dismay, the effort to honor Wainwright was temporarily shelved.

Historians have been equally galled. "It was MacArthur at his vindictive worst," Cole Kingseed wrote in *Old Glory Stories: American Combat Leadership in World War II.* And in his *Americans at War,* Stephen Ambrose described MacArthur's treachery as one of "the pettiest acts of his career."

What prompted the spite? Some believe MacArthur was genuinely appalled by Wainwright's surrender, notwithstanding his role in creating the circumstances that contributed to it. Others speculate it was his reluctance to share even a dribble of glory, to dim for one moment the heroic halo he had placed over his own head.

MacArthur himself had received the Medal of Honor the previous April—a cynical exercise designed less to acknowledge the general's bravery than to counter any enemy perception that he had fled the Philippines in fear. (In fact, he had been ordered to evacuate.) Perhaps it was just too much for him that a subordinate should be similarly recognized. "Poor Wainwright!" Eisenhower noted in his diary the day after the surrender at Corregidor. "He did the fighting . . . [MacArthur] got such glory as the public could find."

After three years in captivity—tormented not only by the Japanese, but also by the belief that his countrymen scorned him for having surrendered the Philippines—Wainwright was finally released at the end of the war and taken to see MacArthur at the Hotel New Grand in Japan. Always lanky—his nickname was "Skinny"—Wainwright was now emaciated. "His eyes were sunken," MacArthur would recall. "His hair was white and his skin looked like old shoe leather."

The two men tearfully hugged, but MacArthur's was a viper's embrace—disguising the contempt he still felt for Wainwright and his decision to raise the white flag at Corregidor. "I ordered them to keep on fighting, and Skinny ordered them to surrender," MacArthur had recently confided to Gen. Robert Eichelberger. "It was not a very creditable thing."

Yet it was more than enough for Wainwright to finally receive the Medal of Honor that MacArthur had successfully sabotaged three years before. President Truman surprised the general with a ceremony in the White House Rose Garden. As the president read the phrase "above and beyond the call of duty," Wainwright "suddenly realized when I heard these magic words that this was the citation for the . . . Medal of Honor . . . Nothing can supplant in my mind that afternoon in the garden of the White House."

Not even the megalomaniacal machinations of Douglas MacArthur.

August

———◆———

Burned by an Old Flame:
Cleveland's Bad Rap

Other than the pathetic Indians—then in the midst of a record-breaking losing baseball season—the woes Cleveland, Ohio, faced were relatively unexceptional in the summer of 1969. Plenty of American cities were likewise starting to earn their "rust belt" label. And given the town's world-class art museum and orchestra—to say nothing of its exceptional Gilded Age architecture—Clevelanders could take justifiable pride in where they lived.

But then, on August 1, 1969, *Time* magazine kicked Cleveland in the crotch. The newsweekly ran a contrived feature that made the city a national laughingstock and saddled it with an enduring reputation as "the Mistake by the Lake."

"Some River!" harrumphed *Time* in describing Cleveland's Cuyahoga, which bisects the city and empties into Lake Erie. "Chocolate-brown, oily, bubbling with subsurface gases, it oozes rather than flows."

After that poetic slap, the magazine went for the city's jugular: "[The river] is also—literally—a fire hazard," referencing the fact that flames had erupted on the Cuyahoga's oily surface the previous June 22. An accompanying photo of the blazing river added punch to the story, and the ultimate blow to Cleveland's reputation.

There was just one problem, though: That damning photo *Time* editors used was nearly two decades old!

Because the June fire had been minor, doused within 20 minutes, no actual photo of it existed. Indeed, it had been a nonstory until *Time* came along. River fires had long been routine in industrial towns such as Buffalo, Detroit, and Chicago—the by-products of unregulated effluents. By 1969, however, Cleveland was already working toward a cleaner Cuyahoga and—ironically—the relatively insignificant June eruption would be the last to occur on that waterway. Thus, the magazine's decision to use a far more dramatic photo from a 1952 conflagration—essentially moving the "news" nearly two decades forward in *Time*.

And with that bit of deception, Cleveland became synonymous with flammable sludge.*

Sure, the fire contributed to the passage of the Clean Water Act of 1972— obviously a good thing—but poor Cleveland suffered inordinate ridicule in its aftermath. Johnny Carson, for one, had a field day at the city's expense. "What's the closest you can come to a week in hell?" he asked. "A day in Cleveland." The city also won the dubious "Flying Fickle Finger of Fate" award from the immensely popular TV series *Laugh-In*. The overhyped blaze even inspired Randy Newman to write a satirical song, "Burn On."

"To me, it was the first great Cleveland punch line," Joe Hannum, co-founder of Cleveland Comedy Fest, said of the fire in 2009. "It is kind of analogous to the first car that rolled off the assembly line in Detroit or the first oil well that anybody struck in Texas. It led to many, many other Cleveland punch lines—and one of our greatest exports, which is our comedy and sense of humor."

---

* Three years after the Cuyahoga River fire and the unfortunate *Time* article, Cleveland was subjected to another strange event that, given the city's combustible history, may be viewed as either a cruel twist or a hilarious postscript. On October 16, 1972, at a convention of the American Society for Metals, Mayor Ralph Perk began to cut the opening ribbon—a metal ribbon—with a blowtorch. Sparks flew as Perk wielded the instrument against the titanium. And the mayor's hair—slathered with product applied by a barber earlier that day—was instantly ignited.

On Second Thought, Part 10:
Wa-a-ay Auto Focus

"With over 50 foreign cars already on sale here, the Japanese auto industry isn't likely to carve out a big slice of the U.S. market."
—Business Week, *August 2, 1968*

Encouraging a Catastrophe:
A Grey Day Indeed

"The lamps are going out all over Europe.
We shall not see them lit again in our lifetime."
—*British foreign secretary Sir Edward Grey, on the eve of the War to [supposedly] End All Wars, August 3, 1914*

He was a man of peace, a quiet gentleman who preferred fly-fishing and the simple pleasures of rural life to the tumult and roar of politics. But now he had to coax his countrymen into a war that would prove to be one of the most devastating in the history of mankind.

On the afternoon of August 3, 1914, with the rest of Europe scrambling madly toward conflict, British Foreign Secretary Sir Edward Grey stood calmly before a divided House of Commons and explained why Britain was morally obligated to join what he knew would be a horrific calamity. That very day, Germany had declared war on France—and was poised to invade neutral Belgium.

Despite having worked tirelessly to maintain the peace, as Grey assured the House he had, war was now on Britain's doorstep. To step into the coming conflagration was surely odious, Grey conceded. But to stand by and do nothing, he argued, was an even worse prospect—a betrayal not only of the nation's interests but of its honor. As Grey reminded the assembled lawmakers, Britain was tied to France by friendship and shared interests, and bound to Belgium by treaty: "If we [said], 'We will have nothing whatever to do with this matter,'. . . we should, I believe, sacrifice our respect and good name and reputation before the world."

An hour and 15 minutes later, when the foreign minister concluded his speech, the House erupted in "a hurricane of applause," as Prime Minister H. H. Asquith's wife, Margaret, described the response. "Grey's speech was very wonderful," wrote Lord Hugh Cecil, "I think in the circumstances one may say the greatest speech delivered in our time or for a very long period."

Yet for all his success in galvanizing the House into action, Grey was feeling far from triumphant. "I hate war," he cried afterward, slamming his fists on a table, "I hate war!"

Later that evening, as he watched a lamplighter going about his business, Sir Edward uttered his now immortal line about the dimming lights of Europe. The next day, Britain was at war. "Thus the efforts of a lifetime go for nothing," Grey, his eyes filling with tears, said to the U.S. ambassador.

"I feel like a man who has wasted his life."

------◆------

AUGUST 4, 2008

On Second Thought, Part ii:
Better Toss That Salad!

"It's a bit embarrassing but there have been no reports
of any casualties. Please do pass on my apologies."
—*British celebrity chef Antony Worrall Thompson in an August 4, 2008,
statement to reporters after suggesting in the August issue of*

Healthy and Organic Living *magazine that henbane,*
a poisonous plant, is "great in salads"

One thing was for certain: It was a lot more than a simple factual error. Here's how Thompson attempted to explain away his potentially lethal advice: "I was thinking of a wild plant with a similar name—fat hen, not henbane," he clarified. In other words, the one that *doesn't* cause hallucinations, convulsions, vomiting, and in extreme cases, death.

Fat hen or henbane, we'll just call Thompson a birdbrain.

AUGUST 5, 1633

Momsters, Part 7: Good Grief! Will You Give It a Rest!

"Since We, God pity Us, were so rarely granted the pleasure of enjoying the living presence of His Majesty, Our adored, dearest master and spouse, of blessed memory, it should at least be granted to Us to stay near His royal corpse and so draw comfort in Our miserable existence."
—*Maria Eleonora, widowed consort of Sweden's King Gustavus Adolphus, February 1633*

Nothing like curling up with Mother for comfort—unless Dad's rotting corpse happens to be in the same room, with his heart encased in a reliquary hanging over the bed. Such was the situation seven-year-old Queen Christina of Sweden was forced to endure thanks to her morbidly neurotic mother, Maria Eleonora.

King Gustavus Adolphus—killed in the Battle of Lützen during the Thirty Years' War—had already been dead eight months when, on August 5, 1633, his decaying body was brought to Maria Eleonora's private castle in Nyköping. There, little Queen Christina, who had been left in the care of an aunt for well over a year, was reunited with her dead father and her excessively grieving mother.

Maria Eleonora had never shown much regard for Christina, reportedly exclaiming at her birth: "Instead of a son, I am given a daughter, dark and ugly, with a great nose and black eyes. Take her from me, I will not have such a monster!" Now, however, the dowager queen fawned over the little girl, who was growing up to be "the living image of the late King," in Maria Eleonora's words.

"I kissed her," Christina later wrote of the reunion, "and she drowned me with tears, and nearly suffocated me in her arms." That flood of maternal attention was just the beginning of the tiny monarch's woes.

Maria Eleonora transformed Nyköping into a virtual mortuary upon the arrival of her dearly departed, whose pearl-adorned coffin was left unsealed to give her ample opportunity to caress his remains. The walls were draped in black, and all light from the windows was blocked by sable.

At first, the overwrought widow was content to have Gustavus Adolphus rest in the castle's Green Hall. But then Maria Eleonora decided she just had to have him in her bedroom—where, she insisted, she and Christina would sleep as well. Nothing like this cozy setting, under the watchful gaze of her father's extracted heart, to raise the spirits of a seven-year-old. Except, perhaps, the spectacle of dwarves and hunchbacks dancing in the flickering candlelight—the one "amusement" Maria Eleonora allowed at Nyköping.

All this, Queen Christina understatedly wrote, was "more insupportable to me than the death of the King, for which I had long been consoled."

And she wasn't the only one disturbed by Maria Eleonora's ghoulish behavior. The Estates General of Sweden sent a petition to the Clerical Estate in 1635, inquiring "whether a Christian could in good conscience apply for and be granted the right to open the graves and the coffins of their dead and gaze at and fondle their bodies in the belief that through these acts they would receive some comfort and solace in their state of great heart-rendering sorrow and distress."

Finally, in June 1634—nearly two years after the king's death—Maria Eleonora at last allowed her overripe husband to be put to rest in an elaborate burial ceremony. Describing her mother's behavior on the occasion, Queen Christina noted laconically: "She carried out her role of mourning to perfection."

※

AUGUST 6, 1945

Gilded Killed It: How a van Gogh Became a Casualty of War

Vincent van Gogh's vision for "Six Sunflowers"—the second of the series he painted in Arles, France, during the summer of 1888— extended beyond the colors on the canvas to the frame itself. "A decoration in which harsh or broken yellows will burst against various BLUE backgrounds, from the palest Veronese to royal blue," would be, he wrote, "framed with thin laths painted in orange lead," creating an effect like that "of *stained-glass windows* of a Gothic church." As van Gogh expert Martin Bailey told the BBC in 2013, "He saw this orange frame as an integral piece of the artwork."

Alas, Koyata Yamamoto, who purchased "Six Sunflowers" in 1920, did not.

The wealthy Japanese cotton merchant slapped an ornately gilded frame around the masterpiece—a decision that would contribute to the painting's ultimate destruction on August 6, 1945.

That day, when the first atomic bomb was dropped on Hiroshima, a separate American attack with conventional bombs was carried out over Ashiya, an affluent town 150 miles to the east. As the resulting fires reached Yamamoto's residence there, the van Gogh hanging over his sofa proved too cumbersome to move—and that heavy added frame didn't help. "Six Sunflowers" was consumed in the flames and lost forever—remembered now only in the very few photographs of it ever taken.

In Spain, 20th-Century Inquisitors

On August 7, 1936, Jesus was symbolically executed just outside Madrid.

A band of radical insurgents took aim at a large statue of Christ, dedicated to the Sacred Heart, and riddled it with bullets. Then, having carried out this blasphemous desecration, they blew the monument to bits. It was perhaps the most jarring representation of the violent antireligious frenzy sweeping Spain at a time when human decency was reduced to rubble and evil viciously unleashed.

The Inquisition and other atrocities the Catholic Church committed in Spain have long been notorious, with images of autos-da-fé and burnings at the stake embedded in the popular imagination. Less well known, however, are the horrors inflicted upon the Spanish clergy in the 20th century—when civil war and revolution simultaneously erupted in the summer of 1936. "At no time in the history of Europe, or even perhaps of the world, has so much passionate hatred of religion and all its works been shown," wrote historian Hugh Thomas, who chronicled the barbarous crusade in his book *The Spanish Civil War.*

Rampaging mobs of anarchists and other extremists took to the streets and, in the murderous spirit of Grand Inquisitor Torquemada himself, slaughtered some seven thousand clergymen. "Many of these crimes were accompanied by a frivolous, sadistic cruelty," Thomas wrote, perhaps understatedly. Bulls gored priests before roaring crowds, with the prelates' ears then lopped off in the tradition of the toreadors. Many were burned or buried alive; one endured a mock crucifixion, complete with a crown of thorns.

In addition to those monstrosities visited upon the living, the dead were subjected to some particularly grotesque defilements. Across Spain, long-deceased nuns were dragged from their graves and propped up on city sidewalks, where passersby could mock and jeer their moldering remains.

"They dug up the nuns' corpses, and displayed the skeletons and mummies," recalled Maria Ochoa, then a 13-year-old schoolgirl, in Ronald Fraser's *Blood of Spain: An Oral History of the Spanish Civil War*. "I found that quite amusing; so did all the kids. When we got bored looking at the same ones in my neighborhood, we'd go to another barrio to see the ones they'd dug up there. In the Passeig de Sant Joan [a Barcelona avenue], they were exhibited in the street. Not for very long, but long enough for us to go and look. We kids would make comments about the different corpses—how this one was well-preserved and that one decomposed, this one older; we got a lot of amusement out of it all."

And with those children skipping merrily among the cadavers, the evil that had crept into Spain passed beyond saturation.

AUGUST 8, 1925

When the Nation's Capital Went to Sheet: The Endless Klan Parade

It was a grand parade down America's Main Street: a celebration of Mom, apple pie, and . . . white power! Klaliffs, Kludds, Klokards, and other awkwardly titled members of the reconstituted Ku Klux Klan—some 35,000 in all, resplendent in their white sheets, American flags unfurled—marched down Pennsylvania Avenue on August 8, 1925, in one of the largest assemblies the nation's capital had ever witnessed.

"The parade was grander and gaudier, by far than anything the wizards had prophesied," wrote renowned journalist H. L. Mencken, who observed the twisted festivities. "It was longer, it was thicker, it was higher in tone. I stood in front of the Treasury for two hours watching the legions pass. They marched in lines of eighteen or twenty, solidly shoulder to shoulder. I retired for refreshment and was gone an hour. When I got back Pennsylvania Avenue was still a mass of white from the Treasury down to the foot of Capitol Hill—a full mile of Klansmen and their ladies."

Unlike their hooded predecessors of the previous century, these Klansmen and Klanswomen were happy to show their faces (though still topped by the traditional white dunce caps) to the cheering crowds. They were in the mainstream now, headquartered at the center of power in Washington, D.C., and embraced by millions since their reemergence a decade earlier as an organization dedicated to the preservation of white, Protestant America. Indeed, many considered the Klan as American as Uncle Sam—assuming, of course, that Uncle Sam was a domestic terrorist determined to suppress blacks, Catholics, Jews, flappers, bootleggers, and purveyors of birth control. (And that he didn't mind homicide as means to an end.)

"Phantom-like hosts of the Ku Klux Klan spread their white robe over the nation's most historic thoroughfare yesterday," *The Washington Post* reported of the mass demonstration—or "the weird procession," as the newspaper called it. The same day the *Post*'s coverage ran, a horde of Klansmen capped off the weekend fun—marred only by scores of the hooded being felled by heatstroke, and a torrential downpour on the grounds of the Washington Monument—by staging one of their signature rituals directly across the Potomac River from the capital: They erected an 80-foot-high cross and lit it. But in a concession to the modern era, the Klan used electric lightbulbs, not flames, to illuminate the crucifix.

A Short Story, Heavier Than Air

"We must fly and fall, and fly and fall,
until we can fly without falling."
—*Otto Lilienthal, German glider pilot and notable source
of inspiration for the Wright brothers. On August 9, 1896,
Lilienthal flew and fell—and broke his neck.*

Quinn Sallies Forth

Were she not so easy to dislike, it would be natural to feel some sympathy for Sally Quinn, the D.C. journalist turned self-appointed doyenne of Washington society. After all, few in the public spotlight have endured so many professional mishaps and humiliating comeuppances—any one of which readily qualifies as a Bad Day.

Quinn's career started with a bang when she was hired—with nary a jot of writing experience—by *Washington Post* executive editor Ben Bradlee, who proceeded to have an affair with her, then make her his third wife. Her bitchy Style-section profiles of Washington blowhards and hypocrites became legendary, landing Quinn a plum spot as television's first female co-anchor on the *CBS Morning News*. But in this unfamiliar milieu, the mean-spirited scribe floundered. Wooden, awkward, and incompetent—unclear even on the meaning of the camera's red light—she became an overnight laughingstock.

Relieved of her broadcasting duties in less than six months, Quinn attempted to salvage her dignity with a book recounting her experiences on the show. It was almost as excruciating as her CBS stint, reflecting what would become a hallmark of the rest of Quinn's career: Sally-on-Sally self-promotion. "It's embarrassing to read if you have any sympathy at all for children or fools," a *Kirkus Reviews* writer noted, "but there's a rule for Quinn's kind of stardom—say anything you like about her, but just say something."

The Sally show droned on over the ensuing decades—in print and on television—with Quinn's "Washington insider" decrees on everything from gracious hostessing to political pecking orders. She also furnished the tinder in many a Sally-centric feud—notably the one she sparked with Bill and Hillary Clinton when they blew off one of her parties.

And even when the topic *wasn't* Sally, she managed to make it so. When her husband and son—named Quinn, of course—co-wrote *A Life's Work: Fathers and Sons,* a banner predictably appeared beneath the authors' names on the cover: "WITH OBSERVATIONS BY SALLY QUINN."

Madame Quinn even managed to insinuate herself into the death of Lauren Bacall, tweeting in 2014: "So so sad about the death of Betty Bacall. I almost lost Ben to her, the only acceptable person. As he would say, she was a spectacular dame." This was followed by a self-serving essay in the *Post,* detailing the angst she felt about Bradlee and Bacall's mutual attraction. The first sentence of the ostensible tribute to the film and stage legend: "It was the night on the dunes in Amagansett that nearly did me in."

With so much Sally spewing forth, it was perhaps kismet that Pulitzer Prize–winning *Post* columnist Gene Weingarten would nominate one of her stories, "The Light and the Labyrinth" (starring guess who?), as the worst that ever appeared in Style. But the most ferocious rebukes of all came when she took a turn as a romance novelist. Several scorching reviews of her debut effort, *Regrets Only,* appeared in the press on August 10, 1986. "Judith Krantz could doubtless have carved a better book out of a banana," wrote L. J. Davis in the *Chicago Tribune.* "There is no excuse for a book like this." The headline on the *Orlando Sentinel* review that same day blared a similar note: "There's No Need to Respond Quickly to 'Regrets Only.'"

Undeterred by the critics, Quinn wrote a sequel, which she titled *Happy Endings.* The verdict of *Kirkus Reviews:* It "may actually outperform its predecessor in tedium and sheer unpleasantness."

So, marvel at Quinn's mountain of schadenfreude, but revel in it not, ye who read these words. As she revealed in her 2017 book, *Finding Magic,* our gal Sal throws a mean hex—several of which, she is certain, have resulted in fatalities.

(Hmm . . . might this be the last volume of *Bad Days in History?*)

AUGUST 11, 1963

Flamed by "the Dragon Lady"

"I would clap hands at seeing another monk barbecue show,
for one cannot be responsible for the madness of others."
—*Madame Ngo Dinh Nhu, on the recent self-immolation by
several Buddhist monks protesting severe government repression,
in a letter composed to* The New York Times *on August 11, 1963*

Her parents named her Tran Le Xuan, or "Beautiful Spring,"* but others had uglier epithets for Madame Nhu, official hostess and influential adviser to South Vietnam president Ngo Dinh Diem, her bachelor brother-in-law. President John F. Kennedy referred to the ferocious first lady who all but ruled South Vietnam as "that goddamn bitch," while *The New York Times* dubbed her "Lucrezia Borgia Nhu."

To many others she was simply "the Dragon Lady"—a trite but apt sobriquet for a monstrous woman who encouraged the persecution of Buddhists, then mocked their drastic self-sacrifice. "What have these so-called 'Buddhist leaders' done?" she said in a television interview before the publication of her *Times* letter. "All they have done is barbecue a bonze [monk]—and that not even with self-sufficient means, since they had to use imported gasoline."

---

* Both of Madame Nhu's parents eventually condemned their dangerously outspoken daughter for her anti-Buddhist cheerleading.

Soon enough, after the assassinations of her husband and brother-in-law, Madame Nhu found herself exported from Vietnam.

AUGUST 12, 1930

Harry J. Anslinger's Reefer Madness

"How many murders, suicides, robberies, criminal assaults, holdups, burglaries, and deeds of maniacal insanity it causes each year, especially among the young, can be only conjectured . . . No one can predict its effect. No one knows, when he places a marijuana cigarette to his lips, whether he will become a philosopher, a joyous reveler in a musical heaven, a mad insensate, a calm philosopher, or a murderer."
—*Anti-marijuana crusader Harry J. Anslinger in a typically frenzied weed warning, published in the July 1937 edition of* The American Magazine. *Upon his appointment as the first commissioner of the Federal Bureau of Narcotics on August 12, 1930, Anslinger was determined to make a name for himself and his new agency by demonizing dope. And tormenting those who used it.**

AUGUST 13, 1823

Flatly Sharp:

Beethoven's Sour Note to His Brother

---

* Singer Billie Holiday, for example, was literally hounded to death by Anslinger—arrested and handcuffed in the very hospital bed on which she subsequently passed away.

Ludwig van Beethoven was feverishly working on his soaring Symphony No. 9 in D Minor throughout the summer of 1823, but there would be no Ode to Joy on August 13. Instead, the often irascible composer diverted himself that day by writing a strongly disharmonious letter to his brother Johann, who had gotten himself embroiled in a mortifying domestic drama.

According to reports that Beethoven had received from his secretary Anton Schindler and others, his brother's wife, Theresa—the "Fat Lump," as the composer called her—had been flagrantly unfaithful while an illness had confined Johann to his bed.

First, as he was in the habit of doing, Beethoven warmed to his main target with some ferociously scattershot finger exercises: His housekeeper was an "arch-swine," his kitchen maid a "beast." The former he accused of upsetting his stomach, the latter of giving him a cold. Nor did the composer neglect to unload on Schindler, calling his secretary a "miserable scoundrel" and a "mean and contemptible fellow."

Ludwig then moved on to attacking his sister-in-law Theresa, whom he detested, as well as her daughter (Johann's stepdaughter), lovingly referred to in the letter as "Bastard."

Finally, Beethoven turned his vitriol on poor, cuckolded Johann:

> However little you may deserve it so far as I'm concerned, yet I shall never forget that you are my brother; and in due course a good spirit will imbue your heart and soul, a good spirit which will separate you from those two canailles [Fat Lump and Bastard]. This former and still active whore [Fat Lump] who received visits from her fellow miscreant no fewer than three times during your illness, and who, moreover, has full control over your money.
>
> "O infamous disgrace! Is there no spark of manhood in you?!!!!"

Nor any dribble of compassion in you, Ludwig, for a brother clearly enduring a few Bad Days of his own?

The Queen of England Who Went Out With a Bang-Bang-Bang

No matter the occasion—whether her wedding night, when her new husband, the future King George IV, was so repulsed that he got drunk and passed out, or her adulterous romps through Europe, when she displayed all the modesty of a nightclub stripper—Caroline of Brunswick always found dignity elusive.

Death was no different.

On August 7, 1821—less than three weeks after the doors of Westminster Abbey were slammed in her face when she tried to attend her estranged husband's coronation—the coarse and unruly queen succumbed to an intestinal blockage. Her demise was a welcome relief to the new king, who hoped to ship Caroline's corpse back to her native Germany as quietly as possible. To that end, it was determined that the funeral procession would be diverted around London on its way to the coastal town of Harwich in Essex. That would avoid the masses who had long supported the ostracized and humiliated queen—mostly because they couldn't abide the profligate king. (Jane Austen reflected popular sentiment when she wrote of Caroline: "Poor woman, I shall support her as long as I can, because she *is* a Woman and because I hate her Husband.")

But on August 14, London mobs made sure the late queen's transfer was anything but discreet. Every time the funeral cortege prepared to exit the city, rioters blockaded the route, forcing the procession to seek another way out. Caroline's coffin became a pinball, caroming about until it had to roll straight through the capital. The ensuing mayhem was a fitting tribute for such an outrageously behaved woman.

The chaos in London was mere prelude to what happened when the procession stopped for a rest in the town of Colchester on the way to the coast. Saving, perhaps, her topless escapades on the continent, rarely had Caroline of Brunswick appeared less regal than on this occasion. Hungry and in need of refreshment, the members of the cortege popped into a local inn to eat, leaving poor Caroline in her coffin outside. "The mourners sat down to dinner, and seemed in high glee," reported the Reverend Samuel Carr, who was present for the meal and what followed. "Dr. Lushington [one of the late queen's executors] sat at the head of the table and the friends on each side seem[ed] to enjoy themselves as fully and as freely as if at a marriage feast." So much for solemnity.

After dinner, it was decided that the weary mourners would spend the night in Colchester and make their way to Harwich the following day. Caroline would rest for the night in the local church of St. Peter's—but only fitfully.

In her will, the queen had requested that a plaque be affixed to her casket, inscribed: DEPOSITED, CAROLINE OF BRUNSWICK, THE INJURED QUEEN OF ENGLAND. Someone decided that the church was the proper place to honor her wishes, which resulted in a minor melee. The government of King George intended a simpler, less inflammatory epitaph, while the queen's executors argued that her will stood paramount. As various officials stood about the church fussing over the matter, a carpenter jumped atop the coffin and started boring holes in it. The controversial plaque was then attached.

"Dr. Lushington highly pleased at having succeeded in fastening on the plate . . . stood shrugging his shoulders and occasionally laughing," reported Reverend Carr. "Lady Anne Hamilton [one of Caroline's ladies-in-waiting] also seemed to forget that she was a mourner, and indulged in an expression of hearty satisfaction that was little beyond a broad grin, and among the whole company of professed mourners I saw no one who even put on the semblance of sorrow . . . The whole scene more resembled the squabbles which sometimes take place at an election than anything connected with a funeral ceremony."

And still the Great Plaque Controversy was unresolved. "The corpse of the Queen of England was lying in a more neglected state than that of any commoner's wife," wrote Reverend Carr. "Every one of her devoted friends had quitted that they might retire to their refreshments at the Inn. The whole scene was one of carelessness and indifference, and the only matter that seemed to be of any consequence was the preventing the removal of an inscription, on the one hand, and the affecting its removal on the other."

The matter was settled later that night, when another laborer was called into the church to unfasten the plate the government found so offensive. While the near-empty church reverberated with the sound of the workman's tools, the plaque remained stubbornly riveted. Eventually it was pried off and hustled away, tucked between the Gentleman Usher's coat and waistcoat. Reverend Carr had the courtesy to sweep the sawdust off Caroline's casket before the government's preferred inscription was attached early the next morning. Then it was finally off to Harwich, where the coffin of England's "injured queen"—like so much cargo—was unceremoniously hoisted by a crane onto the ship that would dump her back in Brunswick.

As for her husband, George IV would endure an unseemly send-off of his own: See his scathing *Times* obit on July 16.

<hr />

AUGUST 15, 1914

Frank Lloyd Wright and the
Price of Free Love

"Those nights in the little back room were black, filled with strange unreasoning terrors. No moon seemed to shine. No stars in the sky. No familiar frog-song coming from the pond below. There was a strange, unnatural silence, while drifts of smoke still rose from the ruin."
—*Frank Lloyd Wright,* An Autobiography

A scandalized press called Taliesin, Frank Lloyd Wright's rural retreat in southern Wisconsin, his "Love Cottage" because the famed architect unapologetically shared the home with his mistress, Martha "Mamah" Borthwick Cheney, the ex-wife of one of his clients. Marriage and family had "conspired against the freedom to which I had come to feel every soul was entitled," Wright, the father of six, wrote in *An Autobiography*. "I meant to live if I could an unconventional life."

Thus was conceived Taliesin, the harmonious blend of nature and adultery in the Wisconsin wilds. "I turned to this hill in the Valley as my Grandfather before me had turned to America—as a hope and haven," he continued, adding, "But I was forgetful, for the time being, of Grandfather's Isaiah. His smiting and punishment."

Divine retribution, if that's what it was, arrived cold-bloodedly on August 15, 1914.

Wright was away in Chicago, overseeing the construction of Midway Gardens, when a servant by the name of Julian Carlton snapped. After serving soup to Mamah and her two young children on Taliesin's veranda, Carlton hacked them to death. Then, having locked a group of estate laborers in the dining room as they were eating lunch, the deranged servant poured gasoline on the floors and set the home ablaze.

Some men managed to escape. Carlton, wielding his bloody weapon, awaited them outside. Only two survived—barely. The murderer, who subsequently swallowed hydrochloric acid in a suicide bid, was found hiding in the furnace. He died of starvation seven weeks later, never to reveal his motive for the mass slaughter.

Meanwhile, Wright returned to a "scene of devastating horror," as he described it. "Thirty-six hours earlier I had left Taliesin leaving all living, friendly, and happy. Now the blow had fallen like a lightning stroke . . . violently swept down and away in a madman's nightmare of flame and murder."

The merciless press compounded the architect's despair. Having condemned Wright's unconventional ménage, it clucked over what it viewed as its inevitable conclusion. The *Ogden Standard,* for one, reported that locals "point to the tragic ruin of the 'Kingdom of Love' as the strongest argument that the Avenging Angel still flies."

"Waves of unkind, stupid publicity had broken over Taliesin again," the architect wrote. "The human sacrifices at Taliesin seemed in vain. Its heroism was ridiculed, its love mocked." But the great house would rise again . . . and again.

"I shall set it all up again," vowed Wright, "for the spirit of the mortals that lived in it and loved it—will live in it still. My home will still be there."

Wright did indeed rebuild Taliesin after the tragedy, only to see it destroyed by an electrical fire in 1925. Its third incarnation, where Wright designed some of his most important projects, endures—at least for now. But who knows where that Avenging Angel might be lurking?

—•—

AUGUST 16, 1812

Home of the Brave? Not at Fort Detroit

"The nation has been deceived by a gasconading booby."
—Richard Rush, confidant of President James Madison,
after Gen. William Hull's surrender of Fort Detroit

William Hull was approaching 60 when, after valiant service to his country in the American Revolution, his reputation was ruined in an instant on August 16, 1812. The fledgling United States had just declared a second war against Great Britain when General Hull surrendered Fort Detroit—and the entire Michigan Territory it protected—without a fight. It was an act so reprehensible to his countrymen that even the Founding Fathers who once esteemed Hull now brayed for his blood.

"[He] will of course be shot for cowardice and treachery," an indignant Thomas Jefferson wrote to President James Madison. Speaker of the House Henry Clay of Kentucky, an ardent voice for commencing the war, added to the murderous chorus: "It was so shameful, so disgraceful a surrender, that whether it proceeded from one or the other cause [treachery or cowardice] he deserves to be shot." Indeed, death by firing squad was the verdict of a military court convened in 1814, with future president Martin Van Buren serving as a prosecutor.

The patriotic vigor during the Revolutionary War that had earned Hull a commendation from George Washington and an abiding friendship with Nathan Hale seems to have been replaced by timidity when Hull was recalled to service in the War of 1812. The general quickly earned the contempt of his men, even weeks before the surrender, when—after making a bold offensive foray into Canada—he decided to slink back to Detroit at the slightest stirring of enemy resistance. "He is a coward," one officer seethed, "and will not risk his person." Terror of the tomahawk and the scalping knife had seized Hull—a condition that British Gen. Isaac Brock learned through intercepted letters and used to his advantage in taking Fort Detroit.

Positioned across the Detroit River, with his Native American allies under the leadership of Shawnee chief Tecumseh, Brock sent a message to Hull designed to stir the American general's deepest fears. "It is far from my inclination to join in a war of extermination," Brock declared, "but you must be aware, that the numerous body of Indians who have attached themselves to my troops, will be beyond my control the moment the contest commences."

By most accounts, the warning (along with some accompanying British incendiaries) had the desired effect. Hull became a dazed and dithering mess. "The general selected the safest place in the fort for his seat," according to the testimony of one witness at Hull's court-martial. "His voice trembled when he spoke—he apparently unconsciously filled his mouth with tobacco, putting in quid after quid, more than he generally did. The spittle colored with tobacco juice ran from his mouth on his neckcloth, beard, cravat and vest—he would rub the lower part of his face, which was apparently covered with spittle; he was repeatedly informed that the enemy were crossing the river, but he took no measures to oppose them."

Far from outnumbered, Hull nevertheless waved the white flag—or, rather, his son Abraham emerged from the fort carrying it, as none of the general's men were willing to perform such a dishonorable duty. General Brock was stunned at the easy capitulation—accomplished, as he triumphantly wrote to his superior, "without the sacrifice of a single drop of British blood."

By contrast, Hull's men—2,500 of whom were handed over as prisoners of war—were mortified. "To see our Colours prostitute," one wrote, "to See and hear the firing from our own battery and the huzzaws of the British troops the yells of the Savages and the Discharge of small arms, as Signals of joy over our disgrace was scenes too horrid to meditate upon with any other view than to Seek revenge." Particularly galling was the sight of British forces kissing a cannon taken from them at Saratoga in 1777—a Revolutionary battle in which, ironically, Hull had fought.

Instant infamy was now the general's lot—no matter that the fate of the villagers who had taken refuge in the citadel had preoccupied him before the surrender. "My God!" he was heard to exclaim. "What shall I do with these women and children?" In Hull's mind, he had saved them from the Indians' merciless savagery. To the rest of the young nation, however, he was a gutless failure—or, worse, a traitor.

"Was it cowardice?" John Quincy Adams wrote to his father, the second president. "I cannot imagine cowardice sufficiently base, for such a trans-action—Was it Treachery?—I should be more reluctant at this conclusion even than at the other—One of them it must have been—Imagination cannot conceive a third alternative."

In fact, there *was* a third: that Hull was a convenient scapegoat for the government's failure to provide naval and other vital reinforcements to the territory. But amid the passions of war, few considered that alternative. Though Hull was ultimately absolved of outright treason, the charge of cowardice stuck. And for that, he was condemned to die. President Madison approved the verdict but mitigated the sentence, leaving Hull to spend the rest of his life striving to vindicate himself.

If Thomas Jefferson had gotten his way, Hull—whom the third president compared to Benedict Arnold—would have perpetually stained the pages of American history. But as one chronicler put it, "a most generous fate allowed this man to sink into obscurity."

Until now!

———❖———

AUGUST 17, 2000

When a Kiss Is Just a Miss

If all the living rooms in America had been mic'd on August 17, 2000, the collective sound from television viewers watching the Democratic

National Convention might have been one heaving gag. For that day in Los Angeles, Vice President Al Gore initiated a mortifying make-out session with his wife, Tipper, right there on the stage.

It was supposed to look like a spontaneous burst of passion, a maneuver designed to make the newly nominated White House contender appear less dull and robotic. But rather than warming the hearts of those watching, the super-smooch left many recoiling in horror. Far from a Democratic Don Juan, Gore looked more like the Tin Man, trying to steal Tipper's heart— through her throat.

Indeed, the cringe-worthy kiss had all the makings of a mauling. And it made the couple's split a decade later seem rather . . . inevitable.

AUGUST 18, 1896

Rough Words From TR, Part 1:

I Like Cowboys Who Don't Get Killed

Theodore Roosevelt was waxing jingoistic in a letter he wrote to novelist Stephen Crane on August 18, 1896. *The Red Badge of Courage* author had sent the future president a rough draft of his short story, "A Man and Some Others," which would appear in *The Century Illustrated Monthly Magazine* the following February. In Crane's story, an Anglo cowboy is gunned down at his campsite after refusing to heed a Mexican vaquero's demand that he leave the area.

That scenario left the race-stratifying Rough Rider appalled. "Some day I want you to write another story of the frontiersman and the Mexican

Greaser," TR responded to Crane, "in which the frontiersman shall come out on top; it is more normal that way!"

Ogre in the Court

On August 19, 1914, President Woodrow Wilson unleashed a beast upon the United States Supreme Court with his successful nomination of James Clark McReynolds—"a savage," as fellow justice Oliver Wendell Holmes, Jr., called him, "with all the irrational impulses of a savage."

"What an intolerable court you have just now," British political theorist Harold Laski wrote to Holmes. "McReynolds and the theory of a beneficent deity are quite incompatible."

Chief Justice William Howard Taft elaborated. McReynolds, he observed in various correspondence, was "selfish to the last degree . . . fuller of prejudice than any man I have ever known . . . one who seems to delight in making others uncomfortable . . . a continual grouch . . . full of the so-called Southern courtesy, but most inconsiderate of his colleagues and others and contemptuous of everybody."

Accounts of McReynolds's cantankerousness during his 26 years on the Court are legion—from petty objections to men wearing wristwatches, which he deemed effeminate, to breathtaking episodes of rabid racism. In one instance, as African-American attorney Charles Hamilton Houston stood before the Court to argue against racial discrimination at the University of Missouri Law School, McReynolds swiveled his chair and kept his back turned for the duration.

Similar courtesies were extended to his own brethren on the Court, especially the Jewish ones. A snarling anti-Semite, McReynolds rarely spoke to Louis Brandeis or Benjamin Cardozo—and sometimes he simply refused to share the same room. "As you know, I am not always to be found when there is a Hebrew abroad," McReynolds wrote to

Chief Justice Taft in declining to accompany the Court to a Philadelphia ceremony in 1922. "Therefore, my 'inability to attend' must not surprise you."

Neither was it surprising that not a single member of the high court bothered to show up at McReynolds's funeral in 1946.* Or that Justice William O. Douglas would invent a card game in his honor. He called it "Son of a Bitch."

<hr/>

AUGUST 20, 1672

Dutch à l'Orange:
The Mob's Grisly Feast

It was known as the Dutch Golden Age—an era of unprecedented trade wealth and military might in the 17th century, when Rembrandt and Vermeer painted their masterpieces, van Leeuwenhoek opened the microscopic world to exploration, and a frenzied mob tore apart the leader of the Dutch Republic and ate him.

Johan de Witt had dominated the governance of the republic for several decades at the expense of the royal House of Orange. But all that changed in 1672, when France invaded the Netherlands and the long-powerless William of Orange (Britain's future King William III) assumed military

<hr/>

* In a bit of historic comeuppance, six Supreme Court Justices later attended the funeral of McReynolds's much put-upon manservant, Harry Parker. "For years Harry did almost everything but breathe for the Justice," noted McReynolds's friend Katherine Ogden Savage—and that apparently included serving as a human bird dog when the justice went hunting on Chesapeake Bay. McReynolds repaid Parker's loyalty with unwavering racism, once admonishing a law clerk for becoming too friendly with Parker and his wife, Mary: "I do wish you would think of my wishes in this matter in your future relations with darkies."

leadership. De Witt was doomed. He resigned his position as grand pensionary (akin to prime minister) in early August, having survived one assassination attempt. But on August 20, Johan and his brother Cornelius were ambushed at the prison where the latter was being held. First, the duo was tortured under a fabricated charge of treason. Then they were clubbed, stabbed, and finally shot by an Orangist mob, incited to a frenzy by false rumors of de Witt's treachery.

And that's when the true monstrosities began.

The two corpses were dragged to a gibbet, hung up by their heels, and stripped naked. Various body parts were sliced off and sold as souvenirs. The brothers were then gutted, after which their spilled entrails and organs were roasted and devoured by the deranged mass. Only long past midnight, when the sated mob had dispersed at last, were family members able to collect and bury what remained of the de Witt brothers.

AUGUST 21, 1818

Some Coarse Human Events: Jefferson's Pain in the Butt

Thomas Jefferson journeyed to Warm Springs, Virginia, in August 1818, hoping to treat his rheumatism by bathing in the region's mineral-rich waters. Rather than basking in relief, however, the former president found himself bored beyond endurance. "So dull a place, and so distressing an ennui I never before knew," he wrote. Worse, he developed festering boils on his backside, a condition he attributed to soaking in the springs. "A large swelling on my seat, increasing for several days past in size and hardness disables me from sitting but on the corner of a chair," Jefferson wrote to his daughter Martha on August 21. "Another swelling begins to manifest itself to-day on the other seat."

The carbuncle made for an agonizing ride home, reducing Jefferson "to the last stages of weakness and exhaustion," as he told his grandson.

But it didn't end there. "The cause of the eruption was mistaken and it was treated with severe unctions of mercury and Sulphur," the Founding Father shared in a letter a year later. "These reduced me to death's door."*

AUGUST 22, 2007

Yerrrr Rout!

Not only did the Baltimore Orioles endure the most lopsided loss in the team's history when, on August 22, 2007, they fell to the Texas Rangers, 30–3, in the first game of a doubleheader. The humiliating rout also allowed the otherwise nondescript Rangers a place in the American League record books for most runs ever scored in a single game.

"This is something freaky," said the Rangers' Marlon Byrd; "you won't see anything like this again for a long, long time." So, for the "long, long time" it would take to erase the Orioles' shame with a new record, manager Dave Trembley had an immediate solution: "You have a real short memory and you let it go." In the meantime, the O's lost the second game, too.

---

* Jefferson wasn't the only Founding Father to cry furuncle. George Washington also suffered from a nasty boil on his backside—"a Bile on his Seat," as William Loughton Smith described it in a letter written to Edward Rutledge in 1789, "which had been so inflamed by his riding on horseback as to grow into an Imposthume as large as my two fists—this occasioned a fever of a threatening nature—it was apprehended that it would turn to a malignant one & the Doctor sat up with him one night—the fever however abated & the Impostune has been opened—he is now considerably better & out of all danger, but will be prevented for some time from sitting up."

AUGUST 23, 1933

All the Fake Soviet News
That Fits, It Prints

*"Any report of a famine in Russia is today
an exaggeration or malignant propaganda."*
—Walter Duranty, Moscow correspondent for The New York Times,
*in an article published on August 23, 1933, as millions starved
to death under Stalin. It would take the* Times *more than
half a century to declare Duranty's articles on the Soviet Union—
a collection of which had won the Pulitzer in 1932—
"some of the worst reporting to appear in this newspaper."*

———

AUGUST 24, 1814

On Second Thought, Part 12:
No, Seriously—the British *Are* Coming!

*"They certainly will not come here. What the devil will they do here? No!
No! Baltimore is the place, sir. That is of so much more consequence."
—Secretary of War John Armstrong during the War of 1812, insisting
that approaching British forces would not attack the nation's capital—
just before they did precisely that on August 24, 1814, torching
the Capitol, the President's House, and other public buildings symbolic
of the fledgling Republic. Then they went to Baltimore.*

"You never saw a drawing room so brilliantly lighted as the whole city
was that night," one resident wrote of the inferno. "Few thought of
going to bed—they spent the night in gazing on the fires, and lamenting
the disgrace of the city." Secretary Armstrong—roundly blamed for the

humiliating fiasco and treated like a new Nero, fiddling while D.C. burned—was hanged in effigy at the burned-out Capitol.* Then, after being thoroughly abraded by President Madison for his failure to defend Washington, he tendered his resignation.

AUGUST 25, 1915

Rough Words From TR, Part 2:
Peace Is for "Sissies"

Theodore Roosevelt had nothing but contempt for Woodrow Wilson—or "that old gray skunk in the White House," as he called his second successor. The famed Rough Rider saw himself as a man of action, equating battlefield bloodshed with vigor and rejuvenation. So as far as the former president was concerned, the incumbent's efforts to keep the United States neutral in the world war then consuming Europe made Wilson a pitiable weakling.

---

* By coincidence, the Visigoths sacked Rome on the same date in A.D. 410. As St. Jerome wrote, "The city which had taken the whole world was itself taken."

"The man who believes in peace at any price or in substituting all-inclusive arbitration treaties for an army and navy should instantly move to China," Roosevelt declared at a military training camp on August 25, 1915. "If he stays here, then more manly people will have to defend him, and he is not worth defending. Let him get out of the country as quickly as possible. To treat elocution as a substitute for action, to rely upon high-sounding words unbacked by deeds, is proof of a mind that dwells only in the realm of shadow and sham."

Lumped in with Wilson that day were "the professional pacifists and the poltroons and college sissies who organize peace-at-any-price societies." Itching for war himself, Roosevelt was denied a military position when the United States at long last entered World War I in 1917. However, he was proud to send overseas his four sons—the youngest of whom, Quentin, was killed in aerial combat over France.

"Poor Quentyquee!" the grieving father was overheard sobbing as he buried his face in the mane of his late son's pony. "What made this loss so devastating to him was the truth it conveyed," Roosevelt biographer Edmund Morris wrote: "that death in battle was no more glamorous than death in an abattoir."

AUGUST 26, 1994

And This Man Used to Work for the FBI

"Well, if the Bureau of Alcohol, Tobacco and Firearms comes
to disarm you and they are bearing arms, resist them with arms.
Go for a head shot; they're going to be wearing bulletproof vests."
—*Watergate burglar cum radio talk-show host G. Gordon Liddy, in an
unhinged broadcast on his nationwide radio program that apparently
endorsed the slaying of federal law-enforcement officers, August 26, 1994*

AUGUST 27, 1792

The Unkindest Cut:
Bad Karma for the Executioner

Few figures in history were more intimate with the mechanics of death than Charles-Henri Sanson. Serving as Paris's chief executioner throughout the latter half of the 18th century, he personally dispatched nearly 3,000 souls—among them, some of Revolutionary France's most prominent personages. Sanson persuaded an indignant Louis XVI, for example, to take off his jacket and permit his hands to be tied, thus removing potential impediments to the guillotine's blade.* And Sanson held high the king's severed head for the edification of the gathered masses—just as he would that of the king's implacable enemy, Robespierre, a year and a half later.†

As he went about his grisly business, Sanson witnessed the extremes of human emotion when confronting violent death—from the icy insouciance of Georges Danton, who told him, "Don't forget to show my head to the people. It's well worth seeing," to the desperate struggle and terrified shrieks of Louis XV's mistress, Madame du Barry, as she approached the guillotine, pleading for her life.

Sanson appears to have derived no sadistic pleasure from his position.

---

* Despite Sanson's precautions, some accounts of the execution indicate that the guillotine did not slice all the way through the king's neck, necessitating a manual push of the blade to complete the job.

† Robespierre's decapitation was likewise less than smooth. Before his rendezvous with the guillotine, the Reign of Terror's prime mover had tried to kill himself with a pistol; he succeeded only in shattering his lower jaw. Upon the scaffold, Sanson ripped off the bloody handkerchief holding Robespierre's face together. "Animal screams of pain escaped," wrote historian Simon Schama, "silenced only by the falling blade."

Indeed, his courtliness toward Jean-Paul Marat's assassin, Charlotte Corday, indicates otherwise: Sanson tried to shield from her view the instrument of her demise. Decapitation was simply a job for him, one he had inherited from three generations of Sanson beheaders before him.

Still, there was a price to pay for participating in so much human carnage. On August 27, 1792, a terrible blow was visited upon the Sanson family.

Call it divine retribution—the sins of the father (and grandfather, and great-grandfather) being visited upon the son—or see it simply as a bit of ghoulish irony: That day, the executioner's son Gabriel—in training to take over the family business—was strutting around the scaffold, holding aloft a freshly severed head, when he slipped on some accumulated gore. With no rail to protect him, poor Gabriel fell to his death. On the bright side, another son, Henri, was familiar enough with the family trade, and sufficiently sure-footed, to step up and oversee the execution of Queen Marie Antoinette the following year.

AUGUST 28, 1968

Hoity vs. Toity: The Buckley-Vidal Showdown

"Now listen, you queer. Stop calling me a crypto-Nazi, or I'll sock you in the goddamn face, and you'll stay plastered."
—*William F. Buckley, Jr., to Gore Vidal, August 28, 1968*

They were two highbrow gladiators—ferocious in wit and intelligence, uncompromising in their opposing political philosophies and mutual loathing—set to clash in the arena of a television studio during the Republican and Democratic conventions of 1968.

On the right was William F. Buckley, Jr., founder of the influential conservative journal *National Review* and renowned for biting ripostes delivered with a clenched Brahmin drawl: a sort of erudite great white shark, with lockjaw. On the left was Buckley's fellow practitioner of linguistic affect, the novelist, playwright, and essayist Gore Vidal, a formidable provocateur with an aristocratic background similar to Buckley's and a well-established history of intellectual brawling.

"In Buckley and Vidal, ABC has a dream television match," *The Washington Post* noted enthusiastically. "They are graceful, shrewd, cool antagonists; paragons of caustic wit and established observers of the American political scene." (Regrettably, the two cerebral combatants were unwitting harbingers of one of TV's worst trends: the emergence of decidedly unlettered talking heads, screeching over one another in what passes for political debate today.)

To the delight of executives at the low-rated ABC network, Buckley and Vidal performed exactly as expected during the Republican National Convention in Miami—dueling with what reporter Dean Gysel described as "waspish bitchery" while drawing an increasing number of viewers to the spectacle. But their verbal sparring took a nasty turn at the Democratic convention in Chicago on August 28. Against a back-drop of Vietnam War protesters being clobbered and teargassed by police outside the convention hall, Buckley and Vidal resorted to parallel savagery inside the studio while arguing over that very violence.

It started when moderator Howard K. Smith asked if the protesters' raising a Vietcong flag in Chicago might be analogous to Americans' raising a Nazi flag during World War II. There were pro-Nazis in the 1940s, Buckley insisted, and they had received what they deserved. To which Vidal responded: "As far as I am concerned, the only sort of pro- or crypto-Nazi I can think of is yourself."

And with that "cherry bomb," as Christopher Hitchens called it, Buckley turned ferociously on Vidal, hurling his homophobic slur and threatening physical violence. Vidal stoically weathered the attack, chuckling, "Oh, Bill, you're too extraordinary." In a later *Esquire* mag-azine essay, he re-created the moment with malicious glee: "The little door in William F. Buckley, Jr.'s forehead suddenly opened and out sprang that wild cuckoo which I had always known was there but had wanted so much for others, preferably millions of others, to get a good look at. I think those few seconds of madness, to use his word, were well worth a great deal of patient effort on my part."

Buckley, on the other hand, seems to have genuinely regretted his frothing loss of control. After a lengthy *Esquire* piece of his own—super-ficially apologetic, but mostly self-justifying—he did his best to put the episode behind him.* Indeed, Buckley was apparently distressed to discover years later that a tape of the exchange still existed. It was as if he knew a single sound bite had eclipsed his legacy of cool, cerebral detachment—that the Egghead had cracked.

⸻

AUGUST 29, 1526

The (Slippery) Fall of a Hungarian King

Suleiman the Magnificent, sultan of the Ottoman Empire, was up to his neck in hacked-off heads—literally thousands of them, piled in a pyramid or perched on spikes. They were war trophies, taken during the Turks' crushing defeat of Hungarian forces at the Battle of Mohács on August 29, 1526.

Conspicuously absent from those grisly souvenirs was the crowned head of King Louis II of Hungary, who had led his army into the disastrous battle. Watching the Ottoman rout of his forces, the 20-year-old Louis simply rode away from the battlefield. Attempting to scramble up a steep riverbank, however, his horse fell over backward, crushing the king beneath it.

Thus it was that the deep mire became both hiding place and tomb for

---

* But not before lobbing a libel suit against Vidal, whose *Esquire* essay implied that Buckley was an anti-Semite and a homosexual. The suit was settled after three years.

the beaten monarch. Mercifully, the location of this temporary resting place would not be discovered until well after Suleiman had left the scene.

———

AUGUST 30, 1904

Run Ragged—and Dry: The 1904 Olympic Marathon Comes to a Staggering Finish

Thomas Hicks stumbled across the marathon finish line at the 1904 Olympic Games in St. Louis—eight pounds lighter than when he started the event and barely alive, his dehydrated body surging with strychnine, raw eggs, and brandy. Yet despite his dire condition, Hicks was the winner of what must be considered one of the most preposterous races in Olympic history, when athletes of vastly divergent levels of talent and training were deliberately deprived of water on a ragged, dust-clogged course that left them dazed, and in some cases, utterly debilitated and dangerously ill.

Thirty-two men began the 24.85-mile marathon* on August 30 at 3 p.m., just about the hottest point of an already scorching day. Nearly half of them would not finish; conditions simply would not allow it. The deliberate lack of water was a significant factor: Organizer James Sullivan wanted to test the limits of dehydration on the athletes, the results of which soon became apparent as man after man was left writhing and vomiting by the roadside.

The already treacherous route caused quite a dustup—literally. Men on horseback rode ahead of the runners to clear the country road of

---

* The now standard distance of 26 miles, 385 yards, was adopted at the 1908 Games in London.

spectators, wagons, and any other obstacles, raising massive clouds of dirt. Medical personnel, Olympic officials, and scientists rode alongside the parched athletes in automobiles, enveloping them in noxious fumes. So severe was the situation that one runner, William Garcia, had to be rushed to the hospital for emergency surgery midway through the race; the airborne debris had shredded his esophagus and stomach.

Others fared only slightly better. Cuban runner Andarín Carvajal walked and hitchhiked his way to St. Louis, having gambled away his train fare in New Orleans. Arriving at the last minute, he ran the marathon in his street clothes and street shoes, taking time only to cut his long pants short with a pair of borrowed scissors. Severely deprived of nutrition en route, Carvajal created his own feed zone by wandering into an orchard and gobbling down some apples. They were rotten. The resulting stomach cramps forced him to lie down on the roadside to recover. He finished fourth—an indication of just how physically compromised his competitors were.

American Fred Lorz, a bricklayer by trade, likewise succumbed to the grueling conditions but still managed to finish the race. Problem was, he did it by cheating: After collapsing midway, Lorz caught a ride in a passing automobile and hopped out near the finish line to lope across it. It appeared that Lorz had won. Indeed, he was just about to accept the laurels from President Theodore Roosevelt's daughter Alice when someone flagged his deception.*

That left Hicks the winner—if a hallucinating athlete, juiced on booze and what amounted to performance-enhancing rat poison, propped up by two assistants as he crossed the finish line of a marathon that has gone down as the slowest ever in Olympic history can really be considered a winner.

———

* Lorz claimed it was all a joke, which he said he was on the verge of revealing just before he was busted. Olympic officials didn't find it funny; they temporarily suspended Lorz from amateur competition.

AUGUST 31, A.D. 12 AND 161

Dawn of the Deadly:
Two Monsters Hatched

Happy Birthday to our two favorite megalomaniacal Roman emperors, Caligula and Commodus!

September

Just Plane Dumb: Malaysia Airlines
Promo Dead on Arrival

"My Ultimate Bucket List"
—Promotional campaign by Malaysia Airlines, asking customers to describe their ideal activities and destinations before they die, in exchange for prizes. Launched on September 1, 2014—just after the airline's catastrophic loss of two planes and, with them, 537 lives—the woefully ill-conceived advertising stunt was abruptly withdrawn several days later.

A Teetotal Flop:
Carrie Nation's Dry Reception

Visitors to Coney Island on Labor Day of 1901 were prepared to pay for their amusements at the popular New York resort—but not for the Carrie Nation sideshow. The hatchet-wielding teetotaler had made quite a name for herself over the past year, smashing saloons and railing against demon alcohol. But her September 2 arrival at "the most iniquitous resort in America," as she called it, was generally met with a shrug.

"The thousands of people who took their Labor Day outing at Coney Island were all made acquainted in various ways of the fact that Mrs. Nation was the island's particular freak of the day," *The New York Times* reported. "From early morning a man made up as a Kansas farmer, and leading a billygoat and mangy dog, paraded up and down the Bowery, the goat and the dog bearing placards on their sides announcing Mrs. Nation's lecture."

No one, it seemed, cared. Ticket sales for her lecture that afternoon were anemic. Even a last-minute price slash did little to swell the audience. "Well, this is a small crowd," the Bible-wielding booze buster observed from the stage. "But the Scripture tells us that we must not despise small things, and what we lack in quantity we make up in quality." Yet Mrs. Nation offered the sparse gathering little of that quality—and certainly none of the violent antics for which she had become famous. "She is not an interesting talker," the *Times* reporter observed. "The vehemence which her career suggests is altogether lacking in her speech."

With a week still to go in her engagement, something exciting would have to be done to pull in paying crowds. So Mrs. Nation dutifully launched into Full Maniac mode, attacking a tobacco store with her trusty hatchet and getting herself arrested. But then she went just a tad too far, even for her: She told an audience that she hoped President William McKinley—recently shot by an anarchist in Buffalo—would die from his wounds. That would be a just fate for this "friend to the rum sellers," she insisted. Her listeners hissed her right out of town.

SEPTEMBER 3, 1980

Double, Double—Blood and Bad Acting Both Cause Trouble

The best known legend in theater circles is that Shakespeare's *Macbeth* is cursed. (Some say it's by the incantations chanted by the play's three witches.) Coincidental or not, certain unfortunate incidents have bedeviled various productions over the years: stage accidents, untimely deaths, even a bloody riot.

On September 3, 1980, the curse of "the Scottish play" (superstitious performers refuse to utter its name) became manifest in the form of howling, derisive laughter from the audience. Perhaps the evil spell was at work again. More likely, though, it was simply Peter O'Toole's uproariously bad performance in the title role, mixed with some very silly stage effects.

For the famed actor, who had been given complete artistic control over the production at London's Old Vic theater, after himself, it was all about the blood—buckets and buckets of blood. "Do you know how many times the word 'blood' appears in the text, old darling?" the actor asked director Bryan Forbes, who recalled the conversation in his book *A Divided Life*. "If you stab a living man, blood spurts seventeen feet."

Being the boss, O'Toole got all the gore he craved, slathering himself with the stuff to unintentionally hilarious effect on opening night. "In the wings was a tin bath with about a foot of [stage blood] inside it," co-star Kevin Quarmby told O'Toole biographer Robert Sellers. "Peter would stand in it and douse himself from head to foot, walk on stage with everything dripping, looking like [Stephen King's] Carrie, and say, 'I have done the deed.'" Despite audience titters over the excessive goop—in which the other actors found themselves slipping—O'Toole was adamant about retaining the absurd effect. "No blood! No show!" Forbes recalled him declaring.

The real problem with the production, however, was O'Toole's over-the-top acting. "The performance is not so much downright bad as heroically ludicrous," wrote Jack Tinker in the next day's *Daily Mail*. "The voice is pure Bette Davis in her Baby Jane mood, the manner is Vincent Price hamming it up in a Hammer horror." When read excerpts from one particularly vicious review, in which his voice was described as "thick, hoarse and full of abrupt sledgehammer emphasis," O'Toole growled, "arseholes." Told that it came from the august *Times,* the actor punctuated his thoughts, "double arseholes."

With theatergoers lining up to laugh, the artistic fiasco made lots of money. "It's in many ways a funny play, full of irony," said O'Toole. "But the trouble is that many in the audience laughed at the wrong times. They did not see the real humor."

Tragically, they did.

SEPTEMBER 4, 1666

Of Burning Embers and Missing Members

St. Paul's Cathedral had loomed high over London for six centuries when a massive conflagration roared through the city in 1666. Many believed the ancient edifice, perched atop Ludgate Hill, would survive the all-consuming combustion. But when the flames arrived on September 4, the sacred place became a hellish inferno, the heat so intense it sent huge chunks of the building's stone walls hurtling through the air.

The unslakable fire left little in its wake. "Thus lay in ashes that most venerable Church," wrote diarist John Evelyn, who visited the site afterward, "one of the most antient [sic] pieces of early piety in the Christian world."

Impiety came next.

Rising from the ashes was the proverbial phoenix—two, in fact. The first was a near-perfect analogue of the perpetually self-regenerating bird of myth: a memorial statue that John Donne, the Dean of St. Paul's, had commissioned for himself before his death in 1631, featuring the poet rising from an urn, still in his death shroud, yet looking toward new life in heaven. It was retrieved undamaged from the smoldering ruins and is now displayed at the rebuilt St. Paul's Cathedral, the classic baroque landmark designed by Sir Christopher Wren and consecrated in 1697.

The second phoenix would have been better off incinerated in its nest. Yet somehow the corpse of Robert Braybrooke, bishop of London in the 14th century, withstood the flames and was placed on ghoulish public display. Samuel Pepys, another famous diarist of the era, viewed the remains two months after the centuries-dead bishop emerged from the wreckage of St. Paul's. The sight did not exactly inspire reverence—"his skeleton with the flesh on," Pepys recorded; "but all tough and dry like a spongy dry leather, or touchwood upon all his bones. His head turned aside. A great man in his time, and Lord Chancellor . . . [his remnants] now exposed to be handled and derided by some, though admired for its duration by others. Many flocking to see it."

The gawking and grabbing were hardly the worst indignities the reclaimed Braybrooke endured, however. There was also a most unsavory mutilation—at least according to an account written by the antiquary Henry Hare, Second Baron Coleraine, in 1675. That December, Coleraine had gone to inspect the desiccated bishop—still on display nine years after the Great Fire—and noted several wounds laborers retrieving it from the cathedral ruins inadvertently inflicted upon the corpse. Worse, he reported, the body had also recently suffered "a greater maim . . . by a female's defrauding (shall I say?) or deroding of the virile instrument." With her teeth.

The alleged culprit: King Charles II's mistress, Barbara Palmer, Duchess of Cleveland.

Thomas Boys, keeper of the Chapter House that held Braybrooke's remains, told Coleraine that the duchess had asked to be left alone with the corpse—tipping Boys handsomely for the privilege—and returned with quite the souvenir to share with her companions. Boys "returned to shut up the carcase," wrote Coleraine, "but unexpectedly found it served like a Turkish eunuch, and dismembered of as much of the privity as the lady could get into her mouth to bite (for want of a circumcising penknife)."

Commenting upon this unsavory tidbit, Coleraine couldn't resist adding his own perverse paronomasia: "Though some ladies of late have got bishopricks for others, yet I have not heard of any but this that got one for herself."

Clever, but we'll just call it robbing a peter at St. Paul's.

SEPTEMBER 5, 1992

Put to the Testes, Part 6:
A Whole New Ball Game

On September 5, 1992, Mississippi State coach Jackie Sherrill apparently confused castration with inspiration. Hoping to rouse (or terrify) his team to victory over the University of Texas Longhorns, Sherrill arranged to have his Bulldogs observe the moment every bull calf undoubtedly dreads: a good old-fashioned gelding. (Whether the poor animal dragged onto the practice field was a longhorn remains unverified.)

Sherrill did not urge his boys to "win one for the clipper," observed *Orlando Sentinel* columnist Larry Guest at the time, but the Bulldogs did triumph over the Longhorns that day.

To critics of the stunt, the coach had this to say: "I don't think that calf was embarrassed." Alas, neither was Coach Sherrill.

SEPTEMBER 6, 1872

A Future President Executes His Duties

Future president Grover Cleveland faced a terrible task: one that would horrify any decent man. On September 6, 1872, he was set to purposely and methodically kill a fellow human being. That Patrick Morrissey was a vicious murderer, and of his own mother, made little difference in terms of what had to be done: Yes, the law decreed that he deserved to die, but it was something else entirely to be the instrument of his doom—to trigger the trapdoor that would suddenly swing open and send Morrissey hurtling to eternity at the end of a rope.

Cleveland, then serving as sheriff of Erie County, New York, could have delegated the gruesome job to someone else—for a $10 fee. Indeed, his mother suggested he do just that. Though tempting, for a man of honor such as Cleveland, it was ultimately unthinkable to saddle someone else with the soul-searing anguish he felt. "He recognized his duty," recalled a contemporary, Judge Albert Haight of Buffalo, "and was not disposed to shirk it or transfer his own responsibility to the shoulders of a subordinate."

Nevertheless, Cleveland took steps to make Morrissey's execution as dignified as possible. He would be hanged behind a canvas wall, depriving the crowds of the entertaining spectacle of death. And in designing the scaffold, the sheriff made certain that he, too, would not see Morrisey swing when he pulled the lethal lever.

Despite doing his duty as best he could, Cleveland was deeply distressed by the deed—"a sick man for several days after," as *The New York Times* reported. Even more disturbing for the man who would one day be denigrated by his political opponent as "the Buffalo Hangman," Cleveland was obligated to complete one more judicial killing before his term as sheriff ended. And it went even worse.

Jack Gaffney had murdered a man over a card game and was sentenced to death. Facing the noose, though, Gaffney feigned insanity. It appears Cleveland fell for his ruse, or at least took Gaffney's supposed instability seriously enough to request a jury determination of the condemned man's mental state. The deception bought Gaffney time, and buttressed Cleveland's hope that another dreadful appointment at the gallows might be unnecessary.

It was not to be. A new execution date was set for February 14, 1873. In an instance of grim irony that day, Cleveland managed to prolong Gaffney's life yet again—albeit unwittingly, and much to his dismay. Something went wrong with the mechanics of the hanging, and Gaffney dangled without dying for nearly half an hour.

SEPTEMBER 7, 1941

O-bitch-uary, Part 4: Eleanor Roosevelt's Not-So-Dearly Departed

"I looked at my mother-in-law's face after she was dead
& understood so many things I had never seen before. It is
dreadful to have lived so close to someone for 36 years
and to feel no deep affection or sense of loss."
—*First Lady Eleanor Roosevelt's cold but understandable response to the
September 7, 1941, death of Sara Delano Roosevelt. That pathologically
controlling, ruthlessly undermining matriarch had once informed her
grandchildren: "I was your real mother; Eleanor merely bore you."*

SEPTEMBER 8, 1906

Bronx Bomb: When Man Becomes Animal

"The whole episode is good comic-opera material. When the
history of the Zoological Park is written, this incident
will form its most amusing passage."
—*William Temple Hornaday, director of
the New York Zoological Park (the Bronx Zoo)*

Fresh from the horrors of the Belgian Congo, where his wife and
children were slaughtered and he was sold into slavery, a Mbuti man
by the name of Ota Benga found refuge in the United States—occupying
a cage at the Bronx Zoo. Beginning on September 8, 1906, visitors were
welcomed to gawk at the diminutive man—the main attraction in a
"purely ethnological exhibit," as zoo director William T. Hornaday

described it, with Darwinian evolution as a backdrop. "It is probably a good thing that Benga doesn't think very deeply," a *New York Times* reporter opined. "If he did it isn't likely that he was very proud of himself when he woke in the morning and found himself under the same roof with the orang-outangs and monkeys, for that is where he really is."

Hornaday stressed, however, that Benga "has one of the best rooms in the primate house." Furthermore, he wasn't necessarily confined there; sometimes, under the supervision of his "keeper," he was permitted to roam freely through the park. The *Times* reported all the fun to be had one Sunday in September, when 40,000 people headed to the zoo: "Nearly every man, woman, and child of this crowd made for the monkey house to see the star attraction in the park—the wild man from Africa. They chased him about the grounds all day, howling, jeering, and yelling. Some of them poked him in the ribs, others tripped him up, all laughed at him."

Objections to this sadistic mistreatment took curiously decorous forms, with *The New York Times* reporting a vague unease among visitors on the first day. "The human being happened to be a Bushman, one of a race that scientists do not rate high in the human scale," the newspaper noted, "but to the average non-scientific person in the crowd of sightseers there was something about the display that was unpleasant." Reverend James H. Gordon, superintendent of the Howard Colored Orphan Asylum in Brooklyn, was more specific in his dissent: "Our race, we think, is depressed enough, without exhibiting one of us with the apes. We think we are worthy of being considered human beings, with souls."

Hornaday bridled at the criticism. "This is the most ridiculous thing I have ever heard of," he fumed. "Why, we are taking excellent care of the little fellow and he is a great favorite with everybody connected with the zoo." As for the way Benga was displayed, Hornaday had an answer for that, too: "We have no platform that we could place him on, and this big open air cage was the best place we could find to put him where everybody could see him."

The *Times* likewise seemed unable to figure out the fuss. "Not feeling particularly vehement excitement ourselves over the exhibition of an African 'pigmy' in the Primate House of the Zoological Park," read one editorial, "we do not quite understand all the emotion which others are expressing in the matter. As for Benga himself, he is probably enjoying himself as well as he could anywhere in his country, and it is absurd to make moan over the imagined humiliation and degradation he is suffering."

Plus, the paper reported, the zoo was having one undeniably civilizing effect on "the Bushman," as it insisted on referring to Benga: "He loves soda."

SEPTEMBER 9, 1911

His Harping Will Go On

Seven months before John Jacob Astor IV sailed to his doom aboard the *Titanic,* he hit another iceberg—a metaphorical one—when the recently divorced real estate scion, one of the world's richest men, married for a second time, on September 9, 1911. High society snickered at his choice of a bride: Madeleine Talmadge Force, a teenager half his age and far beneath his station. Newspaper editorials *tsk-tsk*ed the union, some assuming it was transactional—an example of the "selling of daughters to worthless inheritors of wealth or rank," as the New York *Evening Post* put it. Others clucked at the couple's social incongruity.

But the Episcopal Church, with its strict rules against remarriage after divorce, proved most obnoxiously opposed. "We abhor this Astor alliance," the Reverend George Chalmers Richmond fulminated from the pulpit. "It is unholy in its origin, and its end will be a defiance of God's laws and of our holy religion." Richmond predicted, correctly, that no Episcopal clergyman would perform the ceremony.

For all his wealth, Astor couldn't even buy one. At one point he was prepared to retain the services of a Free Baptist carpenter/clergyman by the name of George Straight, but at the last minute he opted instead for the Reverend Joseph Lambert, pastor of the Elwood

Temple Congregational Church in Providence, Rhode Island. Report-edly humiliated by the substitution, Straight nonetheless fared better than Lambert—who, amid a torrent of criticism for having officiated, resigned his ministry several months later.

By then, the much maligned newlyweds were on their honeymoon in Egypt and Europe. In April 1912, they were sailing home aboard the *Titanic*. Madeleine, pregnant with their son (who would be born four months later), was rescued. Astor, however, went down with the ship—bravely, by every available account.

The world was horrified by the tragedy—with one exception: Having once condemned the Astor marriage as "an outrage on decency," the very Reverend Richmond now summoned all his Christian charity to revel smugly in what he believed were its consequences. "Mr. Astor and his crowd of New York and Newport associates have for years paid not the slightest attention to the laws of church or state which have seemed to contravene their personal pleasures or sensual delights," Richmond declared, before Astor's body had even been recovered. "But you can't defy God all the time. The day of reckoning comes and comes not in our own way."

SEPTEMBER 10, 2001

The Eve of Destruction

John P. O'Neill had spent a quarter century working his way up the ranks at the FBI, eventually becoming the bureau's counterterrorism chief—and therefore an expert on Osama bin Laden. But after years of bureaucratic infighting that he saw as having compromised his efforts, a frustrated O'Neill left the FBI in the summer of 2001, to head up security at New York's World Trade Center.

The career pivot did nothing to dull the former agent's internal alarm sensors. On the evening before the 9/11 attacks, O'Neill confided to his colleague Raymond Powers, director of security at Rockefeller Center,

"It's going to happen, and it looks like something big is brewing." That same night, he told his friend Jerry Hauer, the director of emergency management for New York City, "We're due—and we're due for something big."

O'Neill would take the reasons for his certainty of a cataclysm in the making to the grave: He died the next day in the collapse of the twin towers.

"He chased bin Laden all over the world," Louis Napoli, a detective on the FBI-NYPD Joint Terrorism Task Force told author Murray Weiss, author of *The Man Who Warned America.* "And bin Laden caught up with him."

———

SEPTEMBER 11, 1968

The Beach Boys: Pickin' Up
Manson's Bad Vibrations

"I gave Dennis Wilson a bullet [on his bed], didn't I?
I gave him a bullet because he changed the words to my song."
*—Murderous cult leader Charles Manson on Beach Boys drummer Dennis
Wilson, in a 1994 interview on the ABC News program* Turning Point

The Beach Boys weren't having much fun, fun, fun in the late summer of 1968 when, on September 11, they entered a recording studio to lay down a new track, "Never Learn Not to Love." The sunny sounds that had made them so popular earlier in the decade seemed outmoded now, eclipsed by music more suited for darker days of war and assassination.

The band's most recent album, *Friends,* had flopped. Fans no longer flocked to their shows. Perhaps saddest of all, Brian Wilson, the Beach Boys' musical visionary, had all but withdrawn from his bandmates and taken to his bed—the victim of massive drug consumption and a tortured mind. Not surprisingly, the group had become fractured and unmoored. Only drummer Dennis Wilson, one of Brian's brothers, appeared to be in tune with the times. And that meant real trouble.

In addition to being the only band member who was really a surfer, the handsome and hard-partying Dennis had always been the bad boy of the Beach Boys. Girls loved him, but the band tended to dismiss his talents. As the 1960s progressed, however, the drummer long relegated to the background started to emerge as a songwriter in his own right.

Unfortunately, "Never Learn Not to Love"—the number the Beach Boys were recording on September 11 and credited to Dennis—was not actually his. It had been written by Charles Manson. And that future maestro of murder was not happy with the Beach Boy's treatment of his tune.

Wilson had become enamored of the wild-eyed pseudo-guru, whom he came to call the Wizard, after some of Manson's female followers introduced him earlier in the year. Dennis dug the ex-convict's hippie-dippie love vibe (not to mention his stable of willing young women and easy access to drugs). Having convinced himself that Manson possessed real talent as a musician, Dennis helped him record a number of songs.

One Manson composition, "Cease to Exist," was reportedly written specifically for the broken Beach Boys—"imagining that his vision of love as a soul-consuming act of submission would make them feel better about themselves," as biographer Peter Ames Carlin noted. But when Dennis essentially co-opted the song—renaming it "Never Learn Not to Love" and, most egregiously, switching the lyric "cease to exist" to "cease to resist"—the Wizard became incensed.

Manson and his "family" had already consumed a good chunk of Dennis's fortune, occupying his home and crashing his cars. But upon hearing the altered lyrics of "Never Learn Not to Love"—first released as the B-side of the single "Bluebirds Over the Mountain"—he threatened the drummer's life, leaving a bullet on his bed as a warning.

But that bloodbath was only implied. The real one came the next summer, when Manson's minions slaughtered actress Sharon Tate and four others at the former home of Terry Melcher, the record producer to whom Dennis had introduced the Wizard in hopes of advancing his music career. Melcher had snubbed Manson, and innocent people lost their lives as a result.

Dennis Wilson was all too aware of the fate he had been spared. "I'm the luckiest guy in the world," he told Manson prosecutor Vincent Bugliosi, "because I got off only losing my money."

SEPTEMBER 12, 1869

Put to the Testes, Part 7:
The Eunuch's Too-Ballsy Behavior

An Dehai, a palace eunuch in Qing dynasty China, seemed to have it all (well . . . *almost* all). At a time when these emasculated servants were often thought of as slithery, conspiring creatures—"the lowest and basest, more worms and ants than men," as the Kangxi emperor described them—An Dehai (or Little An, as he came to be called) was special. Or at least *he* thought so.

Like many of his fellow eunuchs, Little An had been born into poverty and sexually maimed at a young age in the hope that he would find a place in the imperial court—where, following an ancient tradition, neutered men by the thousands performed every task necessary to keep the palaces of the Forbidden City running. The eunuchs had no legal protections—they could be whipped or killed on a whim—but their proximity to power presented unique opportunities for bribery and graft.

Little An gained the favor of Cixi (or Tzu Hsi), the formidable dowager empress who virtually ruled China—albeit from behind a curtain, given the strictures imposed on her gender—during the reigns of two successive Qing emperors in the second half of the 19th century. Cixi's unlikely rise from imperial concubine to the pinnacle of power made her an extraordinary figure in Chinese history; her four-inch-long nails made her an unmistakable one.

Little An's fatal error was to believe that the patronage of the empress dowager made him invincible. And for that false sense of security, he lost more than just his genitalia.

At a time when a eunuch's failure to remember his lowly status was considered an egregious breach of propriety, some members of the imperial court found Little An's arrogance, scheming, and contempt for China's puppet ruler (Cixi's young son, the Tongzhi emperor) intolerable. Clearly, something would have to be done about this abhorrent creature.

Cixi sent her adored eunuch to the city of Suzhou, famed for its fine silk, to procure garments for her. Eunuchs had never been permitted to stray very far beyond the Forbidden City, so it was a novel mission—"a most bizarre thing," as the Tongzhi emperor's tutor wrote in his diary. By allowing Little An such freedom of movement, the empress dowager was stomping on tradition—and putting her pet's life in peril.

Disaster might have been averted had the favored eunuch not made such a spectacle of himself en route to Suzhou. Gathering a sizable retinue about him, Little An set off for the city along China's Grand Canal, music wafting from his large barge festooned with flags. Convinced the emperor himself must be passing, crowds turned out along the canal banks.

Unfortunately for Little An, one of the onlookers was the conservative governor of Shandong Province, who had him arrested and reported his shenanigans to Beijing. Sensing opportunity, Little An's enemies at court pounced. A message was sent to the Shandong governor: The captive "must not be allowed to defend himself with cunning explanations." Rather, he should be executed immediately.

For all her guile, the empress dowager was powerless to save her favorite. The proper order of things had been upended, and Cixi was considered too close to the situation to have a credible voice in restoring the natural balance. So Little An was beheaded. Then, to dispel rumors that he had been the empress dowager's intact lover, his naked corpse was put on public display.

Cixi could not be consoled at the loss of her chosen one. Instead, reported a chief secretary of the Grand Council named Zhu, she took "out her anger on the servants around her," beheading on the spot a eunuch who suggested she could have done more to save Little An. "Brimming over with regret," as Zhu wrote, the empress dowager took to her bed for weeks. Eventually, she would recover. But, thereafter, Cixi lopped off all relations with eunuchs.

SEPTEMBER 13, 1898, 1964, *and* 2001

Critical Mess:
Century After Century of Disses

What is it about September 13 that makes critics so cranky? Just listen to them snarl:

"I often want to criticise Jane Austen, but her books madden me so that I can't conceal my frenzy from the reader; and therefore I have to stop every time I begin. Every time I read 'Pride and Prejudice' I want to dig her up and beat her over the skull with her own shin-bone."
—*Mark Twain, in a letter of September 13, 1898, to his close friend, Reverend Joseph Twichell*

And from literary loathing to musical depreciation . . .

"The Beatles are not merely awful; I would consider it sacrilegious to say anything less than that they are god-awful. They are so unbelievably horrible, so appallingly unmusical, so dogmatically insensitive to the

magic of the art that they qualify as crowned heads of anti-music, even as the impostor popes went down in history as 'anti-popes.'"
—*William F. Buckley, Jr., September 13, 1964*

Finally, how about this gem from Reverend Jerry Falwell and his pal, televangelist Pat Robertson—two pillars of religious tolerance—disgorged just two days after the terrorist attacks of September 11, 2001:

FALWELL: I really believe that the pagans, and the abortionists, and the feminists, and the gays and the lesbians who are actively trying to make that an alternative lifestyle, the ACLU, People for the American Way—all of them who have tried to secularize America—I point the finger in their face and say, "You helped this happen."
ROBERTSON: Well, I totally concur, and the problem is we have adopted that agenda at the highest levels of our government. And so we're responsible as a free society for what the top people do. And the top people, of course, is the court system.
—*The 700 Club, September 13, 2001*

SEPTEMBER 14, 1521

When Henry VIII's Book Came Back to Bite

Henry VIII, notorious for his gargantuan meals, almost certainly wanted to wolf down his own words as well when looking back on September 14, 1521—the date when a grandiloquent if rash book written by the king, *Declaration of the Seven Sacraments Against Martin Luther*, was formally presented to Pope Leo X. In it the English king vigorously upheld papal supremacy—a position he would come to sorely regret when Pope Clement VII later refused to approve the annulment of Henry's first marriage to Katharine of Aragon.

Similarly, Leo X's successors most certainly rued a decision the pope made a month after he received that regal book: He bestowed upon Henry the title of "Defender of the Faith" as a reward for his fealty. But his loyalty was of an inconstant sort. The defiant monarch eventually broke away from Rome and declared himself Supreme Head of the Church of England.

SEPTEMBER 15, 1916

The Tank Tanks

"My poor 'land battleships' have been
let off prematurely and on a petty scale."
—*Winston Churchill, on the inauspicious debut of the tank
at the Battle of the Somme on September 15, 1916*

The armada of invincible mechanical behemoths that British Field Marshal Douglas Haig envisioned—smashing through entrenched German lines on the Western Front and opening the way to a glorious cavalry charge straight to Berlin—turned out to be something significantly less impressive. Sure, the tank, as it came to be called,* intimidated the enemy when it was unveiled on September 15, 1916, amid the carnage of the Somme. "The devil is coming!" came shouts from the German trenches as the death-spewing metal-clad monster loomed into view. But the real hell was *inside* this latest addition to the weaponry introduced during World War I. It was unbearably hot, noisy, and cramped, jarring in the extreme, filled with noxious engine fumes, and potentially lethal when shelled as metal scraps whizzed around the interior.

---

* The name "tank" arose from the extreme secrecy surrounding the development of this new war machine, which was initially disguised to resemble a water tank.

"After a few hours the crews were good for nothing," wrote historian Peter Hart in *The Somme: The Darkest Hour on the Western Front*. "Unfortunately, the sheer mechanical unreliability of the tanks meant that this was usually of little importance, as [they] often broke down well before the crew's health became a problem."

Indeed, the first tanks were like brainless beasts aimlessly lumbering about, with no properly trained crews to guide them. Visibility was limited. Communications with the men inside were sometimes dependent on decidedly old-school carrier pigeons. Often they simply didn't work, or got bogged down in mud and debris. Of the 49 British tanks that arrived in France—far fewer than Field Marshal Haig had wanted—many never made it to the front lines. Others failed to move when called into action.

Bert Chaney, a signaler with the Seventh London Territorial Battalion, recalled his first sight of the "huge mechanical monsters" on September 15: "It was most heartening to watch their advance, we were almost ready to cheer," Chaney recalled. "But there was a surprise in store for us. Instead of going on to the German lines the three tanks assigned to us straddled our front line, stopped and then opened up a murderous machine-gun fire, enfilading us left and right. There they sat, squat monstrous things, noses stuck up in the air, crushing the sides of our trench out of shape with their machine-guns swiveling around

and firing like mad." Though the tank operators finally realized their mistake and moved on, the success of the ungainly vehicles hardly improved.

"One of the tanks got caught up on a tree stump and never reached their front line and a second had its rear steering wheels shot off and could not guide itself," Chaney continued. "The four men in the tank that had got itself hung up dismounted, all in the heat of the battle, stretching themselves, scratching their heads, then slowly and deliberately walked round their vehicle inspecting it from every angle and appeared to hold a conference among themselves. After standing around for a few minutes, looking somewhat lost, they calmly took out from the inside of the tank a primus stove and, using the side of the tank as a cover from enemy fire, sat down on the ground and made themselves some tea. The battle was over as far as they were concerned."

The third tank managed to plow its way through, into the village of Flers. But for wartime leaders looking back on the occasion, such small victories were insignificant. As they saw it, the tank, which would later prove to be far more formidable, was simply not yet ready for battle. Haig's premature use of it, and in such small numbers, was "a foolish blunder," as former Prime Minister David Lloyd George wrote in his *War Memoirs*—notwithstanding the fact that, since July, the Somme had become a stalemated charnel house, with every foot of advance costing thousands of lives.

Winston Churchill, an early champion of the tank's development, was equally critical. "The first twenty tanks . . . were improvidently exposed to the enemy at the Battle of the Somme," he wrote in *The World Crisis*. "The immense advantage of novelty and surprise was thus squandered while the number of tanks was small, their conditions experimental and their crews almost untrained. This priceless conception, containing if used in its integrity and on a sufficient scale, the certainty of a great and brilliant victory, was revealed to the Germans for the mere petty purpose of taking a few ruined villages."

SEPTEMBER 16, 1929

Beantown: Not Good for the Arts

"I would rather be banned in Boston than read anywhere else because
when you are banned in Boston, you are read everywhere else."
—*American novelist Upton Sinclair*

Three centuries after Christmas celebrations were made illegal in Massachusetts (see December 25), the city of Boston continued to wriggle under the heel of the Puritan boot. On September 16, 1929, Mayor Malcolm Nichols decreed that Eugene O'Neill's Pulitzer Prize–winning play *Strange Interlude* was filth—and therefore unfit for local audiences. Despite having never seen the nine-act, five-hour-long experimental drama featuring controversial themes of premarital sex and abortion, Nichols insisted that it was "a plea for the murder of unborn children, a breeding ground for atheism and domestic infidelity, and a disgusting spectacle of immorality."

So in a strange prelude, the curtain fell on *Strange Interlude* before a single syllable of O'Neill's overflowing dialogue had been uttered on a Boston stage.

It made no difference to the crusading executive that his city— purportedly the "Cradle of Liberty"—had become a notorious cultural backwater, thanks to his attempts to legislate its morals. (Indeed, "Banned in Boston" had become a byword for artistic repression—one that publicists gleefully employed to draw paying customers to any work thus stigmatized.)

Nichols would not budge from his anointed duty to shield the populace from the depravity of *Strange Interlude*—just as he had already ensured they would never see O'Neill's earlier play *Desire Under the Elms*. Or read Hemingway's *The Sun Also Rises*. Or Theodore Dreiser's *An American Tragedy*. Or Sinclair Lewis's *Elmer Gantry*.

In an editorial that appeared two days after the play was shuttered, *The Boston Globe* gave a sarcastic nod to both the city's doctrinaire mayor and its rich tradition of censorship: "Till the last Hottentot and the ultimate

Eskimo have heard, till the denizens of farthest Siberia and Terra Del Fuego are familiar with the stimulating slogan ["Banned in Boston"], we must not rest. We must, like Columbus, go on and on, and on."

Several weeks later, *Strange Interlude* opened 10 miles south of Boston in Quincy and ran for nearly a month of sold-out performances—a boon not only to the town but also to an obscure restaurant near the theater named Howard Johnson's.

SEPTEMBER 17, 1941

Cultural Vandalism, Part 2:
Harried Treasure

The curators of the Catherine Palace just outside Leningrad were frantic. The Nazis were coming. And though they never could have conceived the horrors that awaited Peter the Great's grand city during the ensuing 900-day siege—when some one million souls perished*— they knew that one of the world's most precious treasures was in peril.

"What shall we do with Amber Room? What can we do?" recorded Anatoly Kuchumov, guardian of the glowing, gem-encrusted showcase sometimes called the Eighth Wonder of the World. "A trial moving of one of the [wall] panels has resulted in disaster. The amber facing has come off the mount and shattered completely. We cannot move the Amber Room. We dare not move it."

Kuchumov's trepidation was understandable; the unique masterwork was admired the world over. "The room is rather large, with . . . walls

---

* "Leningrad must die of starvation," Hitler publicly declared in 1941, and the city (since restored to its original name of St. Petersburg) very nearly did. The statistics are staggering, as are the recorded travails of doomed individuals reduced to eating scraps of wallpaper paste, leather, and even each other.

wholly adorned with amber mosaic from top to bottom, including a frieze," Theophile Gautier wrote in his 1866 travelogue *Voyage en Russie*. "The eye, which has not adapted to seeing this material applied in such scale, is amazed and is blinded by the wealth and warmth of tints, representing all colors of the spectrum of yellow—from smoky topaz up to a light lemon. The gold of carvings seems dim and false in this neighborhood, especially when the sun falls on the walls and runs through transparent veins as those sliding on them."

The only available solution for preserving the Amber Room from certain pillaging was a long shot: hiding the precious panels behind a false wall. The completed effect was an empty room—precisely resembling most other spaces in the palace turned museum, from which irreplaceable collections of the bygone tsarist era had been evacuated and hidden.

But the ruse was exposed when the Germans stormed the Catherine Palace on September 17, 1941. "Two privates in curiosity toiled in tearing protective . . . covers off [the walls]," one Nazi later told author Paul Enke. "They revealed wonderfully shining amber carvings, the frames of a mosaic picture."

The work of art—ironically, a gift of peace from a Prussian king to Peter the Great in 1716—was packed up by the invaders and shipped back to Prussia, where it was triumphantly displayed at Königsberg Castle. It was, as one German newspaper gleefully reported, "a return to its true home, the real place of origination of the amber."

But in 1945, coinciding roughly with the final days of the Third Reich, the famed Amber Room disappeared again—perhaps forever. Treasure hunters have been salivating for decades over the missing masterpiece, while many a conspiracy theorist has spun tales of intrigue about its likely fate. However, most historians believe in the simplest answer: that the Amber Room was destroyed at the end of World War II—perhaps even inadvertently by Soviet troops rampaging through Königsberg.

As if to acknowledge that the original is gone for good, Russia unveiled a re-created chamber of amber at the Catherine Palace in 2003. But as anyone who has encountered the Las Vegas Sphinx knows, a replica Wonder of the World does not always fill viewers with wonder.

Oh Man! What a Mess!

"Oh man! Oh God! Oh man! Oh God! Oh man!
Oh God! Oh man! Oh God! Oh man! Oh God!"
—One of the more god-awful line readings from Norman Mailer's
box-office bomb, Tough Guys Don't Dance, *released on September 18,*
1987. The 20 words—well, three words, really—are vomited forth by
Ryan O'Neal's character upon learning from his ex-girlfriend
that his wife is sleeping with her husband.

The Mickey Mouse Move That Kept Khrushchev out of Disneyland

The Cold War threat of nuclear annihilation was all too real in 1959. Nevertheless, the hot ticket in Hollywood that summer was lunch with the very man who repeatedly bragged about his power to push a button marked *Oblivion.*

Soviet premier Nikita Khrushchev was in the middle of a bizarre two-week tour across the United States—"a surreal extravaganza," historian John Lewis Gaddis would call it—when he swooped into Tinseltown on September 19 and made a scene so absurd that even the most imaginative scriptwriter would have deemed it too fanciful for the screen.

While dining with a panoply of A-list movie stars at the 20th Century Fox commissary—Elizabeth Taylor and Frank Sinatra among them—the roly-poly premier received word that a trip to Disneyland planned for later that day would have to be canceled for security reasons. The ensuing explosion, though not quite atomic, would have put the most petulant five-year-old to shame.

"What is it?" Khrushchev demanded. "Is there an epidemic of cholera there? Have gangsters taken hold of the place? Your policemen are so tough they could lift a bull by the horns. Surely they can restore order if there are any gangsters around! I say, 'I would very much like to see Disneyland.' They say, 'We cannot guarantee your security.' Then what must I do—commit suicide?"

The bald cauldron of fury before them—his face reddening, his fist punching the air—started to make the gathered celebrities uneasy. "Were they really watching the sixty-five-year-old dictator of the world's largest country throw a temper tantrum because he wasn't allowed to go to Disneyland?" wrote Peter Carlson in his 2009 book *K Blows Top: A Cold War Comic Interlude, Starring Nikita Khrushchev, America's Most Unlikely Tourist.*

Yes, they really were.

Meeting Marilyn Monroe afterward, however, seemed to mollify the Soviet Grumpy. "You're a very lovely young lady," he purred to the Hollywood sex goddess. The love from Russia was not reciprocated: "He was fat and ugly and had warts on his face and he growled," Monroe complained to her maid and confidant, Lena Pepitone. "He squeezed my hand so long and so hard that I thought he would break it. I guess it was better than having to kiss him."

No doubt Snow White would have felt the same way.

SEPTEMBER 20, 2006

On Second Thought, Part 13: The iFlub

*N*ew York Times technology columnist David Pogue set himself up for a massive blunder on September 20, 2006, when he merrily provided his readers a list of failed predictions about Apple, Inc. from rival publications. *Fortune* magazine's declaration from 1996—"By the time you read this story, the quirky cult company . . . will end its wild ride as an independent enterprise"—was just one example Pogue cited to illustrate how "wildly, hilariously, embarrassingly wrong" his fellow analysts had been.

But Pogue intended to make a larger point about those misguided oracles.

"This is why, when anyone asks me what the future of technology holds, or what kids will be bringing to school in 2016, I politely decline to answer," he wrote. "In the end, this story really isn't about Apple—or any one company . . . This story is about the journalists and commentators. It's one thing to report what's happening to a flailing company, and quite another to announce what's *going* to happen. In the technology business, that's a fool's game."

In another column just one week after that preening pronouncement, Pogue played the fool's game himself: "Everyone's always asking me when Apple will come out with a cellphone. My answer is, 'Probably never.'"

———◆———

SEPTEMBER 21, 1796

The Captain and the Terrible Tar, or Why Not to Hire an Entitled Snot for an Entry-Level Job

Capt. George Vancouver stands today as one of Britain's preeminent explorers—perhaps most notable for having meticulously charted the Pacific coast of North America in the late-18th century. But his reputation was nearly ruined in his own time by a surly midshipman with a title, lofty connections, and an obsessive grudge. Thomas Pitt, the Baron of Camelford, was a cousin of the prime minister, a brother-in-law of the foreign secretary, and an all-around jackass.

Pitt, it seems, had been an obstreperous twerp during Vancouver's four-year grand voyage of exploration around the globe. This was only a short time after the infamous mutiny aboard the H.M.S. *Bounty* (see

April 28), when naval discipline—already notoriously harsh—was even more rigorously enforced. Thus the grossly insubordinate sailor was regularly lashed for a multitude of infractions—and eventually dismissed from the expedition.

That left Pitt seething, his rage compounded by Vancouver's lesser social status. Revenge became the outcast's blinding passion.

No sooner had Vancouver completed his explorations and settled in a village outside London in 1796 than Pitt (now Lord Camelford, having inherited the peerage from his recently deceased father) wrote him an abusive letter challenging him to a duel. Vancouver demurred, explaining that he was not honor-bound to answer for his official actions in a private capacity. He did, however, offer to present himself before a board of inquiry. Pitt would have none of it. First he showed up on Vancouver's doorstep, spewing insults and demanding satisfaction. Then, after three weeks of relentlessly stalking his former captain, he viciously attacked him in public.

On September 21, 1796, as Vancouver and his brother Charles were walking along Conduit Street on their way to see the Lord Chancellor (the only peer powerful enough to wield any influence over his deranged fellow member of the House of Lords), Pitt ran up and began wildly striking Vancouver with his cane. Charles stepped in to defend his brother, who had grown increasingly ill since his return to Britain, and the melee ended only when onlookers dragged the screeching Lord Camelford away.

The brutal beating was not Pitt's final insult, however. His friend, popular satirical cartoonist James Gillray, would see to that.

Just over a week after the assault, Gillray's "The Caneing in Conduit Street" appeared in print. It was a devastating broadside, featuring Vancouver meekly submitting to the blows while his brother is forced to defend him. "Give me satisfaction, rascal!" Pitt yells, "draw your sword, coward! What, you won't! why then, take that, lubber! and that, and that, and that!" Vancouver, for his part, cries "Murder! murder! Watch! constable! Keep him off, brother, while I run to my Lord Chancellor for protection! Murder! murder! murder!" From Vancouver's pocket hangs "A List of those degraded during the voyage; put under arrest, all the ship's crew; put into irons, every gentleman on board; broke, every man of honour and spirit."

For a man whose seafaring accomplishments rivaled those of his esteemed contemporary Capt. James Cook, the derision to which the cartoon subjected Vancouver was almost too much to endure. Broken in body and spirit, he died less than two years after the caricature appeared. As for Thomas Pitt—the quarrelsome "Half-Mad Lord," as one biographer described him—he finally got his duel, in a spat with his friend Capt. Thomas Best. He also got himself killed.

———◆———

SEPTEMBER 22, 1846

The Blight Side of History:
When the Snakes Came Back to Ireland

"The Irish peasant had tasted of famine and found that it was good.
He saw the cloud looming in the distance and he hailed its approach.

To him it teemed with goodly manna and salient waters. He wrapped himself up in the ragged mantle of inert expediency and said that he trusted to Providence. But the deity of his faith was the Government—the manna of his hopes was a Parliamentary grant."
—*Editorial in* The Times *of London, published September 22, 1846, amid the Great Famine in Ireland that resulted, by some estimates, in one million deaths*

As far as *The Times* was concerned, the mass starvation had nothing to do with the British government's oppressive (and arguably genocidal) policies toward the Irish. Rather, "it was the same rooted and innate disposition which thwarts, and baffles, and depresses them whithersoever they turn."

And so, the paper insisted, there should be no government-funded relief for these intransigently indolent people, who opted to live in "hereditary squalor." Come to think of it, why not look on the bright side of famine? Perhaps now the Irish would actually get busy and scrounge something more nutritious to eat than the lowly spud.

"For our parts," *The Times* concluded, "we regard the potato blight as a blessing."

SEPTEMBER 23, 1908

"Merkle's Boner":
The Rise of a Terrible Tag

"A Boner Buries the Giants"
—New York Times *headline for a September 23, 1908, story detailing a baserunning blunder committed that day by 19-year-old New York Giants rookie Fred Merkle. The phrase "Merkle's boner," reprinted in thousands of newspapers, would dog the ill-starred player for the rest of his life—and beyond.*

I t's the bottom of the ninth with two outs and a man on in this pivotal game between the New York Giants and the Chicago Cubs. The score is all tied up at 1 apiece. At stake: the National League pennant.

Now approaching the plate is the Giants' backup first baseman, Fred Merkle. He's played in only 38 games this year, but—oh! Merkle hits a scorcher down the right-field line, advancing outfielder Moose McCormick to third base! Then, another single—this one by shortstop Al Bridwell—and McCormick trots home!! The Giants have won it!!!

Oops . . . no, they hadn't.

As delirious New York fans rushed the field, Merkle pivoted on his cleats halfway between first and second and headed back to the dugout. There was just one problem, and it would become the "boner" (for "bonehead play") of lore: Perhaps hoping to avoid the stampeding crowd, Merkle never bothered to step on second base.

Recognizing this as a potential violation of official baseball rule #4.09 ("A run is not scored if the runner advances to home base during a play in which the third out is made . . . by any runner being forced out"), Cubs second baseman Johnny Evers shouted for the ball. How he got it amid the jubilant chaos on the field—and whether it was indeed the game ball or a stand-in—has been hotly debated ever since. Regardless, Evers used the ball to tag second base. Umpire Hank O'Day then called Merkle out, nullifying McCormick's winning run.

The Giants' victory vanished in an instant.* With it went the blissful period during which Fred Merkle had enjoyed being known simply as Fred Merkle; forever after, the "boner" would be fused to his name. Indeed, a less-than-subtle *Toronto Star* headline on the anniversary of the game blared: "40 Years Haven't Softened 'Boner' Blow for Merkle."

And even death offered no surcease from the turgid tag: A 1956 obituary headline by the Associated Press read, "Fred Merkle, of 'Boner' Fame, Dies."

---

* The game was ruled a 1–1 tie. The Cubs defeated the Giants in the rematch and went on to win the World Series.

SEPTEMBER 24, 2002

Monster's Ball:
A Gala to Honor Jerry Sandusky

"**G**ive him the young guys any day," reporter Rob Amen innocently wrote in the September 16, 1995, edition of *The Daily Collegian,* the student newspaper at Pennsylvania State University. Alas, it was in a feature on assistant football coach Jerry Sandusky—later revealed to be a serial child molester—with the unfortunate headline: "Defensive Coordinator Jerry Sandusky's Love for Kids Keeps Him at Penn State Instead of Pros."

Prior to being unmasked as a monster, Sandusky was lauded at every turn. President George H. W. Bush singled out The Second Mile, Sandusky's charity/grooming ground, as one of his "thousand points of light."* ("It's about time, George!" Sandusky recalled telling the president in *Touched,* his regrettably titled autobiography. "This is long overdue.") Later, in 1995, the predatory football coach was awarded the YMCA Service to Youth Award.

On September 24, 2002, came the ultimate ironic salute. That day the Congressional Coalition on Adoption Institute held its annual Angels in Adoption Awards Gala—"the crown jewel of our awareness programming," as director Kerry Hasenbalg described the event, "a celebration of those committed individuals making a difference in the lives of children and families." With award recipients from each state selected by their congressional representative, Sandusky was recognized as an "Angel" by Senator Rick Santorum of Pennsylvania.

It was the perfect disguise for a devil at work.

---

* Perhaps equally mortifying was President George W. Bush's praise for Florida Representative Mark Foley on July 27, 2006. The Republican congressman was part of a "SWAT team for kids," the president proudly declared. Two months later, Foley—a leading member of the House Caucus on Missing and Exploited Children—resigned in disgrace when it was revealed that he had been sending sexually explicit texts and emails to teenage boys working as Capitol Hill pages.

SEPTEMBER 25, 2018

That Time the Donald
Made the Whole World Smile

"In less than two years, my administration has
accomplished more than almost any administration
in the history of our country."
—*President Donald Trump in an address to the*
United Nations on September 25, 2018. The response—
from an international audience clearly more familiar with
American history than the president*—was raucous laughter.
"Didn't expect that reaction," a rattled Trump responded
to the titters, "but that's okay."

———◆———

SEPTEMBER 26, 2010

What a Segway to Go:
First He Bought the Company,
Then He Bought the Farm

On September 26, 2010—less than a year after acquiring Segway,
Inc.—British entrepreneur Jimi Heselden died of injuries sustained
after accidentally driving one of the company's gyroscope-powered,
self-balancing scooters off a cliff.

———◆———

* See March 31 for another example of Trump's extraordinary historical insight.

SEPTEMBER 27, 1589

Put to the Testes, Part 8: Such a Fan of the Sopranos

Pope Sixtus V was an inexorable opponent of contraception in any form—so much so that he promulgated a decree equating it with homicide and calling for a commensurate punishment. Ironic, then, that this pope would also promote the ultimate in birth control: castration. On September 27, 1589, Sixtus issued the papal bull *Cum pro nostro pastorali munere,* which called for a reorganization of the pope's official choir to include four emasculated men (castrati) to sing the soaring high notes.

The low note: Gonads for the greater glory were continuously sacrificed over the next three centuries.

SEPTEMBER 28, 1972

Anatomically Incorrect: John Mitchell Delivers *Post* Publisher His Breast Shot

"All that crap, you're putting it in the paper? It's all been denied. Katie Graham's gonna get her tit caught in a big fat wringer if that's published. Good Christ! That's the most sickening thing I ever heard."
—*John Mitchell, former attorney general and director of President Richard*
  Nixon's 1972 reelection campaign, threatening The Washington Post
  publisher in response to Post *reporter Carl Bernstein's late-night phone call*
  seeking comment on a story—set to run the next day—that Mitchell con-
  trolled a slush fund for use in undermining Nixon's Democratic opposition

More details of the conversation with Mitchell—duly reported in the *Post* on September 29, 1972, minus the words "her tit"—were furnished in *All the President's Men,* the book Bernstein co-wrote with his investigative partner on Watergate, Bob Woodward: "For Bernstein, the only constant had been an adrenal feeling that began with Mitchell's first JEEEEEEEEESUS—some sort of primal scream. As the cry of JEEEEEEEEESUS was repeated, Bernstein had perceived the excruciating depth of Mitchell's hurt. For a moment, he had been afraid that Mitchell might die on the telephone . . . [His] tone was so filled with hate and loathing that Bernstein had felt threatened."

"It was quite a temper tantrum on Mitchell's part," Katharine Graham later wrote in her Pulitzer Prize–winning autobiography, *Personal History.* And though she recalled being shocked,* "so personal and offensive were the threat and the message," the renowned publisher did manage to find a glint of humor in the situation: She had a gold charm made in the shape of a washing-machine wringer, then wore it on a necklace. Dangling beside it was a miniature gold breast that her friend Art Buchwald had given her.

And of course Mrs. Graham got to savor the fact that in the end it was a sensitive part of John Mitchell's anatomy that ended up being squeezed—behind bars.

---

* Mitchell's crude personal attack on Katharine Graham was hardly an aberration among all the president's men. The year before, Nixon himself had launched a sexist tirade against the powerful publisher in a telephone conversation with the equally abhorrent FBI director, J. Edgar Hoover. "She's a terrible old bag," the president fumed on July 1, two weeks after the *Post* began publishing articles based on the infamous Pentagon Papers. Hoover was quick to agree: "Oh, she's an old bitch in my estimation." Yet as Jack Shafer pointed out in *Slate*, Graham was only 54 at the time. "The 75-year-old Hoover, on the other hand, resembled nothing more than sun-rotted, wormy calabash."

SEPTEMBER 29, 1853

Two Terms Before Lincoln, Malice Toward Some

"If there be any purpose more fixed than another in the mind
of the President and those with whom he is accustomed to consult,
it is that the dangerous element of Abolitionism, under whatever
guise or form it may present itself, shall be crushed out,
so far as his administration is concerned."
—*Caleb Cushing, President Franklin Pierce's attorney general, in a letter
to the* Boston Post *on September 29, 1853. Cushing had added fangs to
the Fugitive Slave Law of 1850 by declaring that all methods and resources
were acceptable in the apprehension effort. That included the use of "any
and all organized force, whether militia of the state, or officers, sailors,
soldiers, and marines of the United States."*

SEPTEMBER 30, 1957

Crying Uncle . . . Tom

"He's the Number One Uncle Tom! The worst in the U.S.!"
—*Thurgood Marshall, head of the NAACP Legal Defense and Educa-
tional Fund and future Supreme Court justice, speaking of jazz pioneer
Louis Armstrong in a September 30, 1957
interview with the* New York Post

"Uncle Tom," the title character of Harriet Beecher Stowe's influential
1852 novel, is also a nasty slur, traditionally used by African Americans to stigmatize other African Americans deemed overly subservient
to whites, or perceived to be traitors to their own race. Marshall was in
the habit of tossing the term about quite casually. Indeed, one year

before insulting Armstrong, he went after singer Nat King Cole, who had just been attacked on stage during a performance for a white audience in Birmingham: "All Cole needs to complete his role as an Uncle Tom is a banjo."

Call it historic comeuppance or Uncle Tom's curse, but Marshall's legal triumphs in public-school desegregation were anathema to firebrands such as Malcolm X and Bobby Seale, who branded his efforts too accommodating of a corrupt, white-dominated system. As a result, they slapped the Supreme Court's first African-American justice with the same inflammatory epithet he had so blithely hurled at others.

Thurgood Marshall's legacy—both as an iconic seeker of justice and as a base peddler of odious insults—is perhaps best represented by the law school at Texas Southern University in Houston, which today bears his name in worthy tribute. Yet upon its 1946 founding as a separate institution for training black lawyers, the law school bore the brunt of his worst instincts: Marshall's derisive nickname for the school was "Uncle Tom's Cabin."

October

Foundering Son:
A Duel That Ended in a Living Death

"**D**ear Sir!" Dr. Benjamin Rush wrote to his fellow Founding Father Alexander Hamilton on November 26, 1801, three days after Hamilton's beloved son Philip had engaged in a fatal duel at Weehawken, New Jersey.* "Permit a whole family to mingle their tears with yours upon the late distressing event that has taken place in your family."

The sympathetic Dr. Rush would come to experience paternal agony of the very kind that had left Alexander Hamilton debilitated by grief. On October 1, 1807, Rush's son John was involved in a duel of his own, with his fellow naval officer and friend Lt. Benjamin Turner aboard a gunboat in port at New Orleans. The affair of honor would leave one man dead and the other permanently unhinged.

---

* Alexander Hamilton, who would be fatally shot by Aaron Burr on the same dueling ground three years later, rushed to the bedside of his dying son. Dr. David Hosack, attending Philip—as he later would his father—recalled the moment: "He instantly turned from the bed and, taking me by the hand, which he grasped with all the agony of grief, he exclaimed in a tone and manner that can never be effaced from my memory, 'Doctor, I despair.'"

The lethal spat was over Shakespeare, of all things. "A number of officers were amusing themselves in their quarters last evening playing cards when Lieut. Rush came in and was asked to play," one witness reported. "He declined, with a quotation from Shakespeare. Some criticism was made on it by Turner, and an argument of some warmth took place—disagreeable reflections were made, bad language ensued, and this morning Turner sent Rush a challenge."

It seems that Turner had something to prove. He had recently rebuffed a challenge to meet on the field of honor—which, in the duel-crazed U.S. Navy of the time, marked him as a coward. Ironically, Turner's friend John Rush had supported his demurral as proper for an officer and a gentleman. Thus, it was quite a surprise when Turner challenged his own champion.

Rush was determined not to fire directly at his friend in the ensuing encounter, until he learned of Turner's kill-or-be-killed mindset. With little choice left, Rush fired the shot that fatally tore through Turner. "My dear friend!" he wailed. "Why would you force me to do this? Let me declare in your dying ear . . . that I did not wish to meet you, and . . . shall mourn your death as that of a brother!"

Though cleared of wrongdoing by the Navy, which tended to wink at the practice of dueling, John Rush could not clear his own conscience. Never the steadiest fellow to begin with—he described himself as "the degenerate son of an eminent and respectful father . . . a blackguard"— Rush unraveled after killing Turner.

"The situation of your son is at present the most deplorable," Commandant David Porter wrote to Benjamin Rush from New Orleans in March 1809. "He is now and has been for some time past in a state of insanity." Not only had the disturbed man attacked a surgeon and others in a hospital, but he also had slit his own throat.

John Rush returned home to Philadelphia in what his father described in a letter to another son, James, as "a deep state of melancholy. Neither the embraces nor tears of your mother, father, sister, nor brothers could obtain a word nor even a look from him." Furthermore, he presented a frightful picture. "His appearance when he entered his father's house was that of the King of Babylon described in the old testament," Benjamin

Rush wrote to John Adams. "His long and uncombed hair and his long nails and beard rendered him an object of horror to his afflicted parents and family."

Adams understood. Like Alexander Hamilton and other Founders, he was all too familiar with the vicissitudes of fatherhood. "John's Misfortune I deplore," the retired second president wrote to Rush, referencing his own deeply troubled son, Charles, who had died of alcoholism nine years earlier. "I Sympathize with you, and with the keener sensibility as I have experienced the Feelings and Reflections of a Father in Circumstances perhaps Still more desperate calamitous, and afflicting. Parents must have their Tryals."

The "Tryals" of Benjamin Rush ended long before his son's: He died in 1813, lauded as the "father of American psychiatry." John Rush, by contrast, spent the rest of his life endlessly pacing an asylum, tormented to the end by the knowledge that a superficial chivalry had obligated him to slay his own friend.*

OCTOBER 2, 1980

Defeat of Clay: When Ali Got Stung

"Holmes must go. I'll eat him up. I'll hit him with jabs and right crosses. He can't dance. I'm gonna dance fifteen rounds. This old man will whup his butt. Pow! Pow! Pow! I see it all now. He's exhausted. Bam! The right hand over the tired jab. And Holmes is down!

---

* Samuel Coates, a colleague of Benjamin Rush's in the pioneering treatment of mental illness, related an incident at the Pennsylvania Hospital where John Rush was confined until his death in 1837: "The Barber on combing his [Rush's] hair pleasantly remarked to him that it was becoming quite Grey, 'but never Mind,' added he, 'grey hairs are honourable, you know.' 'Yes,' replied the patient emphatically, 'and sometimes honour makes grey hairs.'"

Ali goes to a neutral corner. Seven, eight, nine, ten!
And for the world-record-setting never-to-be-broken fourth time,
Muhammad Ali is the heavyweight champion of the world!"
—*Boxing legend Muhammad Ali, on his upcoming fight*
with Larry Holmes, 1980

He had always been The Greatest at the verbal strut, and he was still just as lean as when he fought—and beat—Joe Frazier in 1974. But behind the bravado and the superficial appearance of fitness, Muhammad Ali's 38-year-old body was beginning to betray him when he emerged from a short-lived retirement in 1980 to fight his former sparring partner, Larry Holmes.

A pre-match examination at the Mayo Clinic indicated slowing reflexes and diminished dexterity. (Both were early signs of Parkinson's disease, it would tragically turn out.) But that didn't stop Ali from returning to the ring—or the Nevada State Athletic Commission from shamefully allowing him to do so.

What resulted on October 2, 1980—a Vegas encounter ironically billed as "the Last Hurrah"—was a sad spectacle, akin to a once noble lion limping away from the pride after being mauled by a younger rival.

It was clear from the beginning that something was seriously off with Ali. He barely reacted to the Holmes onslaught and, as he remembered thinking while slouched in his corner at the end of Round 1, "Oh, God,

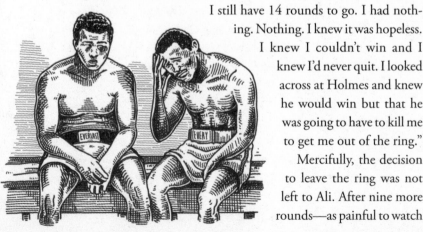

I still have 14 rounds to go. I had nothing. Nothing. I knew it was hopeless. I knew I couldn't win and I knew I'd never quit. I looked across at Holmes and knew he would win but that he was going to have to kill me to get me out of the ring."

Mercifully, the decision to leave the ring was not left to Ali. After nine more rounds—as painful to watch as they must have been to endure, with Ali repeatedly pummeled and left staggering, even cowering at one point—the bout was called in Holmes's favor.

It was an appalling dethronement. And given the former champ's diminished physical state, insisted his former ring physician, Ferdie Pacheco, it never should have been allowed. "All the people involved in this fight should have been arrested," he said. "This fight was an abomination, a crime." As for Larry Holmes, who pulled many of his punches in the later rounds, there was no triumph in defeating his idol and mentor.

"I went to his room and I told him, 'I love you, man,'" Holmes recalled after the lopsided clash. "He said, 'If you loved me, why'd you beat me up like that?' I was laughing and crying at the same time."

OCTOBER 3, 1952

With McCarthy Screaming "Red," Ike Turns Yellow

The text of presidential candidate Dwight D. Eisenhower's speech was typed and ready as the campaign train approached Milwaukee. And it was going to be a doozy—a stinging rebuke to Red-baiting demagogue Joseph McCarthy, delivered smack in the Wisconsin senator's home state, for having maligned World War II hero Gen. George C. Marshall. "Just wait till we get to Milwaukee," Eisenhower's aides told reporters, "and you will find out what he thinks of McCarthy."

Ike had long been repulsed by Senator McCarthy, who had catapulted himself to national prominence by claiming that the U.S. government was crawling with Communists, then threatening the individuals he named with removal from their jobs. Eisenhower's loathing did not fully crystallize until 1951, however, when McCarthy stood before the Senate and accused Marshall—Ike's mentor and friend—of being part of a

Communist conspiracy "so immense as to dwarf any previous such venture in the history of man. A conspiracy of infamy so black that, when it is finally exposed, its principals shall be forever deserving of the maledictions of all honest men."

Now, on October 3, 1952, Eisenhower was set to volley that vilification right back.

"I know [Marshall], as a man and a soldier, to be dedicated with singular selflessness and the profoundest patriotism to the service of America," the text of Ike's speech read in part. And as far as McCarthy's spurious charges of treason: "Here we have a sobering lesson of the way freedom must *not* defend itself."

Yet Eisenhower never spoke the words that had been written. Instead—on what his staffers came to call "that terrible day"—he stood in Milwaukee and delivered the same sort of anticommunist pap for which the snarling Wisconsin senator had become notorious. General Marshall's name was not mentioned once.

Sitting several rows behind the candidate, Joe McCarthy was so pleased with the speech that he leaped over the seats blocking his way to grab Ike's hand and, no doubt, to bask in the photographic opportunity—two anti-Red warriors united.

The backlash against Ike's capitulation to McCarthy (and the Republican Party leaders who had prevailed on him to defang his speech) was fierce. President Harry Truman, for one, declared that Eisenhower had surrendered to a "moral scoundrel." And indeed, it appeared that he had. But why would a man unafraid to invade Nazi-held Europe crumple before someone as craven as McCarthy—especially when he genuinely despised him?*

For Eisenhower biographer Stephen E. Ambrose, the answer was simple: Ike wanted to be president. And if the price of votes was curbing his criticism of McCarthy in the senator's home state, so be it—even at the sacrifice of Marshall's good name.

---

* Milton Eisenhower stated that his brother "loathed McCarthy as much as any human being could loathe another."

Nonetheless, Eisenhower seemed to regret the decision—and struggled to justify it in his memoirs, where he maintained that his support of Marshall had never wavered. Any capitulation to McCarthy was simply a woeful misperception. "Indeed," he wrote, after scrapping a number of drafts, "if I could have foreseen this distortion of the facts, a distortion that even led some to question my loyalty to General Marshall, I would never have acceded to the [speech modifications], logical as they sounded at the time."

Marshall himself, however, best captured the essence of the matter: "Eisenhower was forced into a corner," the general told a reporter in one of his few comments on the issue. "There is no more independence in politics than there is in jail."

───────

OCTOBER 4, 1609

When the Jamestown Settlers Ate Their Words— and Each Other

Capt. John Smith may have been a domineering blowhard—"an Ambityous unworthy and vayneglorious fellowe," as his rival George Percy put it—but he was key to the stability of the fledgling Virginia Colony based at Jamestown. Regrettably, those who sought to undermine him did not grasp his value until it was too late.

On October 4, 1609, Smith departed the settlement he had helped establish two and a half years earlier, sailing back to England to undergo treatment for the severe burns he had sustained when a stray spark ignited his gunpowder sack. Thus began a season of horrors in Jamestown known as "the Starving Time."

Captain Smith would have left earlier, but his enemies detained his ship while they compiled a dossier of his alleged misdeeds to be sent back to England. Meanwhile, they neglected essential winter preparations such as stockpiling food—a discipline that Smith had enforced with a rigor some resented. The Native Americans of the region had plenty to eat, but with Smith gone they were less willing to trade—or coexist. In fact, they set out to annihilate the invasive English through terror and starvation.

John Ratcliffe, a member of the anti-Smith clique, suffered a horrific fate when he went to Chief Powhatan to negotiate for food: Tied to a stake, Ratcliffe watched helplessly as his flesh was slowly torn off with mussel shells and tossed bit by bit into a waiting fire.

"Now we all found the want of Captain Smith," an anonymous Jamestown chronicler wrote, "yea his greatest maligners could then curse his loss. Now for corn, provision, and contribution from the savages, we had nothing but mortal wounds with clubs and arrows."

Afraid to forage beyond the Jamestown perimeter, the colonists were reduced to eating cats, dogs, rats, snakes, and even the leather from their shoes. Then they began to eat each other. Graves were dug up for the human flesh they contained. And in at least several instances, the living became nourishment:* A colonist named Collins chopped up his pregnant wife and consumed her, an abomination for which he was executed. (Whether he too was eaten afterward is not recorded.)

By March, six months after Smith left Jamestown, only 60 of the original 500 colonists remained alive.

"It were too vile to say what we endured," the anonymous reporter wrote. "but the occasion was only our own, for want of providence, industry, and government, and not the barrenness and defect of the country, as is generally supposed . . . Had we been in Paradise itself . . . it would not have been much better with us."

———◆———

* Historians doubted accounts of cannibalism at Jamestown until 2013, when it was revealed that portions of a young girl's skeleton uncovered at the settlement showed she had been methodically butchered.

Drug Rush

"**D**rug use destroys societies. Drug use, some might say, is destroying this country. And we have laws against selling drugs, pushing drugs, using drugs, importing drugs."

And there you have pill-popping blowhard Rush Limbaugh, ranting into a studio microphone on his eponymous radio show on October 5, 1995. When he was later charged with obtaining prescription painkillers illegally, another bombastic pronouncement from that same harangue would ring especially hypocritical: "[I]f people are violating the law by doing drugs, they ought to be accused and they ought to be convicted and they ought to be sent up."

Yet Limbaugh himself never served a single second of "sent-up" time—largely because he had cloaked himself in the language of recovery. "The idea is to help the person overcome the addiction," Limbaugh's lawyer insisted after the drug charges had been settled.* "There should be a recognition that people like Rush really should not be prosecuted."

Hmm . . . instead "people like Rush" should be awarded the Presidential Medal of Freedom?

Worse Than the Apple: The Fall of "Adam"

Biblical Adam didn't get off easy after defying God and eating that forbidden fruit. Banished from Eden, he had to resort to subsistence

---

* Luckily for Limbaugh, the bottle of Viagra subsequently discovered in his luggage—and prescribed under another person's name—was found not to be a violation of his settlement agreement.

farming on bad soil for the remaining 600 years or so of his life. But at least he wasn't smashed to pieces: That fate was reserved for the life-size marble sculpture of him carved in the late 15th century by Tullio Lombardo.

Sometime around 6 p.m. on October 6, 2002, the plywood base upon which "Adam" stood in New York's Metropolitan Museum of Art buckled and collapsed, causing the exquisite masterpiece—"the first life-sized nude marble statue since antiquity," as the Met described it, "and the most important Italian Renaissance sculpture in North America"—to come crashing down. It was a catastrophic loss—"about the worst thing that could happen" to a museum, in the words of Met Director Philippe de Montebello.

"Adam" was decapitated, the floor lit-
tered with hundreds of marble shards.
But after a meticulous, 12-year
restoration, "Adam" stood tall
once more—forever com-
promised, just like the original sinner, but with repairs
so deft that, as de Montebello had promised at the
time of The Fall, "frankly
only the cognoscenti will know."

OCTOBER 7, 1916

Note: No Nails Were Bitten
During This Game

"As a general rule the only thing necessary for a touchdown was to give
a Tech back the ball and holler, 'Here he comes' and 'There he goes.'"
—The Atlanta Journal

O n October 7, 1916, the most lopsided game in college football history was played between Georgia Tech and Cumberland College. Georgia Tech prevailed, 220-0. "With all due regard to the Tech team," the *Journal* noted, "it must be admitted that the tremendous score was due more to the pitifully weak opposition than to any unnatural strength on the part of the victors."

Indeed, Cumberland College had recently discontinued its football program in the midst of financial difficulties. But rather than pay a hefty fine for canceling the Tech game, the Tennessee Presbyterian school hastily assembled a group of fraternity brothers. The players were "absolutely minus any apparent football virtues," the *Journal* continued. "They couldn't run with the ball, they couldn't block and they couldn't tackle. At spasmodic intervals they were able to down a runner, but they were decidedly too light and green to be effective any stage of the game."

Farce that it was, the drubbing satisfied Georgia Tech coach John Heisman (he of the famed trophy). The previous year, Tech's baseball team, also coached by Heisman, had been routed 22-0 by Cumberland, allegedly with the help of professional ringers. Indeed, it has been suggested that Tech's 220-point win—exactly 10 times the size of its baseball loss—was Heisman's deliberately precise revenge.

OCTOBER 8, 1625

The Raid in Spain Goes Mainly Down the Drain

"A force never left England so full of wants and defects."
—*Sir Edward Cecil, commander of the doomed*
1625 English expedition against Spain

K ing James I left not just a throne to his son Charles upon his death in 1625. He left his boyfriend, too. Together, the new monarch and the old favorite, George Villiers, First Duke of Buckingham (James's "sweet child and wife"), forged a deep bond of their own—a brotherhood born of romantic attraction and sustained by bellicosity toward Spain.

Just as Sir Francis Drake had famously "singed the King of Spain's beard" during the glorious days of Queen Elizabeth I nearly three decades before, so Charles I and his best buddy Buckingham sought to do so again as the new reign dawned.

Regrettably, neither man knew a thing about waging war. And even if they had, Parliament was not about to spend a thruppence for it. Undaunted, king and duke scraped together what they could for an expedition against Spain, launched on October 8, 1625.

It wasn't nearly enough. "Men, ships, and stores were all defective," wrote historian Francis Charles Montague; "skill, discipline and devotion were wanting; and the history of the expedition was an unbroken tale of shame and loss."

The worst of it was an abortive assault on the city of Cádiz—the very place where Drake had shattered Spain's might in 1587. Now, thanks to one of the more absurd fiascoes in military history, it was the king of England's turn to be flamed. An ill-provisioned landing party found Cádiz heavily fortified and unassailable (Spain had learned its lesson from the last English foray onto its turf). So instead of taking the city, the would-be invaders raided the ample supplies of wine outside it.

Thus, the walls of Cádiz stood sturdy, but the English got bombed.

"The worser sort set on the rest, and grew to demand more wine, in such disorder and with such violence that they contemned all command," John Glanville, secretary to expedition commander Sir Edward Cecil, recorded in his journal. "No words of exhortation, no blows of correction, would restrain them, but breaking with violence into the rooms where the wines were, crying out that they were King Charles's men and fought for him, caring for no man else, they claimed all the wine as their own . . . The whole army, except only the commanders, was all drunken and in one common confusion, some of them shooting at one another among themselves."

Sir William St. Leger echoed Glanville's account, reporting to Buckingham that a mere 500 of the enemy ". . . would have cut our throats.

And there was no hope to see things in a better condition, for our men were subject to no command. Such dissolute wretches the earth never brought forth."

With the remainder of the meager food supplies rotted—and not one Spanish treasure ship captured—the mismanaged armada limped away to infamy. Like the killing field that inaugurated Tsar Nicholas II's disastrous reign in Russia (see May 30), the Cádiz expedition prefigured Charles I's. Both the duke and the king would die violently: Buckingham by an assassin's knife in 1628, Charles by a headsman's ax two decades later.

OCTOBER 9, 1849

O-bitch-uary, Part 5: Poe's Foe, the Author's 19th-Century Troll

Mystery—fittingly—surrounds the death of Edgar Allan Poe. Just days before his demise, he had been found roaming the streets of Baltimore, delirious and incoherent. Poe never recovered enough from that state to explain what had befallen him.

But there is no question at all about who killed the writer's reputation just days after his death. This assassination was perpetrated with the poisoned pen of poet and critic Rufus Wilmot Griswold. The depth of Griswold's animosity toward Poe, his literary rival, is reflected in the biting obituary he published in the *New-York Tribune* on October 9, 1849. A choice excerpt appears as follows:

> Passion, in him, comprehended many of the worst emotions, which militate against human happiness. You could not contradict him, but you raised quick choler. You could not speak of wealth, but his cheek paled with gnawing envy. The astonishing natural advantage of this poor boy, his beauty, his readiness, the

daring spirit that breathed around him like a fiery atmosphere, had raised his constitutional self-confidence into an arrogance that turned his very claims to admiration into prejudice against him. Irascible, envious, bad enough, but not the worst, for these salient angles were all varnished over with a cold repellent synicism [sic] while his passions vented themselves in sneers. There seemed to him no moral susceptibility. And what was more remarkable in a proud nature, little or nothing of the true point of honor. He had, to a morbid excess, that desire to rise which is vulgarly called ambition, but no wish for the esteem or the love of his species, only the hard wish to succeed, not shine, not serve, but succeed, that he might have the right to despise a world which galled his self-conceit.

Thus quoth the raver.*

⎯⎯⎯✦⎯⎯⎯

OCTOBER 10, 1963

Uncivil Wrong: When RFK Eavesdropped the Ball at Justice

Martin Luther King, Jr., had a dream of achieving racial unity when he came to the nation's capital for the famed March on Washington for Jobs and Freedom in August 1963. But he also had some powerful enemies prepared to derail it.

---

* Lest anyone feel *too* sorry for the pitiable Mr. Poe, it should be remembered that he often wielded quite a savage quill himself. On fellow scribe Thomas Carlyle, for example: "We can only say he is an ass—and this, to be brief, is our private opinion of Mr. Carlyle, which we now take the liberty of making public."

One of them was nakedly apparent: FBI Director J. Edgar Hoover despised the civil rights leader—"the most dangerous and effective Negro leader in the country," as King was described in a bureau memo shortly after his "demagogic" address from the steps of the Lincoln Memorial. Another foe was far more subtle—and surprising: an ice-cold political pragmatist hiding behind the friendly face of a civil rights champion. On October 10, 1963—less than two months after King's iconic "I Have a Dream" speech—Attorney General Robert Kennedy authorized an FBI wiretap on the Georgia minister's phones.

Kennedy clearly didn't think much of King at the time. "He's not a serious person," the attorney general reportedly told Marietta Tree, U.S. delegate to the United Nations, on the eve of the March on Washington. "If the country knew what we know about King's goings-on"—presumably his serial adultery—"he'd be finished."* But fear, not animus, had motivated him to approve the secret FBI invasion of King's home and offices, for Hoover had boxed Bobby Kennedy into a corner.

Even though previous wiretaps had proved otherwise, the FBI director stated that some of King's closest associates were active Communists. Kennedy was loath to have his brother's administration appear soft on subversive Reds, yet he dreaded a revelation that would be much more explosive. Hoover had dirt on yet another of President Kennedy's many mistresses (see February 27)—this one a suspected East German spy named Ellen Rometsch. The attorney general had quietly engineered Rometsch's deportation two months earlier, but the specter of a scandal that could bring down the administration lingered. Thus, Hoover held the fate of Camelot in his claws.

"This was no time for Robert Kennedy to cross the FBI director," wrote biographer Evan Thomas. So the attorney general approved the wiretap that would fuel Hoover's vendetta to discredit King, whom the director had slandered as "a tom cat with obsessive degenerate sexual urges."

---

* "The quote as remembered by Marietta doesn't sound much like RFK to me," Kennedy intimate Arthur Schlesinger told his fellow biographer Evan Thomas, "but she is a respectable witness."

Privately—and anonymously, by mail—Hoover also urged King to kill himself.

Manufactured by the FBI and written in the voice of a disenchanted African-American admirer, the so-called "suicide letter" overflowed with condemnations of King's extramarital sex life. Accompanying it was an allegedly compromising tape recording, to which the bogus sender urged King to lend his "sexually psychotic ear . . . You will find yourself and in all your dirt, filth, evil and moronic talk exposed on the record for all time." The faked letter (a copy of which resides in Hoover's confidential files at the National Archives) concludes: "You are done. There is only one way out for you. You better take it before your filthy, abnormal fraudulent self is bared to the nation."

Ironically, that was precisely the fate that befell Hoover.

OCTOBER 11, 1913

Jack London's Call of the Riled

"At the present moment I am up against it hard, and fighting
for my very life—my financial life, I mean. A bunch of financial
pirates and robber lawyers have joined together, and are at the
present moment trying to take away every bit of copyright
I possess in everything I have ever written."
—*Author Jack London, writing to his former brother-in-law
Ernest Matthews on October 11, 1913—
one Bad Day in a year fraught with them*

World-famous writer Jack London called 1913 his "bad year" for good reason. "It seemed as if almost everything that could hurt him befell him," recalled his second wife, Charmian.

Her use of "almost" was a bit too beamy. There was that soul-sapping copyright struggle, of course, but also a plague of grasshoppers, which swarmed London's financially failing farm in Glen Ellen, California. Then a catastrophic fire broke out in his recently completed dream home on the same property—a loss that "killed something in Jack," Charmian wrote, and from which "he never ceased to feel the tragic inner sense of loss."

Also that year:

- The removal of all his upper teeth.
- An emergency appendectomy revealing the dangerously diseased kidneys that would contribute to his death at age 40 three years later.
- The severely strained relationship with his elder daughter, Joan, who, despite his pleas, refused to visit him out of loyalty to her mother—London's ex-wife Bess.
- The emotional affair second wife Charmian conducted with a sweet-talking thief.
- The accidental shooting by a passing hunter of his favorite broodmare.
- Disastrous investments, an incompetent agent . . .

And capping it all off: A very crappy Christmas.

Writing to Joan at the end of his *annus horribilis* of 1913, London apologized for not sending her any extra money for the holiday. "I did not have it," he explained. "Let me tell you about my Christmas. I sent only 2 presents all told . . . So far I have received one Christmas present—it was an advertising calendar."

OCTOBER 12, 1793

For the Rulers of France, the Rest Is History

Let us purge the patriot soil,
By kings still infected.
The land of liberty

Rejects the bones of despots.
Of these monsters deified
Let all the coffins be destroyed!
—Ponce Denis Écouchard Lebrun, official (bad) poet of The Terror, 1793

The Reign of Terror unleashed by the Revolutionary government of France visited its grisly excesses not just on the living but the dead—including 43 kings and 32 queens interred at the Basilica of Saint-Denis outside Paris. Bertrand Barère, a prominent member of the National Convention—known as "the Anacreon of the Guillotine" for his lyrical calls to slaughter—pushed for a mass desecration of the royal graves.

"These tombs under the tyrants," Barère inveighed, "had flattered monarchy by their pompous descriptions, and seem, even now, to swell with a vanished grandeur. Let the hand of the Republic destroy these proud epitaphs and sumptuous mausoleums, which recall the frightful souvenirs of royalty; and of the coffins of our old tyrants, let us make bullets to hurl at our enemies."

The ensuing raid on the royal necropolis began on October 12, 1793. "Gentlemen," the commissioner in charge of the ghoulish proceedings announced, "we are about to empty the rathole under the high altar." After a rousing cheer, the first coffin was dragged out. It contained the remarkably well-preserved body of King Henri IV, the first monarch of the House of Bourbon, assassinated almost two centuries before.

"I had the pleasure of touching these venerable remains," reported Alexandre Lenoir, an archaeologist who saved many of the marble monuments in Saint-Denis—if not those memorialized. "I took his hands with a certain respect that I could not resist, as true a Republican as I am."

Somewhat less reverentially, one tomb raider snipped off a portion of the Bourbon king's still luxurious beard—fanned and fluffed, as it had been in life—and applied it to his own face. "I am a French soldier and henceforth I shall have no other moustache!" he exclaimed. "Now I am sure to vanquish the enemies of France and I march to victory."

The dead king was then propped up against a pillar, where for the next few days he served as a silent sentinel over a macabre procession:

The monarch's descendants, in various states of decay,* were carried one by one to a hastily dug lime pit outside the medieval abbey church. Finally, the long-expired (but still remarkably good-looking 239-year-old) King Henri IV was allowed to join his fellow lifeless Bourbons in their designated trench. Members of the earlier Valois dynasty—including Catherine de' Medici (see January 5)—were hurled into a ditch of their own.†

As Alphonse de Lamartine would later write in his *Histoire des Girondins,* "Death itself was not an inviolable asylum for the relics of kings . . . The people, savage over these tombs, seemed to exhume their own history and cast it to the winds."

Or dump it into a ditch.

⟶•⟵

OCTOBER 13, A.D. 54

Nero Fiddled; His Family Got Burned

It's hard to say which of Nero's family members fared the worst when that lunatic became the fifth ruler of the Roman Empire on October 13, A.D. 54. You decide:

1) The first contender would have to be his half brother

---

* The corpse of Louis XIV—he of anal-fistula fame (see November 18)—was reportedly intact, but the Sun King had turned entirely black. The carcass of Louis XV, meanwhile, was described by a witness as "in a perfectly fresh condition," with buttocks "red like those of a newborn infant."

† Only after the restoration of the Bourbon monarchy in 1814 were the scattered remains of the insulted sovereigns gathered up, placed in several ossuaries, and ceremoniously returned to Saint-Denis. There they were joined by what was left of Louis XVI and Marie Antoinette, whose decapitated corpses had been buried 21 years earlier in a mass grave at Paris's Madeleine Cemetery.

Britannicus, whom Nero had poisoned at a dinner party, delighting as the dying man foamed at the mouth.*

2) Rivaling Britannicus's demise was the emperor's mother (and reputed lover), Agrippina the Younger, whom he murdered, simply because she reportedly nagged him too much.

3) And then there was his first wife, Claudia Octavia, steamed to death in a hot bath after Nero tired of her and falsely accused her of adultery. Claudia's severed head was sent to the emperor's second wife, Poppaea Sabina, as a wedding present. Yet poor Poppaea ultimately fared no better than her predecessor. Nero reportedly kicked the pregnant woman in the stomach, killing her.

Incidentally, Poppaea Sabina was replaced in turn by Statilia Messalina—and, concurrently, by a poor soul known as Sporus, who bore an uncanny resemblance to the emperor's dead wife. Only problem was, Sporus was a boy—a beautiful one, to be sure, but a boy nonetheless. Nero solved that problem by having Sporus castrated—less to fiddle with, we suppose. Then, in a lavish wedding ceremony, he made the maimed young man his bride.

OCTOBER 14, 1971

Party at Persepolis:
The Shah's Desert Debacle

The 50,000 dead songbirds said it all.

The poor creatures had been removed from their native European

---

* The concoction that killed Britannicus was prepared by a professional poisoner named Locusta—the same woman who had whipped up the batch of toxic mushrooms that dispatched Nero's father, Claudius.

forests and plopped down in the middle of the Iranian desert to serve as props in a lavishly artificial setting—a faux oasis amid the ancient ruins of Persepolis, constructed for the shah of Iran's decadent commemoration of himself on October 14, 1971. The shah's human guests—kings, queens, sheikhs, presidents, and other world leaders, all imported to toast the oil-rich "king of kings" and housed in elaborate tents on site—fared only slightly better than the birds.

But the host of the event himself—Iran's second-generation monarch Mohammad Reza Pahlavi, upstart occupier of the so-called Peacock Throne—suffered the most in the aftermath of "the Devil's Festival," as his archenemy Ayatollah Ruhollah Khomeini denounced the extravaganza. Indeed, many historians trace the 1979 collapse of the shah's regime to this opulent, breathtakingly gaudy desert banquet.

Ostensibly a celebration of the establishment of Iran (or Persia) 2,500 years prior, the festivities were noticeably light on touches of true Iranian culture. The scrumptious many-course meal, catered by Maxim's of Paris, featured fully plumed roast peacock (ironic, given the eventual fate of the shah's throne). The vintage wine was French too, as was most of the kitschy dining-tent decor—all flown in from Europe at colossal cost.

But most conspicuous of all by their absence were any actual Iranians. Like the scorpions and snakes that had been swept from Persepolis in anticipation of the party, many citizens deemed overly critical of the shah were rounded up and jailed in advance by SAVAK, his secret police. Others simply weren't invited. This created a superabundance of foreign dignitaries—some of whom appeared less than pleased to be present.

Among them was Vice President Spiro Agnew, who endured a bowel-churning case of what was indelicately called "the Shah's Revenge." Agnew was also in a snit over precedence: In a long-obsolete form of protocol, all royals—headed by Ethiopian emperor Haile Selassie and his diamond-collared Chihuahua—were deemed more important than a mere American veep. Or, as it turned out, a Filipina first lady: Imelda Marcos (she of the 1,000 shoes) was informed that tiaras like the one she was sporting were permitted on royal heads only. Defiantly, she wore hers backward and upside down.

When a desert sandstorm blew up, monarchs and lesser mortals alike jostled to get inside the banquet pavilion before the sabulous squall could wreak havoc on their hairdos. In the ensuing crush of bodies, Agnew was announced as the official representative of . . . Afghanistan.

Once inside, the elites must have wondered why they had squabbled to gain entry. The cavernous tent was oddly silent, with no music playing—only the forlorn sound of the wind whipping the canvas walls and rattling the plastic chandeliers overhead. "Does anyone know where the hell I have to go?" barked a flustered King Frederick of Denmark. At the 200-foot-long serpentine table, the awkward silence continued. Most of the invited guests "had remarkably little to say to one another, at least before the wines were served," *The Washington Post* reported. "Most remained wooden faced."

"When Marie Antoinette said, 'Let them eat cake,' she could never have dreamed of this performance," a member of Maxim's catering staff told *Newsweek* magazine. Indeed, with so many Iranians living in poverty, the entire display was not so much ostentatious as obscene. And the shah seemed as deaf to the criticism as France's doomed queen had been two centuries before. "What am I supposed to feed these leaders," he snorted, "bread and radishes?"

Only his wife, Farah, appeared to grasp the lethal implications of the five-hour feast. Asked by a court minister if she wished to attend the screening of a film about the fete, she emphatically squelched the idea: "For goodness' sake, leave me alone. I want our names to be utterly disassociated with those ghastly celebrations."

OCTOBER 15, 2004

"Butt Boy" Jon Stewart Makes an Ass Out of His *Crossfire* Hosts

"Stop, stop, stop, stop hurting America."

—Jon Stewart, host of Comedy Central's The Daily Show,
to Tucker Carlson and Paul Begala, co-hosts of CNN's Crossfire,
during a guest appearance on their program, October 15, 2004

Jon Stewart smashed his way through his October 15, 2004, appearance on *Crossfire* like a marauding Visigoth, pummeling both the program and its hosts with such relentless precision that, three months later, CNN canceled the show. *Crossfire,* Stewart announced on air that night, was nothing more than "theater" that was "hurting America." As for the hosts who had invited him on—liberal Paul Begala and conservative Tucker Carlson—they were nothing more than "partisan, what do you call it . . . hacks."*

Both hosts appeared rattled by Stewart's "disemboweling" of "my show," as Begala later termed it. But only Carlson—*Crossfire's* bow tie–wearing standard-bearer of the right—opted to return fire, thereby attracting the bulk of Stewart's contempt. Carlson's first mistake was to disparage what he deemed *The Daily Show's* soft content:

"I want to contrast our questions with some questions you asked John Kerry recently," Carlson ventured.

"If you want to compare your show to a comedy show, you're more than welcome to," Stewart retorted.

CARLSON: You have a chance to interview the Democratic nominee [for president]. You asked him questions such as—quote—"How are you holding up? Is it hard not to take the attacks personally?"

STEWART: Yes.

CARLSON: Didn't you feel like—you got the chance to interview the guy. Why not ask him a real question, instead of just suck up to him?

---

* "I agree wholeheartedly with Jon Stewart's overall premise," CNN President Jonathan Klein told *The New York Times* in January 2005.

STEWART: Yes. "How are you holding up?" is a real suck-up. And I was actually giving him a hot stone massage as we were doing it.

As Carlson continued to jab at *The Daily Show*'s delicate treatment of Kerry, Stewart responded: "You're on CNN. The show that leads into me is puppets making crank phone calls. What is wrong with you?" Then, after saying that Stewart was Kerry's "butt boy"—and receiving a devastating indictment of *Crossfire*'s coarsening of public discourse in reply— Carlson tacked into the wind: He accused comedian Stewart of being a humorless guest. "I do think you're more fun on your show," he opined. "Just my opinion."

Prompting Stewart to deliver his deathblow: "You know what's interesting, though? You're as big a dick on your show as you are on any show."

OCTOBER 16, 1644

Not to Be Minimized: When Teasing a Real-Life Boy Toy Turned Lethal

Seven-year-old Jeffrey Hudson—a lowly butcher's son— became an instant sensation among England's elite in 1626. Did he possess some special talent? No—but he *was* tiny enough to pop out of a pie.

The Duke of Buckingham had thrown a royal banquet for his buddy King Charles I (see October 8) and his teenage wife, Henrietta Maria of France. The astonishingly diminutive child, standing only 18 inches high, was the human door prize. Upon emerging from the pastry dressed in a miniature suit of armor, Hudson solemnly marched across the table—and right into Henrietta Maria's heart. For the next two decades, "Lord Minimus" was the queen's darling—a close companion both in the luxurious splendor of the Stuart court and later, in the midst of the English Civil War, when she endured exile in France.

But on October 16, 1644, their storied relationship came to an abrupt and violent end.

Dwarfs had long been a staple of royal entertainment, but Hudson was something else: His body was perfectly miniaturized, the result of a growth-hormone deficiency. He was, a contemporary wrote, "one of the prettiest, neatest and well-proportioned small men that ever Nature bred, or was ever seen, or heard beyond the memory of man."

Unfortunately for Hudson, his humanity was secondary to his status as an adorable little toy—a plaything who learned to ride, shoot, fence, and perform in masques for the amusement of Henrietta Maria and her court.

Being a pampered member of the queen's menagerie was better than being shoved in a cage and displayed as a circus freak (a fate to which many little people were then consigned). But as he grew in years if not stature, Hudson naturally began to resent being treated as a pet. Indeed, by 1644, he was a man—one who had loyally stood by his queen as darkness descended upon the English court and civil war threatened her very life. Though Henrietta Maria honored Hudson's service by naming him Captain of Horse, some of her court-in-exile apparently found it difficult to reconcile the wee jester they had long known with the person of significance he now viewed himself to be. And for one of those courtiers, that underestimation would prove fatal.

Hudson had made it clear that any further insults about his size would be met with a challenge on the field of honor. Rather than discouraging Queen Henrietta Maria's rowdy young hangers-on, the warning only enticed them to further torment Lord Minimus and revel in his outrage. Charles Croft, brother of the queen's Master of Horse, was selected by his friends to provoke Hudson, which he apparently did well enough. The proverbial gauntlet was thrown down. *How hilarious this will be,* they all thought: *a foot and a half of impotent fury, squaring off against his full-size opponent on horseback.* To compound the mirth, Croft arrived at the dueling grounds with his "weapon" of choice, a primitive water gun known as a "squirt." But the laughing stopped when Hudson showed up—armed with a real pistol.

Recovering himself, Croft took his place on horseback opposite his opponent, who was barely visible in the saddle. The flag was dropped and the two charged at one another. All the training Hudson had received in riding and shooting—once meant to amuse—now made him a mortal threat.

One shot to the forehead as Croft galloped past and it was all over. No one would ever look down on Lord Minimus again.

Just as the little man finally stood tall, sadly, life as he had known it since the age of seven came to an unceremonious end. Dueling was officially frowned upon in France, which persuaded Henrietta Maria, a guest in the kingdom of her birth, that she must dismiss her beloved Jeffrey. And so they parted, neither to see the other again.

Queen Henrietta Maria endured the execution of her husband, the king, in 1649, and the death of her 14-year-old daughter Elizabeth (who had been imprisoned by the Parliamentarians) a year after that. Jeffrey Hudson was captured by Barbary pirates immediately after leaving the queen's court and spent the next quarter century a slave. Later imprisoned as a suspected participant in a Catholic plot against King Charles II, Lord Minimus died a pauper on an unknown date, circa 1682.

Beneficently, British author Nick Page restored Hudson's historic stature with his 2002 biography, *Lord Minimus: The Extraordinary Life of Britain's Smallest Man.*

OCTOBER 17, 1535

The Holy Father's Unholy Son

Pope Paul III had just about had it with his eldest son (that's right . . . his son), Pier Luigi Farnese.* As if the Holy Father didn't have enough

---

* Sired, like his siblings, while the pope was still sowing his wild oats as Cardinal Alessandro Farnese.

to worry about with the Protestant Reformation rapidly possessing Europe at the time, Pier Luigi's scandalous dalliances with younger men only amplified his vexations.

So on October 17, 1535, just a year into his reign, the pope vented his frustrations in a letter to his wayward offspring. Paul was, he wrote, "so annoyed that I cannot easily express" over Pier Luigi's ongoing affairs, especially considering that he had banned such lustful indulgences. Furthermore, Pier Luigi was scheduled to visit Emperor Charles V, "who hates such kind of vice," and "it will be more than certain that you cannot take [the young men] with you without a great infamy and shame."

And besides all that, the pontiff might have asked, what kind of example was Pier Luigi setting for his own 15-year-old son, Alessandro, whom proud grandpa Paul had just made a cardinal, a Prince of the Church?

Typical of many a parental admonition, the pope's letter had little effect on Pier Luigi, who garnered even greater notoriety by allegedly raping Cosimo Gheri, the young bishop of Fano, two years later. Next in Farnese's chain of outrages came a "manhunt" for a boy who had spurned his advances. Yet despite his son's continued sinful conduct, Paul III was, as might be expected of the Vicar of Christ, a forgiving father. And in that spirit—with just a dash of simony added—he carved the duchies of Parma and Piacenza out of the Papal States and handed them over to his degenerate progeny.

Regrettably, the rivals of the newly created duke were not nearly as benevolent as his dad had been. They stabbed Pier Luigi to death in 1547, then hung the corpse outside his palace.

OCTOBER 18, 1956

Warhol's "Shoe" Gets the Boot

"In the future, everyone will be world-famous for 15 minutes," Andy Warhol famously said. And indeed, the clock started ticking on the pop artist's first brush with fame in 1956, when one of his "Shoe" drawings was included in a temporary exhibit of new works at New York's Museum of Modern Art.

But time ran out when the emerging artist tried to donate the work to the museum's permanent collection. "I regret that I must report to you that the Committee [on the Museum Collections] decided . . . that they ought not accept it," wrote Alfred H. Barr, Jr., director of collections, in a curt letter to Warhol dated October 18, 1956. Grinding the rejected artist even further under his heel, Barr added icily: "The drawing may be picked up from the Museum at your convenience."

These days, Andy Warhol's "Shoe" collection cannot be picked up at all; it sold at auction in 2016 for more than $400,000.

OCTOBER 19, 1781

Calling In Sick to Your Surrender: Cornwallis the Wuss

"Cornwallis held himself back from the humiliating scene; obeying sensations which his great character ought to have stifled."
—The Revolutionary War Memoirs of General Henry Lee

The ignominious British defeat at the Battle of Yorktown, which effectively ended the Revolutionary War, was a stain that Gen. Charles Cornwallis could not escape. But the ritual of surrender, set for October 19, 1781, was another matter entirely: That humiliating ordeal Cornwallis would skip by pretending to be sick.

"There is no display of magnanimity when a great commander shrinks from the inevitable misfortunes of war," wrote Dr. James Thatcher, a member of the Continental Army who witnessed the British surrender, "and when it is considered that Lord Cornwallis has frequently appeared in splendid triumph at the head of his army by which he is almost *adored,* we conceive it as incumbent on him cheerfully to participate in their misfortunes and degradations, however humiliating; but it is said he gives himself up entirely to vexation and despair."

The general's feigned indisposition was indeed a gross violation of the code of honor that bound gentlemen in those days. For Cornwallis, though, these were extraordinary circumstances. He saw the victorious Americans not as equals, but as a rabble of traitorous rebels who had robbed him of the dignity he deserved.

With Cornwallis cowering elsewhere, the British surrender became something of a farce. The disaffected general appointed his adjunct, Charles O'Hara, to represent him at the ceremony—with instructions not to acknowledge the Americans in any way. Thus O'Hara rode up to the commander of the allied French forces, the comte de Rochambeau, and tried to present his sword. Rochambeau, however, recognized the intended insult and refused the gesture. He directed O'Hara instead to the American commander, George Washington. Approaching the general, O'Hara was rebuffed yet again: Washington made it clear that he would accept the sword of surrender only from his equal, Cornwallis. Because the British commander had deigned not to participate, neither would Washington.

At long last, O'Hara found someone who would accept the sword of surrender: his opposite number, Washington's adjunct, Benjamin Lincoln, characterized by historian Clifford K. Shipton as "fat, lame, and undramatic."

O'Hara, no doubt drained from the ordeal of being bounced around, wrote the next day: "America is irretrievably lost."

OCTOBER 20, 1928

Too Much to Bear:
Winnie-the-Pooh-Poohed

A. A. Milne created an adorably dim-witted, eternally sunny character in Winnie-the-Pooh. Surrounded by Piglet, Eeyore, and the rest of his gang, Pooh has enchanted generations of readers—with one notable exception.

Dorothy Parker despised the bear. Unable to stomach Winnie the Ninny's cloying preciousness, the brilliantly acidic critic—whose *New Yorker* reviews were bylined "Constant Reader"—took particular exception to Pooh's "Hums," those dollops of "*tiddely pom*" he popped into a song for Eeyore. It "seemed to him a Good Hum, such as is Hummed Hopefully to Others," Milne wrote. And that's where Parker invested the text of the story with her own irresistible commentary on October 20, 1928:

> "Well, you'll see, Piglet, when you listen. Because this is how it begins. *The more it snows, tiddely pom*—"
>
> "Tiddely what?" said Piglet. (He took, as you might say, the very words out of your correspondent's mouth.)
>
> "Pom," said Pooh. "I put that in to make it more hummy."
>
> And it is that word "hummy," my darlings, that marks the first place in "The House at Pooh Corner" at which Tonstant Weader Fwowed up.

OCTOBER 21, 1032

Holy Unsuitable:
Three Strikes and He's Out

> "His life as a pope was so vile, so foul,
> so execrable, that I shudder to think of it."
> —*Pope Victor III,* Dialogues, *in reference
> to his predecessor, Pope Benedict IX*

Given the spectacular variety of misbehaving medieval popes, it would take an especially wicked one to earn the opprobrium that

Benedict IX received from Victor III. But with *three* stints upon the chair of St. Peter, this papal bad boy had no problem garnering such recognition.

Thanks to his powerful father's persuasive palm greasing, Benedict was elevated to the papacy—for the first time—on October 21, 1032, while still in his early 20s. He would rule, off and on, for the next 15 years—each time making a complete mockery of his holy office. "It seemed as if a demon from hell, in the disguise of a priest, occupied the chair of Peter and profaned the sacred mysteries of religion by his insolent courses," wrote historian Ferdinand Gregorovius in the 19th century.

Torture, rape, and murder typified so much of Benedict's first tenure as pope that he was driven out of Rome in 1044 and replaced by Sylvester III. Benedict would be back the following year to reclaim the throne, only to sell it to his uncle, who became Gregory VI. But when his marriage plans fell through, the ex-pope decided he wasn't suited to life on the sidelines. So he resolved to become the Vicar of Christ once more. Only problem was, Sylvester III and Gregory VI had maintained their individual claims to the papacy as well. Now there were three competing pontiffs, each ensconced in his own palace. A group of influential Romans therefore appealed to the German king Henry III to swoop in over the Alps and cleanse Rome of its redundant popes.

Benedict and Sylvester were both deposed at the Council of Sutri in 1046, while Gregory resigned in recognition of having immorally purchased the papacy. All three were then replaced by Henry III's personal confessor, who became Pope Clement II. The matter seemed settled—until Clement died of lead poisoning less than a year later. And with that, Benedict IX came roaring back to Rome to reclaim the papacy for a third time. He held on for six months before finally being driven out of the Lateran Palace for good in July 1048.

What became of the threepeat pope? History is largely silent on that score. Some sources claim that Benedict retreated to the Abbey of Grottaferrata, where he is buried, and there repented of all his sins. If true, the move may have saved his soul, but not his legacy. Nearly a millennium later, even the circumspect *Catholic Encyclopedia* calls the debauched Benedict IX "a disgrace to the Chair of Peter."

OCTOBER 22, 1937

Fasc Friends: Hitler and
the Duke of Windsor

"The world is in a very troubled state,
and David seems to loom ever larger on the horizon."
—*King George VI on his brother David, formerly King Edward VIII,*
who had abdicated the British throne in 1936
and now bore the lesser title of Duke of Windsor

Less than a year after relinquishing the throne to marry twice-divorced American Wallis Simpson—"the woman I love"—Britain's former king Edward VIII and his bride arrived in Germany to a warm Nazi reception in the fall of 1937. It had been a wildly romantic (if unpatriotic) gesture, but Life After Abdication was proving anticlimactic for the Duke and Duchess of Windsor (the titles to which they had been relegated). The couple was unwelcome at home in England, with Wallis particularly despised and denied the coveted designation of "Her Royal Highness." Therefore, the regal trappings offered by Goebbels, Göring, and the rest of the gang represented a tonic to the otherwise cast-off Windsors: Nothing like a band of bowing and scraping Nazis to make a duke feel like a king again!

During a grand tour—which did not include the newly opened Buchenwald concentration camp—the duke and duchess were feted everywhere they went. (No wonder the former king was moved to give a stiff-armed Nazi salute.) The highlight of the trip came on October 22, when the Windsors popped in to see the führer at the Berghof, his alpine lair. Hitler seemed more than happy to take a little time away from plotting the conquest of Europe and the annihilation of the Jews to greet his guests. After all, it was a golden propaganda opportunity in the midst of what Winston Churchill referred to as the Gathering Storm: a member of the British royal family—a former king, no less—deeply sympathetic to Germany and eager to embrace the Third Reich.

If Hitler had one regret, it was that easy-to-manipulate Edward no longer wore the British crown. As for his wife, Wallis, the führer remarked after she departed his home: "She would have made a good queen."

———

OCTOBER 23, 1844

Oh, Well—It's Not the End of the World

William Miller awoke to a disaster on October 23, 1844: The world, which the evangelical preacher had predicted would end in a fiery apocalypse the day before, was still there—humming right along, without the slightest indication of the Lord's destructive hand.

For Miller, the consequences of survival were devastating.

Sometime in the 1830s—during an intense Protestant revival in America known as the Second Great Awakening—the New York farmer had founded the eponymous Millerism, an influential religious movement based on the biblically inspired prognostication that the Second Coming of Jesus Christ (also known as Advent) was just around the corner.

Through numerous publications and sermons, Miller attracted hundreds of thousands of adherents to his creed. Many of them put so much faith in one of his blithe forecasts—Christ's fire-and-brimstone return would occur precisely on October 22, 1844—that they abandoned their homes and possessions in anticipation of the blessed event. What need would there be in heaven, after all, for such worldly impedimenta as mere shelter and clothing?

The Lord's failure to materialize at the appointed time led to what became known as the Great Disappointment—and an avalanche of ridicule. "And the next day it seemed as though all the demons from the bottomless pit were let loose upon us," Miller wrote as satirical cartoons and broadsides proliferated. "The same ones and many more who were crying for mercy two days before, were now mixed with the rabble and mocking, scoffing, and threatening in a most blasphemous manner."

But what's a little sacrilege when you've survived the world's end?

OCTOBER 24, 2000

Fools' Gold

"Lads, move down a gear or they'll figure out you're not disabled."
—Reported instruction to members of Spain's Paralympic
(Intellectual Disability) basketball team from their coach

The members of Spain's Paralympic basketball team posed proudly with the gold medals they won on October 24, 2000, at the games in Sydney, Australia. The Spanish athletes had triumphed over adversity—but alas, not their own.

Spain had used a secret edge to defeat Russia for the first-place medal among athletes with mental challenges: Only two of the team's 12 players actually had the requisite low IQs. The rest were just playing dumb—and they looked it, too, when they inevitably got busted for the pretense and had to return the meaningless medals.

OCTOBER 25, 2000

Mierda, Mierda, On the Wall

There are art movements, and then there are bowel movements. Curators at Britain's Tate Modern gallery didn't see the difference.

On October 25, 2000, the museum paid £22,350 (about $32,000 at the time) for a creation by controversial Italian artist Piero Manzoni that was literally a piece of crap. Entitled "Merda d'artista" ("Artist's Shit"), the work consists of nothing more than a tin can stuffed with Piero's own poop.*

Manzoni apparently dumped a total of 90 cans on the public two years before his death from a heart attack at age 29 in 1963; Tate Modern is the proud owner of the fourth in the series. (No. 33 stinks up the Centre Pompidou in Paris, and No. 14 has been plopped down in New York's Museum of Modern Art. It remains uncertain, however, who owns the most distinguished can of them all: No. 2.) Each of the coveted artifacts is labeled—in Italian, English, French, and German—"CONTENTS: 30GR NET FRESHLY PRESERVED, PRODUCED AND TINNED IN MAY 1961."

(And actually, yeah—you *could* have done that!)

A decade after acquiring Manzoni's droppings—and arguably wiping away its credibility in the process—Tate Modern purchased the perfect complement to the masterpiece: a roll of toilet paper by Slovakian artist Julius Koller.

OCTOBER 26, 2010

No Satisfaction?

"Anyway, she had no fun with the tiny todger."
—*Rolling Stones lead guitarist Keith Richards, reflecting on the brief affair between his girlfriend Anita Pallenberg and his minimally endowed (as he alleged) bandmate Mick Jagger, in Richards's autobiography* Life, *published October 26, 2010*

---

* It is perhaps worth noting that on the same date Tate Modern purchased "Artist's Shit," Britain's king George II died while producing his own work of art—on the toilet—in 1760.

OCTOBER 27, 1921

Congress's Censured Version

The Speaker of the House loomed before Congressman Thomas L. Blanton like a basilisk, prepared to deliver a public rebuke almost as poisonous to a lawmaker's reputation as expulsion. "Mr. Blanton," the speaker gravely intoned on October 27, 1921, "I have been directed to pronounce, and I hereby pronounce upon you, the censure of the House." Having absorbed that bit of ritualized humiliation, the normally feisty representative from Texas "turned ashen and fled the chamber," as *The New York Times* reported.

His offense: inserting into the *Congressional Record* a letter containing language one colleague described as "unspeakable, vile, foul, filthy, profane, blasphemous and obscene."

The reason for the letter's insertion is a boring sidebar to the story (some kind of squabble between union and nonunion printers), and the language it contained (already censored before printing) was tame by modern standards.*

The consequences for Blanton, however, were horrific. He narrowly missed being expelled from Congress by just eight votes—which, given his reaction to being censured, might well have been fatal: The traumatized congressman "fell exhausted [in the corridor outside the House chamber], striking his head on the marble floor," the *Times* report continued. "He rested a few minutes on a couch, refused medical aid and shuffled to his office, tears running down his face as he forced his way between spectators and members who were leaving the session."

Alone in the end, Blanton might have entertained some "unspeakable,

---

* An excerpt from the "foul" printer's letter, as it appeared in the *Congressional Record:*

"G_d D_ _ n your black heart, you ought to have it torn out of you, you u _ _ _ s _ _ of a b _ _ _ _. You and the Public Printer has [sic] no sense. You k _ _ _ _ _ his a _ _ and he is a d _ _ _ _ d fool for letting you do it."

vile, foul, filthy, profane, blasphemous and obscene" thoughts that *really* fit the occasion.

OCTOBER 28, 1963

Cultural Vandalism, Part 3: Razing Hell at Penn Station

"It's not easy to knock down nine acres of travertine and granite, 84 Doric columns, a vaulted concourse of extravagant, weighty grandeur, classical splendor modeled after royal Roman baths, rich detail and solid stone, architectural quality in precious materials that set the stamp of excellence on a city. But it can be done. It can be done if the motivation is great enough, and it has been demonstrated that the profit motive in this instance was great enough."

—New York Times *editorial on the demolition of the original Pennsylvania Station, which began on October 28, 1963*

The destruction of New York City's celebrated Penn Station was, for many people, nothing less than an obscenity: "a monumental act of vandalism . . . the shame of New York," as the paper of record went on to describe it. The shattered remnants of the 1910 beaux arts masterpiece were unceremoniously dumped in the wastelands of New Jersey. In its place between 7th and 8th Avenues in Manhattan, meanwhile, rose the concrete monstrosity that is Madison Square Garden.

Penn Station's subterranean tracks remain a well-traveled hub today. But as architectural historian Vincent Scully has noted, New York City lost some irreplaceable magic with the obliteration of this magnificent edifice. "Through it one entered the city like a god," wrote Scully. "One scuttles in now like a rat."

OCTOBER 29, 1958

Somewhere, My Love, but Not at Home: Boris Pasternak's Nobel Nightmare

"An ignominious end waits for this Judas who has risen again."
—Literaturnaya Gazeta, *1958*

Korney Chukovsky, often described as the Dr. Seuss of Russian children's literature, rushed to the neighboring home of Boris Pasternak in the fall of 1958, excited to share the joy of his fellow writer's Nobel Prize (announced on October 23). "I threw my arms around him and smothered him with kisses," Chukovsky related in his diary, recounting how Pasternak "was happy, thrilled with his conquest."

It was an understandably exhilarating moment for the *Doctor Zhivago* author, who never expected his novel would be published, let alone propel him to international literary acclaim. "Immensely grateful, touched, proud, astonished, abashed. Pasternak," he telegraphed the Swedish Academy, which selects each year's literature winner.

The elation was fleeting. As Chukovsky wrote, "No one foresaw the imminent catastrophe." Indeed, Pasternak was about to face an excruciating ordeal precipitated by his prize, with the might of the entire Soviet state arrayed against him.

Both Chukovsky and Pasternak lived in a rarefied world. In Peredelkino, their writers' village outside Moscow, they enjoyed privileges their countrymen could scarcely imagine. But they paid a high price to live there: Members of this select literary circle were expected to inspire and uphold the socialist ideal in the works they produced. Whereas failure to do so no longer meant a bullet to the back of the head (as it occasionally had in the Stalin era), livelihoods and reputations were still at stake.

Pasternak's *Doctor Zhivago*—with its themes of loss and alienation amid the Bolshevik Revolution—failed to meet the criteria for well-crafted socialist propaganda, besmirching as it did the seminal event in Soviet history. Recognizing this, Pasternak seemed reconciled to the fact that

his work—"my final happi-
ness and madness," he called
it—might never find read-
ers. Only when a literary
scout secretly approached
him about publishing the
novel in Italy did the author
see some hope. "This is
Doctor Zhivago," he wrote
on the manuscript before
the agent spirited it away.

"May it make its way around the world."

That's just what happened—with a little help from the U.S. Central
Intelligence Agency, engaging in a cultural skirmish in the middle of the
Cold War by covertly distributing the book. And it all culminated in the
1958 Nobel Prize.

The first intimation of trouble after that happy event came from Pasternak's own brethren. An emergency meeting was called of the
4,000-strong U.S.S.R. Writers' Union—which, Pasternak knew, boded
ill for him. Like other Soviet citizens, the members of the group were
ultimately slaves to the system, and they would destroy him if necessary
to protect themselves. "His face grew dark," Chukovsky described Pasternak's receipt of the news, "he clutched his heart and could barely climb
the stairs to his room."

Predictably, Pasternak was excoriated at the meeting, then expelled
from the union. "The novel *Doctor Zhivago* . . . only reveals the author's
immeasurable self-conceit coupled with a dearth of ideas," declared the
group's formal resolution; "it is the cry of a frightened philistine, offended
and terrified by the fact that history did not follow the crooked path that
he would have liked to allot it. The idea of the novel is false and paltry,
fished out of a rubbish heap."

It was merely the first salvo in a relentless campaign of repression.

"The radio, from five in the morning until twelve at night, the television, the newspapers, the journals, magazines, even for children, were
full of articles and attacks on the renegade writer," reported Albanian

More Bad Days *in* History

writer Ismail Kadare, then studying at the Maxim Gorky Literary Institute in Moscow. Especially fierce in its condemnation was the journal *Literaturnaya Gazeta,* which dismissed as "low-grade reactionary hackwork" the novel that critic Edmund Wilson had hailed as "one of the great events in man's literary and moral history." Branding Pasternak as a "malicious literary snob" and "the ally of those who hate our country and hate our system," the journal's caustic editorial concluded that "he is a weed."*

Though Pasternak had told his son he would "willingly endure any deprivations for the honor of becoming a Nobel laureate," the ferocity of the state-mandated war against him—particularly the threat of exile from his beloved country—had its desired official effect. Less than a week after accepting the honor, the beleaguered author felt obliged to send the Nobel Committee a second telegram: "Considering the meaning this award has been given in the society to which I belong, I must refuse it," he cabled on October 29. "Please do not take offense at my voluntary rejection."†

❦

OCTOBER 30, 1940

It Smelled Vichy Even Then

"I today enter the road of collaboration."
—*Marshal Philippe Pétain, in an address delivered on October 30, 1940*

---

* Not to be outdone in the name-calling arena, Soviet premier Nikita Khrushchev, through a mouthpiece, publicly fired off one of the most memorable insults in his prodigious arsenal: "If you compare Pasternak to a pig, a pig would not do what he did," because a pig "never shits where it eats."

† Boris Pasternak's Nobel Prize medal was presented to the writer's son in Sweden on December 9, 1989—nearly three decades after the author's death. In Russia, *Doctor Zhivago* is now part of official classroom curricula.

After France fell to Nazi Germany in the summer of 1940, it consented to set up a puppet government in Vichy, a town 200 miles south of Paris. As head of the new authoritarian state, Marshal Philippe Pétain—a revered World War I hero—meant what he said about working with Hitler in the aftermath of a one-sided armistice. Indeed, his infamous collaboration would later earn him a treason conviction and a death sentence (reduced to life in prison because of his age and war record).

Pétain labored under a German yoke—yet he needed no prompting from Berlin to persecute his Jewish countrymen. As his chief of staff noted, "Germany was not at the origin of the anti-Jewish legislation of Vichy. That legislation was spontaneous and autonomous."

Indeed, this particular strain of anti-Semitism was entirely homegrown.

OCTOBER 31, 2000

On This Day in History...
Eternity Came to an End

German chancellor Gerhard Schröder meant his visit to Israel's Yad Vashem Holocaust memorial on October 31, 2000, to be a profoundly solemn occasion of healing and reconciliation for both nations.

It had the opposite effect.

Schröder inadvertently turned the dial on the memorial's eternal flame in the wrong direction. Rather than boosting the bright light of remembrance, he snuffed it out.

November

---※---

Bernini's Bust

The year was 1670, and Gian Lorenzo Bernini needed a hit. The renowned architect and sculptor—who had breathed life into the cavernous St. Peter's Basilica and refashioned Rome into a city of baroque splendor—appeared to be falling out of favor with Pope Clement X, who had fired Bernini from a refurbishment project at the church of Santa Maria Maggiore earlier that year. His dismissal coincided with savage press criticism of his extravagance on the job, with some even calling for the artist to personally reimburse what had been spent. So Bernini was sweating as he prepared to debut his colossal equestrian sculpture, "The Vision of Constantine," on November 1. It did not go well.

Some appreciated the work, to be sure. Others, however, ruthlessly picked at nearly every element—from "the absurd length of [the horse's] body and legs" and its "emaciated belly and thin, crane-like neck" to the shaggy beard Bernini had opted to give Constantine. "The reaction was mixed," wrote biographer Franco Mormando, "and for Bernini at that juncture in his career, the fact of mixed reviews was almost as undesirable as universally bad reviews. He needed an unqualified, universal, crowd-pleasing success."

The critical quibbling was hardly the worst of it. As Bernini fielded the tepid appraisals of "The Vision of Constantine," his brother and right-hand man, Luigi, violently raped a young boy right in the shadow of the recently unveiled statue. And not just any child: The youngster was the godson of powerful Cardinal Albrizzi, who "is raising hell over this crime," according to one report, and "seeking punishment of the guilty party."

Now Bernini faced not just the collapse of his career but also the mortifying shame that Luigi's sexual assault had brought down on the Bernini family. Oh, and there was this very practical consideration: Luigi, an engineering expert, was most likely about to be burned at the stake. Gian Lorenzo's masterpieces could not stand on their own two feet without his brother's brain.

Fortunately for the dastardly Luigi—whom, incidentally, Bernini had once tried to kill*—his brother had some powerful friends in Rome. And it was to one of them, Christina of Sweden (see August 5), that Bernini now turned for help. The ex-queen, who had abdicated her throne 16 years before and was living in Rome, appealed to the pope on Luigi's behalf. As some had cynically predicted would happen, the rapist had his assets restored. He would not have to face trial. "The sodomites of Rome in particular have their great protectors and defenders," one editorial read, "since this is a tasty dish enjoyed in Rome by the upper and lower classes alike."

Still, Luigi would need a full papal pardon to return home and resume work by his brother's side. Bernini ultimately secured that, but it took some abject begging—and numerous statues sculpted free of charge for the pope's family. The Bernini reputation, however, continued to be assailed. According to one critic, Bernini had given his sculpture of Constantine that shaggy beard because "were he smooth-shaven, he would not be safe from Luigi, Bernini's brother."

---

* Back in 1638 Bernini was having an affair with a married woman, Costanza Bonarelli. As it turned out, Luigi was sharing her bed as well. When the artist discovered this, he chased his brother all over Rome in a bid to batter him to death. (He also ordered a slave to slash Costanza's face—the same face he had once immortalized in marble.)

NOVEMBER 2, 1979

Margaret Thatcher Issues a Flatulence Denial

Those who embrace the magnificence of a masterpiece are often unable to emotionally separate the sublimity of what they experience from the nature of the creator; art and artist are assumed to possess the same transcendent qualities. Thus when confronted with the murderous brutality of Caravaggio, say, or T. S. Eliot's anti-Semitism, they are left dumbfounded—or in aggressive denial, as was British prime minister Margaret Thatcher after seeing one of her musical heroes humanized.

On November 2, 1979, Peter Shaffer's play *Amadeus,* depicting Mozart as a filthy-minded twit who happened to compose the world's most superb music, premiered at London's Royal National Theatre. Mozart's letters overflow with his deep fondness for—how to put this decorously?—fart talk*, but Lady Thatcher was in no mood to learn of his flatulophilia.

"She was not pleased," wrote the National's director at the time, Sir Peter Hall. "In her best headmistress style, she gave me a severe wigging

---

* "Now I must relate to you a sad story that happened just this minute," wrote Mozart to his cousin Marianne in just one of his many anal-obsessive missives. "As I am in the middle of my best writing, I hear a noise in the street. I stop writing—get up, go to the window—and—the noise is gone—I sit down again, start writing once more—I have barely written ten words when I hear the noise again—I rise—but as I rise, I can still hear something but very faint—it smells like something burning—wherever I go it stinks, when I look out the window, the smell goes away, when I turn my head back to the room, the smell comes back—finally My Mama says to me: 'I bet you let one go?'—'I don't think so, Mama,' I replied. 'Well, I am certain that you have,' she insisted. Well, I thought, 'Let's see,' stick my finger in my ass, then put it to my nose, and—there is the proof! Mama was right!"(And Maggie was wrong.)

for putting on a play that depicted Mozart as a scatological imp with a love of four-letter words. It was inconceivable, she said, that a man who wrote such exquisite and elegant music could be so foul-mouthed." When

Hall attempted to explain the historical genesis of what the appalled prime minister had just witnessed on the stage, Mrs. Thatcher dismissed him: "I don't think you heard what I said," she replied firmly. "He couldn't have been like that."

On Second Thought, Part 14: Strike Three!

"The tide seems to be running in our favor still, and I do not know how they are going to stop it."
—*Three-time Democratic nominee for president**
William Jennings Bryan, just weeks before his third and final election defeat (this time to William Howard Taft) on November 3, 1908

Having confidently made "the worst prediction of his long career," as Bryan's biographer Michael Kazin called it, the candidate was baffled

---

* And posthumous target of H. L. Mencken—see July 27.

by his electoral loss. Indeed, in the first postelection edition of his weekly newspaper, *The Commoner,* Bryan implored his readers: "HOW DID IT HAPPEN?"

◆––◆––◆

Worse Than Pimples: The Death Penalty for Disobedient Teens

Woe to the surly teenager in colonial Massachusetts. It was Ye Olde Daye of Reckoninge on November 4, 1646, when the General Court enacted a new law that prescribed death for the chronically misbehaved adolescent who "will not obey ye voice of his father or ye voice of his mother."

That same day, incidentally, the court ruled that "no Indian shall at any time pawwaw or pforme outward wor[ship] to their falce gods or to [the] devil." As for anyone who denied that the Bible was the word of God, the court further decreed, they would be put to death.

◆––◆––◆

A Nighttime Jolt From Joe DiMaggio

Florence Kotz was sleeping soundly in her Los Angeles apartment on the night of November 5, 1954, when a group of thugs smashed through her door and snapped a photo of the screaming woman, who they thought was Marilyn Monroe. One of the invaders was the "Yankee Clipper" himself, Joe DiMaggio—freshly divorced from Monroe after only nine months of marriage, but still seething with possessive jealousy. Another was reportedly his pal Frank Sinatra, who, as one participating witness later testified, flipped on the bedroom lights only to find not a Hollywood sex goddess but poor Florence Kotz in curlers. "It's the wrong apartment!" one of the men yelled. Then, the witness continued, "There was a scramble for the door."

Whereas police initially treated the break-in as a botched burglary (Kotz couldn't identify the men), the salacious *Confidential* magazine later printed an entirely different story—one resulting in a California State Senate investigation that utterly humiliated both DiMaggio and Sinatra.

It turned out that DiMaggio had retained a private investigator, Barney Ruditsky, to follow his estranged wife. At dinner with Sinatra on the evening of the 5th, Joltin' Joe got word that Ruditsky had tracked Monroe to a West Hollywood apartment building—and that she had gone inside with an unidentified man. A raging DiMaggio grabbed Sinatra and several others and raced to the scene. But the building contained three apartments, and the panicked posse hadn't bothered to ascertain which one might harbor Marilyn and her mystery companion.

"I was terrified," said Kotz, the inadvertently besieged neighbor, who eventually won a settlement brokered by Sinatra's lawyer. But perhaps not nearly as frightened as Hal Schaefer, Monroe's vocal coach and the gentleman enjoying her company that evening. As DiMaggio and Sinatra* began their raid, he and the actress managed to

---

* Sinatra denied any part in the home invasion, claiming that he merely drove DiMaggio to the apartment building and waited outside. When a young investigator hired by Ruditsky (and present at the scene) sharply contradicted this—once in front of the State Senate committee and again before a grand jury—Sinatra challenged the district attorney: "Who are you going to believe, me or a guy who makes a living kicking down bedroom doors?"

scurry out a back door. "It was so lucky they got the wrong door," Schaefer later said. "I think they would have done me terrible injury."

Put to the Testes, Part 9: The Founding Father's Moby Dick Moment

G ouverneur Morris was a man of many talents:

- An eloquent writer, he was credited by James Madison for "the *finish* given to the style and arrangement of the Constitution."
- A charming bon vivant, Morris was so adept at seduction that when he had to have his lower leg amputated after an accident, John Jay was moved to write: "I am almost tempted to wish he had lost *something else.*"
- A successful businessman, he was a visionary champion of digging the Erie Canal to link Albany and Buffalo, New York.

The accolades go on. Indeed, as Theodore Roosevelt exuberantly concluded in his 1888 biography of Morris: "There has never been an American statesman of keener intellect or more brilliant genius."

But in one arena—do-it-yourself catheterization—the Founding Father was a total flop. We'll let Morris's friend and fellow Founder Rufus King tell *that* unsettling story:

"He has been long subject to a stricture in the urinary Passage; and have unskillfully forced a whale bone thro' the Canal so lacerated the parts, as to create a very high degree of inflammation, which has been followed by a mortification that I am told will prove fatal. Some years ago . . . he performed the same operation with a flexible piece of hickory; the success on this occasion probably emboldened him to repeat the experiment, that is now to prove fatal."

On November 6, 1816—the day after Rufus King's missive—Gouverneur Morris succumbed to the hideous effects of his cetacean self-surgery.

NOVEMBER 7, 1940

The Tacoma Narrows Bridge Collapse: A Doggone Tragedy

Leonard Coatsworth, an editor at *The Tacoma News Tribune,* was driving across the recently opened Tacoma Narrows Bridge on November 7, 1940, when the span—already dubbed "Galloping Gertie" for its tendency to bend and sway in the wind—began experiencing the extraordinarily violent undulations for which it became infamous.

"I jammed on the brakes and got out, only to be thrown onto my face against the curb," Coatsworth reported. "Around me I could hear concrete cracking . . . The car itself began to slide from side to side on the roadway." Coatsworth crawled back to the toll plaza, bloodying his palms and knees, just in time to watch the buckling bridge collapse into Puget Sound. He was lucky to be alive.

His passenger, however, was less fortunate.

Engineers have long studied and debated the physics of this catastrophic failure. But far less attention has been paid to its single fatality: a little cocker spaniel named Tubby. Trapped in Coatsworth's car when it plunged from the bridge, the beloved pet of his 15-year-old daughter, Gerry, was washed away in the powerful tide.

Coatsworth was just one of Tubby's would-be rescuers. He had tried to retrieve the dog as soon as the bridge began to tremble, but the wildly roiling roadway kept him from reaching it. Next was *News Tribune* photographer Howard Clifford, who had rushed to the scene after Coatsworth called the paper. Clifford ran directly onto the twisting center span. "I probably wouldn't have gone out there if it hadn't been for the dog," he later told *Arches* magazine. "I liked dogs and had seen the Coatsworths' dog at a company picnic recently." But as the structural convulsions became life threatening, Clifford too had to turn back.

Frederick Burt Farquharson, an engineering professor at the University of Washington, came closest to retrieving the pooch. He too made it as far as Coatsworth's car, only to be bitten by a terrified Tubby when he tried to coax him out. By then it was too late, and Farquharson had to retreat. He barely made it off the bridge alive. "I saw the suspenders [vertical cables] snap off and a whole section caved in," Farquharson told the *Seattle Post-Intelligencer*. "The bridge dropped from under me. I fell and broke one of my cameras. The portion where I was had dropped 30 feet when the tension was released." A photo of Farquharson displaying his bandaged—and nipped—left index finger appeared in the *Post-Intelligencer* the next day, above a photo caption reading "Token of 'Gratitude.'"

For Coatsworth, the bridge collapse had a double impact. He deeply sympathized with project engineer Clark Eldridge, who was on the scene, "his face white as paper." Yet "with real tragedy, disaster and blasted dreams all around me, I believe that right at this minute what appalls me most is that within a few hours I must tell my daughter that her dog is dead, when I might have saved him."

Neither Tubby nor the 1936 Studebaker in which he perished was ever recovered. Gerry did, however, receive a new cocker spaniel from a sympathetic breeder in Virginia. She named the puppy Cobina after her dad nixed her first choice: Bridget.

NOVEMBER 8, 1932

Hoover Damned:
The President Meets His Breadline

"Democracy is a harsh employer."
—*President Herbert Hoover*

Herbert Hoover was beyond weary in the weeks leading up to the 1932 presidential election. The Great Depression, heralded three years earlier by a massive stock-market collapse, had become an economic tsunami that defied the president's every effort to contain it, sapping both his vigor and his public standing. "I am so exhausted," an ashen, hollow-eyed Hoover confided to his wife, Lou, as they prepared to make a final cross-country campaign push by train. "I do not believe I will survive this trip."

Few believed the once popular president, swept into office four years earlier as a well-regarded businessman and humanitarian, stood any chance of being reelected now. Every bread line, every foreclosed farm was blamed on him. Hoover appeared helpless in the face of the economic calamity—and, worse, indifferent to the suffering it caused. No matter how much care and toil he expended on the crisis, Hoover found himself hated.

"At this time we are very badly whipped," press secretary Ted Joslin recorded in his diary that October. "We are as blue as wet stones." Nevertheless, the president was determined—"frantic," as Joslin put it—to plow forward and win a second term, not only to vindicate his own policies but also to save the nation from his Democratic opponent, Franklin D. Roosevelt. "He fully realizes the predicament he is in," the press secretary wrote, "but he just doesn't know the meaning of defeat. He is plugging right along as though victory was assured."

On that transcontinental rail trek, Hoover came face-to-face with the anger and despair Americans were feeling. Rotten tomatoes and eggs pelted his train; hecklers jeered him. At one point, someone was caught pulling up the iron spikes of the train track in an effort to derail the president's locomotive.

Weeks earlier, a reporter had described Hoover's face as that "of a human creature deeply hurt and pained . . . tortured intolerably and interminably." Now the strain was all but unendurable, a condition made especially manifest during a speech in St. Paul. "He spoke haltingly and without emphasis," Joslin reported. "He lost his place in the manuscript again and again . . . A man sat directly behind him gripping an empty chair throughout the time he was speaking, so that, if he should collapse, the chair could be pushed under him and he would not fall to the platform." Watching the sad spectacle in St. Paul, a local party official asked the head of Hoover's Secret Service, "Why don't they make him quit? He's not doing the party or himself any good. It's turning into a farce."

After crossing into his native California, Hoover was greeted by stink bombs in San Francisco and a cheeky telegram from an unnamed citizen: "VOTE FOR ROOSEVELT AND MAKE IT UNANIMOUS." At his home in Palo Alto on November 8, "President Reject" (*Time* magazine) received the first reports of his drubbing by Roosevelt. He could do nothing now but sleep. "Good night," the broken man said to his closest advisers. "That's it."

NOVEMBER 9, 1737

Unholy Matrimony, Part 6:
In Sickness and in Hell

"Why do you stare like that? Your eyes are like those
of a cow whose throat has just been cut."
—*Britain's King George II, addressing his dying wife,
Queen Caroline of Ansbach*

Caroline of Ansbach was in for a hideous ordeal when, on November 9, 1737, she collapsed at St. James's Palace after being seized by violent abdominal pain. And what made the next 11 days so unbearable wasn't just the relatively barbaric medical treatment the queen consort received (eventual diagnosis: umbilical hernia). It was her husband, George II—the bulgy-eyed martinet of the Hanoverian line of British kings who, despite his professed devotion to Caroline, seemed unable to modify his brutish behavior toward her.

While the queen suffered amid what Lady Catherine Jones described as "a throng of the killing profession [doctors] trying their utmost skill to prolong her life in adding more torment to it"—slicing open poor

Caroline, without benefit of anesthesia, to cut away portions of protruding bowel—King George demanded her attention. He slept beside his wife but reprimanded her for her restlessness, insisted she eat yet scolded her for vomiting up the food she could not stomach. Plus, his shirts needed sewing.

Throughout Caroline's torment, the king held forth interminably about how brave *he* was in enduring it—equating his current bearing to the fearlessness he had once demonstrated at sea during a violent storm, or in the face of his own health tribulations. "How tiresome he is!" remarked George and Caroline's daughter Princess Amelia in a conversation recorded by family intimate Lord Hervey. "In the first place, I am sick to death of hearing of his great courage every day of my life; in the next place, one thinks now of mama, and not of him. Who cares for his old storm? I believe, too, it is a great lie, and that he was as much afraid as I should have been, for all what he says now; and as to his not being afraid when he was ill, I know that is a lie, for I saw him, and I heard all his sighs and groans, when he was in no more danger than I am at this moment."

In the end, though, King George demonstrated his true love for Caroline when the dying woman begged him to remarry after her passing. "No," the notoriously unfaithful monarch replied, sobbing. "I shall only have mistresses."

———◆———

NOVEMBER 10, 2007

A Diplomatic Faux Paw

Foo Foo, the air chief marshal of the Thai Royal Air Force, was feeling frisky on the night of November 10, 2007. And at a party hosted by U.S. Ambassador to Thailand Ralph Boyce, he made quite the spectacle of himself: "At one point," Boyce reported,* "he jumped up onto the

---

* Boyce's report was published by WikiLeaks.

head table and began lapping from the guests' water glasses, including my own."

Turns out the "marshal" was a miniature poodle—the beloved pet of Thailand's future king, Maha Vajiralongkorn.* The oft wed, crop-top-wearing crown prince—known for his penchant of adorning his body with full-color if temporary tattoos—had bestowed the exalted military title on Foo Foo. Prince Vajiralongkorn also decked out the dog for the evening's festivities in what Boyce described as "formal evening attire complete with paw mitts."

<hr/>

Nothing to Fear
but Indifference Itself

"No, I think not . . . you better handle that through the State Department."
—President Franklin D. Roosevelt, during a press conference on November 11, 1938, when asked if he had anything to say about the massive terror campaign the Nazis unleashed on German Jews two days earlier

The state-sponsored pogroms, about which President Roosevelt declined to comment—or to act—were a frenzied and brutal assault

<hr/>

* Vajiralongkorn would ascend to the Thai throne in 2016.

upon Jewish culture and commerce all across Germany, as well as in occupied Austria and Czechoslovakia. On November 9–10—a date that will live in infamy as *Kristallnacht,* or "the Night of Broken Glass"—synagogues were burned, cemeteries were desecrated, and shops had their windows smashed and their contents looted. And in a chilling preview of the coming Holocaust, some 30,000 Jewish men were arrested and hauled off to concentration camps.

Equally chilling was President Roosevelt's continued refusal to take a firm stance against the burgeoning Nazi menace. Indeed, FDR couldn't even bring himself to utter the word "Nazi." Or "menace." But his silence wasn't a function of personal prejudice. It was a by-product of something equally odious: Politics.

NOVEMBER 12, 1914

Oval Offense:

Wilson's Prickly Reception

Woodrow Wilson had always prided himself on his self-control. But on November 12, 1914—three months after the death of his wife, Ellen—the president completely lost it.

His outburst stemmed not from grief but from bigotry. A delegation of African Americans headed by William Monroe Trotter, editor of the activist newspaper the *Guardian,* met with Wilson that day to protest the president's approval of segregated facilities for federal workers in Washington. "Tense" was one word for the convocation.

Trotter began with a fierce rebuke of the president. "Only two years ago you were heralded as perhaps the second Lincoln," he said, "and now the Afro-American leaders who supported you are hounded as false leaders and traitors to their race. What a change segregation has wrought!"

Wilson bristled. A son of the South, the Virginia-born president possessed many of the deeply ingrained prejudices of the time. Nevertheless, he believed—or had convinced himself—that separating the races in government offices would allow blacks to prove their worth as workers while "rendering them more safe in their offices and less likely to be discriminated against." Racial disharmony ran deep, the president reminded his visitors. "It takes the world generations to outlive all its prejudices."

To Trotter, though, segregated work spaces were degrading—and a betrayal of Wilson's promises. "You said that your 'colored fellow citizens could depend on you for everything which would assist in advancing the interest of their race in the United States,'" he retorted. Was there now a "new freedom for white Americans and a new slavery for your Afro-American fellow citizens?"

"Your tone, sir, offends me," Wilson scolded Trotter. "You are an American citizen, as fully an American citizen as I am, but you are the only American citizen that has ever come into this office who has talked to me with a tone . . . of passion that was evident."

If the *Guardian's* delegation was to approach him again, the agitated president made clear, a different spokesman would have to head it. Then, angrily dismissing the group, the fuming president said to Trotter: "You have spoiled the whole cause for which you came."

The unpleasant White House encounter sparked outrage in African-American newspapers. In the pages of *The New York Age,* for example, editor James Weldon Johnson addressed the president directly: "Mr. Wilson, the men who waited upon you did not go to ask you any favors; neither did they go . . . to be patted on the head and told to be 'good little niggers and run home.'" Their goal, Johnson insisted, was to have their "Chief Magistrate" correct a gross injustice. The editorial concluded that Wilson "bears the discreditable distinction of being the first President of the United States, since Emancipation, who openly condoned and vindicated prejudice against the Negro."

Wilson regretted his behavior in the Oval Office that day—not for the obvious reason that he had failed to acknowledge his visitors' valid concerns, but only because he had exploded. "I was damn fool enough to lose my temper and point them to the door," he later told Secretary of the Navy Josephus Daniels. "What I ought to have done would have been to have listened, restrained my resentment, and, when they finished, to have said to them that, of course, their petition would receive consideration. They would have withdrawn quietly and no more would have been heard about the matter . . . But I lost my temper and played the fool."

The Berlin Guffaw

"The devil . . . that proud spirit . . .
cannot endure to be mocked."
—*St. Thomas More*

Erich Mielke was losing his audience on November 13, 1989, just as surely as he was losing his grip on power. For decades, the head of East Germany's secret police, known as the Stasi, had inspired dread—infiltrating, probing, and ruthlessly punishing a population kept perpetually on edge under his iron thumb. But now, with his beloved Berlin Wall permanently breached and his police state hurtling toward extinction, the so-called Master of Terror was being scorned—on live television.

It started with jeers and boos as Mielke opened an address to the East German parliament with overly confident pronouncements about conditions in the collapsing communist country. He then made the retro mistake of repeatedly referring to those assembled as "Comrades." Shouts of derision rang forth, and one brave dissenter rose from his chair to detail his objections: "As a point of order," the bold Parliamentarian declared to a roar of approval, "let me remind you that there are more people sitting in this House than just your Comrades!"

By now the bloodthirsty Stasi chief was beginning to pale, stunned to find himself sinking in this unfamiliar sea of hostility. He sputtered and flailed, and then—in a moment of desperate lunacy—Erich Mielke became a laughingstock. Raising his arms, Mielke proclaimed, "I love all—all Humanity! I really do! I set myself before you!"

The audience howled.

NOVEMBER 14, 1957

The Mafia Summit
They Shoulda Refused

"I should have broken both my legs
before I accepted that invitation."
—*Mafia don Vito Genovese, quoted in the*
New York Daily News *about the disastrous mob summit
held in Apalachin, New York, on November 14, 1957*

The gang was all there: "Don Carlo" Gambino. "Joe Bananas" Bonanno. "Big Paul" Castellano. Santo Trafficante, Jr. Joe Profaci, the so-called "Olive Oil King." Salvatore "Sam" Giancana. Not to mention close to 100 other Mafia bosses, underbosses, enforcers, soldiers, and consiglieri. Decked out in fedoras and camel-hair coats, bedizened with diamonds and gaudy gold watches, mobsters from across the country had descended on the upstate rural home of Joe "the Barber" Barbara, 200 miles from New York City, to participate in a major crime confab—perhaps the largest ever.

But as the aroma of barbecued meat wafted over small-group discussions of murder techniques, trouble lurked nearby.

State Police Sgt. Edgar Croswell and his partner, Trooper Vince Vasisko, thought the influx of luxury cars with out-of-state plates looked suspicious, so they called in reinforcements. Alerted to the police presence, the mafiosi scattered into the surrounding woods and fields like so many silk-clad cockroaches. "They poured out of the doors, windows—everywhere," noted an officer on the scene.

While some eluded capture simply by sitting still—there had been no time to secure search warrants—dozens of others were snared in the wilds into which they had fled in a panic. "Those city boys didn't have a chance," Sergeant Croswell told reporters. "With their fancy shoes and their hats and coats snagging on branches, we could grab them easy . . . One by one we rounded them up, bedraggled, soaking wet, and tired . . . There are no sidewalks in the woods."

For supposedly hardened hoodlums bound by a criminal code of honor, it was a sorry spectacle. Indeed, the egg on their faces exceeded the muck on their shoes. "I'll tell you the reaction of all of us soldiers when we heard about the raid," gangster turned informant Joseph Valachi told author Peter Maas. "If soldiers got arrested in a meet like that, you can imagine what the bosses would have done. There they are, running through the woods like scared rabbits, throwing away money so they won't get caught with a lot of cash, and some of them throwing away guns. So who are they kidding when they say we got to respect them?"

Yet the Apalachin rout had consequences far beyond unrest in the ranks. The secrecy that had always shrouded mob actions was shattered—and the interest of Department of Justice investigators was piqued. "It was horrendous," Joe Bonanno wrote in his ironically titled autobiography, *A Man of Honor.* "All those men caught in the same place, a ton of publicity, a public relations coup for law enforcement, a field day for journalists."

And a nightmare for FBI Director J. Edgar Hoover, who had long denied the Mafia's mere existence. ("Baloney," he had scrawled across one report detailing mob activities.) Communist infiltration was the pugnacious director's raison d'être, and while his files bulged with dirt on suspected Reds, they contained little on the murderous thugs ravaging American cities. Now, an incensed Hoover faced a highly organized mess.

"He recognized Apalachin for what it was," wrote *Mafia Summit* author Gil Reavill, "the most serious challenge ever to his reputation as the nation's top law enforcement officer. Dozens of top Mafia leaders gathered from all over the country, and he and his vaunted bureau of mythic G-men were caught flat-footed. The fact called into question not only the air of omniscience that Hoover took pains to project, but more basically his competency."

No one questioned the competence of the state police officer who first smelled a rat, however. Unintentionally capturing the significance of what proved to be a turning point in America's battle with organized crime, Sergeant Croswell mordantly observed, "This is going to be a bad day for a whole lot of people."

NOVEMBER 15, 1902

The Assassin's Tangled Crosshairs

The turn of the 20th century was a dangerous time for the world's heads of state. Bloodthirsty anarchists had already assassinated Elisabeth, Empress of Austria and Queen of Hungary (1898), King Umberto I of Italy (1900), and U.S. President William McKinley (1901). Then, on November 15, 1902, anarchist Gennaro Rubino took a shot at King Leopold II of Belgium—familiar to readers of the first volume of *Bad Days* for his rapacious rampage through the Congo Free State in search of rubber.

Alas, he missed.

"My dear senator," King Leopold was quoted in the newspaper *La Meuse* two days after the failed attempt on his life, "if fate wants me shot, too bad!"

Invigorated by Rubino's unintended reprieve, the monstrous monarch continued his atrocities in the personal fiefdom he had carved out for himself in Africa—maiming and slaughtering his way to a fortune, at the cost of an estimated 10 million lives. Indeed, two years after the assassin missed, British diplomat Roger Casement delivered a devastating report of the barbarities—including this excerpted interview with a forced laborer who had somehow managed to survive:

> We begged the white man to leave us alone, saying we could get no more rubber, but the white men and their soldiers said: "Go! You are only beasts yourselves; you are nyama [meat]." We tried, always going further into the forest, and when we failed . . . soldiers came up our towns and shot us. Many were shot; some

had their ears cut off . . . We were killed and starved and worked beyond endurance to get rubber.

On November 15, 1908, exactly six years after the attempted assassination, an international outcry forced Leopold II to give up his bloodstained territory. He did so most grudgingly.

"The day had been for him one of definitive abdication from his personal overseas empire, and he felt a deep resentment at the manner in which the transfer of sovereignty [from Leopold personally to the Belgian state] had come about," noted the king's equerry. The annexation had not been carried out as the grateful acceptance of a generous and patriotic gesture by the sovereign, but in an atmosphere of distrust that almost appeared as a reprobation of his rule.

"It was base and unjust."

And—thanks to that assassin's lousy aim—six years overdue.

NOVEMBER 16, 1973

Retch for the Stars!

Space exploration had perhaps lost some of its luster by the time rookie astronauts Lt. Col. Gerald Carr (U.S. Marines), Col. William Pogue (Air Force), and civilian scientist Dr. Edward Gibson rocketed to the Skylab space station on November 16, 1973. Men had landed on the moon six times already, and the crew for this expedition was the third in a series of scientific missions to the United States' first space station.

Sure, there were wonders to behold as the craft circled Earth—but NASA saw to it that the Skylabbers would have little time to contemplate them: The space agency packed their daily schedule so full of tasks that even a peek out the window became an unaffordable luxury. Nevertheless, the men managed to liven things up on their first day in orbit when one of them puked.

Mission pilot Pogue had earned the nickname "Iron Belly" for his extraordinary imperviousness to nausea during training. But Pogue's "cement inner ear" betrayed him in outer space: Weightlessness made him queasy.

Uh-oh—maybe I shouldn't have had those stewed tomatoes for lunch.

With NASA Mission Control responsible for detecting any sign of physical distress on the part of the astronauts, Pogue and his fellow crew members knew that deploying an onboard barf bag would put them in a tizzy. The trio therefore orchestrated an upchuck cover-up.

"Well, Bill," Carr told Pogue, "I think we better tell the truth tonight [in the evening report to Houston] since we're going to have a full vomitus bag to turn in." Then, to Gibson: "Although I guess we could throw it down the trash lock and forget the whole thing, and just say Bill doesn't feel well and is not eating."

Gibson liked that idea. "I think all the managers would be happy," he said.

"Well, let's do it, then," Carr replied. "We won't mention the barf, and we'll just throw it down the trash airlock."

A short time later, Gibson added: "It's just between you, me, and the couch. You know damn well every manager in NASA, under his breath, would want you to do that."

Alas, the couch wasn't the only listener. In hatching their scheme, the astronauts had forgotten that every word they said was being recorded. A humiliating reprimand followed—broadcast for all the world to hear— from the first American in space himself, Alan Shepard, now employed by NASA as a mission controller.

"I just wanted to tell you," Shepard said, "we think you made a fairly serious error in judgment here."

"Okay, Al, I agree with you," Carr responded. "It was a dumb decision."

That "dumb decision" would hardly be the crew's last. Late the next month, the astronauts staged a daylong mini-mutiny: To protest NASA's merciless work schedule, they cut off all radio communications with Earth, then put their feet up (or was it down?).

None of the three was ever allowed to leave the planet again.

NOVEMBER 17, 2003

Oldest Living
Confederate Widow Tells Some

Lucy Marsden, the incomparable storyteller in Allan Gurganus's 1989 novel, *Oldest Living Confederate Widow Tells All,* was a sprightly 99-year-old. Regrettably, her stint on the stage lasted nowhere near that long. The Broadway adaptation of the book, with Ellen Burstyn playing Lucy in a one-woman show, opened on November 17, 2003—and closed the same day.

———◆———

NOVEMBER 18, 1686

The Bottom Line for King Louis?
A Hole Lot of Agony

For a monarch obsessed with his own dignity—notwithstanding the fact that pooping in front of his courtiers was part of an elaborate daily ritual—France's self-styled Sun King, Louis XIV, found himself in an unenviable position on November 18, 1686. After suffering for several months from an anal fistula (a condition so superlatively disgusting that we'd rather you look it up than describe it here), he was undoubtedly mortified to find himself positioned moon-side-up as barber-surgeon Charles-François Félix prepared to excise the suppurating tunnel that had formed inside Louis's rear end. Having spread the king's not insubstantial cheeks, Félix inserted the sickle-shaped scalpel he had devised specially for the occasion, pushed it through the fistula, and then, with a yank, sliced the whole thing open.

To his eternal credit, the prone king, suffering without the benefit of anesthesia, barely let out a yowl. Indeed, the surgery was so successful that some subjects—lacking anal fistulas but eager to kiss their sovereign's royal derriere—swaddled their own behinds in bandages. In some cases they even elected to receive themselves what became known as *"la grande opération du roi"*—a truly asinine way to curry favor.*

NOVEMBER 19, 2014

She Who Cast First:
A Reporter Sinks Like a Rolling Stone

Sabrina Rubin Erdely was appalled by the sin: Her former University of Pennsylvania classmate and fellow journalist Stephen Glass had fabricated a number of the prominent stories he wrote for *The New Republic* and other publications. She called Glass "a sociopathic creep" in her 2004 review of *Shattered Glass,* a film detailing the young journalist's elaborate deceptions. "Why did he do it?" Erdely wondered in the middle of her indignant screed, published in the alumni magazine *The Pennsylvania Gazette.* Why go to such lengths to deceive when it would have been easier simply to report the story? Ultimately, she grumbled, the film had failed to answer that question.

Erdely was still in a froth nearly a full decade after her review ran in the *Gazette.* When Glass was denied a law license despite having declared himself a changed man, she tweeted: "Stephen Glass' argument proving his rehabilitation boiled down to: 'But I haven't betrayed the public trust in a WHILE!'"

---

* Almost as mortifying as the Sun King's anal ordeal were the testicular travails of Kaiser Wilhelm II of Germany, infamous for his role in starting World War I. The emperor's withered arm (a birth defect) was counterbalanced later in life by a grotesque swelling of the crown jewels—just over 12 inches in circumference, as John C. G. Röhl recorded in his biography of the emperor, and nearly 7.5 inches in length.

A year after that ill-tempered tweet, on November 19, 2014, *Rolling Stone* published Erdely's astonishing account of a young woman's sexual assault by a gang of fraternity brothers at the University of Virginia. The piece was an immediate sensation—a call to arms against the culture of misogyny and abuse infecting the nation's campuses. It was also a complete sham—a toxic mix of shoddy reporting and, as a jury determined, malicious falsehoods conjured to fit the narrative, all of which fell apart under scrutiny and forced *Rolling Stone* to retract the story.

Why did I do it? Erdely might have asked herself. *Why?*

NOVEMBER 20, 1997

Tripped Up by Treachery: Monica's (Tor)Mentor

"I'd be careful what I said on the phone."
—*Linda Tripp to Monica Lewinsky*

They were just two girlfriends chatting away, covering everything from diets to fashion to sex with the president of the United States. But only one of them knew there was a third party on the line as well: the entire world.

One of those two gal pals, Linda Tripp, was eager to engineer Bill Clinton's destruction by documenting the fact of his affair with her friend and co-worker, Monica Lewinsky. Unaware that Tripp was taping her every word, the president's 24-year-old former mistress prattled away about "the creep," as she sometimes referred to the man she had dallied with nine times in the Oval Office from November 1995 to March 1997. The treacherous Tripp, a quarter century Lewinsky's senior, adopted the guise of concerned mother confessor—all while inciting her to reveal more and more presidential details. "Monica,

Monica, Monica," Tripp can be heard in one recording, clucking in faux exasperation.

Hours and hours of the taped conversations—"a breathtaking study in betrayal," as Marc Fisher of *The Washington Post* called them—were spent on banalities. But on November 20, 1997, Tripp—salivating over a blue dress—set a trap that would plunge Lewinsky into a pit of shame and Clinton into an impeachment trial.

The garment in question, as Tripp well knew, retained a splotch of the president's semen after Lewinsky wore it during a White House encounter. Moral Avenger Tripp was desperate to have this specimen preserved as proof of the president's sexual improprieties. Making that happen—without her naive young target suspecting an agenda—became even more urgent when Lewinsky told Tripp she was planning to dry-clean the dress.

Tripp was all calculation in the November 20 conversation as she manipulated and cajoled the clueless Lewinsky to stash away the presidential souvenir. Her only (perhaps unconscious) concession to being a lying snake was her frequently repeated admonition, "Believe me." It would be in Lewinsky's best interests, Tripp argued with feigned sincerity, to capture DNA evidence of the affair—just in case Clinton ever tried to discredit her, or worse. And this, Tripp said over and over, "is something I would say to my own daughter."

"I—I just—I—I don't trust the people around him and I just want you to have that for you," the false friend continued. "Put it in a baggie, put it in a ziplock bag, and you pack it in with your treasures, for what I care. I mean, whatever. Put it in one of your little antiques." And there was one more thing: ". . . you don't label it, obviously." Having delivered that amusing aside, Linda Tripp just had to laugh.

Eight months after the fateful conversation—with the blue dress now logged as evidence in the Office of the Independent Counsel—Monica Lewinsky made her second appearance before a grand jury. "I'm really sorry for everything that's happened," the sobbing witness said as she wrapped up her testimony. "And I hate Linda Tripp."

NOVEMBER 21, 1954

Portraits in Outrage:
Churchill's Finest Glower

British artist Graham Sutherland was pleased to find that his portrait of Winston Churchill—commissioned by both Houses of Parliament as a gift to the legendary prime minister on his 80th birthday—had met with the approval of Churchill's wife, Clementine, who had asked to see it before its official unveiling. She "liked the portrait very much," Sutherland later told the *Daily Telegraph,* "she was very moved and full of praise for it."

But the golden glow of approbation quickly turned a ghastly gray.

The very next day—November 21, 1954—Sutherland received a hand-delivered letter from the prime minister. Churchill had seen a photograph of the portrait, taken by his wife, and he was underwhelmed: "I am of the opinion that the painting, however masterly in execution, is not suitable as a presentation." Whereas the birthday celebration slated for November 30 at Westminster Hall could proceed as planned, Winston added, "it is sad there will be no portrait."

Churchill indeed despised the work, which depicted him naturalisti-

cally, leaning back slightly in his armchair, his rumpled waistcoat straining at its buttons. "I look like a down-and-out drunk who has been picked out of the gutter in the Strand," he blustered. Taking her husband's cue, Clementine's prior admiration of the painting—confirmed by author W. Somerset Maugham, who had accompanied her to the preview*—vanished. As she informed Lord Beaverbrook, the prime minister was "very hurt" that this "brilliant painter with whom he had made friends . . . should see him as a gross and cruel monster."

Revulsion aside, Churchill ultimately conceded that it would be a gross insult to the members of Parliament, who had paid for the portrait from their own pockets, for him to attend the event but block the presentation of their generous gift.

Lord Hailsham, for one, was aghast when the painting was unveiled. "If I had my way, I'd throw Mr. Graham Sutherland into the Thames," he was heard to say. "The portrait is a complete disgrace . . . I have wasted my money—we have all wasted our money . . . It is bad mannered [and] a filthy colour." Churchill, though far more benevolent that day, did take a subtle swipe at Sutherland's work. "The portrait is a striking example of *modern* art," he said with a slight grin as his listeners erupted in laughter.

Though the painting was intended to hang in the Palace of Westminster, the Churchills opted to take it home with them that evening instead. It was stashed in their basement until Clementine secretly arranged for it to be whisked away under cover of night—and burned.

——◆——

NOVEMBER 22, 1963

The Eerie Premonition of the *Post*

"Help us to bear patiently this day's sorrow . . .
We ask for light for today's darkness."
—*A prayer published in* The Washington Post *on November 22, 1963,
just hours before the assassination of President John F. Kennedy*

——◆——

* "I liked it and so at the time did she," Maugham later wrote.

NOVEMBER 23, 1906

Sure, Blame It on the Monkey: #MeToo at the Zoo

Was a saucy simian named Knocko to blame for an unwelcome pinch at the monkey house of the Central Park Zoo? Or was the culprit actually opera superstar Enrico Caruso?

The female victim maintained it was the world-famous performer, in town for his third annual engagement at New York's Metropolitan Opera House. And so did a policeman on the scene, who arrested the singer on the spot.

Caruso strenuously denied the charge. "I swear on your sacred white hairs that I am innocent," the overwrought tenor reportedly cabled his father back in Italy. Now a magistrate had to determine if the man with a voice described as "gold swathed in velvet" had gone to the zoo to look at the animals or behave like one.

The trial sparked a frenzy.* Spectators swarmed the entrance to the Yorkville Police Court, some greeting the renowned defendant with huzzahs—"Bravo! Viva Caruso!"—and others with hisses.

An insatiable press lapped up every bizarre detail that unfolded inside the packed hearing room. There was the nonappearance of the complaining witness, for example, prompting accusations of a frame-up. A mysterious veiled woman appeared in the courtroom—allegedly a second Caruso victim—yet said nothing. And there was the creepy technique Caruso purportedly used to cop a feel, slipping his hand through a slit in his coat pocket, then out the front toward his unwary target.

---

* "The event gained immortality when [James] Joyce drew upon it for scenes of Leopold's trial in *Ulysses* and for themes of the sin in the park and the fall of man in *Finnegans Wake*," scholar Ruth Bauerle wrote in the University of Tulsa's *James Joyce Quarterly*. "Caruso himself, with his appropriate initials, became one model for E. C. Earwicker."

On November 23, 1906, the magistrate was due to render his decision. But not before a lunchtime visit to see the monkey house for himself—as well as an incendiary closing argument by William L. Mathot, the deputy police commissioner who doubled as prosecutor. In addition to classifying Caruso, a native Neapolitan, as among those whose practices "are prompted by the devil," Mathot pointed to the singer's countrymen as the real reason his star witness had failed to appear for the proceedings.

"It is because of the crowd of moral perverts and dogs and curs out there in the courtroom who come here to listen," he declared. "Our mothers and our sisters are not safe in the streets; they cannot go about without being subjected to insult by this scum from the lazaretto of Naples."

Whether or not he was inspired by Mathot's xenophobic rant, the magistrate pronounced Caruso guilty and fined him $10. The tenor vowed to appeal, but never bothered. After all, a week after the conviction, a jury of concertgoers gave their own rousing verdict as they cheered Caruso's debut performance of the season in *La bohème*.

Sadly, Knocko fared not so well. At the same time Caruso was being cheered onstage, the exonerated monkey—apparently overexcited by the extra attention he'd received from sensation-seeking zoo visitors—dropped dead.

NOVEMBER 24, 1966

Too Hot for the Heartland

Police in Kansas City, Missouri, called an early end to a November 24, 1966, James Brown concert after the audience erupted in a riot that spilled out into the city streets. *The New York Times* came up with the only possible explanation for such behavior:

"Mr. Brown, as part of his act, wails, 'Do you love me, baby?' and invariably teen-age girls wail back: 'Yeah, baby, yeah.' At one point in his act, the girls are encouraged to rush onto the stage and rip his jacket off.

"They invariably do."

NOVEMBER 25, 1120

A Dark Day Aboard the *White Ship:* The Party Boat That Wiped Out a Dynasty

"No ship ever brought so much misery to England;
none was ever so notorious in the history of the world."
—*William of Malmesbury,* Gesta Regum Anglorum, *1125*

I t was history's most fateful booze cruise.

Most of the passengers and crew were thoroughly soused long before they boarded the *Blanche-Nef,* or *White Ship,* in Normandy and set sail for England on November 25, 1120. Among the revelers—many of them from the top echelons of English society—was King Henry I's son and heir, William Adelin, as well as two of the monarch's numerous illegitimate children.* Not on board: King Henry's nephew, Stephen of Blois, who left the ship at the last minute because of diarrhea.

Stephen's case of the runs would have far-reaching consequences.

Meanwhile out in the English Channel, the drunken merrymakers were urging the sleek *White Ship* to faster and faster speeds. Hilarity and exhilaration ensued—until the ship plowed into a submerged boulder and began to sink. Nearly everyone aboard drowned, including King Henry's three children. And though early historians described William Adelin as an overindulged brat, he did apparently shine at the end; the heir lost his life trying to rescue his drowning half sister.

---

* Perhaps the king regretted that his illegitimate daughter Juliana, who had tried to kill him with a crossbow, was not aboard the *White Ship* as well. Juliana's hatred of her father is a fraught story involving rebellion, betrayal, and the blinding of children. See C. Warren Hollister's biography of Henry I for the full details of the story, based on an account by Orderic Vitalis.

The disaster devastated Henry I, who saw his dynastic dreams go down with the ship. Contemporary chronicler Orderic Vitalis recorded the king's reaction to the news: "So sudden was the shock, and so severe his anguish, that he instantly fell to the ground, but being raised up by his friends, he was conducted to his chamber, and gave free course to the bitterness of his grief." It was said the king never smiled again.

When Henry I died 15 years later (from a "surfeit of lampreys," as the Henry of Huntington famously described the king's eel-induced demise), England was hurled into nearly two decades of anarchy and civil war. The opposing principals in this internecine battle were King Henry's sole legitimate daughter, Empress Matilda, and her first cousin, Stephen of Blois—he of the well-timed loose stools, who took the English crown. (Stephen emerged from the clash still king, but Matilda's hot-tempered son—see July 12—would succeed him as Henry II.)

According to historian Dan Jones, the English survivors of this violent and chaotic time coined an appropriately nautical nickname for it: They called it "the Shipwreck."

NOVEMBER 26, 1840

Hobbled in Kabul

"My command I do not think enviable."
—*British major general William Elphinstone,*
upon his arrival in Afghanistan, April 1841

There was only one thing worse than the job offer to command the British garrison in Kabul, Afghanistan: Maj. Gen. William Elphinstone's decision on November 26, 1840, to accept it. He would regret his choice for what little remained of his life.

"We are . . . of the opinion that [the command] could not be given to anyone who would exercise its functions so efficiently as you would,"

Lord Auckland, Governor-General of India, had written to Elphinstone with apparent sincerity.

Precisely which leadership qualities Auckland recognized in the general remains an open question.

Plagued by gout and rheumatism, Elphinstone had last seen action more than a quarter century earlier at Waterloo. Infirmities aside, he also happened to be, in the estimation of Gen. William Nott, "the most incompetent soldier that was to be found among all the officers of requisite rank."

General Elphinstone considered Kabul "very dirty & crowded," as he noted upon his arrival there in April 1841, making its British garrison appear Edenic by comparison. Gardens flourished; fine furnishings, expensive wines, and scores of servants filled the homes of high-ranking officials. "You will have nothing to do here," the departing commander, Sir Willoughby Cotton, assured his replacement. "All is peace."

Yet it was a deceptive calm. This was Afghanistan, after all—a region then, and consistently ever since, allergic to foreign occupation. And in 1841, it was seething. Even the doddering Elphinstone immediately sensed danger. The British garrison was ill situated, he noted, "not very defensible without a number of men, as people can come in from without at many points." This could prove "very inconvenient," he continued. "I am a good deal puzzled what is the best thing to be done."

Regrettably, Elphinstone remained at sea—physically wrecked and mentally adrift—as a tribal rebellion erupted that fall.

Military engineer George Broadfoot found the general in "a pitiable state of health, absolutely unfit for duty" at the time. Indeed, he seemed so "lost and perplexed" that Broadfoot questioned his sanity. Elphinstone implored the engineer for safe passage out of Kabul should events escalate: "For, if anything were to turn up I am unfit for it, done up body and mind, and I have told Lord Auckland so." The distressed commander repeated this two or three times, according to Broadfoot. Then, in an apparent moment of resignation, Elphinstone added that "he doubted very much he would ever see home, even if he did get away."

Very few of his charges would.

Elphinstone dithered as the situation in Kabul deteriorated—especially after the British envoy, Sir William Macnaghten, had his head hacked off and his corpse dragged through the streets before it was hung up for display in a local marketplace.

Escape became the only option, but Elphinstone failed to negotiate the deliverance he had so presciently sought: In exchange for the garrison's armory, he received only a vague promise of protection as some 4,500 Anglo-Indian troops and 12,000 camp followers prepared a winter retreat through the Hindu Kush mountain range to the relative safety of Jalalabad, 90 miles away.

On January 6, 1842, the fleeing contingent entered what became an ice-encrusted charnel house. The guarantee of safety was disregarded, and thousands of soldiers and civilians were systematically slaughtered as they trudged through the range's treacherous passes. "A night of starvation, cold, exhaustion, death," Maj. Gen. Vincent Eyre wrote of just a single episode in a week filled with horrors, "and of all the deaths I can imagine none more agonizing than where a nipping frost tortures every sensitive limb until the tenacious spirit itself sinks under the exquisite extreme of human suffering."

Of the thousands who entered the mountains' merciless maw, only a pitiable few emerged. As to their hapless commander, historian Thomas Archer, writing later in the 19th century, had this to say: "It was a happy thing for Elphinstone that he died."

NOVEMBER 27, 1724

Peter Packs a Pickled Head

Peter the Great, Russia's hulking, nearly seven-foot-tall tsar, was unacquainted with nuance. Take, for example, the unmistakable message he sent to his second wife, the peasant-born Empress Catherine: the chopped-off head of her reputed lover, Willem Mons, preserved in alcohol and delivered to her bedroom.

Mons, a member of the empress's household, was publicly decapitated on November 27, 1724. Though his ostensible offense was corruption,

everyone knew the real reason why Mons had lost his head. It was therefore essential that Catherine not show the slightest hint of grief at his fate, lest she confirm the tsar's suspicions of infidelity.

Catherine took her regular dance lesson the day Mons died, which mollified Peter not one bit. He then accompanied Catherine on a carriage ride through St. Petersburg, arranging to pass within a few feet of the scaffold upon which Mons's headless corpse had been left to rot. Still the empress refused to flinch, prompting her husband to send her that ghoulish souvenir for her bedside table. Fortunately for Catherine, Peter died just a few months later and she inherited the crown.

The pickled head of poor Willem Mons ended up in Peter the Great's famed cabinet of curiosities, where it joined that of Mary Hamilton, the tsar's onetime lover. Decades would pass before another Catherine—the Great, who had married Peter's grandson—stumbled upon her predecessor's monstrous mementos and had them buried.

NOVEMBER 28, 2010

No Other Way to Spin It:
Spider-Man's Sticky Mess

"Break a leg" is theater-speak for "Good luck." But actors' bones had in fact already been broken during the troubling prelude to the much hyped musical *Spider-Man: Turn Off the Dark*. Fortunately, no ticket holders had been present to witness those crippling rehearsal accidents.

Not until November 28, 2010—the date of the first preview of the $65 million extravaganza—was the public finally able to see how the comic-book hero was weathering his transition to the Broadway stage. They found Spider-Man ensnared in an epic fiasco.

Preview performances are considered works in progress, so the occasional production glitch is expected. But it was clear from curtain rise that this wildly ambitious production was spinning out of control. Actors supposed to soar above the heads of the audience instead got tangled in their stage wires midflight. Such was the case with Natalie Mendoza, playing the villainess Arachne. She also suffered a backstage concussion that night, forcing her eventual withdrawal from the show.

In his book *Song of Spider-Man: The Inside Story of the Most Controversial Musical in Broadway History,* the musical's co-writer Glen Berger recounted every mortifying moment of Mendoza's tangled suspension:

> After a minute, all of the show's momentum had gone *pffft.* After two minutes, the quiet in the auditorium felt like the quiet in a library. After three minutes, I closed my eyes and concentrated on my breathing, as if I were in the last minutes of a yoga class. After four minutes, the auditorium didn't sound like a library anymore. It sounded exactly like an auditorium full of people enduring an indefinite delay while looking at a spider-lady suspended in the air. Murmurs. Some titters and bubbly noises. After five minutes, Randall [stage manager Randall White] went on the God Mike. "Give it up for Natalie Mendoza, for hanging in there!" Surprisingly boisterous applause. Natalie acknowledged the applause with a subtle nod and smile. The applause subsided until silence reigned again, punctuated with murmurs and some coughing. After six minutes, I was digging fingernails into my skin. After seven minutes, I seriously began to worry that this weirdness was going to trigger an acid flashback in me. After eight minutes, I felt on the verge of a spiritual epiphany, but it was disrupted by the sudden resumption of music, and Natalie ascending into the flies.

The evening's performance finally concluded after three seemingly interminable hours, permitting the underwhelmed but visibly relieved audience members to begin filing out into the lobby. Among them was a no-holds-barred heckler, Denise Chastain, who had shouted out, "I don't know how everyone else feels, but I feel like a guinea pig today! I feel like it's a dress rehearsal!"

New York Post theater critic Michael Riedel then made a point of seeking out Chastain and asking her to expand on the frustrations she had voiced during the show.

"I was like the frog in the boiling water," Chastain told Riedel. "The slow simmer just got to me, and by the second act I just lost it."*

NOVEMBER 29, 1961

Space Chimp Goes Apeshit

"**E**nos the Penis" did not earn his nickname by being nice. In fact, the second chimpanzee launched into space (and the first to orbit Earth) was, as his veterinarian Jerry Fineg circumspectly described him to *Packing for Mars* author Mary Roach, "just a son of a gun."

"Meaning he was a dick," Roach said.

"Yeah," Fineg conceded.

More than 1,000 hours of strenuous mission preparation undoubtedly contributed to the primate's irascible nature—resulting at one point in a bite on Jerry Fineg's behind. "His personality had not responded well to civilization, much less to training for orbital flight," wrote NASA physician Lawrence E. Lamb. "Enos did not like school."

But if Enos was cranky in the classroom, his horrendous experience in

---

* After 182 preview performances, *Spider-Man* officially opened on June 14, 2011, to poisonous reviews, additional cast injuries, and eventual financial losses topping $60 million.

space on November 29, 1961, gave the already surly simian every excuse to go ballistic. As the sole passenger aboard the Mercury-Atlas 5 rocket that day, Enos had performed each of his tasks admirably—pulling the right levers and pushing the right buttons in a test of brain function under the extraordinary conditions that astronaut John Glenn would experience early the next year. But something went terribly wrong.

Rather than the banana-pellet rewards the chimp had been conditioned to expect after each success, Enos instead received a nasty electrical shock from an electrode attached to his feet. A system malfunction caused the poor animal to get zapped over and over again, in essence punishing him no matter how well he did.

And all the while, the cabin was overheating.

Mercifully, NASA ended the one-day mission after just two orbits, not the three that had been planned. And though Enos's rescuers found him to be "excitable but in good shape" after his space capsule splashed down in the Atlantic, the chimp was in no mood for monkeyshines during the press conference that followed. He would not even turn a cartwheel, the Associated Press ruefully noted, perhaps unaware that Enos had just spent more than three hours strapped to his seat in literally shocking conditions.

"He's really quite a cool guy," the butt-bitten vet said at the time, "and not the performing type at all."

NOVEMBER 30, 1864

The Uncivil War, Part 5:
Hood's Bitter Angels

"General Hood has betrayed us. This is not the kind of fighting he promised us . . . This was not 'a fight with equal numbers and choice of the ground' by no means. And the wails and cries of widows and orphans made at Franklin November 30th 1864 will

heat up the fires of a bottomless pit to burn the soul of Gen J B Hood for Murdering their husbands and fathers at that place that day. It can't be called anything else but cold-blooded Murder."
—*Confederate captain Samuel T. Foster, 24th Texas Cavalry (dismounted)*

Though historians have long wrestled with the possible motives and mental state of Confederate general John Bell Hood when he ordered a suicidal assault upon well-entrenched and advantageously positioned Union forces outside Franklin, Tennessee—a foolhardy decision that nearly annihilated the Confederacy's vital western forces in the waning months of the Civil War—Captain Foster left no doubt about what he thought of the man he held responsible for the gruesome debacle that resulted in nearly 6,000 Confederate casualties, including six dead generals: The fiery one-legged commander, he wrote, "sacrificed those men to make the name Hood famous." In the end, though, "it will make him *infamous.*"

December

Voyeur of the Damned

"Dreadful propensity of our nature, which often leads us to exult in
the vilest deeds, provided they be adroitly executed!"
—*Alexander Slidell Mackenzie,* A Year in Spain, *volume 1, 1831*

The spectacle of death aboard the U.S.S. *Somers* on December 1, 1842,
was meticulously choreographed by the brig's commander, Alexander
Slidell Mackenzie. Three men—condemned without a hearing for plotting a mutiny aboard a ship then being used to train young naval appren-
tices—stood in their assigned places on the quarterdeck, each with a hood
over his head and a rope tied around his neck. Above them loomed the
ship's yardarm, part of the designated machinery of their demise.

Mackenzie detailed the precise order of events to one of the doomed,
Midshipman Philip Spencer, the 19-year-old son of Secretary of War
John C. Spencer: "I told him that being desirous to hoist the colors at
the moment of execution, at once to give solemnity to the act and to
indicate that by it the colors of the *Somers* were fixed to the masthead, I
had intended to beat the call as for hoisting the colors, then roll off, and
at the third roll fire a gun."

The moment the gun was fired, the group of seamen assigned as exe-
cutioners did their duty with the steady coordination Mackenzie

demanded—pulling on the ropes looped over the yardarm and hoisting Spencer and his struggling companions. And there, high above the *Somers,* they strangled to death as Mackenzie gave orders for a rousing cheer from the novice crew—some as young as 13. This he followed with an edifying sermon on the perils of disobedience.

The summary executions aboard the *Somers*—which inspired not only Herman Melville's *Billy Budd* but also the creation of the more structured and supervised U.S. Naval Academy in Annapolis, Maryland—shocked the sensibilities of many Americans, including novelist James Fenimore Cooper. Why had Mackenzie deemed it necessary, demanded an outraged public, to kill three men, already subdued and shackled, aboard a peace-time training vessel close enough to home to allow for due process?*

While this question festered, one aspect of the story in particular captured the attention of historian Philip McFarland and others: The executions appear to have fulfilled a ceremonial death fetish Alexander Slidell Mackenzie long harbored.

In his 1831 book, *A Year in Spain,* volume 1, Mackenzie revealed that after witnessing an execution in France, "the feeling of oppression and abasement, of utter disgust, with which I came from it, was such as to make me form a tacit resolution never to be present at another." Nevertheless, he managed "to overcome, or at least to stifle, my repugnance" and soon attend another public killing in Spain.

Over 13 vividly lurid pages, Mackenzie described the violent end of two criminals—with all the "persevering and conscientious fidelity of a Flemish picture," as *Sleepy Hollow* author Washington Irving described the Navy man's prose. Despite his professed "disgust" at the scene, Mackenzie clearly delighted in every grim detail—from the "lips of the miserable man turned blue with terror" to the executioner knocking the condemned off a ladder, then clinging "to his prey with a resolute grasp" and bouncing up and down on his shoulders as the doomed soul choked to death.

---

* Although Mackenzie was exonerated at a court-martial, the question dogged the commander for the rest of his career.

"Surely there can be nothing in such a spectacle to promote morality, nothing to make us either better or happier," Mackenzie continued with manufactured sobriety: "a spectacle which serves but to create despondency, and array man in enmity with his condition.

"I hurried at once from the spot," Mackenzie continued, "determined to seek some society which might rid me of my thoughts and reconcile me to my species." But first he had to take one more look—one more *lo-o-ong* look, of course—and relay that eyeful to his readers as well.

Returning to Spain a few years later, Mackenzie completed his catalog of butchery by witnessing a garroting. "It was sure to be a spectacle full of horror and painful excitement," he wrote in 1836, "yet I was determined to witness it. I felt sad and melancholy, and yet, by a strange perversion, I was ready to feel more so."

Finally, at the extrajudicial killing he orchestrated aboard the *Somers* in 1842, Mackenzie did what his "strange perversion" compelled him to do: "I now placed myself on the trunk, in a situation from which my eye could take in everything."

DECEMBER 2, 1991

Living Up to His Name:
Senator Packwood's Lechery Log

He was a delusional lothario, convinced that his "kamikaze kissing attacks," as *New York Times* columnist Maureen Dowd described them, were irresistible to the women upon whom he inflicted them. Indeed, Senator Bob Packwood kept a detailed record of his manly prowess—enhanced by hair having "just the right amount of bounce to it and wave to it," as he recorded, not to mention "the well-defined musculature of my sinewy arms which are always bulging with desire." In Packwood's warped view, what woman wouldn't want that probing tongue shoved down her throat?

Given all his crave-worthy qualities—the boozy breath, the stealthy hand up the skirt—it must have come as a shock to the senator that women found him repulsive. All the more appalling, some dared to come forward and publicly accuse him of sexual harassment.

The senator detailed his bewilderment at this bizarre betrayal in his diary entry of December 2, 1991:

> Grabbed Tracy Gorman behind the Xerox machine today and she got a little pissed. What's the big deal? I was smiling while I did it. She made this big stink about it and it took me about two hours and a couple of thousand dollars to calm her down. I have one question—if she didn't want me to feather her nest, why did she come into the Xerox room? Sure, she used that old excuse that she had to make copies of the Brady Bill, but if you believe that, I have a room full of radical feminists you can boff. She knew I was copying stuff in there. I had my jacket off and my sleeves rolled up . . . I know what she wanted. This didn't require a lot of thought.

Nor did it require much thought to understand Packwood's resignation from the Senate in 1995, after a total of 19 women had come forward: The alternative was expulsion. Perhaps the most astonishing thing about the whole sloppy episode is that Packwood had *edited* his diaries upon being compelled to produce them. How those pages must have pulsated with slime before they were sanitized.

DECEMBER 3, 2003

Mary Tyler Moore Onstage:
She Didn't Make It After All

Curtain time for the Wednesday matinee at the Manhattan Theatre Club was fast approaching. But Mary Tyler Moore was struggling with a bit of stagecraft—specifically, learning her lines—essential to the success of Neil Simon's final play, *Rose's Dilemma*. In it, a widowed novelist, Rose Steiner, invokes the ghost of her late husband to complete the book he left unfinished at his death.

With only four actors in the cast, the 66-year-old Moore had plenty of dialogue to memorize, and playwright Simon was unhappy with her progress: During the play's preview run—its official opening would be December 18—Moore had been receiving line prompts through an ear mic. So Simon, known for his killer comedic writing, dashed off a one-liner that was cuttingly humorless: "Learn your lines or get out of my play."

He entrusted this nastygram to his fourth (or fifth, depending on how you count them) wife, Elaine Joyce, who hand-delivered it to Moore shortly before the 2 p.m. preview performance.

The actress could not hide the fact that she was crushed. Stage-door vultures reported her storming out the theater's rear entrance minutes before the lights went down. In a press release shortly after, Moore's publicist, Mara Buxbaum, confirmed her client's psychic injury: "Mary was devastated and completely debilitated personally and professionally. Mary has been working tirelessly for months but feels pushed out of this production."

Cue the understudy!

Patricia Hodges, stepping into the role on literally a moment's notice, delivered a "courageous [but] artificial-seeming" performance, according to *New York Times* critic Ben Brantley.

But really, what stand-in could ever fill the shoes of one of the nation's most beloved actresses? "There is, most conspicuously, the nagging phantom of the Star Who Isn't There," Brantley's mostly unfavorable review opined. "But Ms. Moore's spirit still lingers, exhaling what sounds like a sigh of relief."

DECEMBER 4, 1926

Momsters, Part 8:
Mrs. Hemingway Sets on Her Son

"My mother is an all-time, all-American bitch."
—*Ernest Hemingway on his mother, Grace Hall Hemingway*

Freud would have had a field day examining the roots of Ernest Hemingway's lifelong loathing for his mother, Grace—or "that bitch," as he often referred to her. The domineering, admonishing matriarch dressed her oldest boy like a girl, yet she expected him to be a man of her molding.

Plenty to psychoanalyze there, certainly—but maybe it was all so much simpler than that. Perhaps Grace Hemingway was, as her son consistently maintained, really just a bitch. It's nearly impossible to tweeze apart the deepest dynamics of any family, of course. Yet what Grace left on paper may say enough—or say it all.

On December 4, 1926, she wrote to her darling boy after the publication of *The Sun Also Rises,* one of his most widely acclaimed novels:

> I belong to a current Book Study Class and we have lectures from the literary critics of the various newspapers.
>
> I could not face being present when your book was to be reviewed, but one of the class told me afterwards what was said. That you were prostituting a really great ability to the lowest uses. It is a doubtful honor to produce one of the filthiest books of the year.
>
> What is the matter? Have you ceased to be interested in loyalty, nobility, honor and fineness in life . . . surely you have other words in your vocabulary besides "damn" and "bitch"—Every page fills

me with a sick loathing—if I should pick up a book by any other writer with such words in it, I should read no more—but pitch it in the fire.

We wonder: Would that be an all-time, all-American pitch?

DECEMBER 5, 1938

Hateful? *Ja.* Original? *Nein.*

Plagiarism took a diabolically perverse turn in the December 5, 1938, issue of *Social Justice,* a weekly newsletter published by Father Charles Coughlin, the ordained demagogue and fervent anti-Semite whose radio program attracted millions of listeners in the United States. The edition contained an article entitled "Background of Persecution," in which the Roman Catholic priest recounted a slew of outrages communistic Jews allegedly visited upon Christians.

Coughlin's rabid readers were no doubt reinvigorated in their anti-Semitism—just as so many Nazis had been at Nuremberg three years earlier, when the Third Reich's propaganda minister Joseph Goebbels had vomited forth many of the exact same sentences in his speech, "Communism with the Mask Off."

Another mask removed: A hate-spewing fanatic posing as an original-thinking Christian.

DECEMBER 6, 1950

Harry Gives Him Hell

"I love criticism just so long as it is unqualified praise," the playwright Nöel Coward once said. And anything short of that sentiment often makes artists bristle. In 1877, for example, James Abbott McNeill Whistler (of "Whistler's Mother" fame) sued John Ruskin (of repulsed groom fame; see April 10) for libel after the critic accused him of "flinging a pot of paint in the public's face" with the work "Nocturne in Black and Gold: The Falling Rocket."* And pioneering impressionist Édouard Manet went so far as to fight a duel with Louis Edmond Duranty in 1870 over a minor critical comment.†

In the case of Margaret Truman, though, it wasn't the artist who went ballistic over the bad review of her singing performance that ran in *The Washington Post* on December 6, 1950: It was the artist's father, the president of the United States, who responded to critic Paul Hume by letter the same day.

"Mr. Hume," Harry S. Truman wrote. "I've just read your lousy review of Margaret's concert. I've come to the conclusion that you are an 'eight ulcer man on four ulcer pay.' It seems to me that you are a frustrated old man who wishes he could have been successful. When you write such poppy-cock as was in the back section of the paper you work for, it shows conclusively that you're off the beam and at least four of your ulcers are at work. Some day I hope to meet you. When that happens you'll need a new nose, a lot of beefsteak for black eyes, and perhaps a supporter below!"

In response, Hume took the high (paying) road: He sold Truman's screed for $3,500.

—◆—

---

* Whistler won the suit but was awarded derisory damages of a single farthing—about a quarter of a penny.

† Duranty was wounded above the right breast in the sword fight, which ended the duel. Considering his honor satisfied, Manet quickly revived his friendship with Duranty.

DECEMBER 7, 43 B.C.

When Cicero Got His Silver Tongue Pierced

Marcus Tullius Cicero was one of the world's greatest orators. But to his rival Mark Antony, the eloquent Roman senator was nothing more than an odious loudmouth who needed to be silenced —permanently.

The trouble began in earnest after the assassination of Julius Caesar in 44 B.C. In a series of speeches known as the Philippics, Cicero railed at what he saw as Antony's increasingly tyrannical behavior and urged his annihilation by military means. Cicero's message received widespread support, but Antony and his autocratic allies ultimately prevailed. And they did so in a ghastly fashion that involved the orator's most vital instrument.

With the Roman Republic doomed to dictatorship—and the enemies of the emergent masters liable to forfeit their lives and fortunes in a ruthless practice known as proscription—Cicero made a feeble attempt to flee the coming retribution. He was easily intercepted, however, and bowed to the inevitable. "I am stopping

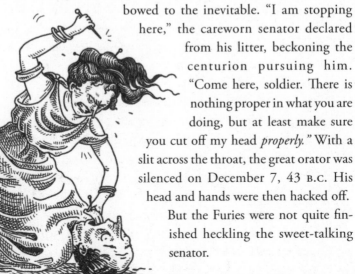

here," the careworn senator declared from his litter, beckoning the centurion pursuing him. "Come here, soldier. There is nothing proper in what you are doing, but at least make sure you cut off my head *properly.*" With a slit across the throat, the great orator was silenced on December 7, 43 B.C. His head and hands were then hacked off.

But the Furies were not quite finished heckling the sweet-talking senator.

According to the ancient historian Cassius Dio, Mark Antony's third wife, Fulvia, took her revenge upon Cicero and his fulminations against her husband in a most gruesome manner. Just before the statesman's severed head was put on public display in the Roman Forum, Fulvia took it, "and after abusing it spitefully and spitting upon it," Dio wrote, set it between her knees, forced open the mouth, and pulled the tongue forward. She then used her own hairpins to puncture the offending organ of speech while "uttering many brutal jests."

DECEMBER 8, 2008

On Second Thought, Part 15:
Better Rein In That Forecast

"I don't believe there's any cloud that hangs over me. I think there's nothing but sunshine hanging over me," Illinois governor Rod Blagojevich confidently declared on December 8, 2008—the day when reports surfaced that federal investigators had been secretly recording his conversations. Topping off his plummy forecast, Blagojevich added this weather-resistant note of defiance: "I appreciate anybody who wants to tape me openly and notoriously, and those who feel like they want to sneakily and wear taping devices, I would remind them that it kind of smells like Nixon and Watergate."

He was arrested on corruption charges the next day.

The governor's Watergate comparison was apt—if inexact. Just a month earlier, Blagojevich had come off as positively Nixonian when he was captured on tape musing about the monetary value of his power to appoint the successor to Barack Obama's recently vacated Senate seat. "I've got this thing, and it's fucking golden," the governor told aide Doug Scofield. "I'm just not giving it up for fucking nothing."

Ultimately the gold would come from Blagojevich's own pocket: The greedy governor was ordered to cough up $21,800—and spend the next

14 years of his life in prison*—upon being convicted on 18 felony counts of corruption in 2011.

Mother Nature, it seems, did not appreciate being misrepresented.

DECEMBER 9, 1984

ABC You Later, Suckers!

"This is our last and final show," Michael Jackson declared from the concert stage at Dodger Stadium on December 9, 1984. "It's been a long 20 years and we love you all." And with that, Jackie, Tito, Jermaine, and Marlon—the brothers with whom the now stratospherically successful Michael had first risen to fame as the Jackson 5—officially became irrelevant.

Sadly, none of them saw it coming: Michael made the announcement in front of 50,000 people without bothering to inform his brothers first. And with that, the *Thriller* was gone.

DECEMBER 10, 2013

No Words to Describe
Mandela Memorial

The memorial service for 95-year-old South African president Nelson Mandela on December 10, 2013, was supposed to be a solemn

---

* Blagojevich ultimately served nearly eight years before his former *Celebrity Apprentice* boss, President Donald Trump, commuted the sentence in February 2020. The convict governor, grateful for the suddenly clement weather, promptly declared himself a "Trumpocrat."

occasion. In attendance were world dignitaries including U.S. president Barack Obama.

Yet there was one stridently discordant—though utterly silent—note in the chorus of encomiums delivered from the podium: Supposed interpreter for the deaf Thamsanqa Jantjie, sporting an official-looking blue lanyard and ID badge, knew not the first gesture of International Sign. Instead, fluent only in Bogus, he delivered gibberish translations of the tributes being offered up by various world leaders.

"It was hours of complete nonsense," an outraged David Buxton, CEO of the British Deaf Association, told Britain's *Telegraph* newspaper. "He is clearly a fraud who wanted to stand onstage with big and important people. It's quite audacious if you think about it."

Or perhaps it's best *not* to think about how Jantjie—a street thug who later claimed to have schizophrenia—had infiltrated security and made his way onto the stage, where he performed what Buxton described as "childish hand gestures and clapping."

A year after the imposture, it emerged that Jantjie had taken up a new and clearly more natural career: acting. Though the professional organization Deaf South Africa had barred him from working as a sign-language interpreter anywhere in the country, Jantjie sounded more philosophical than remorseful: "It's difficult," he told a South African radio station, "but men have to do what men have to do."

Including, it would seem, desecrating the memory of the apartheid-plagued nation's first black head of state.

DECEMBER 11, 1861

The Uncivil War, Part 6:

Sherman's Reputation Tanks

William Tecumseh Sherman was in the grip of a gloomy despondency in the first months of the Civil War—far removed from the spirited general who would, just three years later, effectively snap both the spine and the spirit of the South with what he called "the hard hand of war."

The United States was woefully unprepared for combat, Sherman insisted in 1861, and deaf to the true dangers of a determined enemy. "Tis folly to underestimate the task [of decidedly defeating the South], and you see how far already the nation has miscalculated," he wrote to his wife, Ellen, after the Union's disastrous July defeat at the Battle of Bull Run. "The Real war," he added, "has not yet begun."

Sherman's appointment as second-in-command (and eventually commander) of the Department of the Cumberland, based in the strategic state of Kentucky, reinforced his conviction that Washington was taking the rebel threat far too lightly. "Some terrible disaster is inevitable," he wrote. Yet as Sherman became increasingly strident in his calls for more, better-trained and better-equipped men to defend the region—a prescient demand, it turned out—he was met with derision. Worse, some in the administration began to question the stability of this wailing lone voice, physically and emotionally sick from sleeplessness and worry. The general was relieved of his command and sent home to rest.

Then, on December 11, 1861, *The Cincinnati Commercial* published a mortifying story that was not just misleading but libelous: "GENERAL WILLIAM T. SHERMAN INSANE," the headline trumpeted. "It appears that [Sherman] was, at the time while commanding in Kentucky, stark mad," read the accompanying story. The paper then added how "providential" it was that the nation "has not to mourn the loss of an army, through the loss of mind of a general into whose hands was committed such vast responsibility."

For a man of honor, no deeper stake could be driven into his soul. "The idea of having brought disgrace on all associated with me is so horrible to contemplate that I cannot really endure it," Sherman wrote Ellen. In fact, as he shared with his brother John, "I am so sensible now of my disgrace . . . that I do think I should have committed suicide were it not for my children." The general correctly predicted that the dismaying story would spread across the country. However, his fear that it would "impair my personal influence for much time to come, if not always" proved unfounded.

Recovering his vigor after a brief rest, Sherman returned to service. Less than four months after the *Commercial* declared him insane, he distinguished himself at the Battle of Shiloh—"contributing largely to the glorious victory," as Maj. Gen. Henry Halleck informed Secretary of War Edwin Stanton, recommending a promotion. "So at last I Stand redeemed from the vile slanders of that Cincinnati paper," Sherman wrote his wife. And those malicious newspaper reporters? "They keep shy of me as I have said that the first one I catch I will hang as a Spy."

DECEMBER 12, 1950

Put to the Testes, Part 10:
McCarthy Didn't Go Just for the Jugular

"I just kicked Drew Pearson in the nuts!"
—*Senator Joseph McCarthy of Wisconsin, crowing to Frank Waldrop,
executive editor of the Washington* Times-Herald, *about his assault
on columnist and radio broadcaster Drew Pearson*

Washington socialite Louise Tinsley "Tinnie" Steinman thought it would be a hoot to seat Senator Joe McCarthy and reporter Drew Pearson at the same table during a party at D.C.'s Sulgrave Club on December 12, 1950. The two men loathed each other.

Pearson had spent the past year relentlessly mocking McCarthy for his recently launched Red hunt, as well as for his tax troubles in Wisconsin. A fuming McCarthy, meanwhile, had repeatedly threatened the influential journalist with bodily harm. The boozed-up pol finally got his chance to do just that at Tinnie's exclusive soiree.

The dueling duo spent the evening trading insults. They were "the two biggest billygoats in the onion patch," as *Time* magazine described them at the time, "and when they began butting, all present knew history was being made."

"You know, I'm going to put you out of business with a speech in the Senate tomorrow," McCarthy hissed at Pearson. "There isn't going to be anything left of you professionally or personally by the time I get finished with you."

"Joe," Pearson shot back. "Have you paid your income taxes yet?"

As the party concluded, McCarthy encountered Pearson in the club cloakroom, grabbed him by the neck, and kneed him in the groin—twice. Gasping for breath, Pearson managed to cough out, "When are they going to put you in the booby hatch?"

Just then, a recently elected senator entered the room. His name was Richard Nixon. Like Pearson, he was a Quaker, and like McCarthy, his shady politics had been the target of Pearson's journalistic investigations. Apparently the sight of Nixon incited McCarthy to even greater violence, for now he raised his hand, slapped Pearson hard enough to snap his head back, and proudly announced: "That one was for you, Dick."

DECEMBER 13, 1978

Suff-Reject:
Susan B. Anthony Strikes Out

"Susan B. Anthony has good reason to look as grim
as she does. In her shining moment upon the new dollar coin,
the noted suffragist is falling flatter than her face."
—The Philadelphia Inquirer

Numismatic history was made at the U.S. Mint in Philadelphia on December 13, 1978. A new one-dollar coin was being struck, and for the first time ever it featured a female figure who was *not* that mythic composite known as Lady Liberty. So it was understandable why excitement ran high among the dignitaries gathered for the unveiling of the metallic dollar stamped with the visage of crusading suffragist and social reformer Susan B. Anthony.

"We've had live eagles on our coins, live buffaloes, but we've never had a live woman," exulted U.S. Representative Patricia Schroeder of Colorado, who ceremoniously stood at one of the pressing machines. "Now we've got her."

A million "Susie B's" were minted in Philadelphia that day, with hundreds of millions more subsequently turned out in Denver and San Francisco. The massive accumulation—seven months before the coin's official debut—arose from officials' concern that collectors would gobble up the supply as soon as it was released, creating a shortage.

They needn't have worried.

The Susie B. was a bomb. "There is no way to overestimate how badly that coin was received," Michael Brown, a spokesman for the U.S. Mint, told *Chicago Tribune* columnist Bob Greene years later. "I suppose there may have been other disasters in the history of our nation's currency. But never anything this bad. Never rejection by the public that is this complete."

Most commentators attribute the failure of the coin to its size and color—it was easily mistaken for a quarter. Others see something darker: Might some members of the public have spurned the Susan B. Anthony dollar for the feminist agenda they perceived lurking behind it?

The truth may lie in a more prosaic tradition: Americans have simply never taken to using dollar coins over bills.

Whatever the reason for the public's rejection of Susan B. Anthony, one man took it especially hard. Frank Gasparro, chief engraver of the Mint—and creator of the cast-off coin—told Bob Greene at the time: "It hurts my feelings."

When Studio 54 Got 86'ed

The snapshots from Studio 54's late-1970s heyday are nothing short of surreal. There's Bianca Jagger, Mick's wife, celebrating her 30th birthday astride a white charger inside the famed New York nightclub. Truman Capote's on the dance floor—seemingly oblivious to the pounding disco beat—whistling to a sound track only he can hear. Liza Minnelli's all over the place—including on a stained sofa she shares with First Lady Betty Ford. Dolly Parton arrives to find a barnyard created in her honor. Cher, Halston, and Salvador Dalí rub elbows with their fellow glitterati up and down the chronological spectrum, from silent-no-more film star Gloria Swanson to Academy Award–winning tot Tatum O'Neal.

So much for the participants. What about the observers? Well, there's spectral, waiflike Andy Warhol, silently absorbing it all—and later confiding his bitchy observations to his diary. "Liz [Taylor] looked like a—bellybutton," the pop-art progenitor wrote in an entry from March 1978. "Like a fat little Kewpie doll."

Orchestrating the entire scene was 54's coked-up munchkin of a co-owner, Steve Rubell. The tiny tyrant stood guard at the door, mercilessly turning away the uncool and the overeager. Though Studio 54 was Rubell's empire—his entrée to the elite—he was also the accelerant of the nightclub's implosion. And all because of his big, fat mouth.

"What the IRS doesn't know won't hurt them," the cocky King of the Dark Hours joked with a radio host. And to *New York* magazine he boasted: "Only the Mafia makes more money." Then, on December 14, 1978, the IRS mobilized against the gnome dumb enough to dismiss them: Thirty-one agents raided Studio 54, seizing bags stuffed with skimmed cash. Rubell and his partner, Ian Schrager, wound up in the slammer—and their prized club staggered to an ignoble end.

It was a shame, really, with so much wholesome fun to be had: dust clouds of cocaine; quaaludes in abundance; celebrities mixing with carefully chosen civilian revelers—and their secretions—in the easy-to-clean Rubber Room. And, of course, that dingy but very private basement—epicenter of Studio 54's most depraved excesses—where a future president of the United States turned sex into a spectator sport: "I would watch supermodels getting screwed . . . on a bench in the middle of the room," club regular Donald Trump breathlessly recalled to writer Timothy O'Brien. "There were seven of them and each one was getting screwed by a different guy."

The perfect playground for a future politician.

———

DECEMBER 15, 1950

A Whole Lot of *Hooey*

"One homosexual can pollute a Government office."
—Employment of Homosexuals and Other Sex Perverts,
a report by the Investigations Subcommittee, delivered to the
United States Senate on December 15, 1950

Oh, and another thing:

"The lack of emotional stability which is found in most sex perverts, [along with] the weakness of their moral fiber, makes them susceptible to the blandishments of the foreign espionage agent."

The Hoey Report, as it was called (after Subcommittee Chairman Clyde R. Hoey, D–NC), was issued amid the infamous "Lavender Scare," whose persecution of gay people had consequences arguably exceeding those of the contemporaneous "Red Scare." Thousands of men and women accused of homosexuality were forced out of their jobs in the federal government as potential subversives, further marginalizing a minority already grappling with societal rejection. And, unlike the scapegoats of the government's witch hunt for Communists, which abated significantly by the 1960s, gays and lesbians would remain official targets for decades to come.

Many of their oppressors were congressional closet cases themselves. We're talking to you, Larry Craig. And you, Bob Bauman. Yes, and you, too, Mark Foley.

<hr>

DECEMBER 16, 1949

Red Square-Off: Murderers' Row

The peak of Everest was positively balmy compared with this icy postwar summit between two megalomaniacs. Soviet premier Joseph Stalin and China's Chairman Mao Zedong were both major communist leaders—Stalin, a seasoned murderer of millions, and Mao about to be—so at least they should have had some war stories to swap. But by refusing to meet Mao's train when it arrived in Moscow on December 16, 1949, Stalin made it clear that the Russian bear intended to swat aside the Chinese panda.

The chore of welcoming the newly empowered Mao—a "margarine communist," the Soviet dictator derisively called him—was delegated instead to several senior officials from the Politburo. They took Stalin's cue and refused to eat lunch with the Chinese leader or escort him to the dacha where he would stay.

"[Mao] was treated not as the leader of a great revolution bringing into the Communist orbit one of the world's great nations," wrote David Halberstam, but (quoting historian Adam Ulam) "'as if he were, say, the head of the Bulgarian party.'"

Stalin did deign to meet Mao on the evening of his arrival. It was not at the Kremlin—that would have been commensurately august for the man who had just turned China Red—but at the relatively undistinguished Metropol Hotel. And audiences with Uncle Joe were only sporadic after that, leaving Mao stewing alone in his dacha and fuming that he had come to Moscow to do more than "eat and shit." (The scatological reference was unknowingly ironic, for Stalin had ordered that the Chinese leader's feces be secretly removed for scientific analysis.)

"Mao began to show his dissatisfaction that he was sitting behind lock and key in a residence that was assigned to him," future Soviet leader Nikita Khrushchev later wrote, "[and] that they did not show him anything, that no one met with him. He declared that if things continued that way, he would leave."

Though a lopsided pact was eventually signed—two months after Mao's arrival in Moscow—Sino-Soviet relations were ultimately doomed. As Ulam wrote, "It is no wonder that Mao conceived, if he had not nurtured it before, an abiding hatred of the Soviet Union."

When Stalin's successor visited China nine years later, in 1958, Mao got a measure of revenge. Knowing that Khrushchev couldn't swim, Mao arranged to meet him in a swimming pool, where the chairman swanned effortlessly across the water while the Butcher of the Ukraine (and future Disneyland reject; see September 19) was kept afloat by inflatable plastic water wings. According to Mao's personal physician, "the chairman was deliberately playing the role of emperor, treating Khrushchev like a barbarian come to pay tribute. It was a way, Mao told me . . . of 'sticking a needle up his ass.'"

DECEMBER 17, 1965

It *Did* Amount to a Hill of Beans: Garbanzo Beans!

Trouble had been simmering in the White House kitchen since early December 1963, when Lyndon and Lady Bird Johnson, with their down-home Texas tastes, had moved into the residence. Resident chef René Verdon, originally hired by Jackie Kennedy to bring French elegance to the president's table, simmered as his meticulously prepared dishes were supplanted by more common fare. He also bristled at being placed under the watchful glare of a new, economy-minded "food coordinator," who deemed fresh ingredients an unnecessary extravagance, directing Verdon to use canned and frozen instead.

Understandably, the top chef stewed under these constraints. "I don't think you can economize on food in the White House," he sniffed.

In the end, an order for a cold puree of garbanzo beans (a dish Verdon described as "already bad hot") sent his refined senses reeling—and right out the door. On December 17, 1965, in what *Time* magazine described as "a Gallic huff," Verdon hung up his apron and walked. "The Johnsons liked to have certain foods, but I think people coming to the White House are not expecting hamburgers, chili con queso or spareribs," he later told *The New York Times*. "Those foods belong to the land; they do not belong in the dining room."*

---

* Although Verdon lived long enough to witness the desecration of the Louvre Museum when a McDonald's opened there in 2009, he was mercifully spared *le horreur* of fast-food hamburgers being served at the White House a decade later.

DECEMBER 18, 1989

An Invasion of Privates: The (Icky) Inside Story of Charles and Camilla

Centuries after Henry VIII expressed his desire to kiss Anne Boleyn's breasts—her "pretty duckies," as the king called them in a letter to his future wife (now held in the Vatican Archive, of all places)—Charles, Prince of Wales, took royal cooing to another level. On December 18, 1989, he engaged in an intimate phone chat with his then mistress (now wife) Camilla Parker Bowles. Alas, some rat had surreptitiously taped the carnal conversation, in which the hapless prince expressed a longing to be constantly and conveniently close to his lover (complete with a vision of being reborn as her feminine hygiene product). His reputation in the aftermath? Flushed.

DECEMBER 19, 2008

That'll Be Ten Trillion Dollars, Please

"Zimbabwe is mine."
—*President Robert Mugabe, telling it like it*
(regrettably) was on December 19, 2008

After helping to establish the independent nation of Zimbabwe (formerly Rhodesia) in 1980, Marxist and former schoolteacher Robert Mugabe proceeded to snap its economic spine. Pursuing a policy of decolonization over the next two decades, he morphed into an autocratic strongman who deputized his goons to seize large commercial farms starting in 2000 and redistribute them to inexperienced owners—often elites in the government or military. The beneficiaries' predictable failure to produce sufficient crop yields unleashed famine and hyperinflation across the country.

Indeed, on that December day when Mugabe claimed to own his native land, Zimbabwe's inflation—second highest in world history, according to a Cato Institute report—had just peaked at a staggering *monthly* rate of 79.6 billion percent. Which meant a trillion-dollar Zimbabwean bill might buy you a slice of bread—but forget about using it to take home a whole loaf.

━━◆━━

DECEMBER 20, 1956

Don't Believe a Word He Suez

On December 20, 1956, British prime minister Anthony Eden stood before the House of Commons and used the occasion of his final address to tell a whopping lie. Less than two months had passed since Israel attacked Egypt, an event followed immediately by an ill-conceived Anglo-French military incursion into the area around the Suez Canal. Just a few days later, however, the two European nations were forced to withdraw.

Disgraced by the debacle and about to lose his job, Eden maintained the fiction that Israel had acted unilaterally, with Britain and France merely responding to events as peacekeepers: "I want to say this on the question of foreknowledge, and to say it quite bluntly to the House, that there was not foreknowledge that Israel would attack Egypt. There was not."

Ah, but there was. In fact, Israel, France, and Britain had secretly gathered to plot the entire Egyptian offense.

Eden nursed a nearly pathological hatred for Egyptian president Gamal Abdel Nasser, who in July 1956 had nationalized the Suez Canal (built and operated by Britain and France). The oil that fueled Europe passed through the canal—but more than that, it was powerfully symbolic of Britain's imperial past. By snatching it away, Nasser threatened both Britain's economic stability and its standing in the world.

The canal's seizure nearly gave Eden one of his own. "I want him destroyed," the prime minister railed, "can't you understand?" Such was the recall of Anthony Nutting, minister of state for foreign affairs, whose later account revealed that Eden's rage escalated from hysterical to homicidal: "I want him murdered, and if you and the Foreign Office don't agree, then you'd better come to the cabinet and explain why."

An alternative to assassination presented itself when Israel's plans to invade Egypt, with French backing, were revealed to Eden, resulting in the scheme that ended so disastrously. Under the guise of simply maintaining order in the region, Britain and France would follow Israel's invasion with an air and ground offensive of their own. "We were to take part in a cynical act of aggression," recalled Nutting, "dressing ourselves for the part as fireman or policeman, while making sure that our firehoses spouted petrol and not water."

There was just one snag, and its name was President Dwight D. Eisenhower. Having been systematically deceived by Eden about British intentions, Ike made an unexpected and emphatic declaration of U.S. opposition to European aggression in Egypt as soon as the operation got under way.

Facing the specter of economic devastation and global isolation, the English and French called off their ill-advised foray shortly thereafter. With it went any notions that Britain might return to its pre–World War II preeminence.

Anthony Eden endured the full brunt of the fiasco. Just 21 months after succeeding Winston Churchill, the humiliated prime minister left office. He never varied from his pretense that Israel's attack on Egypt had been plotted without his knowledge—until an interview in 1967, when he finally admitted that, yes, there had been collusion.* "I am still

---

* Still stage-managing events from beyond the grave, Eden would not permit this confession to be published until after his death, which came on January 14, 1977.

unrepentant about Suez," Eden stated at the time. "People never look at what would have happened if we had done nothing. There is a parallel with the '30s. If you allow people to break agreements with impunity, the appetite grows to feed on such things.

"I have no apologies to offer."

'Tis the Season to Be Hateful

"Therefore be on your guard against the Jews, knowing that
wherever they have their synagogues, nothing is found but a den
of devils in which sheer self-glory, conceit, lies, blasphemy,
and defaming of God and men are practiced most maliciously."
—*Martin Luther,* On the Jews and Their Lies, *1543*

Martin Luther usually loved Christmas. But yuletide cheer was not present on December 21, 1542—when, as the German theologian wrote to his confidant Justus Jonas, he found himself "immersed in the madness of the Jews." Indeed, the renowned usher of the Protestant Reformation was in the midst of furiously completing his anti-Semitic screed, *On the Jews and Their Lies.* Published early in 1543, the diatribe contained enough hate to fill the stockings of bigots for the next five centuries.

When Stalin's on the Phone: Can You Fear Me Now?

"Imagine Genghis Khan with a telephone!"
—*Leo Tolstoy*

Nadezhda Krupskaya was tending her ailing husband, Vladimir Ilyich Lenin—recently debilitated by a second stroke—when the phone rang on December 22, 1922. On the line was Joseph Stalin, seething with rage. Though the emergent monster with the yellow eyes and pock-marked skin had yet to rack up the body count that would ultimately number in the tens of millions, his barbarian disposition was already on display. And the venom he spewed over the phone that day left a shattered Krupskaya sobbing on the floor.

"Because of a short letter which I had written in words dictated to me by Vladimir Ilyich by permission of the doctors, Stalin allowed himself yesterday an unusually rude outburst directed at me," she wrote to party leaders (and future Great Purge victims) Grigory Zinoviev and Lev Kamenev. "I beg you to protect me from rude interference with my private life and from vile invectives and threats."

Stalin's ostensible reason for the call was concern for Lenin's health, and that attending to party business while ill might make him worse. But the embryonic dictator was also busy consolidating his political power—and the last thing he needed was Lenin's interfering letters, transcribed by his wife and confidant—a "syphilitic whore," as Stalin reportedly called Krupskaya during his telephonic tantrum.

Lenin rallied enough to rebuke Stalin by yet another letter. That followed his public "Testament," in which he declared Stalin "too rude" to be general secretary of the Communist Party and urged his removal from the position. But the testament lacked teeth, and soon enough Lenin succumbed to a final stroke, leaving his wife at Stalin's mercy.

Miraculously, Krupskaya was allowed not just to live but also to serve Mother Russia, working as deputy education commissar from 1929 until her death in 1939. It was always under a malicious but unstated menace, however: Watch your step or we'll find someone else to play the part of Lenin's widow.

DECEMBER 23, 1750

Nice Fry, Ben!

"I am Ashamed to have been Guilty of so Notorious A Blunder."
*—Benjamin Franklin, writing of an electrical experiment
gone embarrassingly wrong*

Contrary to popular myth, Ben Franklin never championed the turkey over the bald eagle as the emblematic avian of the newly formed United States.* In fact, the inventive Founding Father made life miserable for the poor birds in question when he aimed to shock them to death in his electrical experiments.

"The Turkies," he wrote, "tho' thrown into violent Convulsions, and then lying as dead for some Minutes, would recover in less than a quarter of an Hour." Fortunately, a sufficiently lethal surge was eventually

---

* The common misconception of Franklin as turkey touter arose from a letter he wrote his daughter in 1784, observing that the bird adopted for the seal of the Society of the Cincinnati looked less like a bald eagle than a turkey—which, he noted, was "a much more respectable Bird, and withal a true original Native of America . . . a Bird of Courage." The eagle, by contrast, was "of bad moral Character. He does not get his Living honestly. You may have seen him perched on some dead Tree near the River, where, too lazy to fish for himself, he watches the Labour of the Fishing Hawk; and when that diligent Bird has at length taken a Fish, and is bearing it to his Nest for the Support of his Mate and young Ones, the Bald Eagle pursues him and takes it from him."

found. "I conceit that the Birds kill'd in this Manner eat uncommonly tender," Franklin recounted.

However, on December 23, 1750, the electrocuted turkeys got to stick one in Ben's gizzard.

"I have lately made an Experiment in Electricity that I desire never to repeat," Franklin wrote of that day, when a group had gathered to watch him zap a bird into oblivion and partake of its succulent flesh. But as things turned out, the would-be killer, holding a metal chain, was the one who received the staggering jolt.

"I . . . felt what I know not how well to describe," Franklin wrote several days later; "an universal Blow thro'out my whole Body from head to foot which seem'd within as well as without; after which the first thing I took notice of was a violent quick Shaking of my body which gradually remitting, my sense as gradually return'd . . . that part of my hand and fingers which held the Chain was left white as tho' the Blood had been Driven Out, and Remained so 8 or 10 Minutes After, feeling like Dead flesh, and I had a Numbness in my Arms and the back of my Neck, which Continued till the Next Morning but wore off. Nothing Remains now of this Shock but a Soreness in my breast Bone, which feels As if it had been Brused. I Did not fall, but Suppose I should have been Knocked Down if I had Received the Stroke in my head: the whole was Over in less than a minute."

To the relief of the wildfowl (and the benefit of humanity), Franklin would soon redirect his electrical experiments from turkeys to turnkeys.

DECEMBER 24, 2007

A Christmas Affair:

For a Senator, What Could Be Verse?

'Twas the night before Christmas at John Ensign's house,

When his cross wife confronted her louse of a spouse;
Ensign's mistress was there; her husband as well,
Four old bosom buddies—a summit from hell;
Ensign's cuckolded pal, his office assistant
Went on *Nightline* to paint his boss as an infant;
"Johnny cries like a kid; holds his head in his hand,"
And yet ending the fling was not part of his plan;
Nevada's senator, evangelic Christian,
Wouldn't quit the forbidden fruit that he'd bitten;
Ensign never flagged; how his colleagues they brayed!
On learning how much the canoodlers got paid;
A congressional probe scrutinized every clue,
Yet its damning report was not pursued;
Though Ensign evaded a stint in the clink,
His voters took note of the scandal's high stink;
He went back to Nevada, his profession quite dead,
And banished that Christmas Eve dance from his head.
—*with apologies to Clement Moore*

DECEMBER 25, 1659

'Tis the Season to Be Sullen:
Yule Be Sorry if You Celebrate

Never rabid fun seekers, the Puritans of New England loathed the occasion of Christmas in particular. Given that there was no scripturally sanctioned observance of the Nativity—and, worse, that December 25 had pagan associations dating back to the Saturnalia revelries of ancient Rome—they contemptuously called the day "Foolstide."

From the *Mayflower's* arrival in 1620 forward, the traditional celebration of Christ's birth was deliberately ignored. Indeed, Governor William Bradford was quite pleased with himself when, after observing some recently arrived colonists playing in the street "on the day called Christmas day" in 1621, he snatched away their toys.

Party-pooper though he was, Bradford was a positively gleeful North Pole elf compared with the Puritan leaders of the Massachusetts Bay Colony: In 1659 they made it illegal to celebrate Christmas, with anyone caught in the act of decking the halls subject to a five-shilling fine.

DECEMBER 26, 2008

Towering Babble: In Short There's Simply Not, a Jot of Camelot

Caroline Kennedy found herself confounded by her own verbal clutter on December 26, 2008. The former first daughter—lobbying for an appointment to replace former first lady (and incoming secretary of state) Hillary Clinton in the U.S. Senate—managed to squeeze 80 verbal attends (distracting temporizers such as "um," "uh," and "you know") into a 30-minute interview with New York cable channel NY1.

Lacking any political experience when she sought Clinton's vacated seat, and having inherited evidently little of JFK's eloquence, Kennedy the Younger repeated her sorry performance the next day. In what Christopher Hitchens described as "'filler' words being used as props, to shore up a lame sentence," Kennedy uttered "you know" 130 times in an interview with *The New York Times,* and more than 200 times in a 30-minute chat with the New York *Daily News.*

Here, for example, candidate Caroline shares her insights on the Bush tax cut: "Well, you know, that's something, obviously, that, you know, in principle and in the campaign, you know, I think that, um, the tax cuts, you know, were expiring and needed to be repealed."

Flensed for her verbal stumbling—as well as her apparent lack of substance—Kennedy eventually removed her name from election consideration for "personal reasons." All was not lost, however. In 2013 President Barack Obama appointed her U.S. ambassador to Japan because of, um, well, you know . . . her name.

DECEMBER 27, 1933

Before Fala:
Meggie's Reign of Terrier

Turns out that Poll, Andrew Jackson's foulmouthed parrot (see June 10), wasn't the only problematic presidential pet. Indeed, some animal occupants of the White House have been truly bestial—especially Meggie, a member of FDR's canine menagerie. Whereas Roosevelt's beloved Scottish terrier, Fala, is enshrined at the feet of his master at the president's memorial in Washington, D.C.—a moving tribute to abiding friendship—his predecessor Meggie, another Scottie, was a monster. She quickly found herself banished from the White House—and into historical obscurity.

Immediately upon moving to Washington with the Roosevelts in March 1933, Meggie made her presence in the capital known. United Press International described her as being "possessed of plenty of nerve and fighting spirit"—a nice way of saying she was a snarly little bitch. In fact, they could have just ended their appraisal at "possessed." That would have better captured Meggie's vicious disposition, given that she terrorized everyone within biting distance.

Yet no matter how nasty she was, Eleanor Roosevelt adored the dog. Meggie became "very obstreperous," the first lady wrote to a friend in that indulgent way certain pet owners have. "Barking loudly," she chased "a rather terrified woman with a little boy, who was peacefully walking home past the White House." The growling and biting were all too cute—until December 27, 1933, when Meggie took a chunk out of Associated Press reporter Bess Furman's face.

Horrified by the incident,* Mrs. Roosevelt accompanied Furman to the hospital, stayed with her while the cut on her nose was stitched up, and even offered to write a dispatch about the encounter for the AP, which an editor there graciously (though in retrospect foolishly) declined. Now deemed an unpredictable menace, the demon Meggie was exiled from the Executive Mansion within just a few days. "That was a sad day for me," the first lady recalled, "and no one thought it wise to say too much to me about dogs for a long time."

———————

DECEMBER 28, 1793

The Days That Tried Tom Paine's Soul

"You folded your arms, forgot your friend, and became silent."
—*Thomas Paine to his former compatriot George Washington*

Thomas Paine had every reason to expect loyalty from the young nation he helped create: The rousing prose of his pamphlet *Common Sense* had fueled America's march toward independence from Britain, while *The American Crisis* revived the flagging spirit of the Revolution during its early days of defeat and despair. "Without the pen of the author of 'Common Sense,'" declared future president John Adams, "the sword of Washington would have been raised in vain."

---

* The first lady could console herself that she was not the first Roosevelt in the White House to experience pet peeves. Her uncle Teddy Roosevelt's bull terrier, Pete, had set an ornery precedent. "Pete has not a particle of humor and little reverence for anybody but his master," *The Washington Post* observed in 1907. That included the French ambassador, chased up a tree by the cantankerous canine. "The ambassador was attired in a stunning flannel suit," the *Post* reported. "He was only rescued by the heroic efforts of several sturdy policemen, who rushed upon the scene."

In 1783 Washington had honored Paine by having him ride by his side at the head of a celebratory parade as the last British garrisons evacuated New York. A decade later, however, when the raging furies of another Revolution screamed for Paine's head, Washington deserted the faithful scribe in his most desperate hour.

In the early morning hours of December 28, 1793, Paine was arrested and dumped in Luxembourg prison in Paris. He had journeyed to France to advance the cause of freedom there, taking a seat (despite speaking no French) in the first government of the French Revolution, the National Convention. But soon the appropriately dubbed Apostle of Liberty found himself on the wrong side of Robespierre and his bloody radicals—particularly when he urged the convention to spare the life of the deposed king, Louis XVI.

With a faction calling for his head, Paine desperately appealed to Gouverneur Morris, the American minister to France (and urethral self-surgeon; see November 6). Thus far, Morris's only response to his fellow founder's plight had been to pass along to him—unremarked—a notice from Chemin Deforgues, the French minister of foreign affairs, stating that Paine was subject to the laws of France. "You must not leave me in the situation in which this letter places me," Paine wrote to Morris. "You know I do not deserve it, and you see the unpleasant situation in which I am thrown." If the American minister failed to respond to Deforgues, Paine pleaded, "your silence will be a sort of consent to his observations."

Morris did nothing. "Lest I should forget it," he nonchalantly wrote to Thomas Jefferson, "I must mention that Thomas Paine is in prison, where he amuses himself with publishing a pamphlet [*The Age of Reason*] against Jesus Christ* . . . I incline to think that if he is quiet in prison he

---

* Thomas Paine's *The Age of Reason* was less an attack on Jesus than a treatise against organized religion in general: "All national institutions of churches," he wrote, "whether Jewish, Christian, or Turkish, appear to me no other than human inventions, set up to terrify and enslave mankind, and monopolize power and profit."

may have the good luck to be forgotten, whereas, should he be brought into notice, the long suspended axe might fall on him."

Worse than Gouverneur Morris's indifference was George Washington's. As Paine endured nearly a year of what he described as "a continued scene of horror"—with the Reign of Terror creeping through the bleak Luxembourg, sending anguished victims to the guillotine in a nearly nonstop procession—there came not a peep from the president whose greatness Paine had once trumpeted to the world.

Understandably, Paine's reverence now turned to rancor.

"He thinks the President winked at his imprisonment and wished he might die in gaol," wrote another future president, James Monroe, who replaced Morris as the American minister and would finally help secure Paine's release in November 1794. "Also, he is preparing an attack upon [Washington] of the most virulent kind."

Paine's public rebuke of the first president's character was stinging indeed: "And to you, Sir, treacherous in private friendship (for so you have been to me, and that in the day of danger) and a hypocrite in public life, the world will be puzzled to decide whether you are an apostate or an imposter; whether you have abandoned good principles or whether you ever had any."

The Founding Fathers never spoke again.

DECEMBER 29, 1978

Woody Hayes: Knocking Himself Out With His Own Punch

"I didn't hit him to hurt him. It only hurt me.
You see, it only hurt me. But you can't always explain
everything. Some things are beyond you."
—*Legendary Ohio State University coach Woody Hayes, speaking to*
The Washington Post *in 1984, on the career-ending throat punch*

he delivered to Clemson nose guard Charlie Bauman
at the Gator Bowl on December 29, 1978

W oody Hayes didn't like to lose—or tie, for that matter. And on those occasions when he did, the Ohio State coach was known to stage a nude spectacle of himself. "He was an ugly guy, so it would clear the locker room out pretty fast," recalled Leonard Downie, former executive editor of *The Washington Post,* as quoted in *The Lantern,* the Ohio State student newspaper where the budding journalist covered Hayes in the early 1960s.

More disturbing, if possible, was the coach's propensity for violence—most often directed at his own players. Downie remembered one occasion when Hayes instructed a player to take off his helmet so the coach could strike his bare head.

"Everybody who played for Ohio State probably got slugged in the stomach or slapped by Coach Hayes," former OSU guard Jim Savoca told ESPN.com. "It was the era. We would joke about it and say, 'Circle right to get away from that left hook.'"

Ohio State players may have taken Hayes's fits—and fists—of fury in stride. But it was a different matter at the 1978 Gator Bowl, when the coach turned his wrath on a player from the opposing team.

With two minutes to go in the game and Clemson leading 17–15, Tiger nose guard Charlie Bauman intercepted a pass from Ohio State freshman quarterback Art Schlichter at the Clemson 24 and ran it back into Buckeye territory before being tackled out of bounds—right at the feet of the combative Coach Hayes. "You SOB, I just lost my job," he screamed at Bauman, according to Clemson linebacker Bubba Brown. Then the 65-year-old Hayes swung at the neck of the giant lineman, who chose not to retaliate. But as Bauman retreated to the Clemson bench, a brawl erupted on the field.

Hayes was right to worry about his future with Ohio State if the Buckeyes lost the game—which they soon did. (Indeed, some pinned the defeat on the longtime coach's stubborn adherence to a tired playbook.) But Woody guaranteed his own departure when he threw that sucker punch. "He didn't hurt Charlie," former OSU linebacker Tom Cousineau told ESPN some years later. "It was like a mosquito. But it was the intent. You couldn't cross that line. It's different when you kick a sideline marker or push a cameraman. We expected him to be that animated with us—but never with the opponent."

"I knew he was done," Jim Savoca recalled of his coach's moment of madness. "I knew it was over." And the next day, it was.

DECEMBER 30, 1511

Cultural Vandalism, Part 4:
The Agony and the ... Agony

The crowd roared its approval when, on December 30, 1511, the 11-foot-high bronze statue of Pope Julius II, which adorned the facade of Bologna's Basilica of San Petronio, was pulled from its perch and came crashing to the ground, penetrating the pavement with its weight. It was an awesome display of defiance against the so-called Warrior Pope, who had subjugated the city only five years before. But the metal figure's downfall also represented a terrible cultural loss, for this wasn't just any statue: Michelangelo himself had created the masterpiece in a torturous process that was ultimately all for naught.

The artist had approached the project with trepidation late in 1506—and not only because he was inexperienced sculpting with bronze, a complicated medium that had stymied even Leonardo da Vinci.* More intimidating still was Pope Julius II, who commissioned the statue of himself.

---

* Leonardo struggled with this notoriously unforgiving medium. Trying to create a massive bronze equestrian statue for the Duke of Milan, he got no further than casting it in clay. Michelangelo was anything but understanding, calling out his rival as a "horse-modeller . . . unable to cast a statue in bronze [and] forced to give up the attempt in shame."

Michelangelo had a tense relationship with this fearsome pontiff, whose explosive temper rivaled the artist's. Earlier that year, for example, Michelangelo had left Rome in a huff after a money dispute with Julius about an elaborate tomb—the one the pope had commissioned for his very own eternal rest. The artist ignored as many papal pleas as he safely could before finally reporting for duty in Bologna, where Pope Julius was administering his vanquished domain. "I was forced to go there with a rope round my neck, to ask his pardon," he later said.

Though peeved at Michelangelo's repeated defiance, the pope recognized the artist's genius. Plus he wanted him to execute that giant bronze—an unmistakable reminder to the rebellious Bolognese of just who was boss. Julius was therefore in a conciliatory mood, and Michelangelo was wise enough not to decline the commission. Soon after, he had a model of the work completed.

That was the easy part.

In fact, artist and pope were almost jocular when discussing the details. Michelangelo had devised a seated figure with one arm raised, but Julius demanded to know if it was offering a blessing or a curse. The statue "threatens the people, Holy Father," the artist responded, "lest they be foolish." The figure's other hand had been left empty, but Michelangelo's suggestion that it could hold a book seemed only to offend the Warrior Pope:

"A book?" Julius responded. "A sword! I am no scholar!"

Then, the drudgery of completing the bronze behemoth began. Michelangelo complained about the process in letter after letter to his brother. "I live here in the greatest discomfort, subject to the greatest anxieties, and do nothing but labor day and night," he wrote in November 1507, a year into the project. "I have undergone and am undergoing so much strain that, if I were obliged to make another figure, I do not believe my life would suffice for it, as the undertaking has been one of enormous difficulty; had it been entrusted to anyone else it would have turned out a failure."

After a number of setbacks—including removing the statue from the oven to find it melted from the waist up—Michelangelo finally completed the massive work: one of the very few bronzes he would ever sculpt. Installed at the basilica in February 1508, the likeness of Julius stood scanning the Piazza Maggiore for signs of impudence for less than four years before it was toppled and destroyed. The bronze fragments were then melted down and recast to form a massive cannon that the Duke of Ferrara dubbed "La Giulia"—an insolent play on the pope's name.

Michelangelo's reaction to the desecration of his "undertaking . . . of enormous difficulty" is not known. By that time he was absorbed in a more promising project for Pope Julius: the frescoed ceiling of the Sistine Chapel.

DECEMBER 31, 1986

Still More *Bad Days* Just Around the Corner: Jim and Tammy Faye Bakker on the Brink

Tammy Faye Bakker, the mascara-slathered spouse of cloyingly avaricious televangelist Jim Bakker, was filled with cheery, saccharine hope during the couple's New Year's Eve broadcast in 1986. Right before bursting into the song "(Don't Give Up) On the Brink of a Miracle," Tammy Faye had this to say: "You know, your miracle might be just around the corner. And you can't see around the corner, Jim. But you may be right at that corner and your miracle may be just around that corner. And so, people, don't give up on the brink of a miracle. Your healing may be just around the corner. Your financial success may be just around the corner. Your job may be just around the corner. You know everything good for you could be just around the corner. So don't you dare give up on the brink of your miracles. Amen!"

But sometimes the light at the end of the tunnel is the high beam of an onrushing freight train. What lay in wait for Tammy Faye "just around the corner" was a stint in drug rehab, where she hallucinated "demons coming at me." For husband Jim, it was the loss of his sprawling ministerial empire—brought on by the revelation of his sexual encounter with a young church secretary (and subsequent payments to cover it up). And just around the corner from *that* would loom a grand-jury indictment and prison sentence for bilking his only-too-believing followers out of millions to fund the couple's lavish lifestyle.

Acknowledgments

———✦———

Although nothing can ever be done to change history, there are many ways to recount it. Indeed, the Bad Days assembled here were made considerably brighter in the telling by the valuable contributions of some very clever people.

I want to thank Pat Myers, who has consistently earned her distinction as "the world's funniest copy editor," bestowed by two-time Pulitzer Prize winner Gene Weingarten. I am also grateful to Giulia Ghigini for her brilliant illustrations, and to Allan Fallow, aka "Conan the Grammarian." As his tag suggests, Allan wields his blue pen as ruthlessly as a (smart) barbarian's sword—and thank goodness for that! "Conan" had a very skilled accomplice in forcing the best possible prose onto these pages: National Geographic editor Hilary Black, who steadfastly managed this project with grace, good humor, and an abundance of patience.

And speaking of that wild planet over at National Geographic: I am forever indebted to Publisher and Editorial Director Lisa Thomas for originating this Bad Days concept and allowing me to wallow in it again. And to Daneen "the Marketing Queen" Goodwin, whose attention-drawing artistry helped ensure this second volume. Many thanks as well to the rest of the Bad Days Team: Ann Day, Melissa Farris, Nicole Miller, Judith Klein, and Heather McElwain.

A number of my former colleagues at *The Washington Post* also contributed to this collection: Mary Hadar, Rita Kempley, Patricia Dane Rogers, and Megan Rosenfeld. Thank you!

And thank you, too, Stefanie Reponen, for the May 6 inspiration I'm sure you have no idea you provided.

Finally, a huge hug of gratitude to my wonderful friends and family— the people who make my days so happy, and yet added their wit and wisdom to make these days so *Bad:* Mary Farquhar, John Foote, Jeff Larroca, Kevin Murphy, and Casey O'Neil.

Selected Bibliography

January

Gaines, Caseen. *We Don't Need Roads: The Making of the Back to the Future Trilogy*. New York: Plume, 2015.

Lacey, Robert. *Monarch: The Life and Reign of Elizabeth II*. New York: Free Press, 2003.

February

Barrier, Michael. *Hollywood Cartoons: American Animation in Its Golden Age*. Oxford, New York: Oxford Press, 1999.

Broder, David S. *Behind the Front Page: A Candid Look at How the News Is Made*. New York: Simon & Schuster, 1987.

Davies, Hunter. *The Beatles: The Authorized Biography*. London: Heinemann, 1979.

Haldeman, H. R. *The Haldeman Diaries: Inside the Nixon White House*. New York: Berkley, 1994.

Hendrickson, Paul. *The Living and the Dead: Robert McNamara and Five Lives of a Lost War*. New York: Knopf, 1996.

Jacobs, George, and William Stadiem. *Mr. S: My Life with Frank Sinatra*. New York: HarperEntertainment, 2004.

Lash, Joseph P. *Eleanor and Franklin: The Story of Their Relationship, Based on Eleanor Roosevelt's Private Papers*. New York: Norton, 1971.

Remini, Robert V. *Henry Clay: Statesman for the Union*. New York: Norton, 1991.

Sinatra, Tina (with Jeff Coplon). *My Father's Daughter: A Memoir*. New York: Simon & Schuster, 2000.

Womack, Kenneth. *Long and Winding Roads: The Evolving Artistry of The Beatles*. New York: Bloomsbury Academic, 2007.

March

Cook, Kevin. *Kitty Genovese: The Murder, the Bystanders, the Crime that Changed America*. New York and London: W. W. Norton & Company, 2014.

Finucci, Valeria. *The Prince's Body: Vincenzo Gonzaga and Renaissance Medicine (I Tatti Studies in Italian Renaissance History)*. Cambridge, MA: President and Fellows of Harvard College, 2015.

Miller, James Andrew, and Tom Shales. *Live From New York: The Complete, Uncensored History of Saturday Night Live as Told by Its Stars, Writers, and Guests*. New York: Little, Brown, 2002.

Seale, William. *The President's House*. Washington, D.C.: White House Historical Association, 1986.

Speiser, Stuart M. *Lawsuit*. New York: Horizon Press, 1980.

April

Brownell, Robert. *Marriage of Inconvenience*. London: Pallas Athene, 2015.

Miller, James Andrew, and Tom Shales. *Live From New York: The Complete, Uncensored History of Saturday Night Live as Told by Its Stars, Writers, and Guests*. New York: Little, Brown, 2002.

O'Keeffe, Paul. *A Genius for Failure: The Life of Benjamin Robert Haydon*. London: The Bodley Head, 2009.

May

Bradlee, Ben, Jr. *The Kid: The Immortal Life of Ted Williams*. New York, Boston, London: Little, Brown, 2013.

Higginbotham, Adam. *Midnight in Chernobyl: The Untold Story of the World's Greatest Nuclear Disaster*. New York: Simon & Schuster, 2019.

McElroy, Robert McNutt. *Jefferson Davis: The Unreal and the Real*. New York: Harper, 1937.

Neely, Mark E., Jr., Harold Holzer, and Gabor S. Boritt. *The Confederate Image: Prints of the Lost Cause (Civil War America)*. Chapel Hill: The University of North Carolina Press, 1987.

Reagan, Ronald, and Richard G. Hubler. *Where's the Rest of Me? The Ronald Reagan Story*. New York: Duell, Sloan and Pearce, 1965.

Treglown, Jeremy. *Roald Dahl: A Biography*. Boston: Faber & Faber, 1994.

June

Hernon, Ian. *Britain's Forgotten Wars: Colonial Campaigns of the 19th Century*. Stroud, England: Sutton, 2003.

Morgan, Chester M. *Redneck Liberal: Theodore G. Bilbo and the New Deal*. Baton Rouge: Louisiana State University Press, 1985.

Reagan, Nancy (with William Novak). *My Turn: The Memoirs of Nancy Reagan*. New York: Random House, 1989.

July

Ambrose, Stephen E. *Americans at War*. Jackson: University Press of Mississippi, 1997.

Isaacson, Walter. *Einstein: His Life and Universe*. New York: Simon & Schuster, 2007.

Kingseed, Cole C. *Old Glory Stories: American Combat Leadership in World War II*. Annapolis, MD: Naval Institute Press, 2006.

McManus, John C. *Fire and Fortitude: The US Army in the Pacific War, 1941–1943*. New York: Dutton Caliber, 2019.

August

Fraser, Ronald. *Blood of Spain: An Oral History of the Spanish Civil War*. New York: Pantheon, 1979.

Morris, Edmund. *Colonel Roosevelt*. New York: Random House, 2010.

Quinn, Sally. *Finding Magic: A Spiritual Memoir*. New York: HarperOne, 2017.

Schama, Simon. *Citizens: A Chronicle of the French Revolution.* New York: Knopf, 1991.

Thomas, Hugh. *The Spanish Civil War.* New York: Harper, 1977.

September

Bernstein, Carl, and Bob Woodward. *All the President's Men.* New York: Simon & Schuster, 1974.

Carlin, Peter Ames. *Catch a Wave: The Rise, Fall, and Redemption of the Beach Boys' Brian Wilson.* New York: Rodale Books, 2006.

Carlson, Peter. *K Blows Top: A Cold War Comic Interlude Starring Nikita Khrushchev, America's Most Unlikely Tourist.* New York: PublicAffairs, 2009.

Chernow, Ron. *Alexander Hamilton.* New York: Penguin Press, 2004.

Ellis, Joseph J. *American Sphinx: The Character of Thomas Jefferson.* New York: Knopf, 1997.

Forbes, Bryan. *A Divided Life.* London: Heinemann, 1992.

George, David Lloyd. *War Memoirs of David Lloyd George.* London: Odhams Press, 1938.

Graham, Katharine. *Personal History.* New York: Knopf, 1997.

Hart, Peter. *The Somme: The Darkest Hour on the Western Front.* New York: Pegasus Books, 2009.

Pepitone, Lena, and William Stadiem. *Marilyn Monroe Confidential: An Intimate Personal Account.* New York: Simon & Schuster, 1979.

Sellers, Robert. *Peter O'Toole: The Definitive Biography.* New York: Thomas Dunne Books, 2016.

Weiss, Murray. *The Man Who Warned America: The Life and Death of John O'Neill, the FBI's Embattled Counterterror Warrior.* New York: ReganBooks, 2003.

October

Ambrose, Stephen E. *Eisenhower: Soldier and President.* Newtown, CT: American Political Biography Press, 2007.

Montague, Francis Charles. *Political History of England,* vol. VII, *From the Accession of James First to the Restoration, 1603–1660.* London: Longmans, Green, 1907.

Richards, Keith, and James Fox. *Life.* New York: Little, Brown, 2010.

Thomas, Evan. *Robert Kennedy: His Life.* New York: Simon & Schuster, 2000.

Ziegler, Philip. *King Edward VIII: A Biography.* New York: Knopf, 1991.

November

Berger, Glen. *Song of Spider-Man: The Inside Story of the Most Controversial Musical in Broadway History.* New York: Simon & Schuster, 2013.

Bonanno, Joseph (with Sergio Lalli). *A Man of Honor: The Autobiography of Joseph Bonanno.* New York: Simon & Schuster, 1983.

Hollister, C. Warren. *Henry I.* New Haven: Yale University Press, 2001.

Jones, Dan. *The Plantagenets: The Warrior Kings and Queens Who Made England.* New York: Viking, 2012.

Kazin, Michael. *A Godly Hero: The Life of William Jennings Bryan.* New York: Knopf, 2006.

Lamb, Lawrence E., M.D. *Inside the Space Race: A Space Surgeon's Diary.* Austin, Texas: Synergy Books, 2006.

Maas, Peter. *The Valachi Papers.* New York: Putnam, 1968.

Mormando, Franco. *Bernini: His Life and His Rome.* Chicago: University of Chicago Press, 2011.

Reavill, Gil. *Mafia Summit: J. Edgar Hoover, the Kennedy Brothers, and the Meeting That Unmasked the Mob.* New York: Thomas Dunne Books—St. Martin's, 2013.

Roach, Mary. *Packing for Mars: The Curious Science of Life in the Void.* New York: Norton, 2010.

Röhl, John C. G. (translation by Sheila de Bellaigue and Roy Bridge). *Wilhelm II: Into the Abyss of War and Exile, 1900–1941.* Cambridge: Cambridge University Press, 2014.

December

Halberstam, David: *The Coldest Winter: America and the Korean War.* New York: Hyperion, 2007.

McFarland, Philip. *Sea Dangers: The Affair of the* Somers. New York: Schocken Books, 1985.

O'Brien, Timothy L. *TrumpNation: The Art of Being the Donald.* New York: Warner Books, 2005.

Ulam, Adam B. *Stalin: The Man and His Era.* Boston: Beacon Press, 1973.

Index